Gazetteer of Coorg

Rev. G Richter

Low Price Publications
Delhi-110052

First Published 1870

ISBN 10: 81-7536-531-5
ISBN 13: 978-81-7536-531-5

Published by

Low Price Publications

A-6, 2nd Floor, Nimri Commercial Centre,
Ashok Vihar Phase 4, Delhi 110052 (INDIA)
telephone: +91-11-47061936
website: www.LPPindia.com
e-mail: info@LPPindia.com

Printed at
Balaji Offset
Delhi

PRINTED IN INDIA

PREFACE.

THIS Manual aims at a truthful sketch of the past history and the present physical and political position of the interesting Province of Coorg which has for the last 36 years been under the sway of the British Government.

Great changes have taken place during this period. Coorg, though for a long time a jealously guarded *imperium in imperio*, had gradually to yield to the onward march of civilization, in spite of the antagonism of its conservative Headmen. Good roads in every direction opened up this once impenetrable mountain-girt tract, and numbers of enterprising British settlers with capital and national energy have already stamped a new character upon the country. By three opposite lines the electric wire has linked Coorg with the grand net of the South-Indian telegraph and consequently with Europe and far distant America. Education is firmly and extensively established, and the administration of the country compares most favourably with that of any well-governed province in India.

By the kind permission of the Superintendent and the Chief-Commissioner of Coorg, I had access for the compilation of this Gazetteer to all the official records bearing on the subject. Amongst these I have found the "Rájéndranáme" and the "Memoir of the Coorg Survey" of great service. The former contains the history of the Coorg Rájahs from 1633 to 1808, composed under the eye of Dodda-Vírájender, the hero of Coorg history. The latter was written by Lieut. Connor of the Royal Engineers in 1817. Though drawn up under the most untoward circumstances, it exhibits a clear and comprehensive insight into the state of Coorg half a century since and reflects great credit upon the intelligence and ability of that Officer.

In 1855 Dr. H. Moegling, the first Protestant Missionary in Coorg, wrote a little book, entitled "Coorg Memoirs" which in 1866 was republished in German in an enlarged and amended edition. This book intended for a Missionary public furnishes extensive and correct information on social and religious topics and has been largely made use of in this volume.

I am also indebted to my late Assistant, Mr. A. Graeter, for his communications on the Coorg language which he has successfully studied.

But whatever source of information has been made use of — and I am under obligation to several Gentlemen for special communications and references, to whom I herewith offer my thanks — the materials have been worked with the view of forming a homogenous whole.

The Compiler's residence of 14 years amongst the Coorgs and his familiar intercourse with them in every part of the country as Inspector of the Government Vernacular Schools, may be accepted as a further guarantee for the reliable character of the information in this Gazetteer.

The greater portion of the Manual having been read in manuscript by Mr. Bowring, the late Chief-Commissioner, it may be considered as having passed official censorship.

In the spelling of native words, which are based upon their etymological roots, as far as these could be ascertained, an attempt has been made at a uniform system according to the one usually received by English Orientalists, except where established English usage has otherwise fixed the orthography. The short vowels are unaccented, the long have an acute accent above them and are pronounced with their natural sound as in German or Italian.

The distance of the Press rendering it impracticable for the author to correct the proofsheets, sundry misprints have been left which, however, are noted in the Errata.

G. Richter.

CONTENTS.

I. PART.

THE COORG COUNTRY AND ITS NATURAL PRODUCTIONS.

	Page.
1. *Geographical Features*	3—4
2. *General description of Coorg*	4—81
its mountains and their formation	4—11
its rivers and their course	11—16
its forests and their general flora	16—36
its forests and their general fauna	36—81
Mammalia	36—52
Birds	53—61
Reptiles	61—64
Fishes	64—66
Molluscae	67
Insects	67—79
Spiders and Scorpions	79—80
Crabs	80
Leeches	80—81
3. *Metereological and climatic conditions*	81—86
4. *Cultivation of the principal productions*	86—109
Rice	86—91
Cardamom	91—94
Coffee	94—101
Chinchona	101—102

	Page.
Tea, Sugarcane, Cotton	102—103
Plantain	103—104
Manilla Hemp and Assam Nettle	104—106
Chocolate and Nutmeg tree	106—107
Fruit trees and Vegetables	107—109

II. PART.

THE PEOPLE OF COORG.

1. Composition and density of the population	110—117
A. Tribes who speak Kodagu.	
Coorgs and Amma-Coorgs	110
Eimbókalas	110—111
Hegadés	111
Bénepadas	111
Airis	111
Madiválas	111
Kávatis	111
Naindas	111
Koyuvas	111
Kudiyas	111
Médas	112
Holeyas	112
B. Tribes who speak seperate languages.	
Roman Catholic Christians	112—113
Siváchåries	113
Gaudas	113
Páléyas	113
Maleyas	113
Kurubas	113—114
Adias	114
Yeravas	114—115

Page.

Káplas 115

Kádavas or Bodavas 373

2. Personal appearance, occupation and general character of the Coorgs . . . . 117—127

3. Social life of the Coorgs 128

The Coorg house . . . . 128—131

Prescriptive law of inheritance . . . . . . 131—132

Wedding and married life . . . . 132—140

Childbirth . . . . 141—142

Death and funeral ceremonies . . . . 142—146

4. Popular Festivals of the Coorgs . . . . 146—162

The Kávéri-feast . . . . 146—151

The Huttári-feast . . . . 151—156

The Bhagavati-feast . . . . 157—160

The Keilmúrta-feast . . . . 160—162

5. Religious Observances and popular Superstition . . 162

The Sanctuaries of a Coorg community . . . . . 162—163

Ancestral and Demon-worship . . . . 163—167

Astrology and Sorcery . . . . 167—168

• Substitutes for human sacrifices and other peculiar rites. 168—170

Pilgrimages of the Coorgs within and outside their own country . . . . 170—175

Tale-Kávéri-Játre . . . . 146—151

Irpu-Játre . . . . 171—173

Iggudappa-Játre 173

Kuntada-betta-Játre . . . . 173—174

Pálúr-Játre 174

Subramanya-Játre 174

Baitur-Játre 175

Payávur-Játre 175

Nanchanagódu-Játre 175

Dévastánas, Mattas and Musjids . . . . 175—177

Page.

6. The Amma-Codagas . . . . 177—180

7. Architectural Structures and archæological remains in Coorg 180

Palaces . . . . 180—182

Mausoleums . . . . 182—184

Antique Sepulchres or Cairns . . . . 184—186

Monumental Stones . . . . 187—190

The Coorg Cadangas . . . . 190—191

Forts . . . . 191—193

8. The Coorg language and its literature . . . . . 193—214

III. PART.

THE HISTORY OF COORG.

1. The Legendary Period of the Kávéri-Purána . . . 215—225

2. Popular Tradition . . . . 225—227

3. Conjectures regarding the Origin and early History of the Coorgs . . . . 227—235

4. History of the Coorg Rájahs as delineated in the Rájendranáme and from other documentary Sources . . . . 235—276

Prefatory Remarks . . . . 235—238

Princes of collateral lines . . . . 238—246

Muddurája and his descendents . . . . . 238—240

Dodda-Vírappa . . . . 240—242

Chikka-Vírappa . . . . 242—244

Dévappa and Lingarája . . . . 244—246

Coorg under Dodda-Vírájender Vodeya 246

Vírájender in Mysore captivity . . . . 246—248

Vírájender at liberty 248

Page.

Conflicts with Kóte and Mysore . . . . . 248—252
Virájender's alliance with the East-India Company. . 252—254
First war of the allies with Tippu . . . . . 254—257
An armed peace . . . . 257—263
Second war with Tippu . . . . 263—266
Virájender's relation to the Company after the war . . 266—274
Virájender's last will . . . . 274—276

5. The last years of the independence of Coorg . . . 276—347

Dodda-Virájender's melancholy end . . . . . . 276—287
Lingarájender's intrigues . . . . 287—297
General Welsh's visits to Lingarájender . . . . . 297—314
Lingarájender's character . . . . 314—317
Virarája's tyranny . . . . 317—320
Channa Basava and Dévammájis' flight . . . . . 321—322
Muddaya's murder . . . . 322—323
Complications with the British Government . . . . 323—325
Assassination of the Rájah's family . . . . . . 325—328
The war and the Rájah's surrender . . . . . . 328—347

Proclamations of war . . . . 329—333
The Eastern Column . . . . 333—336
The Northern Column . . . . 336—337
The Western Column . . . . 337—339
The Western Auxiliary Column . . . . 339—341
The Rájah's surrender and Basava's death . . . . 341—345
"General Order" . . . . 345—347

IV. PART.

COORG UNDER THE BRITISH GOVERNMENT.

Since 1834.

A HISTORICAL EVENTS.

1. The Rájah's deposition and the annexation of Coorg . 348—353
The Coorg-Address to General Fraser and his reply . . 351—353

Page.

2. *The Rájah's exile and death. Victoria Gauramma* . 354—355

3. *Vírájender's sons and relatives. Channa Basava* . 356—57

4. *Abhrambára, the Impostor* . . . . 357—360

5. *The Coorg Rebellion* . . . . 360—365

B. THE ADMINISTRATION OF COORG.

1. *Subdivision of Coorg for administrative purposes* . 366—367

Sketch of the several taluqs and towns . . . . . . 368—383

Mercara-taluq and Mercara town . . . . 368—372

Padinálknád-taluq and Nápoklu . . . . 372—374

Yedenálknád-taluq and Virájpet . . . . 374—376

Kiggatnád-taluq and Ponnappet . . . . 376—378

Nanjarájpatna-taluq and Fraserpet and Sómawárpet . . 378—381

Yélusávirashíme-taluq and Kodlipet . . . . . . 381—383

2. *Administration of Justice* . . . . 383—401

In the time of the Rájahs . . . . 383—385

Under the British Government . . . . 385—401

3. *Administration of Revenue* 401

Land-Revenue 401

Jamma-tenure . . . . 401—405

Ságu-tenure . . . . 405—407

Umbali-tenure . . . . 407—408

Jódi-tenure 408

Ghee-, house- and dhúli-paddy-tax . . . . 408—409

Inám-holdings 409

Dry cultivation . . . . 409—410

Assessment on land for coffee cultivation . . . . 410—417

Rents from cardamom jungles . . . . 417—418

Routine for the collection of the Land-Revenue . . . 419—420

Forest Conservancy . . . . 421—422

Revenue Survey . . . . 422—424

Abkári . . . . 424—425

4. *Department of Public Works* . . . . 425—430

Fraserpet-road 426

Page.

Sampáji-Ghat-road 427

Cannanore-road 428

Manjerabad-road 429

Anandapur-road 430

5. *Post Office and Telegraphs* 431

6. *Military Department* . . . . 431—433

7. *Medical Department* . . . . 333—434

8. *Educational Department* . . . . 435—448

C. CHRISTIAN INFLUENCE UPON THE COORGS BY DIRECT AND INDIRECT AGENTS OF CIVILIZATION.

1. *The Roman Catholic Settlement at Virájpet* . . . 448

2. *The English Chaplancy in Mercara* 451

3. *The Protestant Mission of the Basel Society* . . . 452

Appendices:—I. The Chief-Commissioners and Superintendents of Coorg since 1834. 460

II. Comparative Statistics of Revenue . . 461

III. Do. do. of Expenditure . 462

IV. Table of barometrical observations . . 463

V. Do. thermometrical do. . . . 464

VI. Rainfall at Mercara 465

VII. General metereological abstract 466

VIII. Statement of the European Coffee Estates in Coorg 467

I. PART

THE

COORG COUNTRY

AND ITS

Natural Productions

God Almighty, live and rule!
Rule as our Lord and God!
Rule, O glorious sun and moon
In the sky as king and queen!
Land of our fathers, thrive!
Land of houses and of farms!
In the famous Jambudwípa
There are many glorious kingdoms;
Which among them is the finest?
High above the lofty hills
Thrones the snowy Mahaméru;
And among the flowering trees
Is the Sampige the finest;
Thus is *Coorg*, a string of pearls,
Loveliest among the kingdoms;
Live in it, my friend, and prosper!

Coorg Palamé.

The Coorg Country

1. Geographical Features.

The Coorg country is formed by the summits and eastern declivities of the Western Ghats, which separate it on the south and west from the woody tracts of North Malabar (Wynád) and South Canara (Tulu); in the north and east it merges into the table-land of Mysore with the only partially, natural boundary of the rivers Kumáradhári, Hémávati and Kávéri. Its greatest length from north to south, from the river Hémávati to the Brahmagiris, extends over 60 and its greatest width from west to east, from Sampáji to Fraserpet, about 40 English miles. Geographically speaking, the whole country lies between north latitude 11° 55′ and 12° 50′, and east longitude 75° 25′ and 76° 14′. Its area comprises 1,585 square miles. Before the annexation of Coorg by the English, the limits of this little kingdom extended over a larger tract and included the two taluqs of Canara, Amra Sulya and Puttúr, comprising an area of about 580 square miles, which at the request of the inhabitants were separated from Coorg and added to the Collectorate of South Canara.

The present shape of Coorg, as represented on a map, is not unlike a baby's sock, a little contracted at the instep and with a loop at the top, by which it is suspended. In this situation the heel points north-west and the toe south-east, whilst the sole, heel and back seam are formed by the Ghats and the whole length of the instep by the Mysore boundary. Compared with the gigantic extent of the Indian Peninsula, Coorg is but of baby's size, however large it may appear to its inhabitants.

As the Badaga people on the Nilagiris have been named Burghers, so is "Coorg" anglicised from Kodagu or Kodumale, a name which it has borne from the remotest ages and which in its meaning—"Steep mountains" graphically depicts the character of this remarkable alpine land.

2. General description of Coorg,

its mountains and their formation, its rivers and their course, its forests and their general flora and fauna.

Aspect of Coorg. Standing on a bright November morning on the summit of the Brahmagiri near Tala-Kávéri, (tale *Kg.* head) the observer is filled with delight and admiration of the grand and picturesque view, that opens out before him. As far as the eye can reach to the north-west and south-east it beholds ridge after ridge of grassy or forest-clad hills, now gently sloping down in gentle wavy lines, now bold and abrupt, raising their steep summits into the clear, blue air. Kuduremukha-betta, the far seen landmark of the mariner, bursts into view from Canara; the Bettadapur and Chámundi hill in Mysore, the Wynád mountains of Malabar and Dodda-betta of the distant Nilagiris are clearly visible, and in the west at a distance of about 30 miles below the steep precipices of the Ghats the coast-line of North Malabar and South Canara, intersected by broad, bright, serpentine rivers and the dark-blue Indian Ocean with its sailing craft fascinate the spectator.

Coorg itself is covered by forest, save here and there where the clearing of a coffee plantation or ragi patch or the park-like open glades (Báné) with their beautiful green sward and varied foliage afford a charming variety to the landscape.

In vain, however, the eye searches for towns and villages, churches and castles or other indications of civilized life. Only here and there in nooks and corners, ensconced amongst groves and clusters of cultivated trees and betrayed by a wreath of smoke, can one discover the thatched houses of the Coorgs, who love a solitary abode near their fields.

The want of permanent sheets of water, such as extensive tanks or prominent rivers somewhat detracts from the picturesqueness of the landscape, but during a heavy mist or in the monsoon fancy may easily transform the whole country into innumerable islands emerging from a vast agitated sea.

The general appearance of the country varies considerably in the different districts. In the vicinity of Sómwárapet, in the north of Coorg, the hills are gently rounded alternating with sloping glades, interspersed with clumps of forest trees, resembling the finest park scenery in Europe. Near Mercara the hills are closer together and more abrupt, and the ravines deeper and more wild. Towards Fraserpet the country assumes the champaign character of the Mysore plateau, with scattered solitary hills. South of Mercara, in the direction of Virajpet, especially in Beppunád, Katiednád, the country is open, the woods are neither dense nor high, and beautiful grassy doures rise from extensive rice valleys.

The eastern frontier between the Kávéri and the Lakshmana-tírtha river exhibits an almost uninterrupted and impervious forest, inhabited in January, February and March by Kurumbers and Lumbánies and other wandering tribes.

Mountains and their Formation.—The most prominent ridge of mountains in Coorg as to height and extent, is that which culminates in the summits of the Ghats. It stretches in its main outline from Subramanya to the furthest point of the Brahmagiris over or upwards of 60 miles. Seen from the Western Coast near Cannanore the abrupt ascent with the great height and varied configuration of the Ghats present a most grand and imposing spectacle.

The most conspicuous subdivisions of the Ghats are, in the south, the Brahmagiris or Marenád hills, which constitute a formidable natural barrier between Coorg and Wynád. Their height averages some 4,500 feet above the level of the sea. The highest peak of the Brahmagiris is the Brahmagiri hill-station, which towers several hundred feet above a beautiful table-land called Huyále-male (huyále *Kg.* swing) and overlooks the temple of Pemmeya at Tiranelli in Malabar in the deep valley of the Papanashe river and beyond it the extensive coffee plantations and high mountains of North Wynád. Further on, to the west, rise the Hanumán-betta, the Kadanga-male and the Perumále-male. The many spurs that branch off in all directions from the Brahmagiris over the whole of Kigatnád (kiri or ki *Kg.* low) (district of the lower Ghats) and on to the eastern elbow of the river Kávéri produce a ramification of narrow ridged hills, now ascending to almost solitary grandeur, like the Ambate-betta (ambate *Kg.* a kind of mango) near Virájpet, the Bittangala, the Hátur hill or Kundada-betta (kundu *Kg.* height) the Sidéshwara hill and Maukal-betta (mau *Can.* mango, kalloo *Can.* stone) now subsiding into the undulating slopes of the most eastern elevations, and enclosing innumerable paddy-fields, some of which are the most extensive in Coorg.

From the Perambádi-pass near Virájpet to the Todikána-pass, (todia *Kg.* plantain, kána *Kg.* forest) near the source of the Kávéri, the main chain of the Western Ghats extends in a north-westerly direction in almost a straight line of 30 miles in length. Towards the west it falls with great abruptness, the descent from the summit to the foot being generally from 3 to 5 miles, the first part of which is particularly steep. Behind Nalknád palace, the highest mountain of this range, Tadiandamól ("broad-based-hill", tadi *Kg.* broad, molu *Kg.*

hill) raises its gracefully shaped head over its majestic neighbours. Its height is 5,682 feet above the level of the sea, and as it has a central position in the whole range, the panorama commanded by such an elevation is grand beyond description. The ascent is easy, two-thirds of it may be achieved on horseback, and though the topmost portion is rather difficult the persevering climber is richly rewarded for his exertion when in the cool bracing air be stands on the narrow ledge of the giddy summit and gazes over the gloriously diversified highlands and lowlands at his feet.

About 6 miles to the south-east of Tadiandamól rises the Jómamale (jóma *Kg.* ox, male *Kg.* forest), the highest mountain in Katiednád. It is sacred to Maletambiran (Tambiran, a Malayalam god) and overlooks the Kodantora-pass. Two miles to the north-east of Tadiandamól there is another mountain giant, the Iggudappa-kundu (Iggu, a Malayalam god; appa, father; kundu, hill) near the Paditora (Padi, name of a village; tora, pass) and three miles further on the Pérur point and 4 miles still further the Srimangala point. The last notable mountain in the same range is the Brahmagiri in Tavunád (tavu *Kg.* descent, sunset, west) with the source of the river Kávéri.

At an acute angle upon this line the main chain of the Ghats is continued in a due easterly direction as the Benganád range (bengu, to stop) till, nearing Mercara, it makes a sudden turn to the north-west and forms with the latter the Sampáji valley which leads by a gradual slope into the low country of Canara. At the head of the valley and supported by a high ridge with steep abutments on its southern front the Mercara table-land is situated. This ridge branches off in two directions, one towards the south-eastern elbow of the Kávéri, culminating in the pointed peak of Núrokal-betta (núru *Can.* hundred, kallu *Can.* stone, betta hill) and the other, the Horur branch, (hora, outside; uru, town) due east in a zigzag line towards Fraserpet with several rugged hills, the most remarkable of which is Kalluru-betta clothed with teak forest. The Núrokal and Benganád range make up with the Western Ghats the watershed of the upper basin of the Kávéri, a valley, which between Mercara and Nalknád is 15 English miles broad.

From the main chain of the Ghats and the Benganád range, innumerable ridges jut out on either side. These are diminutive when compared with the parent stock; and they decrease in height as they recede, but have almost everywhere narrow summits and steep declivities.

The table-land of Mercara maintains throughout an average altitude of 3500 feet above the sea, and may be said to extend as far as Somawárpet, a distance of 20 miles, but on the east it slopes down towards the Kávéri which near Fraserpet is still at an elevation of 2720 feet above the sea. This plateau, crossed in all directions by minor hills and ridges, is bounded on the west by the continuation of the Ghats which culminate near the Bisly-pass in the Subrahmanya or Pushpagiri hill, 5548 feet above the sea level. This is a remarkable two-pointed hill of precipitous height and peculiar shape, and resembles, as seen from Mercara, a gigantic bullock hump. The ascent, which, on account of the precipices of the southern and western face of the hill, can only be effected by a circuitous route, is more difficult than that of Tadiandamól. Starting from Bhagati, at the base of the Pushpagiri, it is about 6 miles walking, the ascent taking a good walker 2 hours 40 minutes and the descent to the Hiridigadde of the village Bidehalli 2 hours. A dense jungle, dear to wild elephants, has to be penetrated, and the ascent is severe; but the summit commands an extensive prospect over Coorg, Canara and Mysore. There are on this hill numerous Hindu memorials in the shape of stone mounds. Within an enclosure there are two rude stone structures, with the customary imprint of two feet (páda) of celestial origin!

Amongst the many ridges that branch off from the Subramanya range of the Ghats the most remarkable is that, which attains its greatest height in Kóte-betta, about 9 miles north of Mercara. Its elevation is over 5000 feet, and its base covers a very large extent of country. Its summit, which is divided into two peaks, one rather pointed – the Harangal-betta—and the other broad, forms a comparatively flat table-land, while its sides are clothed with forest, and innumerable cultivated valleys occupy the recesses. Close to the apex there are two reservoirs of water, one for the use of the Brahmins and one for the Coorgs, which all the year round retain a constant supply. Close to the summit on a spacious platform is a small temple of rough granite slabs dedicated to Shiva. This hill as well as the Núrokal-betta offer, on account of their height and central position, the finest general view of Coorg, and even to the lover of nature, familiar with mountain glories in Scotland, Switzerland or Italy, no more delightful excursion could be recommended than that to these hills.

From Kóte-betta to the north is another ridge running parallel with it, the Shanthalli hills, and beyond them is a bluff hill with almost a precipitous declivity on its western face—the Múkri-betta (múku, nose) with a fine coffee plantation at its base.

The last remarkable range, that extends from the northern frontier of Coorg down to the Kávéri almost due south, is the Yélusávira hills with the Málimbi and Kanangala peak. The former is distinguished by its beautifully conical shape which strikes the eye in every part of Coorg.

The Geological formation of the Coorg mountains is indicated by the sharply defined outline of the Western Ghats, a feature characteristic of granitic rocks. The constant action of the stormy monsoon rains, however, followed by scorching east winds and a burning sun, has greatly affected the surface of the mountains, and a perpetual process of disintegration of the uppermost portions has imparted to them a somewhat rounded appearance, which does not occur, where the atmospheric influences are less severe, and the alternation of temperature less sudden.

The several members of the metamorphic class of rocks of which the Coorg mountains consist may be found in almost every mountain torrent. They are: granular and foliated or stratified granite (gneiss), which consists of quartz, felspar and mica; syenite, a rock of the appearance of ordinary granite, in which however hornblende is substituted for mica, and mica-schist, a slaty rock chiefly composed of mica and quartz sometimes with imbedded garnets. Near Mercara may be found clay-slate or argillaceous schist of coarse variety. This consists of silica and alumina, combined with a little iron, magnesia potash and carbon; crystalline limestone is present in the neighbourhood of Bellur near Fraserpet and supplies nearly all the requirements for building purposes in Coorg. Among this limestone, which is dug out from the ground in small earthy lumps like the kunkur in the N. W. Provinces and which is perhaps more properly termed magnesian limestone, nodules of magnesite are occasionally met with.

A ferruginous laterite, composed of silicate of alumina and oxyde of iron, appears sporadically in almost every part of Coorg.

The ingredients of all these rocks, which are subject to an unceasing process of decomposition, constitute the nature of the soil all over the country and, as a matter of course, on the predominance of the one or other or several of their constituing parts combined with other conditions depends as elsewhere the fertility or sterility of the ground.

Felspar is very common, and yields a rich soil. Veins of it are laid bare along the banks of the Ghat roads. In many places it is reduced to a white powder, the kaolin or porcelain clay, with which marketable chunam is adulterated. Mica is frequently seen, and here and there the roads glitter with its shining scales. After heavy showers the water channels along the sides of roads which had been metalled with syenite, appear covered with a sparkling blackish sand, the hornblende of the decomposed syenite. Common quartz occurs most frequently in small pieces of uncrystallic form. The considerable amount of carbonate of lime in the ashes of the Matti tree, (Terminalia coriacea) a tree largely distributed all over the eastern parts of Coorg, proves the presence of limestone in the soil of that region.

Mines there are none in Coorg, and it would appear, that except traces of iron in the shape of oxydes no metals exist. The gold ore, which a certain adventurer recently claimed to have discovered in Coorg, proved to be only mica embedded in quartz.

Rivers and their course. From the configuration of the country already described, it is evident, that the main drainage of Coorg is in an easterly direction towards the Bay of Bengal; while the mountain torrents of the western declivities of the Ghats flow into the Indian Ocean.

The Coorg rivers are not remarkable either for width or depth, but their water supply is everywhere abundant throughout the year. As their sources are high up in the mountains and their courses over steep declivities, the streams are impelled with great rapidity over generally very rocky beds; which render them almost wholly useless for navigation of any kind, and owing to the height of their banks and the unevenness of the country, few of them allow of artificial irrigation, but the rivulets are everywhere laid under contribution.

The minor streams vary only in size, which depends upon the length of their course, their general characteristics being the same. They swell with the freshes in the early part of June and flow with violent and boisterous rapidity till October, when they gradually subside in their normal dimensions. The south-westerly monsoon floods the uplands of Coorg against which it partially breaks, with such a torrent of rain, that during its prevalence small rills, out of which a thirsty herd does not care to drink, are suddenly transformed into streams that are impassable for many days.

Of the rivers that flow to the westward the *Barapole* (bare *Can.* empty, bare; pole or hole *Can.* river) is the most considerable. It rises with the *Lakshmana-tírta* and *Pápanáshe* on the same plateau of the Brahmagiri hills in Kiggatnád and flows for several miles in almost a straight line through a deep mountain gorge, where it is joined by a tributary that falls over a perpendicular rock of great height and forms a beautiful cascade near the Kudiál coffee estate. Near the Malayalam frontier the Barapole leaps into a chasm upwards of 200 feet deep, and forms a waterfall that, with the wild gloomy forest scenery around, is remarkably picturesque. Then for two miles this river runs along the Coorg frontier up to the point where the *Kallahole* (kallu *Can.* stone) descending through the Heggala-pass unites with it, when the combined streams enter Malabar and debouch near Chiracal into the sea. The Barapole receives the rainfall of 192 square miles, and is navigable from the sea to within 16 miles off the foot of the Ghats. Near Chávachári on the road to Cannanore it is spanned by a wooden bridge, resting on high stone pillars.

The next stream of importance is the *Nujikal* which drains the Sampáji valley, and follows the main road as far as Sulya, when it turns to the west, receives a tributary that originates on the western slopes of the Todicána-pass and Tala-Kávéri, and falls, under the name of Basavani river, near Kasergóde, into the sea.

The *Kumáradhári* (Kumára *Sans.* son, god of war, the son of Shiva; dháre *Sans.* edge, stream) rises near the Subramanya hill and carries off but little of the Coorg waters. For some distance it forms the northern boundary along the Bisilu-pass (bisilu *Can.* heat). A number of tributaries from north and south swell its waters, the largest of them being the *Nétrávati* (nétra *Sans.* eye) which joins it near the village Uppinangadi (uppu *Can.* salt, angadi mart) and thenceforth gives its own name to the rest of the course of this fine river, which near Mangalore meets the sea. The Nétrávati, though useless for purposes of irrigation, is of considerable commercial value. Boats of large size are safely carried from Mangalore as far as Bantwal or Pánemangalur and smaller craft proceed even beyond Uppinangadi.

The chief of the Coorg rivers, both as to size and importance, is the *Kávéri*; considering the volume of water it gathers during a course of nearly 400 miles through Mysore, along Salem and Coimbatore through Trichinopoly to Tanjore, where it is almost lost in that garden of India; the Kávéri may well be included amongst the principal rivers of the Peninsula. It rises on the Brahmagiri at a place called Tala-Kávéri (tale *Can.* head) on the very verge of the Western Ghats, where they form a sharp angle with the Benganád range. Another stream, the Kánake, starts close by and after a short run joins the Kávéri at the foot of the hill near the village Bhágamandala (bhágia *Sans.* wealth, felicity; mandala, region). At both places on the top and at the foot of the hill there are temples of great repute for sanctity among the Hindus, which are yearly resorted to by thousands of pilgrims from the adjoining countries. The Kávéri is, according to Brahminical legend, the holiest river in India. Even the holy goddess Ganga resorts underground to the all purifying floods of the

Kávéri once a year in Tulámása (tulá *Sans.* the sign of Libra; mása, lunar month) i. e. October, November, to wash away the pollution, contracted from the crowds of sinners, who have bathed in her own waters.

The course of this fine river through Coorg is very tortuous, but below Bhágamandala its current with the exception of a few localities, where it traverses beds of granite rock, is generally tranquil. Its banks which are high and steep are usually formed of rich clay or mould and covered with luxuriant tropical vegetation. The bed over which it flows differs in various places, being alternately sandy, pebbly or rocky, but the latter feature is predominant. In the dry season it is fordable at almost all points, but there is always a good body of water, considering the vicinity of its source.

During the monsoon it rises to an impetuous torrent whose mud-stained waters roll with thundering velocity through its wide channel, floating down shrubs and trees from its crumbling banks and overflowing for a few days the adjoining country. During these freshes the river rises near Fraserpet, where it is spanned by a magnificent stone bridge 516 feet in length, to a height of 20 to 30 feet.

Descending through the great valley between Mercara and Nálkanád, the Kávéri makes a sudden turn near Siddhapur Siddha *Sans.* a divine person) to the north and flows for 25 miles along the eastern frontier, being swollen in its course by several large tributaries. From the Tadiandamól it receives the Kakabe river which separates for some distance Padinálkanád from Katiednád. In Beppunád it is joined by the Kadanur river; and in Yeddenalkanád by the Kummahole.

The Muttáremutta collects the waters of the southern slope of the Mercara ridge, and the Chikkahole those of the valley of Horúrnúrokalnád. The *Háringi* or Suvarnavati (Suvarna *Sans.* gold) with the Kakehole from Sómawarpet, the Chóvanhole from Shanthalli, the Mattapur and Hattehole from Kóte-betta drain the whole northern plateau of Coorg and add an immense bulk of water to the Kávéri. Almost every one of these mountain streams forms in its descent over rocky beds cascades of great beauty. One near Mercara, the Jesse-fall (so called in honor of a daughter of the first chaplain of Mercara) is much admired and frequently visited by picnic parties. Some of the coffee estates along the Sampáji valley are notable for pleasing cataracts.

The rivers of Coorg which fall into the Kávéri beyond the province are Hémavati (héma *Sans.* gold) and the Lakshmanatirtha. The former rises near the Bhadra river, south of Westára in the Kadúr district of Mysore, and after passing Manjarábád, it forms for a few miles the northern boundary of Coorg and joins the Kávéri in the Yedatore taluk of Mysore near the village Tippúr. The Lakshmanatirtha with its tributaries the Kakotta and Kerehole drains nearly the whole of Kiggatnád. It rises in the forest, Munikádu, on the plateau of the Brahmagiris, and in its descent over an almost perpendicular mountain-wall forms a celebrated cataract, which by Brahminical priestcraft has been invested with sin cleansing virtue, and is consequently visited at the Irpu játre by thousands of superstitious devotees. The banks of this river like those of the Kávéri are of clay or mould, steep, with a sandy bottom and shaded by dense forest or bamboo clumps.

Lakes, Tanks, Wells.—Throughout Coorg there is not a lake or tank of any size worth mentioning. In Kiggatnád only there are a few natural reservoirs, called Kolli, enclosed by a belt of small trees and containing water all the year round. A tank 3 miles north of Somawarpet is notable for its picturesque rock scenery and the legend connected with it, which does not however accord with the inscription written upon a stone on the western outlet of the tank. The writing runs thus: "The King Andany has ordered this tank to be built on Tuesday the tenth day of the month of Phálguna in the year Párthiva. This was written by Venkadasya Mallia Bomarsia at the time of Basawalinga Déva Rája Vodea."

The legend is shortly this: "A merchant Malla Shetty of Yelusávirashíme vowed to build this tank. When it was finished, there was no water forthcoming. Animal sacrifices were suggested by the tank diggers and offered, but in vain. In this distress the goddess Ganga appeared and demanded the little finger of the Shetti. Unwilling to make this sacrifice, he offered the life of Akkony, his daughter-in-law instead, whose husband was away on a journey. Akkony agreed, took an affectionate leave of her child and parents, who were ignorant of her intentions, and amidst great solemnities she stepped into the tank, when Ganga made her appearance in rushing water. Akkony's parents, hearing of the impending sacrifice, hastened to rescue their daughter, but she refused to leave the tank, uttered a curse upon her father and mother-in-law and disappeared in the rising water. She then appeared in a dream to her husband, who speedily returned home, and, on hearing what had happened, killed his parents, and with his child in his arms rushed to the tank and in despair threw himself into it, when both were graciously received by Ganga."

Besides the small public tanks, there are only private wells, that yield, if dug deep enough, everywhere sweet and clear water; but it appears, that the natives of Coorg do not bestow enough attention on the great blessing of wholesome water, and are often satisfied with the muddy contents of a hole, carelessly dug by the side of their paddy-fields, though from their own experience they assert, that most of their diseases are owing to the bad quality of their drinking water.

Forests and their general flora and fauna.—In Coorg extensive forests clothe every mountain range almost up to the summit and bamboo jungles, cover the more level eastern districts, interspersed with such trees, as are peculiar to these localities. The flora of Coorg is almost identical with that of Southern India. It is of course beyond the scope of this Gazetteer and equally beyond the knowledge of the compiler, to attempt anything like a full description of the Coorg flora; we can only glance at its distinguishing features and enumerate a few species, that are of practical value, reserving those which fall under the care of the agri-horticulturist for a special consideration.

The first collection of Coorg plants appears to have been made by Captains Munroe and Gough, who probably placed their collections at the disposal of the famous botanist Dr. Wight. Mr. Metz, a German missionary on the Nilagiris, also collected a good many plants about Mercara, which were afterwards distributed in Germany by Hohenacker and named by Miguel. In Major Heber Drury's book on "Useful Plants" and Dr. Bidie's "Timber Trees of India" (1862) much information is given about the principal timber trees in Coorg.

Looking upon Coorg with the eye of the forester, rather than that of the general botanist, the most superficial survey will not fail to discover invaluable treasures of timber trees and their produce, scattered all over the province. Small as the country is, there are nevertheless distinct tracts with trees peculiar to them. The two prominent zones are by the Coorgs called Male-kádu or Hill-forests and Kanive-kádu or Hillock-jungles (Kanive, a ridge between paddy-fields, hillock). Botanically they may perhaps be determined as evergreen and deciduous forests, the former clothing the Ghats, the latter the eastern hill-tracts.

All along the slopes of the Ghats the Poon spar—"Calophyllum augustifolium"—rules as king of the forest. When full grown, it is often upwards of 100 feet in height, its wood is clean, tough and elastic and there is perhaps no other tree so well suited in every respect for making ship's spars and masts. By its side may be seen the black Dammer tree or (*Can.*) Dúppa-mara (Canarium strictum) which attains a great height and may be recognised at a distance by the peculiar red colour of its foliage. The resin obtained from this tree has a brilliant black lustre, when adhering to the ash colored bark, but when held up to the light, it is of a rich brownish yellow tint.

Another resin producing tree is the white Dammer tree (Vateria indica). When an incision is made into the bark of this tree and fire applied to it, the charred trunk yields an increased quantity of the fluid resin.

The Calophyllum inophyllum or Alexandrian Laurel supplies a fragrant resin, and from the seeds is extracted by pressure the Pinnay oil of commerce.

The beautiful order *Guttifera* is also frequently represented by at least 2 species. The *Garcinia pictoria* yields a very superior kind of gamboge, and the other species an inferior sort. The gamboge is obtained from the fruit of the tree by pressure and maceration. A very common tree of the dense forest is the wild cinnamon (Cinnamomum iners) the bark of the branches of which is supposed to form part of the Cassia bark of commerce.

The following trees are noted for the excellence of their timber or other useful qualities: The Sampige—(Champak) Michelia champaca—with its beautiful and sweet scented flowers; the perfection of beauty in the poetical fancy of the Coorg bard, the Ebony—(Diospyros ebenaster) *Can.* Kari-mara, the Wood-oil tree (Dipterocarpus laevis), the Kanagala tree (Dillenia pentagyna), the Jack tree (Artocarpus integrifolius—*Can.* Halasina-mara). The Iron wood (mesua ferrea) with large white fragrant flowers and very hard wood; the Indian Mahogany or White Cedar (Cedrela toona—*Can.* Bellandi-mara), the Red Cedar or Chittagong wood (Chickrassia tabularis), the timber of both trees is little inferior to Mahogany; the wild

Nutmeg (Myristica); the wild Cashew-nut (Anacardium occidentale—*Can.* Géru-mara); the Indian Gutta tree (Isonandra acuminata), a large tree with beautiful foliage and oil yielding nuts; the Bastard Sago (Caryota urens—*Can.* Beini-mara) from which an agreeable toddy is drawn while from the pith sago may be prepared; the Hog-plum tree (Spondias mangifera—*Can.* Ambatte-mara); the wild clove tree (Eugenia).

A most remarkable and truly majestic forest tree is the Lepurandra Saccidora, which deserves to be classed with Thomson's

> "Lofty trees, to ancient song unknown,
> The noble sons of potent heat and floods
> Prone-rushing from the clouds."

It flowers in October in very peculiar catkins, something like a common mulberry. The fruit is in size and shape like a small fig, covered with a beautiful purple coloured down. The Coorgs manufacture very curious sacks from the bark. A branch is cut corresponding to the length and diameter of the sack wanted. It is soaked a little and then beaten with clubs until the liber separates from the wood. This done, the sack formed of the bark is turned inside out and pulled down close to the extremity, where the wood is cut off leaving a thin piece to form the bottom of the sack. These sacks were formerly much used for carrying rice, some of them may be seen in the Mysore Museum. Very different in size, but of far greater importance than the sack tree, is the Poison-nut tree,—"Strychnos nux vomica"—which may be found near it. The wood of this tree is hard and durable, its leaves oval and glossy; the small greenish white flowers appear in February; the fruit is of the size of an orange and in its white harmless pulp are embedded many round flat seeds, from which the powerful poison "Strychnine" is obtained. On open sunny woodsides grow Lobelia nicotianifolia, a stout annual plant with showy white flowers in terminal racemes, and the Brambles: Rubus Lasiocarpus or country raspberry, R. Rugosus a scandent, prickly shrub and R. Wallichiana which yields a delicious fruit. The Conocephalus nivens appears here in great abundance, and proves a troublesome weed on some coffee plantations. Its stem yields a beautiful fibre much resembling that of the Rheea or China grass plant.

The forests in the Ghat region are so dense and tangled by thorny underwood and creepers, that they can only be penetrated by beaten paths and under the guidance of one familiar with their formidable mazes. The many densely shaded mountain rills and torrents are generally lined with a great variety of ferns, prominent amongst which is the stately *Tree fern.* In other places delicate reeds (Wotte) stud the more humid banks of streams. Stout ratans with terrible spines and slender flagelli lashing the air to keep, as it were, intruders at a distance, climb in all directions and surmount with their feathery leaves the highest trees. Favored by the constantly moist atmosphere the stems of many of the trees are speckled with lichens or covered with rare orchids, mosses, and other parasites especially the Mandali-parasite with its large glossy leaves, irregularly cut on one half of the limb. Festoons of wild pepper and gigantic creepers, which again support the more slender herbaceous vines of Convolvulus, Thimbergia, Ipomoea, &c. stretch from tree to tree in the most fantastic interlacings and gorgeously decorate the grand timber trees verdant with their foliage and many hued flowers.

The soil, almost everywhere covered with a humid rich stratum of vegetable mould, highly favors the growth of moisture-loving plants, such as the Indian Arrowroot (Curcuma augustifolia), the long rooted Turmeric (Curcuma longa), the Wild Ginger (Zingiber cassumunar) and especially the highly valued Cardamom.

Wherever the hills are denuded of forest, they are clothed

with a dense coarse grass, which at times greatly impedes their ascent. As the western forests are left and the eastern districts approached, many of the trees just enumerated are still met with, but added thereto others more characteristic of a drier climate. On entering into the more open country, there are found upon the grassy glades (Bánó) smaller trees and shrubs, disposed with an artless grace, that the landscape gardener in vain seeks to imitate. Here spring and summer, in sweet embrace, hold perpetual sway, and the very air, so cool and fresh, seems imbued with life and health.

The aromatic Jasmine with its pure white flowers, the Coorg Rose in its rustic simplicity, the Gloriosa superba with its flaming corolla, the Melastoma malabathricum with its strange looking ribbed leaves and splendid mauve coloured flowers, the Coorg Lilac (Callicarpa Wallichiana) with its small red cymes of flowers, and the Adisia humilis with translucent rose coloured flowers, that look as if they had been cut out of a rare cornelian; these and many other flowering shrubs and herbs greet the eye here.

As we approach the Coorg houses, we come upon groves of Orange, Lime, Guava (Psidium pyriferum), Rose-apple (Jambosa vulgaris), Pomegranate, and clumps of Plantain trees, all of which thrive remarkably well. The Bastard Sago is much esteemed for its toddy and the Areca palm occasionally keeps its company, and their foliage, blended with the dense crown of the stately mango or jack tree, forms a beautiful back ground to the large paddy flats below.

We enter now upon the eastern or bamboo district of Coorg called Kanawé-kádu. The character of this district is indicated by the prevalence of large clumps of bamboo, interspersed with Blackwood, Matti, Hony, Teak, Sandal and other trees. Whoever had the good luck of seeing a Coorg bamboo jungle a few years ago when in its full vigour of growth, cannot have failed to be struck with the elegance and beauty of its general appearance. Captain Basil Hall, who in 1813 entered Coorg from Mysore by way of Siddhapur and Virájpet, thus vividly describes his first impression of a pure bamboo jungle. "It seemed as if I were travelling among the clustered columns of some enormous and enchanted Gothic cathedral. . . . . The ground extended on all sides as smooth and flat and clear of underwood as if the whole had been paved with grave stones. From this level surface rose on every hand and, as far as the eye could penetrate into the forest, immense symmetrical clusters of bamboo, varying in diameter at their base from six feet to twenty or thirty, as I ascertained by actual measurement. For about 8 or 10 feet from the ground each of these clusters or columns preserved a form nearly cylindrical, after which they began gradually to swell outwards, each bamboo assuming for itself a graceful curve and rising to the height some of 60, some of 80 and some even of 100 feet in the air, the extreme end being at times horizontal or even drooping gently over, like the tips of the feathers in the Prince of Wales' plume. These gorgeous clusters stood at a distance of 15 or 20 yards from one another and, being totally free from the interruption of brushwood, could be distinguished at a great distance—more than a mile certainly, in every direction, forming under the influence of an active imagination naves and transepts, aisles and choirs, such as none but a Gothic architect ever dared to conceive . . . ."

A view so grand would now, however, be sought for in vain. The whole of the Coorg bamboo jungles are in a state of decay after the periodical seeding during the last few years. This is a remarkable phenomenon, asserted by the natives, to take place once every 50 or 60 years, though not every where at the same time. In the north-east of Coorg the general seeding took place in 1860, and in the south-west in 1866 and 67, so that there is hardly a green bamboo le in these jungles, but it is said, that on the western slopes of the Ghats the bamboos are still alive and in vigorous health.

The Coorgs have a Canarese proverb:

> "Arvattu warushake ondu katte,
> Yeppattu warushake ondu yette."

which means:

> "Once in 60 years the bamboos will decay,
> Once in 70 years a famine may hold sway."

Lieutenant Connor in his "Coorg Survey" states it as a curious fact, that in 1817 in the whole of the district of Wynád there was scarcely a bamboo clump to be seen, that was not dead, dying or in blossom. Clumps of all ages growing contiguous to or far apart from each other were in the same condition. The same thing happened again there, as well as in Coorg, during the last few years, which occurrence would prove conclusively, that the bamboos, growing from seed and multiplying their reeds from the roots like the grasses, live for a period of about 50 years, when the whole clump with old and young reeds produces flowers and seeds and dies off the same year. From the seed a new progeny springs up, which grows very fast, but not, as has been supposed, to its whole length in one season. This is only true of such shoots as spring up from the main clump, after it has nearly reached maturity, which requires a growth of 12 years. These shoots, being armed at their extremity by a sharp, smooth hornlike cone, and without any lateral branches, force their way through the intricate mass of the parent reeds and contribute to the density, stability and stateliness of the whole clump, which may contain from 50 to 200 reeds. The several reeds are from 5 to 8 inches in diameter, jointed at every 12 or 15 inches, and hollow between the joints where thorny threepartite branches are alternately attached, of which the middle ones are strongest and make good walking sticks. The branches are repeatedly subdivided and present with their delicate light green foliage of linear lanceolate leaves a most graceful feathery appearance. When in blossom the bamboo is leafless and the extremities are covered with flowers like one large compound panicle. The seed is in size and appearance like oats or small paddy. It is eaten by the poorer classes, but considered unwholesome. The birds and rats, however, revel in the feast of plenty. The water into which bamboo seed has largely fallen is said to be particularly noxious.

The cutting of bamboo, is a difficult task that is rarely well done by any other than those expert jungle people, the Yerawas and Kurumbas. For the purpose of cutting a single reed they manage to climb over the lower thorny mass to where the reeds branch out freely about 10 or 15 feet above the ground and cut them at that height. To level the whole clump, the Yerawa has to cut the stem of each bamboo below and above his head, removing each piece from the thorny embrace of the rest; he thus boldly advances into the clump, and the further he progresses in his work the greater is the danger of the whole clump suddenly giving way at the slightest breeze and crushing the unfortunate intruder.

There are several kinds of bamboo, the one described is, however, the most common. The reeds of another kind are much smaller and solid and are known by the name of Male-bamboos.

One of the handsomest trees in the eastern jungles is the *Blackwood* or Dalbergia latifolia with a stem of 2 or 3 feet in diameter and 60 to 80 feet in height. It is one of the most valuable timber trees in India and little, if at all, inferior to the South American Rosewood, which it closely resembles in many particulars. Near neighbours of Blackwood are *Matti* and *Hony*. The *Matti* or Terminalia coriacea is remarkable for its excellent timber, and is easily recognised by its thick ash-coloured bark, cracked into small tablets like the scales of a crocodile. Under the knotty swellings of the bark of the Matti tree small quantities of water are hidden, which the lynx-eyed Kuruba readily discovers in his jungle-wanderings during the hot season and from which providential fountains he draws a thirst-quenching draft. The *Hony* or Kino tree (Pterocarpus marsupium) yields an excellent yellowish timber fit for exposure and a valuable brownish gum, the kino, which oozes out from the wounded stem. Chunam brought in contact with it turns bright yellow.

Teak or Tectonia grandis occupies a distinct girdle along the eastern boundary of Coorg, within the basin of the Lakshmanatirtha and in Nanjarájpatna and Yélusávirashíme taluq; but, with the exception of the Amali-topu in Kiggatnád, the teak forests in Coorg are neither so dense, nor so stately as those in Burmah, where trees of enormous size and height are found. The large and strongly nerved leaves, rough above, whitish and downy beneath, and the numerous white flowers in terminal branches on the high and many branched trunk, mark the beauty and strength of the tree. Both for house and ship building teak is the best of woods, easily worked and almost indestructible by climate or insects owing to its oily nature. Coorg teak is of most excellent quality, oily and free of heart-shake. It is a Government monopoly and sold from wood-yards at the rate of 12 Annas per cubic foot.

In close proximity to teak and in an equally limited tract of dry and elevated slopes grows the *White Sandal-wood*, (Santalum album) scattered between other trees and on cultivated land. It is rather a small tree of a more or less crooked stem, but its spreading branches with tiny, light-green leaves and yellow or purple coloured small flowers give it an elegant appearance and a marked feature in the landscape. The wood is close-grained and hard, especially the duramen or heart-wood, which for these qualities and for its agreeable scent is highly prized and employed for ornamental boxes, card cases, paper cutters, fans, walking sticks, etc. which are made chiefly in Nuggur and North Canara. Sandal-wood is also a Government monopoly and is collected at an expense of one eighth of the value of the wood, trees when from 16 to 40 years old according to the nature of the soil, where grown, are cut down; the best yield a billet of 5 inches square and 4 or 5 feet long. The wood fetches at the public auctions periodically held by Government at the coties or wood stores, from 70 to 98 Rupees per candy of 550 avoirdupois, and is generally exported to Bombay. Natives distinguish 3 kinds according to colour: the "red sandal" (sriganda) which is the most highly scented, the "yellow sandal" (arasana ganda), and the "white sandal" (bili ganda) which possesses but a faint aroma and is least prized. The chips are burnt as perfume, or reduced to powder which enters into the composition for marking the foreheads of natives. The roots, containing the greatest amount of the essential oil, are chiefly used for its production. It is heavier than water and yields an excellent perfume. The sandal tree is propagated from seed and suckers, springing up from the roots.

A stately though not very valuable tree all over these parts of the country is the *Wild Mango tree*, which towers with its lofty crown far above its humbler neighbours. But the giant of these jungles is the *Ajini* or *Wild Jack tree* (Artocarpus hirsuta), the timber of which is most useful for house and ship building. The rosy-tinted, smooth-barked *Ben-teak* or Nandi (Lagerstroemia parviflora) is reputed for its excellent timber.

A splendid jungle tree, when in flower in February and March, is the *Red Cotton tree* or Bombax Malabaricum a very large specimen, stands in front of the Anandapur Mission Church. Its flowers are large and of a deep red colour, and the many seeded capsules contain a silky cotton, which is employed for stuffing pillows and mattresses. The staple is so short as to render this so-called cotton commercially valueless. The wood is soft and spongy and of little value. Another red cotton tree of smaller size and with a prickly trunk is the Salmalia Malabarica (*Can.* Mulu yelava). The Dindul or "Conocarpus latifolius" is a fine timber tree and very frequent in the deciduous jungles. The heart-wood is of a chocolate colour and exceedingly durable. The Kurubas use it for axe-handles. When burning it emits an intense and sustained heat and is therefore highly prized for lime kilns and distilleries. The *Hedde-mara* or "Nauclea cordifolia" yields a beautiful close-grained wood resembling box; but it cannot withstand exposure to damp. Its small yellow flowers appear in November and December. The "Rottleria tinctoria" furnishes an orange dye—the kapela ranga. The *Soap-nut tree* (sapindus) which is here rather common, produces a small fruit, the pulp of which is saponaceous and used by the natives for washing. For marking their cotton clothes the pure black acrid juice of the shell of the "marking nut" is used; it is the fruit of a tree about 50 feet high, the Semercarpas Anacardium. The native ink is chiefly manufactured with the fruit or galls of the Alali-mara and sulphate of iron. This tree, the Terminalia chebula, yields excellent galls produced by insects puncturing the tender leaves. The astringent nuts bruised and mixed with molasses and chunam produce a very strong mortar. They are also larglcy used for tannin purposes.

On the outskirts of bamboo jungles the *Indian Coral tree* (Erythrina Indica) with its brilliant scarlet flowers may be frequently found; its soft wood is much used for toys. On account of its prickly bark the branches make good fences, and where the betel vine is cultivated this tree offers an excellent support. A very pretty tree with spreading pinnate foliage and gooseberry like seeds is the *Nelli-kai-mara* or "Emblica Officinalis." The fruit though hard is welcome to many for its thirst assuaging properties. Sometimes it is preserved in sugar. The Bastard Teak (Butea frondosa), though common, is a very beautiful tree when in flower. Its scarlet flowers dye cotton yellow, and from the bark when cut a gum "Palas-kino" is obtained. A fragrant resin called "Kundricum" is furnished by the Gugula-mara (Boswellia glabra) an erect tall tree covered with greenish ash-coloured bark.

On the table-land of Mercara the Kake-mara or the Coorg laburnum (Cathartocarpus fistula) is particularly conspicuous in April and May by its beautiful long pendulous racemes of yellow flowers. Its long cylindric legumes of dark brown colour and nearly 2 feet in length contain a mucilaginous pulp, which is a valuable laxative when mixed with Cassia. On the same plateau is found the American Aloe (Agave Americana) with its high flower stem and long thick leaves, which might be turned into excellent fibre, but beyond a few experiments no manufacture is carried on. The plant serves for making fences only. It has been superseded, however, by the Lantana shrub (Lantana Aculeata), which within a few years has spread over the whole of Coorg. Its square stem and branches are prickly, its ovate leaves when bruised have a strong smell of black currants, and its orange coloured flowers are more or less in blossom throughout the year, and the shrub when kept within proper bounds makes an excellent fence. But this plant whose vitality is most obstinate, threatens to overrun many a tract of land in Coorg and elsewhere that might be far more profitably occupied. The recognised necessity of shading exposed coffee plantations has brought to notice a tree, chiefly distinguished for its quick growth and shady crown—the *Charcoal tree* (Sponea Wightii) It springs up spontaneously on every new clearing after the burn and mostly so in the eastern districts. Its wood produces a fine charcoal and its bark an excellent fibre. For beauty of shape and foliage the solitary *Nela-mávina-mara*

(Xanthochymus pictorius?) forms a striking contrast to the former. Its branches commence near the ground, and covered with elongated dark green glossy leaves form as they ascend a gently inclined cone. The fruit of the size of an orange and beautifully yellow is rather acid, but it is eagerly sought after and eaten by the natives.

A graceful vegetable beauty of a different character is presented to view by the *Bilwára tree* (Mimosa) which with its spreading airy crown of tiny pinnate leaves and small white fragrant flowers is a graceful jungle ornament. The wood is very hard and strong. Near banks of streams and water courses the Coldera bush or *Fragrant Screwpine* (Pandanus odoratissimus) is commonly found and much used for making mats and umbrellas. In many arid places in the east and north of Coorg the *Dwarf date palm* (Phoenix farinifera) nearly monopolizes the ground. Its leaves are made into mats and baskets and from the small stem a farinaceous substance is prepared for food. A hillock of date palms before the hot season in January presents the appearance of, what we hope may be a thing of the past, a bored coffee estate.

At Fraserpet in the compound of the Coorg Superintendent's Bungalow there are a few trees of the valuable *Divi-divi* or Shumach tree (Caesalpinia Coriaria). It is a small umbrageous tree and would do very well for coffee-shading, and its incurved oblong pods contain about 50 per cent of tannin, the price of which varies in Europe from £ 8 to £ 13 a ton, so that its cultivation might pay as a commercial enterprise.

Thus these eastern jungles contain a number of useful trees. I would now add a few trees, growing in the open, but thriving remarkably well in Coorg, viz: the several representatives of the Ficus tribe, especially the Banian tree (Ficus Indica), of which there are some beautiful specimens near

Fraserpet to which the elegant lines of Southey so truly apply:—

"It was a goodly sight to see
That venerable tree.
For over the lawn irregularly spread,
Fifty straight columns propt its lofty head;
And many a long depending shoot,
Seeking to strike its root,
Straight like a plummet, grew towards the ground,
Some on the lower boughs, which crost their way,
Fixing their bearded fibres, round and round,
Some to the passing wind at times, with sway
Of gentle motion swang.
Others of younger growth, unmoved, were hung
Like stone drops from the cavern's fretted height.
Beneath was smooth and fair to sight,
Nor weeds nor briars deformed the natural floor
And through the leaf-cope which bower'd it over
Came gleams of checkered light.
So like a temple did it seem, that there
A pious heart's first impulse would be prayer."

(*The Curse of Kehama, Book* 13.)

The *Pippal* (Ficus religiosa) is likewise a large tree and found nearly in every temple in Coorg, but growing best in the drier districts. This tree proves most destructive to neglected buildings; when once rooted in crevices, nothing can withstand its progress. More common than both preceding trees is the *Atti-mara* or "Ficus glomerata" with fruit much like the common fig and which is eaten by the natives. The *Indian Caoutchouc tree* "Ficus elastica" also occurs and is not only a useful but highly ornamental tree. The milky juice obtained from incisions into the bark is exposed to the air, when the *Caoutchouc* or elastic substance spontaneously separates, leaving a foetid whey-coloured liquid.

Almost a stranger to Coorg and growing only in several places along the Kávéri between Fraserpet and Sómawarpet, is the *Tamaind tree* (Tamarindus Indica) which Government has reserved and partly made over without tax to certain Brahmins in Ramaswámy Kanawé, partly formed out on yearly rent. It is a stately tree and yields a dense shade, under which however, many plants do not grow and natives do not like to sleep.

It would lead me too far to enter upon a description of the many shrubs, herbs and grasses of these jungles. Suffice it to say, that there are many and very beautiful ones, but most of them are annually swept away by the periodical fires, the purifying messengers of nature, that run through every jungle from February to April. These fires once established in the high coarse hill-grass rush madly in their onward career to the very tops of the mountains, and beautiful is the sight at night of these distant serpentine lines of flame extending over whole ranges of hills.

Coorg is rich in ferns and as these elegant plants will always attract the lover of nature, it may perhaps prove acceptable, if I append a list of such, as have been collected about Mercara and identified according to Major Beddon's work on Ferns by an enthusiastic admirer of these humble productions of nature:—

Alphabetical list of Coorg ferns.

Names.	Where to be found.
Acrophorus immersus	On trees and at the foot of trees, near Ball-practice ground, Falls, etc. common.
Acrophorus pulcher	On trees and rocks; near Ball-practice ground; abundant almost anywhere.
Adiantum capillus veneris	In a wall close to the Fort.
Do. candatum	Near Ramaswámy Kanawé.
Do. hispidulum	Near Ball-practice ground, 3rd milestone, Sunticoppalu Road.

Names.	Where to be found.
Adiantum lunulatum	Common everywhere.
Alsophila glabra	Road to Falls.
Alsophila latebrosa	Road to Falls, (common tree fern.)
Angiopteris evecta	Road to Falls, common in all moist places.
Aspidium polymorphum	Road to Falls, abundant in a deep kadanga.
Aspidium contractum	Same place a former one, also in a lane near 3rd milestone, Sunticoppalu Road.
Asplenium contignum	On trees, between 1st and 2nd milestone, Mangalore Ghat.
Do. *falcatum*	On trees, Sapper Lines, Road to Falls.
Do. *formosum*	On trees, in a deep ditch near Race-course.
Do. *furcatum*	On trees, near Ball-practice ground; common.
Do. *heterocarpum*	In a kadanga on Road to Falls, in moist shady ravines.
Do. *planicaule*	Very common, on trees.
Do. *resectum*	Near 3rd milestone, Sunticoppalu Road in a ravine, also on Road to Falls.
Do. *trapeziforme*	Near 3rd milestone, Sunticoppalu Road, and in a ravine near Race-course.
Athyrium Hohenackerianum	Abundant on all banks during the monsoon.
Blechnum Orientale	Common everywhere.
Botrychium virginicum	On trees, at the foot of Prospect Point Hill on Road to Kadle-kádu.
Do. *Subcarnosum*	Road connecting Cannanore and Mangalore at Louden Valley Estate.
Ceratopteris thalictroides	In a swamp in Muctoom Sahib's Estate, Nalkanád Road, 3 miles from Mercara.
Cheilanthes farinosa	Very common (silver fern).
Do. *tenuifolia*	3 miles out on Nalkanád Road, also Rajah's seat, generally in dry places.
Davallia bullata	5 miles out on Nalkanád Road, on road connecting Cannanore and Mangalore Ghats, grows on trees, pretty common.
Do. *teanifolia*	Common everywhere.
Diflazium dilatatum	On Road to Falls.
Do. *lasiopteris*	On Road to Falls; near Ball-practice ground.

Names.	Where to be found.
Diplazium polypodioides	Between 1st and 2nd milestone Mangalore Ghat; quite a tree fern.
Do. sylvaticum	On Road to Falls.
Drymaria quercifolia	4 miles out on Nalkanád Road on trees.
Gleichenia dichotoma	Very common.
Goniopteris prolifera	Fish river, Kadur-kádu Estate.
Gymnogramma leptophylla	Near 1st milestone Mangalore Ghat. On a bank on Road passing Government School.
Gymnopteris Feei	Muctoom Sahib's Estate, Nalkanád Road; on rocks, trees.
Hemionitis cordata	Very common on Sunticoppalu Road.
Lastrea aristata	Common on Road to Falls.
Do. cochleata	One of the very commonest ferns.
Do. falciloba	Very common.
Do. hirtipes	Near Nalkanád palace.
Do. membraniifolia	Muctoom Sahib's Estate, Nalkanád Road.
Do. ochthodes	Very common.
Do. sparsa	Near Ball-practice ground; on Road to Falls.
Lygodium scandens	In a swamp 3 miles out on Nalkanád Road; 4 miles down Cannanore Ghat.
Microlepia polypodioides	In a ravine near 3rd milestone Mangalore Ghat.
Nephrodium abruptum	Muctoom Sahib's Estate Nalkanád Road.
Do. molle	Very common.
Do. propinquum	Muctoom Sahib's Estate; also Anandapur "Kembu Kolli" Estate.
Do. terminans	Abundant on Nalkanád Road.
Do. unitum	Muctoom Sahib's Estate.
Nephrolepis exaltata	A common wayside fern, in moist places.
Do. tuberosa	Near Rajah's seat; common.
Niphobolus porosus	Nalkanád Road on trees; rather common.
Oleandra neriiformis	On Nalkanád Road; on Road connecting Cannanore and Mangalore Ghats; on trees.
Ophioglossum reticulatum	On Ball-practice ground and in the Fort.
Do. previpes	Near Kaden-kádu on banks of Fish river.
Osmunda regalis	Abundant on banks of Fish river.
Pleocnemia aristata	Two miles beyond Murnad bungalow.
Pleopeltis irioides	On trees and in bamboo clumps, Nalkanád Road.

Names.	Where to be found.
Pleopeltis membranacia	3rd milestone Mangalore Ghat; abundant in moist, shady places, on trees.
Do. oxyloba	Abundant, on trees.
Do. phymatodes	On trees.
Do. wightiana	Very common.
Paecilopteris contaminans	Falls
Do. terminans	Falls.
Polybotrya appendiculata	In ravines near May-male Estate; also Sómawarpet Road.
Do. aspleniifolia	Falls.
Polypodium ornatum	3rd milestone Mangalore Ghat; on Road to Falls.
Do. regulosum	Banks of stream near Post-Office; near Falls, etc. common.
Pteris aquilina	The commonest fern in Coorg.
Do. cretica	On Road to Falls, abundant.
Do. geraniifolia	Near 3rd milestone Sunticoppalu Road; also near Ball-practice ground.
Do. longifolia	Abundant in and about the Fort.
Do. pellucens	Near Nalkanád; also near May-male Estate, Beltamale Estate.
Do. pellucida	Common in all jungles about Mercara.
Do. quadriaurita	Very common.
Do. argentea and rubronerva	Varieties, both abundant especially the latter
Sagenia coadunata	Very common.
Schizoloma ensifolium	At the top of the Falls, very abundant and handsome.
Do. heterophyllum	On Road to Falls; near Sapper Lines.
Do. nitens	Muctoom Sahib's Estate; has not been met with anywhere else as yet.
Trichomanes filicula	On trees near 3rd milestone Sunticoppalu Ghat; Nalkanád Road.
Do. rigidum	On the Bank of the stream that forms the Falls.
Vittaria elongata	On trees, Nalkanád Road about 4 miles out on the right hand side.

To facilitate reference to the vegetable products of Coorg jungle trees and plants, they are here enumerated under the classification of

a. Gums. (soluble in water)—They are obtained from the cashew-nut tree (Anacardium occidentale), the Ambate-mara or hog-plum (Spondias mangifera), the Atti-mara (Ficus glomerosa), the Gambali-mara, the Halumatti-mara, the jack tree (Artocarpus hirsutus), the elephant or wood-apple tree (Feronia elephantum), the bastard teak (Butea frondosa) and the Babul tree (Acacia Arabica).

b. Caoutchouc—or elastic gum is supplied by "Ficus elastica" and "Isonandra acuminata".

c. Gum-resins—the produce of Garcinia pictoria (gamboge), Pterocarpus marsupium (kino), Boswellia glabra (kundricum), Odina wodier (odina gum), Neem tree and Bombax Malabaricum.

d. Oleo-resins—obtained from the Canarium strictum (black dammer), Shorea robusta (rál), Vateria Indica (Indian copal), Dipterocarpus laevis (wood-oil), Calophyllum Inophyllum and Terminalia coreacea.

e. Oils—extracted from the seeds of the Neem tree, the Alexandrian laurel, the Powali, the Nirala and the Kákorate tree.

f. Fibres—obtained from the Kóli, Antupurle, and Bendé-mara, the Indian fig, pippal, banyan and red wooded fig tree (Ficus racemosa), the variegated American aloe, the long aloe (Agave vivipera), the Indian hemp (Crotalaria Juncea), the bow-string hemp (Sanseviera zeilanica). The plantain (musa paradisiaca and textilis), the paddy straw (Oriza sativa), the mat-rush (Cyperus textilis), the broom grass (Aristida setacea), the cotton plant (Gossypium Herbaceum), the silk-cotton tree (Bombax Pentandrum), the Conocephalus nivens, the Sponia Wightii or Charcoal tree, the Nerium grandiflorum and the Isora corylifolia or sham hazel.

g. Tannin—the produce of the bark of the Babool tree, the Neem tree, the Bauhinia variegata, the Buchanania latifolia, the Hymenodyction excelsum, of the pod of the Dividivi tree (Caesalpinia Coriaria), and of the nut of the Alalimara (Terminalia Chebula).

h. Dyes—*Red*, obtained from tne Rottleria tinctoria, the Indian madder (Hedyotis umbellata), Indian mulberry (Morinda citrifolia) the red sandal (Pterocarpus Santalinus). *Yellow*, from the bastard teak (Butea frondosa), the gamboge tree (Garcinia pictoria), the Xanthochymus pictorius and the Berberis tinctoria.

i. Saponaceous matter—yielded by the bark of the Babool tree, the pods of Mimosa saponaria and the fruit of the Soapnut tree (Sapindus).

General fauna of Coorg—It may be easily imagined, that a country, so well watered and wooded and with a vegetation abounding in nourishing produce, will sustain a great variety of animal life. This was still more the case ere the resounding axe of the planter and the still more frequent echo of the sportman's rifle have disturbed the animals' secluded abodes and driven them to remoter regions.

A brief grouping of the more prominent representatives of animal life in Coorg will be all that can be attempted within the small space allotted to the subject. Descending in the scale of zoological classification, it is the monkey tribe, that first claims our attention and there are 3 species for inspection: the black, the grey and the brown monkey. The black monkey or "Wanderoo" (Silenus veter. Linn)—*Kg.* Karingóde—is rather scarce and only found in the Male-kádu or Ghat forests. It has greyish whiskers, chest and belly, and is of small size. Its intelligent look and playful disposition render it a favorite with the natives, but like other monkeys, it is an unsavoury pet, and its capricious and vindictive temper, when getting old, render it a dangerous playmate for children.

The grey or Hanumán monkey (Semnopithecus entellus, Duff)—*Kg.* Kóde—prefers a more open country and does not shun the neighbourhood of native dwellings, where there are Upali trees of the fruit of which it is very fond. Troops of them may sometimes be seen on an open glade near a large tree, gambolling unmindful of the passing by of a native, but quickly disappearing in the dense foliage on the appearance of a European, chattering all the while with their little ones, whose frightened expression is pitiful, clinging to their sides. This monkey is considerably larger than the former species and has a long tail, which is of service in gymnastic feats on slender branches. Its face is bare and rather reddish. It is more docile than the black monkey, but when big more vindictive and dangerous. A case happened in Mercara, where one of these monkeys attacked a baby in its cradle and might have killed it, but for the timely arrival of the parents.

The brown monkey—*Kg.* Mucha—is only found in the Mále-kádu and eagerly hunted by the Coorgs, who eat its flesh roasted and in curry, and consider it a great delicacy. A soup made of its flesh is given to sick and weakly people. When full grown, this monkey is in a sitting posture about two feet high; it has a long tail, a light grey face and chest. It is never kept as a pet by natives. Of the skin of all the three named species the Coorgs make their tom toms or drums.

A little animal of the Lemur kind is the slender *Loris* (Loris gracilis. Linn). The Coorgs call them Chínge-kúli or devils of the Chínge or soapnut shrub which grows all over the central and northern plateau of Coorg. Its silent and slow gait, its thin limbs, its closely set and large protruding eyes and pointed visage are enough to frighten on a sudden encounter any one, who has been attracted by its peculiar noise. It is covered with a light brown woolly fur, whitish beneath, and lives chiefly on fruits, but is not frequently met with. When unobserved, it moves about the tree in a lively manner, but quickly escapes on being noticed.

There appear to be but two species of *Bats* (vespertilio), which are however very common in Coorg houses and temples and on the sago and plantain tree. Their flesh is considered very strengthening, and in cases, where Europeans would give cod liver oil to a delicate child, the Coorgs administer a roasted bat.

Of the ***Carnivora*** there are many representatives foremost the *Royal tiger* (felis tigris) which in former days was much more numerous all over Coorg; but even now it is not scarce, though he seldom attacks man. The large game of the jungles and the herds of cattle roaming about satisfy his appetite. During the reign of the Coorg Rajahs there were annual tiger hunts and Linga Rajah seldom killed fewer than there were days in the year. He was fond of these animals and kept some about his palace as pets. An amusing story about these royal pets is told by Captain Basil Hall, who visited this prince in 1813: "On returning" he writes, "to the great square in the centre of the building (new palace in Mercara) we found 3 chairs placed for us on Turkey carpet, spread on the ground in the open air. The Rajah took a seat and made me come beside him, after placing his son, a nice little boy, nine or ten years of age, on my right hand. This young fellow was gaily dressed with a large overspreading turban. A dark circle about the tenth of an inch broad, was painted round each of his eyes, which gave him a strange staring look; and on his cheeks, brow and chin were placed small black marks, or beautiful spots about twice as large as the head or dot of a note in music.

"The whole area of the court was now begirt with soldiers,

each holding as high as his face, an immense billhook or knife, the blade of which near the extremity could not be less than three inches wide and diminishing gradually towards the hilt. This formidable instrument, well known in Indian warfare under the name of the "Coorg knife", is often used as a sword, and when handled by men, who are not afraid to close with their antagonist, is said to be a most efficient weapon.

"On a signal given by the Rajah a folding door was thrown open on one side of the court, and in stalked two immense royal tigers, held by several men on each side by long ropes, attached to collars round the animals' necks. These beasts appeared very tractable, for they allowed themselves to be led very close to us. I confess, I did not much like this degree of propinquity and eyed the slender cordage with some professional anxiety. Meanwhile the Rajah and his son and the officers of the household appeared quite unconcerned, though the tigers passed within a few yards of them, and, as it seemed to me, might easily have broken loose.

"What degree of training these animals had undergone, I know not, but after a little while, the Rajah, probably to increase the surprise of his guest, directed the men to let go the ropes and to fall back. There we sat in the midst of the open court with a couple of full sized tigers in our company, and nothing on earth to prevent their munching us all up! The well fed and well bred beasts, however, merely lounged about, rubbed their noses together and then tumbling on the ground, rolled about like a couple of kittens at play. I could, however, detect the Rajah spying at me out of the corner of his eye and half smiling at the success of his trick. After a time the men were recalled and the tigers dragged off.

"A pair of lionesses and two furious looking buffaloes were then introduced, but nothing could be more innocent or more respectful to the Rajah and his son. Like Falstaff, indeed, they seemed to have an instinctive knowledge of the true prince. Yet for all this, I caught myself several times edging my chair back a little bit and looking out for a clear place to escape, as the monsters stalked up and down the court, and once or twice actually touched the edge of our carpet with their feet. On these occasions, that part of the circle of guards which stood behind us advanced just so far as to bring our chairs on the outside of their ring and to place themselves between the beasts and us. On clapping their hands and flourishing their knives the lionesses and other beasts moved a little further off, after which the guards again dropped to the rear. Still this seemed rather a poor protection; at least I had my recollection so full of the rapid motions of the same class of animals, which I have seen baited at Mysore, that I could discover nothing which need have prevented the lionesses from whipping off the heads of the Rajah and the heir apparent, or at all events, that of their guest, who having no particular claims to the throne of Coorg, could reckon on none of the benefits of instinctive respect.

"The Rajah gave orders for half a dozen tiger's cubs about eight months old, and as many puppy dogs to be set to play before us on the carpet, while a full grown royal tiger was at the same time dragged forward and pitted against a bear for a real battle in the open court. Any thing more disproportionate or absurd cannot be conceived than this match; and so, perhaps, the poor brutes thought, for fight they would not, although both of them were well thumped and forced against each other by the attendants. At length a brilliant thought struck the Rajah. 'Tie them together!' exclaimed his majesty; and accordingly the rope which was fastened to the tiger's collar was hitched to the belly band of the bear. Neither party liked this. The tiger roared and the bear growled while the Rajah and his son laughed and clapped their hands in ecstacy at their own good joke. Of course the guards and courtiers joined in the mirth and the whole quadrangle rang with mixed shouts of the soldiers, the growl of the bear and the roar of the tiger. Of all the parties in this singular concert, the tiger appeared to be the most discomposed. His eye flashed fire, his tail waved from flank to flank in the most ominous style. I thought at one time, this was to turn out no laughing matter; for, if the angry animal, when at length he lost all patience, had taken a direction towards us, he might have demolished the dynasty of Wadeer, or at least made a vacancy for an officer in his Britannic Majesty's Navy. Fortunately he chose exactly the opposite course, and running furiously across the court, made a flying leap right into one of the low windows of what the Rajah called his English drawing room. The glass and framework of the window were of course dashed to pieces in a moment and the pianos, pictures and book cases must have soon shared the same fate, had not the tiger's progress been checked by the weight of the wretched bear, which hung outside, half way between the window sill and the ground, somewhat after the fashion of the golden fleece over a mercer's door. The tiger we could no longer see, but we could hear him smashing the furniture at a great rate. He was afterwards secured and sent to the rear."

After a successful hunt for a tiger, the natives form a procession and carry the carcass with the band of tomtoms to the mandu or village green. The heroes of the day are the man who shot the beast and he who first touched its tail, a feat which used to be rewarded by the Rajah with the present of a silver bangle. The carcass is then raised on a wooden frame, and according to time-honored Coorg fashion, the lucky sportsman is to be wedded to the departed soul of the tiger and may thenceforth wear the honorable gala-mishi or grand mustachio in Rajah's fashion. In May last such a ceremony took place in Mercara on the occasion of

C. Cariappah, the Subadar of the taluq, having shot a tiger. Under a screen, on a wedding chair, his face towards the carcass sat the hero of the day, clothed in Coorg warrior costume and covered with flower wreaths and gold ornaments. Behind him stood his armour-bearers, in front the sacred house lamp on a heap of rice, poured into a brass dish. First each member of his house, men, women and children, then all his friends, one by one, stepped up to the bridegroom; strewed a handful of rice from the brass dish over his head, gave him from a brass vessel a sip of milk to drink and in making obeisance, dropped a silver coin into his lap. This money is given with a view to defray the impending expenditure on a sumptuous dinner, given to the whole company. A Coorg dance round the tiger concludes the tamásh and the night wears away with singing and feasting.

Government has now fixed a reward of Rupees five for the destruction of a tiger and Rupees three for that of a cheeta; but the unmutilated skin with the clows has to be delivered to the Sirkar. The height of the tiger varies from 3 to 4 and his length from 6 to 7 feet to which 3 feet may be added for the length of the tail. His weight is from 250 to 400 lbs.

Sometimes one sees children with the ornament of 2 tiger's claws, joined together by silver or gold and suspended round the neck. This charm is supposed to keep off the evil eye. The age of a tiger is said to be ascertained by the number of lobes of his liver, one lobe being added every year!

The cheeta (*Can.* kiruba) or panther is more common than the tiger. It is a very destructive beast to smaller domestic animals. In his depredations he is a coward, chiefly attacking his prey by night and fleeing man, if unmolested. Upon the destruction of a cheeta by a Coorg, the same festivities, as on the tiger hunt, take place, but there is less honour to the sportsman. The skin of the cheeta is spotted with black roundish spots. It is 2¼ or 3 feet high and 4 feet long from the tip of the nose to the root of the tail.

The tiger-cat (*Can.* huli-bekku) is a cheeta in miniature and its sleek, glossy, speckled fur renders it a very beautiful animal. It is about 3 feet long and 15 inches high; it is destructive to fowls. The Holeyas eat it.

The black jungle-cat (kabbekku), of the size of a house-cat, but with pointed muzzle, is very common; it lives chiefly on the fruit of the wild fig tree and sago palm. The Coorgs are fond of its flesh. Similar to this in form, but different in colour is the civet-cat (punugina bekku) which yields a peculiar musky secretion.

The hyæna (katte kiruba) is very seldom seen. Of the dog-family there is, besides the Pariah, the wild dog (*Can.* kennai). In resemblance it approaches nearest the wolf. It is a powerful and dangerous brute, remarkable for the strength of its neck and jaws. Its colour is reddish brown, and in size it is like a Pariah dog, whose barking it imitates. It is seldom seen alone but in packs of 10 to 20, and thus united they will attack any beast of the forest, even the tiger. They are swift and never fail in catching what they once give chase to; on coming up with their game, they seize the animal from behind or in front, immediately destroying the eyes and having once fixed themselves, they maintain their position, sucking the blood of their unfortunate victim and never quitting their hold, till it has fallen from pain and fatigue. The samber and other deer are the principal animals they prey upon. Remarkable for his peculiar and piercing yell in moonlight nights is the jackal, so common over the whole of India. Besides feeding on small game and poultry, he is not averse to carrion of any kind. The jackal is no favourite of the planters, for he pilfers a great deal of ripe cherry-coffee, but is honest enough to deposite the beans, which are considered all the better for their transmigration through his body!

The fact is, that, as the jackal eats only the ripest berries, the beans are naturally of a good quality.

The mungoose or Ichneumon Múngos (Viverra mungo *Can.* kíra)—is frequently found on the bánes, where it is seen running from one copse to another. Its elongated, slender body with pearly, ash-grey fur and thick long tail, its pointed head and bright eyes and its rapid movements give it a pretty appearance, and, but for its wanton depredations amongst the poultry, it might become a useful pet, as it destroys rats and snakes. The natives say that after its struggle with a poisonous snake, it takes recourse to the Nágadále (Ruta, Rue) the leaves of which act as an antidote.

Black bears (*Can.* karadi) are found in Marenád on the Pushpagiri, Kóte-betta and Kálur-betta, where there are colonies of beehives, for Master Bruin is very fond of honey. His flesh is not eaten, but pieces of his skin are attached to the necks of horses and cows, to keep off the evil eye.

On the wooded banks of the Hatti and Shóran-hole and elsewhere there are small colonies of a species of otter-hound, which the natives call Nírunái or water-dog (Lutra Nair Cuv.) The animal is deep reddish brown on the back, lightest on the sides and below, lives in artificial burrows and subsists on fish, which it catches with great skill. It is eaten by the Yerawas.

Mice and *rats* there are more of in Coorg, than the farmer and house-owner would wish. The musk-rat betrays itself by its piercing shriek, but has a safeguard in its strong smell against its pursuing enemies. Great havoc has been done on some coffee plantations by the bamboo-rat (Golunda Ellioti) which is gregarious and for want of jungle-food often attacks in great numbers the coffee shrub, selecting the tender and succulent shoots and, to get at them, cutting off the primaries near the stem. Most wary of traps of any kind, this destructive animal is difficult to deal with. The field-rat (*Can.*

kádili) is of a brownish colour; in its provident care against the rainy season it commits great damage to the ripening paddy-fields and stores considerable quantities of grain in its subterraneous burrows, to the great satisfaction, however, of the lynxeyed Wotter (tank digger) who searches after the little granary and carries away in triumph the owner and its property for his own meal. A formidable rat for its destructive burrowing habits is the Bandicoot (*Mus bandicota Can.* Heggana). It grows to the size of a sucking pig, is of a blackish colour and lives near houses. To protect their rice against these enemies, the Coorgs store their grain in enclosures, called pattáya, which are raised 2 feet from the ground with an open space all round. It undermines walls and causes buildings to tumble down. Its flesh is eaten by the Holeyas, Kurubas and Yerawas.

Of squirrels there are 4 species: the striped, the grey, the red and the flying squirrel. The first species (Tamias striatus) is very common in the open and warmer districts of Coorg, especially in Fraserpet, where it familiarly runs along the thatched roofs of the European bungalows and amuses their inmates with its little squeak. It is a pretty tiny creature; with its tail it measures about 9 inches. Its body is of a greyish colour, whitish below and 3 brown longitudinal stripes and 2 white ones on the upper parts. In Hindoo fable, this little animal is said to have been rewarded by Ráma for its services in constructing his bridge over the sea to Ceylon. Passing his hand over its back he said: "Shábás" (well done) and behold, it was marked with indelible streaks!

The grey squirrel is somewhat larger than the former, without stripes, and lives on trees. The red squirrel (Sciurus maximus, *Can.* kenjari) is a remarkably lively and handsome animal, when enjoying its native liberty. In length over two feet, of which its bushy tail measures half, it surpasses its European cousin in size and beauty. All that can be seen of its body from above is of a dark chocolate colour deepening into black along the centre of its back and tail, while the under parts are of a pale yellowish brown. When young, it is easily tamed and proves an amusing pet, but it tries its sharp teeth on most substances, that come within its power, and too confiding children, when ruffling its temper, may suffer harm. The Kurubas, who know the trees of the forest as familiarly as a police man the streets and houses of his beat, catch these squirrels by means of nets which they fix to branches that are in the track of the animals.

The grey flying squirrel or flying cat (Pteromys) has become better known since the destruction of so many forests, when hundreds of the harmless little animals were caught or shot. It is crepuscular in its habits and, unless disturbed, very rarely seen. Its home is in the holes of trees and it lives entirely on fruit, especially that of the wild sago palm, the toddy of which it is very fond of too. Strictly speaking, it cannot be said to fly, but is endowed with a furry membrane between the fore and hind limbs which enables it, when stretched out, to take leaps of almost incredible extent, sometimes 100 yards through which it passes with the swiftness of an arrow. In its flying mode of progression it moves invariably downwards, when it runs up a new tree and takes another leap, which is well sustained owing to the extreme lightness of the animal The flying membrane or parachute cannot be contracted, but is merely a lateral prolongation of the skin and therefore also covered with hair. The squirrel is of a dark grey colour with a black line down its face, which, with its prominent black eyes and grey nose, give it a peculiarly fiendish look, and it bites severely. Its fur is very soft and might be turned to good use. The flesh of all the 4 species of squirrels is eaten by the natives.

The common hare (*Can.* mola) is found chiefly in the open country, where long grass grows. The natives of all classes are fond of its flesh and the poor animal is pursued on all sides by man and beast. It is caught in nets and traps. Rabbits thrive very well and are frequently kept in houses.

There is one kind of porcupine (*Can.* mullu-handi i. e. thorny pig) which like the mungoose lives on shrubby Báne land, and is hunted for its flesh by smoking it out of its holes or by shooting it. The quills are thrown away; for the natives believe, that, if kept in the house, their presence will occasion quarrels amongst the inmates. In the Ghats one may occasionally observe the destructive operations amongst the out-hills of the Badgereit or scaly ant-eater (Manis pendadactyla, *Can.* chippina-bekku i. e. scaly cat). Its flesh is eaten and its scales are used as the supports of fiddle and harp strings.

Homebred horses there are none in Coorg, except those wretched Tats, which are kept by Mussulman residents for carrying loads; but "Young Coorg" is fond of smart Pegu ponies or the powerful Kandahar horses. The damp monsoon climate is, however, not conducive to the health of well bred horses, especially new arrivals from a drier country. The Pegu pony is best suited both to the climate and hilly country. The washerman's donkey and the hybrid goat stand the climate equally well, but sheep do not thrive, except in the eastern districts. The long continued rains and the droughts during March and April which are incidental in these months, are unfavourable to the breeding of horned cattle; but, with proper housing and with an economical saving of the decaying grass, that is annually swept away by the jungle fires, and that should be stored up as hay for stall feeding, the Coorg cattle might be greatly improved. Little care, if any, seems to be bestowed upon the selection of bulls for breeding purposes; beasts of every description and age run promiscuously in the herd, and as there is no check by separating inferior bulls or emasculating them, the progeny must deteriorate. In the Kanawe districts, cattle of the finest description might be reared on sound farming principles. As it is, the cattle of Coorg are of a mediocre breed, better in the north and east, worse in the centre and south-west. The Coorgs procure their cattle partly from Mysore, partly from the annual fair at Subramanya. The ryots have generally too great a number of them, to which they cannot properly attend, and it is not to be wondered, that there is almost annually a great mortality amongst the cattle from what the Coorgs call dodda róga i. e. great disease, the cattle refusing food and being frequently purged, gantlu-kattu i. e. throat swelling disease and the kálu-jwara or foot-sore disease. The increasing coffee cultivation of late years has somewhat limited the pasturage and the constant cattle trespass on coffee plantations is a cause of much vexation and loss, both to planters and ryots. The Coorgs, like other Hindoos, hold the cow sacred; it is a sort of sentimental veneration for the animal which ploughs the fields and, motherlike, gives milk; but does not prevent them from inflicting cruelty upon the sacred beast by ill use, neglect and starvation. The slaughter of kine within the limits of the Coorg Province was distinctly prohibited by General Fraser on the assumption of the administration in the following terms:

To

Lieutenant C. F. Le HARDY,

Superintendent of Coorg.

Sir,

Having ascertained, that it is highly offensive to the religious feelings of the people of Coorg, that cows or bullocks should be killed for the purpose of being used as an article of food, I request, that you will be so good as to prohibit this practice throughout the whole district by any person whether European or native.

J. S. FRASER, *Lt. Col.*
and Commissioner.

Mercara, 16th January 1835.

Whether the sanction of the Government of India was obtained to this prohibition is not apparent, but the Coorgs have always, up to this time, regarded it as binding on the British Government; and, under these circumstances, we must await the dissipation by education of existing prejudices on the subject on the part of the people.

Not venerated like the cow is the bison (*Can.* kádi; Bos cavifrons) which is killed by the Coorgs without hesitation; its flesh, however, is only eaten by the lowest classes. It lives in herds throughout the thickest forests and in the highest hills, especially in Marenád and Hormalnád. The male stands nearly 6 feet high at the shoulder, but disproportionately low behind, and reaches the length of 9 feet from nose to root of tail; the tail itself is almost 3 feet long. Its hump is rather small. When young, the colour of the bison is of a dark reddish hue, which changes with age into a greyish black, the belly, legs as far as the knee-joint, breast and face being, however, of a dirty, whitish tinge. The whole body, especially the dewlap, is covered with long hair and the eyes are of a light blue colour. The horns are short and thick at the base, but gradually become thinner, leaving the tips small and sharp; they are remarkable for the symmetry of their curvature, take a fine polish and the fortunate sportsman may be proud of the trophy. The hide, which is very thick, is used for covering shields. Naturally timid and of retiring habits, preferring shady woods to open glades, except in the cooler parts of the day, the bison, when alarmed or wounded, charges headlong with mad fury his imaginary or real foes, never turning to bay, as long as he has moving space before him. Bison shooting is a favourite sport, both amongst Coorgs and Europeans.

The domesticated buffalo (*Can.* male: kóna; female: yemme) thrives very well in Coorg, but the existing breed is an inferior one; however, some Gaulikas from Dharwar have lately introduced a much larger and more powerful kind which will gradually improve the native stock. Buffaloes are more numerous in the woody districts especially in Kiggatnád and wherever there is marshy land, which is most congenial to their amphibious habits, as they delight during the hot hours of the day in seeking refuge against heat and flies in stagnant pools, where they wallow with supreme gusto with only their noses above water. Buffaloes are a treasure to the farmer; their strength qualifies them for the plough, for the threshing floor and for carrying burdens; they yield more manure and twice the quantity of milk of a common cow and of a far richer kind. With such a list of good qualities one may feel inclined to overlook the extreme ugliness of the beast. It is a bulky, clumsy animal of a greyish colour, with long, annulated horns, lying generally on the back of its thick-set neck; its stupid, motionless look, combined with its gurgling bellow, render its presence unwelcome, though it has nothing of the vicious temper of the hill buffaloes of the Todas.

Of the deer-tribe there are several representatives in Coorg: the samber, spotted deer and jungle-sheep.

The samber or elk, (*Rusa Aristotelis*; *Can.* kadave) is a fine large animal with antlers of great size, resembling those of the stag. It is more frequent in the great mountain forests. It is not gregarious and ruts and drops its horns in spring. The spotted deer (*Axis maculata*; *Can.* sárga) haunts thick jungles in the vicinity of water. It is timid mild and easily domesticated, an elegant pet whilst young, but becomes rather mischievous with age, as it not only butts at children, but eagerly devours any paper within reach. The female has no horns and is smaller than the male, which reaches a hight at the shoulder of 2 feet 6 or 8 inches. The skin is at all times of a rich fawn colour, spotted with white. In almost every Coorg house one finds some horns of the spotted deer, fixed to the walls for hanging clothes on.

The most delicate and beautiful of the deer-tribe is the jungle-sheep—*Can.* kuringi—which somewhat resembles an antelope. It is about 18 inches high, with short horns, a little twisted, their roots for the first inch and a half being enveloped in hair. Its colour is fawn, lighter towards the belly, its legs are very thin, but in speed it is like the passing wind. Its graceful form, mild, bright eye and harmless habits make it an interesting little pet, but it does not long survive its captivity. The flesh of all the deer-tribe is highly esteemed by the natives.

The common pig and the wild hog abound, and their flesh is preferred by the Coorgs to all other meat. Both kinds thrive very well, but the former is not bred with any care and its unsavoury habits do not recommend its flesh for European consumption. What the goat is to the Mussulman, the pig is to the Coorg!

The largest of the Coorg Mammalia is the elephant (áne), but it is so well known, that it needs no particular description. The Coorg elephants are as large and powerful as any others of Southern India. They are gregarious, keeping in droves of 15 to 30, under a leader who directs their movements. They inhabit indiscriminately all the woody parts, but particularly those towards the eastern boundary. They are ferocious and mischievous, destroying garden cultivation and crops of paddy and sugarcane. As they are excellent swimmers, the Kávéri is no barrier to their depredations. When met in droves, they seldom attack the traveller, but it is dangerous to encounter a single elephant. Such brutes, called

"Rogues", are supposed to have been driven from the herd, to which they dare not return, and in consequence become furious in the highest degree.

Elephants in Coorg are caught in pits, covered over with a slight framework to conceal them and placed accross the paths which the animals frequent. It is however no easy màtter to beguile the sagacious creatures into this kind of trap. If caught young they are easily tamed, but when of maturer age, a year and sometimes two are necessary to bring them into subjection. There are now no tame elephants kept in Coorg, but the Rajahs used to maintain many. Wild elephants are now far less numerous and the periodical elephant hunts less productive, though the Coorgs like true highlanders are as eager for sport as ever. The indiscriminate slaughter of these useful beasts has however been forbidden by Government, and they are now only caught alive.

There is a granite slab in the Superintendent's Cutcherry in Mercara with an engraved record of a grand elephant hunt in the beginning of the reign of the late Rajah, which may well excite the jealous astonishment of modern Nimrods. The facts divested of oriental flourish are simply these: In 1822 the ryots complained of the great destruction of their fields and houses, caused by numerous herds of elephants, when the Rajah, "recollecting that it was the duty of a king to destroy the wicked and assist the helpless," resolved upon a wholesale destruction of the beasts and within 38 days he killed with his own hand 233 elephants and his soldiers caught 181 alive! Well may he exclaim in conclusion: "Is this not a great wonder, that men caught elephants alive, as if they were mice, and killed herds of them by using their seven weapons with the destructive force of roaring thunder?"

The *Ornithologist* not less than the Botanist finds in Coorg a fruitful field for his researches, for birds of almost every tribe are plentiful throughout the country. The Mysore Museum already exhibits a goodly number of these, and through the kindness of Dr. Oswald, I have been furnished with a classified list of 30 birds, collected last year in Coorg, but of course there are many more, that are common to Southern India. One would think that, during the heavy south-west monsoon, animal life in the open could scarcely exist, yet hardly does the sun break through the rainy clouds when all around there is life and joy amongst the feathered tribe. They seem to anticipate that happy time, when after the monsoon, in sunny October and November, they pay, dressed in their finest plumage, courtship to their spouses, and warbling and singing, are busy all day long, for the comfort of their expected offspring.

The following survey is arranged according to Mr. Vigor's classification of birds:—Amongst the birds of prey (*Raptores*) the high soaring *Vulture* (*Vultur Indicus*) (*Kg.* adiya paddu), with wings turned obliquely upwards, stands foremost, both for his size and utility, as public scavenger of animal carcasses in which occupation he is assisted by the Pariah dog and the crow. Occasionally a solitary eagle (*Kg.* paddu) may be seen in the mountains; a fine specimen of the golden eagle (Aquila chrysaetos) came into my possession a few years ago; whilst on a mountain slope he was struggling on the ground with a large horned owl, both were caught alive. This eagle was a fine bird, in sitting posture 15 inches high; with outstretched wings 4 feet 5 inches; the upper part of the head and neck light buff, of a light brown and grey down the chest and dark brown, nearly black, on the back, and the wings tinged with brighter spots. The brilliant eye, with its brownish yellow iris and wary look, gave the bird an air of intelligence and its formidable curved and pointed bill and horny talons kept the inquisitive at a respectful distance. He managed to free himself from his chain and escaped.

The Garuda or *Brahmany kite* (Haliastur Indus) is more

frequently seen. His plumage is very handsome, glossy white the head, neck and breast, and beautifully brown the back, wings and tail. In Hindoo mythology it is Vishnu's vehicle and therefore held in high veneration by the natives. He is a useful bird as he devours noxious reptiles, but sometimes he also carries away an unguarded chicken. The *Pariah kite* (Milvus Govinda) is very common and easily recognised by its greyish, brown speckled plumage and short shrill screech whilst soaring over its domain in small circles. He is the scavenger of animal refuse thrown from the cookroom, but preys chiefly on reptiles, which he carries off with a swoop, and devours flying. The sparrow hawk (Accipiter nisus), the Kestrel-falcon (Tinnunculus alandarius), the Sultan and the perigrine falcon (Falco peregrinator and peregrinus) are not unfrequently seen from the hill tops, soaring over the forests in pursuit of their winged prey. The Rajahs used the larger kind of falcon, the Kembakki (red bird) for hunting. The swiftness and majestic flight of the falcon is proverbial with the Coorg bards, who sing of the departed hero: "Like the falcon in the sky, thou wast roaming here on earth." In the eagle-fight we have already been introduced to the *Great Owl* (Bubo maximus; *Can.* guma); but there is also a smaller kind, which on house tops in nightly solitude often disturbs and frightens with its moaning cry: "Waugh O! Waugh O!" the sleeping inmates, by whom the owl is greatly dreaded. My keeping one as a pet some years ago was regarded by the Coorgs with grave apprehension and, afterwards, when I was laid up with jungle fever, the cause was ascribed to the presence of the ominous bird.

The *Insessores* or Perchers are largely represented in each of the five tribes. Amongst the Fissirostres there is the gregarious *Bee-eater* (merops) of both a larger and a smaller green variety. They prey upon insects like the swallows, of which there are also several species found in Coorg. The *Goat-*

sucker (Caprimulgus Asiaticus) in its modest greyish-black plumage is often observed in twilight along hedges or in abandoned buildings. Its flight is short and noiseless. Amongst the beautiful Tragonidae there is the Harpactus fasciatus or Malabar Trogon, a solitary bird of splendid plumage, that delights in the stillness of the forest, where it seizes the flitting insects on the wing. Remarkable for the gaudy brilliancy of its light blue plumage is the Indian roller or blue Jay (Coracias Indicus). It is frequently seen on jungle clearings or coffee estates perched on a solitary dry tree, where it freely surveys its hunting ground and discerns with wary look any approaching danger. It is difficult to get at, though it may be seen all the year round. Nearly allied to the jay are the Kingfishers. Of these brilliant birds, which are rather common along streams and paddy-fields we have three species: the brown headed (Halcyon leucocephalus), the white breasted (H. Smyrnensis) and the common Indian kingfisher (Alcedo Bengalensis; *Kg.* mingotti—fishcatcher). Their habits are similar; they live on small fishes such as stickle-backs and minnows; perched immovably upon some overhanging twig, they watch for a passing fish, upon which they suddenly dart with their long sharp bill, and kill and eat it. Their flight is very swift. They lay their round white eggs in holes of banks.

Amongst the *Scansores* or Climbers foremost are the parrots, which are very numerous in Coorg, especially in bamboo jungles. They are remarkable for their beautiful colours, their climbing skill, their powerful bill, their fleshy tongue and their power of imitating the human voice; they are therefore great pets with natives and Europeans. The large green species (Palæornis torgatus; *Kg.* mále-gini) with a rose coloured ring round its neck, is for its docility and power of imitation most valued. There is also the blue winged Parrokeet (Palæornis columboides), the blue headed parrokeet (P. cynocephalus) and a pretty dwarf parrot, the Indian Lorikeet (Loriculus Vernalis).

The melancholy stillness of the forests is often interrupted by the "tap, tap, tap" of the woodpeckers, of which there are several species; the commonest is the one with rufous, speckled plumage and red crest (Micropternus Gularis), more scarce is the great black woodpecker (Mulleripicus Hodgsoni; *Kg.* Marakotta-pakki) chiefly found in Kiggatnád. The whole plumage is deep black, except the upper part, which, in the male, is of a lively red. In its pursuit of insects under the bark or in holes of trees, it ascends with great rapidity in a screw line, and its tap, tap seems to answer more the purpose of disturbing the hidden insects, which it catches in their precipitous flight, than to peck a hole into the tree. The female deposits 2 or 3 white eggs in the hollows of old trees. The flight of the woodpecker is short and generally only from tree to tree.

The Cuckoo-family is represented by the black cuckoo (Endynamys Orientalis) and the red winged crested cuckoo (Coccystes coromandus) both of which are suspected of parasitic habits regarding the disposal of their eggs.

Of the tribe *Tenuirostres* or Suctorial birds there is the purple honey-sucker (Arachnechtra currucaria), a beautiful little bird, glittering like a humming bird with metallic lustre, as it flutters over the flowers, whose nectar it sucks with its thin long bill. The Indian Loopoe (Upupa Ceylonensis) is an active elegant bird with an arched crest upon the head of a ruddy buff colour, terminating in black. When in search of food, it emits a sound resembling the word hoop, hoop, hence its name. During the monsoon it retreats to a drier district.

The tribe *Dentirostres* has also its representatives in the Malabar Woodshrike (Tephrodornis sylvicola) which resembles a falcon both in form and habits; the black headed

Cuckoo-shrike, the orange Minivet (Pericrotus flammens), the large racked-tailed Drongo and the Paradise Flycatcher (Tchitrea Paradise; *Kg.* Núkare-bála=ribbon tail) which is most elegant in form and plumage. Its dark brown body is ornamented by a greenish black crest on the head and two pure white lateral tail feathers, which, when the bird flies along in wavy curves from bush to bush, present a most graceful appearance.

The *Thrushes* (Merulidae) delight both with their sweet song and their pretty plumage. There is the Malabar whistling thrush (Myiophonus Horsfieldi), the blue headed chat thrush (Orocetes cinclorhyncus) and the white winged ground thrush (Geocichla cyanotus).

The Neilgherry Blackbird (Merula simillima) goes here under the native name of Bhímarája or the Coorg nightingale, so sweet and powerful is its song. An interesting bird of this family is the southern Simitar Babbler, and distinguished for the beauty of its golden plumage, is the Black-naped Indian Oriole (Oriolus Indicus). The common Bulbul (Pycnonotus pygaeus) may be found throughout the year. When pursued, it leads the intruder away from its nest by its short flight to other bushes. It sings very sweetly and its crimson and black crest look very pretty. The Tailor-bird (Orthotomus) is called by the Coorgs "Gíjapakki," in imitation of its sharp cutting cry, which is like the noise of saw-filing and by its frequent repetition, as painful to the nerves. It is common about gardens and groves of trees, and celebrated for the artificial construction of its nest. I have one before me. Three leaves of the guava tree are by many stitches skilfully drawn together, and give throughout their length cover to the nest, the full upper half of one leaf forms a curved roof, completely protecting the entrance. It is a very active little bird, and, whilst hopping about, jerks up its tail, beating time to its piercing cry. It leaves Coorg during the south-west monsoon. Of similar habits is the Wren (Prinia; *Kg.* Chirulichita) of which there are several species. The southern yellow Tit (Machlolophus Jerdoni) and the Indian White-eye (Zosterops) are also found, the latter in great abundance, likewise the Wagtails (Motacilla), which are often seen along reaped paddy-fields feeding among cattle on various insects. The Coorgs call them Bálátimoni (Bála tail, áta play) which coincides with the English name, indicating their peculiar habit of wagging their tails.

Amongst the tribe of *Conirostres* the first place is taken by the most impudent of birds, the common Crow (Corvus splendens; *Can.* kági). In Coorg it is less abundant than in the low country. Less frequent is the pretty rufous Tree Crow, or common Indian Magpie (Dendrocitta rufa), which is found in jungles. It is fond of the fruit of the banian and its cry is like that of the racked-tailed Drongo (Edolius Malabaricus) which frequents coffee estates in the bamboo-district. The well known Mynahs, especially the common mynah and the grey headed species (Temenuchus Malabaricus) are very common, less so the southern Hill-Mynah (Eulabes religiosa). They roost in numerous flocks and feed on berries and grain of various kinds. They also keep company with grazing cattle, feeding on the insects which are disturbed by their footsteps. They are remarkable for their power of repeating words and sentences, of imitating laughing, coughing and sneezing. To Europeans a pleasing acquaintance of the "Old Country" is the "House-Sparrow" (Passer domesticus; *Kg.* mane-pakki=house-bird) which is here as numerous, clamorous and amorous as at home! The yellow necked or Jungle Sparrow (Passer flavicollis) frequents light jungles and chirps exactly like the house-sparrow. The Weaver-bird or bottle-nested Sparrow (Ploceus Baya) is more numerous towards Mysore, but after the monsoon, when the paddy gets ripe, it may be often seen about Mercara in considerable flocks. which perched on a tree keep up a continual chirping. Its pending retort-shaped nest, which is over a foot in length, is woven of long fine grass. The entrance is from below and formed by the two inches wide neck of the retort, the main body of the nest is laterally compressed and divided by an open partition wall into 2 compartments, of which the lower one is occupied by the hatching bird that lays 2 or 3 white little eggs.

There are several species of larks rather common in Coorg. They have much the same plumage and habits as our European warbling lark, and are sometimes caged by the natives.

One of the largest birds here is the Hornbill (Buceros cavatus; *Kg.* Malérapa, malé forest, arapa sound, i. e. the forest resounding bird). It is upwards of 4 feet in length; black on the belly, chin, wings and back, with one band across the tail, the rest of which is white, as also the neck and parts of the wing. The curved, large bill, which now lies before me and which belonged to a male bird, is vermillion above, with a black central line, and yellowish on the sides, the lower mandible is whitish and the base below the eye black. On the upper mandible there is an extraordinary prominence of vermillion colour, 4 inches broad and 8½ inches long, terminating behind in a black curvature and the concave front uniting its dip with the ridge of the beak, so that the two sides rise to a narrow ledge 2 inches above the true bill, from which they are distinguished by a black triangular stripe. The appendage looks as if 2 horizontal horns were superadded to the bill, which from point to gape is in a straight line 11½ inches in length, and from point to the end of the protuberance I measured 16½ inches. The Coorgs make powder flasks of its hollow bill and the quills they use for writing. The noise of its wings, when flying, is very loud and its progress is so slow, that a man can follow it. In its prey it is omnivorous.

Of the third order of birds, the *Rasores* or *Scrapers*, Coorg can make a goodly show with a variety of Pigeons, of which the blue pigeon—*Kg.* tórapakki—is the most common, but the green and the yellow pigeon and the ring-dove are not scarce in the forests. The Peacock (Pavo cristatus; *Kg.* meilu) with its shrill morning call, and the timid jungle fowl (Gallus Sonneratii; *Kg.* kádgóli) with its self-betraying "cockadoodle doo" are numerous in bamboo jungles, especially during the last few years of bamboo seeding. Both species together with the Woodcock and the common Partridge (Perdix cinerea; *Kg.* ganjalakki) and the Quail (Coturnix) are at the time of the ragi crop frequently brought to Mercara for sale by a class of jungle people who are most expert in catching these birds, the voices of which they very cleverly imitate. In the neighbourhood of Subramanya peacocks may not be killed, as they are believed to be the vehicles of the god residing there. The neck-feathers of the jungle cock are much valued for their beauty, each being marked by roundish hornlike plates of various shades of yellow. The Coorgs keep these as trophies, as the Indian does his hairy scalp. The single feathers are turned into artificial flies, to fishes the most attractive bait, and consequently highly prized and dearly paid for by the devotee of "the gentle art." The Crow-pheasant or common Coucal (Centropus rufipennis), distinguished by its cinnamon brown wings, long tail and crow-like head, is very frequently seen on bamboo land, where it hides itself in the dense clumps, uttering as it slowly flies away a deep note like a monkey. It feeds on insects and small reptiles and is eaten by the natives.

A few representatives of the fourth order of birds, the *Grallatores* or *Waders* are: the Egret (Egretta flavirostris; *Kg.* balya-póle=great crane) which towards the end of the monsoon is frequently seen stalking along paddy-fields or streams in search of prey. It is white as snow, about 3 feet high with long yellow legs and straight yellow bill. It keeps in small flocks. The little green Heron (Butstrides Javanicus; *Kg.* kiru-póle=small crane), the Indian Waterhen (Gallinula) and the Plover or Peevit (*Kg.* uppu-títe, imitating its cry) are found in marshy places, likewise the Snipe (Gallinago stenura; *Kg.* bandu-koneya=mud squatter) whose flesh is in great estimation with the Coorgs and Europeans; also the green Sandpiper (Aclitis Ochropus) may occasionally be seen.

As there are no large tanks in Coorg, few of the *Natatores* or *swimming birds* are to be found. There is only the Wild Duck or Teal of a larger and smaller species, which the Coorgs call Kóku and Yerande-pakki; the latter dive under the water, as soon as they observe a hunter and remain submerged for a long time. Geese and Turkeys are kept domesticated, but the cold and wet monsoon weather does not agree with turkeys.

A rapid glance over the remaining portion of the Coorg Fauna will be arrested by but a few species of general interest. The *Reptiles* are represented by two kinds of Tortoises, a variety of Lizards, Snakes and Frogs.

The *Tortoises* are found in paddy-fields and small tanks. The shell of one in my possession is 11 inches long and 7 inches broad, but of a bony nature, unfit for ornamental use. Since the devastations of the coffee-borer common Lizards, Bloodsuckers, and Chameleons, all of them insect-feeders, have become of greater importance to the agriculturist. Alligators are occasionally seen in the Káveri, especially near Rámaswámy Kanawé. Last year one of 9 feet in length was caught in Beppunad with a woman's nose-ring and a silver bracelet in his stomach.

Snakes are rather plentiful in Coorg, but the subject has not yet received sufficient attention, to enable me to give the correct name of the different species. Classifying them as poisonous and harmless snakes, the native name may at least serve to lead the curious upon the right track. The Cobra di capella or Hood Snake (Naia tripudians; *Kg.* Nalla pámbu = good snake, in the sense of Eumenides?) is more frequent in the bamboo than in the mále district, and often takes possession of an out-hill for its habitation, but also deserted huts and the thick thatch of out-houses are its favourite haunts. It is kept and worshipped in demon temples and sometimes in rooms to guard treasure. In a specimen 5 feet long just examined, the hood which is formed by the expanded skin of the neck, when the snake is excited, measured 7 inches in length and 4½ in breadth. It is whitish in front and black on the lower part of the back, shading off into brown and white towards the flattened head; in the middle of the hood there is a peculiar mark resembling a pair of spectacles with the bridge downward, the frame being white and the space of the imaginary glasses black. Before an attack the cobra half raises its coiled body into a graceful curve, dilates its hood and swaying to and fro, its bifid tongue quivering all the while, it keeps its victim spell bound with its fiendish brilliant eyes, till it darts forward and hissing inflicts its deadly wound. In spite of the most strenuous exertions of science, combined with benevolence, no infallible remedy has yet been discovered against the bite of the cobra, and all the boasted native charms have proved worthless, though snake charmers have by their knowledge of the habits of the cobra and by the influence of the melancholy strain of their rude flageolet acquired a great power over the reptile.

The number of the poison fangs of this and all other venomous snakes, is but two, one in front of each side of the upper jaw, and they lie flat along the roof of the serpent's mouth, whilst at rest. The fangs are curved inside and as sharp as the finest needle, yet they are hollow and their root is in direct communication with the venom ducts behind them. In biting the same muscle that raises the fangs compresses the venom ducts and by the force of the actual bite a drop of the venom is injected through the channel of the fangs into the tiny wound and in a few minutes the whole system of the victim is poisoned and inevitable death ensues. Varieties of the cobra with hood and mark are the Pillandi-murga and the kád-murga, the former is greyish white and 1 to 1½ foot long, the latter is dark brown; their bite is less poisonous. The Kare-náda (black snake) with white marks about the throat, is 8 or 10 feet long and very rapid in its movements. It is found in dense forests and is sometimes washed down by the mountain torrents. Its bite causes death within half an hour. The late Rajah is said to have ascertained the power of the venom by experimenting upon sheep and buffaloes. The bite of the Patte-kolaka produces festering sores over the body; the Coorgs string the bones of this snake together and wear them as a charm against sores or swelling of the glands. There are three kinds of Cardamom-snakes: the green, the black and the grey Mandoli or Kummepámbu or Kurudu-mandoli which during the day are in a state of torpor, but active at night. On this account the natives term them "blind snakes"; they are often trodden upon by the cardamom cultivators, but a certain charm is said to render the poison innocuous. The kádu-bale and kére-bale muri or the jungle and tank Bracelet-snakes have white rings round their dark body, which become visible when the snakes are irritated. They are from 4 to 6 feet in length. The Pachi-balli-murga is dangerous to cattle whilst grazing.

Amongst the innocuous snakes the largest is the Perampámbu (big snake) or Rock-snake, a kind of Boa constrictor, which grows to a length of 12 to 15 feet and has in thickness the girth of a man's thigh. It even devours spotted deer and, after the monsoon, is often shot by Coorgs in the cardamom jungles. Next in size is the Black-tank or Rat-snake

(*Kg.* karingere) which catches mice and small reptiles. It frequently lives upon the thatched roofs of native houses and its flesh is eaten by the lower classes. Remarkable for its beauty and graceful evolutions is the green Whip-snake (*Kg.* pache-pámbu), which is commonly seen in shrubs. In native opinion it enjoys the imaginary purity and sanctity of the Brahmin and its skin is said to get blistered by the very shadow of man, falling upon it! An extraordinary forest-snake is the Kánam-pámbu, which is said to have a crest upon its head like a cock. The one foot long Ira-tale or two-headed snake is considered as capable of progressing equally well forwards or backwards, being gifted with a head at either end of its body. The flying snake or Páram-pámbu is very thin, of a brownish black colour and 18 inches long. Equally thin, but shorter is the Elat-áni-murgu or writing-stile-snake, which is black with white spots. Other harmless snakes are: the Billulli, the Niru-kuduma, the Túra-pámbu or cane-snake, etc.

The *Batrachians*, or the family of *Frogs*, fill the air with their croaking concert before the monsoon and during the occasional breaks, prognosticating impending rain. There is the large bull-frog, which makes itself heard at night, the common brown frog, which chiefly infests paddy-fields and tanks, and a small green frog, that lives on shrubs and trees; but all of them are feeders on insects, which they catch very cleverly. Toads, very ugly and very large, are found wherever there is a convenient hiding place on damp ground.

The river Kávéri and its affluents and the small native tanks and even the paddy-field rills are well stocked with a great variety of *Fishes*, which are caught by every class of natives, who have leisure for and take pleasure in the sport. Shooting, angling, netting, basketing and poisoning with Cocculus Indicus are the usual methods of fishing. For the following remarks I am chiefly indebted to Dr. Nash's list of

14 Coorg fishes and Colonel Puckle's "Memorandum" on Fishes about Bangalore.

The queen of Coorg fishes in size and quality is the *Lady-Fish*, Callichrous (Silurus) chekra H. B. or Bále-mínu as the Coorgs call it, on account of its resemblance in whiteness and smoothness to the inside of the plantain-tree-bark. They distinguish 3 kinds of decreasing size: the Patna-bále, the Bále and the Kincha-bále. Next in size and excellence of its flesh is the *Black Cat-Fish*, Clarias magur H. B.—*Kg.* Kulla-bare?—of a dark green colour approaching to blakish purple on the back and fading to a greenish white; it is chiefly reared in tanks, spawns in the mud and is full of eggs in April, May and June.

Similar in appearance and size is the *Black Murl*—Ophiocephalus striatus—*Kg.* Bare-mínu. It lives in muddy tanks, guards its young till they are about 2 inches long, before which they may be seen swimming in two lines above their parent. It grows up to 2 feet in length and is of a dull brownish green on the sides, darker on the back and whitish beneath. The *Painted Murl*—Ophiocephalus marulius H. B. (*Kg.* Kávéri-bare?) is a very handsomely marked fish of 4 feet in length; upon the darkish grey ground there are white markings like flowers, hence its name "Flower Murl". It is found in the Kávéri and other deep river pools. They spawn in April and May.

The *Black Dhok* (Ophiocephalus gachua H. B.) grows to within one foot in length and is commonly found in clear tanks. Its colour is greyish green with irregular herring bone bands of lighter colour. The anal and dorsal fins are dark grey, the edges being tipped with the light green belly colour, but the pectoral fins are dull orange and strongly marked with dark grey dotted bars.

The *Painted Dhok* is like the former in shape, size and colour, but the head is handsomely mottled and banded and or 10 distinct blotched bands below and 8 or 9 dark coloured bands above them run along the sides of the body. The lower jaw is marked on each side by 4 black dots.

The *Stone Loach* (Nemacheilus striatus. Day; *Kg.* Pálavari?) is found in sandy and stony river bottoms, where they lie hidden until disturbed or rising for air, when they quickly come to the surface and as speedily return. It is a small fish; its silvery sides and yellowish brown back are dotted with black. There is a well defined dot at the base of the caudal fin, which gives at the first glance the appearance of the little fish having an eye at each end. If well dressed it is fair eating.

The *Manincha* or Malanchi-mínu (slimy fish) is a kind of Eel, that grows to a length of 6 feet and is perhaps identical with the Murana maculata. Its flesh is very good eating and highly esteemed by the natives for its medicinal qualities against piles.

The *Indian Trout* (Garra Jerdoni. Day; *Kg.* Pandi-mínu i. e. Pig-fish) may be found in all the mountain nullahs; it is about 6 inches long, its head and neck are thick like those of a pig, hence its name. Its colour is a mottled green and grey. It has a suctorial dish under the chin, by which it can attach itself to rocks.

The *Carp or Roach* (Puntius) occurs in several varieties all of which are esteemed good eating.

The *Banded Gold-fin* (Barilius cocsa) is an exceedingly pretty fish about 5 inches long and found only in shallow running streams. The back is greyish blue, with 8 or 9 lateral darker bands, the sides are silvery with blue reflections and fading to white below.

The *Silver-fish* (Chella cultellus) is of about the same size as the former, handsomely shaped and covered with brilliant, silvery scales, which are easily rubbed off.

From August till November the flooded paddy-fields give

shelter to numerous little fishes from half an inch to 4 inches in length, the smallest is the bitter Keipe, next the Kumbalakotte, the Koile, the Ponakani and the Avari. They are eagerly caught by the natives who are very fond of fish curry.

The shells, which I have been able to collect in Coorg comprise the following: 3 species of the Genus Unio, 2 species of the Genus Helix, the Genus Melania, the Genus Paludina, the Cyrena Malaccensis and the Cyclophorus excellens. The Helicidae are eaten by the natives.

With the termination of the monsoon the insect world, in its varied and often brilliant array, asserts its dominion in the sunny air, the reinvigorated vegetation, on the placid waters and the warm ground. Then is the time for the entomologist to enrich his collection with fresh specimens of the different insect forms, and certainly Coorg offers a rich reward to the enthusiastic lover of nature. A small collection of Coorg Beetles, sent to a German entomologist, was highly appreciated for the variety and beauty of its species. Almost every family of the Coleoptera has its numerous representatives and even a glance over them all, were I able to enumerate them, would be too much for the patience of the reader. Passing over the beautiful family of the Cicindelidæ or Sand-runners and the still more brilliant Buprestidæ and Elateridæ, the powerful family of the Scarabaeidæ with the giant Stag-beetle (Lucanus Malabaricus) over 3 inches in length and with light brown elytra; our attention will be arrested by the formidable looking Cerambycidæ or Long-horns, for amongst this family we find the contemptible and yet terrible little enemy of the coffee planters in Coorg and Southern India generally: the Coffee-Borer (Clytus Coffeophagus or Xylotrechus quadrupes) of which our woodcut gives a very good representation. The

The Coffee-Borer-beetle (*Xylotrechus quadrupes*) slightly enlarged.

full grown beetle is about three quarters of an inch long and the male is considerably smaller; both have an elongated cylindrical body and are equally marked. The head is small and depressed; the eyes are large and brilliant with a small whitish indentation near the root of the antenna, which are of moderate length, filiform, eleven jointed and pointed at the tip, the first joint being thicker and the second shorter than the rest. The mandibles are short, strong and incurved. The prothorax is slightly oval, nearly as broad as long, covered with greyish green minute hairs and marked by three black roundish spots, the middle one being four times larger than those on the sides. The elytra are thin but horny, long and slightly tapering; on a black ground there are three symmetrically curved, greenish, transverse lines and a perpendicular one at the base forming on the left wing with the first curve the letter **y**. The last pair of legs are particularly long and indicate by their strong light brown femora considerable walking and jumping powers; the other joints are black and the tarsi armed with bifid claws. The beetles are most numerous directly after the monsoon, but many stragglers appear all the year round. They are diurnal in their habits, not gregarious or migratory and unaffected by light at night.

The telescopic Ovipositor, highly magnified.

They are generally quiescent during the cool hours of the day, reposing on the bark of the coffee stem or under the leaves, but the warm sunshine calls forth their full activity. The female beetle is more plentiful and constantly busy with depositing her eggs on the sunny side of the stem alongside and into the natural fissures of the bark. As the beetle moves over the stem, the ovipositor which is a telescopic tube is in constant activity, sweeping like the finest hair-brush over and into every little cavity, and with unerring instinct she stops at the proper place and securely fastens one or several eggs; but it is difficult to say how many altogether, perhaps not over 100. The beetle does not attack the tree and dies after a fortnight. The ova, just perceptible to the naked eye and in groups of 3 to 8 appear under the microscope whitish, elongated and pointed at the top and are so securely hidden, that they become visible only on removing part of the corky layers of the bark. The ova gradually enlarge till after 12 or 15 days the white membrane bursts and the young grub of the size of a maggot begins to exercise its mandibles, eating its way into the juicy part of the soft bark and gradually into the hard wood of the tree. It is in this state of the larva that the insect has its longest existence of about 9 months and commits such fearful havoc. The full grown larva is about three-fourths to one inch in length, broadest at the head and tapering behind; of a pale yellow or whitish colour and fleshy appearance. The body consists of eleven segments, has no legs, but some of the abdominal rings have small tubercles on the back, which aid the insect in moving forward. The head is hard, flattened above, of a brown colour and armed with powerful mandibles, with which it reduces the wood to a fine powder for its food and, having passed it through its body, the glutinous powder is accumulated behind and so closely packed, that the tunnel is completely filled up and inaccessible from without. The first working of the larva in and under the bark leaves an unmistakable trace behind in a clearly defined swelling of the wounded bark, which sometimes cracks along the course of the larva. With the growth of the larva the tunnel also enlarges and its progress is in a most irregular manner winding up and down the tree and penetrating to the very end of the tap root, but though there may be as many as 20 or 30 larvæ at a time in one tree, their tunnels do neither coalesce, nor do they emerge on its surface. When near its transformation into the pupa state, the larva turns towards the bark and often makes a clear horizontal sweep round the alburnum, so that the tree must die and snaps off at the least touch. This last operation of the borer accounts for the sudden sickly change in a tree, seeming shortly before to be in perfect health and frequently occurs shortly after the March and April showers, succeeding a period of very dry weather. The flow of sap in the reinvigorated tree may also induce the larva to turn towards the bark, for, contrary to other boring insects, the Coffee-xylotrechus revels in the most juicy green-wood and dies in a dry stem. In its last lodgement the pupa occupies a spacious cell, prepared by the larva and separated from the outside by merely the bark or a thin layer of wood. The pupa is yellowish white like the larva exhibiting the outlines of the future beetle shining through the covering membrane. In this quiescent state, the head towards the bark, the pupa remains for about two months in its dark chamber, when it emerges from its pupa covering, matures its beetle nature and with its powerful jaws eats its way through the bark, where afterwards a small round hole will indicate its departure, to perpetrate its pernicious work on an extended scale by a numerous progeny. The whole existence of the coffee borer from the egg to the death of the beetle does not exceed 12 months. Its presence in a coffee tree becomes apparent by the sickly look of the tree, the older leaves of which become yellow and the young shoots peculiarly twisted. The formed coffee berries do not ripen and fall off with the leaves and the tree dries up or lingers in a sickly, unfertile condition. Its destructive operations are not confined to particular localities, but spread almost all over the coffee growing districts in Southern India, and the devastations and consequent loss on many coffee estates are the more lamentable, the less chance there is of finding an immediate and reliable remedy. The insect, which is no doubt indigenous, has through various collateral causes, real and hypothetical, such as: the destruction of forests, abnormal seasons, dying of bamboos, disturbance of the balance in the local fauna etc. increased to an enormous extent, so as to render its presence a pest to coffee cultivation since the year 1865, a pest which spread to an alarming degree all over the Province. The removal and destruction of far gone trees, the scraping, rubbing and washing with acids healthy ones, to remove or destroy the ova, the shading in dry localities with permanent shade trees such as the charcoal and jack trees, proper cultivation—these and others are the remedial and preventive measures, recommended by practical agriculturists and also by the Commissioner, whom the Government deputed to investigate this important subject.

A beetle, neither notorious for destructive habits nor particularly useful, but interesting on account of the brilliant phenomenon it affords, when swarming in myriads on trees and shrubs during the warm April and May nights, is the *Fire-fly* (Lampyris splendidula; *Ky*. Minambulu i. e. glittering insect). It is not peculiar to Coorg, but in abundance and brilliancy no where else seen like here. A thunder storm, succeeded by a rich shower, has closed a sultry day. The sun has set unobserved. The western sky is overhung with clouds. In the cloudless east, the full moon rises slowly. The air perfectly pellucid, the stars glittering in fresh glory; not a breath of wind; all still. You turn from the broad red orb of the rising moon to the host of golden stars on the deep azure, from them to the massive banks of clouds, lit up here by faint lightnings, there by the pale beams of the moon their bold edges fringed with silver, and wonder at the beauties of the world above, where on the dark blue depths of heaven light seems to vie with light in the illumination of the vast dome, built by the unseen Master. Now, as by magic, a curtain of clouds is drawn over this glorious view above; but a scene of strange beauty is spread below. Shrub and bush and tree, as far as the eye can reach, burn with fairy light. The ground, the air, teem with lustre, every leaf seems to have its own enchanting lamp. The valley at your feet, the wooded hills at your right and left, the dark distant forest, all are lit up and gleam in ever varying splendour, as if every departed star had sent a representative to bear his part in this nightly illumination of the dark earth. Whence all at once these innumerable lights? No sound is heard, silently all these shining throngs pass before you in fantastic confusion. Look at this bush, that tree! Myriads of fiery sparks brighten up with phosphoric glare through the labyrinth of leaves and branches; a moment and they vanish. Now they flash up brighter than ever, as if this world of magic lustre was animated by pulsations keeping regular time. You sit and look, and think you could sit all night beholding the fairy scene!

Among the membrane winged Insects (Hymenoptera) we must pay a grateful tribute to the *Honey-bee*, for the Coorg honey is plentiful and of an excellent flavour. Some bees build their hives in hollow trees (Tude-jénu) some in rocks (Hed-jénu) others on shrubs (Kólu-jénu), they are most frequently found in Surlabi-muttu-nád, in Yeddava-nád, Gaddi-nád, Mudikéri-nád and Kiggat-nád, where I saw a rock called Tembare, on which from 200 to 300 beehives are to be found. In the forests on some trees, especially the Gony-mara, there are from 100 to 200 hives. A jungle tribe, the Jénu-kurubas, gather the honey in the month of June. Having hit upon a hive in a hollow tree, they tie a bamboo, the short cut branches of which form a convenient ladder, to the tree during the day time and at night, provided with a basket attached to a long rope and lined with leaves, they climb up with a strongly smoking torch which they hold near the hive. The alarmed and half stunned bees fly away and their honeycombs are removed and let down in the basket. Whilst thus engaged, the Kurubas have a peculiar song, made for the occasion and expressing their feigned sympathy with the spoliated bees, so rudely disturbed of their nightly rest. The Kurubas sell the honey at 2½ seers for the rupee. The wax has to be delivered for a pittance to the contractor of jungle produce, who as Government agent is alone entitled to sell it at the rate of 2½ annas per seer of 24 rupees weight.

Wasp and Hornet-nests, suspended from trees like inverted cabbage-heads, are frequently met with in jungles and are better left alone, for their inmates attack any intruder with painful stings. Small and large Ants of a black and red colour are very numerous and maintain the ferocious character of the family, pursuing the disturber of the domicile of their bustling community and inflicting severe bites upon the unfortunate victim. They play an important part in the cleansing and purifying department of the economy of nature. Their structures, domestic economy and transport operations of objects many times larger than their own bodies, excite admiration.

Of the numerous and most beautiful family of *Lepidoptera* or *Butterflies* and *Moths* Coorg presents a goodly show, but though fine collections of them have been made, their classification is still uncompleted. With the close of the monsoon the Lantana hedges and especially the sandy banks of streams seem to be the rendezvous of a great variety of butterflies, of which some are distinguished for their size and brilliant colouring. Three species of similar size and shape chiefly attract our attention: the . . . .
with black velvety upper wings of about 6 inches in width and light blue under wings; the . . . .
with similar upper wings and the swallow tailed lower wings ornamented with a pale yellow satin-like spot; the most beautiful, however, is the . . . .
the black upper and lower wings of which are dotted all over

with minute brilliant green little dots, in addition to which the tailed lower wing is marked with a brilliant greenish blue large spot. A darting showy butterfly is the green mottled . . . . A slowly moving but high soaring butterfly is the large winged yellow speckled . . . . Distinguished amongst the moths for the swiftness and power of their flight are those that appear in the twilight (Crespuscularia), called Hawk-moths, which include the remarkable Death's-head-moth, the Sesia; the Sphinx of the vine, of the oleander, the caterpillar of which I found in great numbers on Cinchona trees, and many others. Amongst those that come forth at night (Nocturna), the largest perhaps amongst all the moths is the Atlas . . . . a beautiful specimen of which I caught only a few days ago on a Lantana hedge and which measures nearly 10 inches across the wings; the ground colour of the wings is a warm brown, with reddish brown curved bands faced by white black lines dividing the wings nearly into halves, a similar band running across the body and a little over the wings with an outward curve. The whole space encircled by these bands is of a deeper brown colour and ornamented by four triangular transparent mica-like spots set in black rims and by a small, elyptical second spot on each of the upper wings. These are curved downwards, tipped with an orange band and a black eye, which gives the extremities of the wings a striking resemblance to a serpent's head. The upper wings are edged with a fine black wavy line and the lower wings with black dots surrounded by yellowish bands. The male is of a darker hue than the female and whilst the antennæ of the former are broad bipectinate and like a feather in miniature, those of the female are narrow. Another large and beautiful moth of the same group is the greenish-white swallow tailed Lithosia sanguinobuta, 6 inches in width. Its upper wings are ornamented with a crimson line on the front edge and two lunular ocelli or spots of a black and crimson, shading off into a pale rose colour; the lower wings, which terminate in long twisted tails, are marked with similar spots. The Bombycidæ, to which the former moths seem to belong are represented by several other fine species, especially the genus Saturnia. There are some moths, of a light brown colour, belonging to the same genus, the caterpillars of which attach their silken cocoons, to the branches of the "Careya arborea". They are chiefly found in the open parts of Kiggatnád, and the trees are sometimes covered with clusters of these pale yellow cocoons. The thread of this silk is so interwoven and gummed together that the cocoons seem to be worthless for any practical purpose.

The larva of the Zeuzera Coffeophaga, commonly called "Red Borer" on account of its colour, is found in coffee and young Casuarina trees. It burrows its tunnel chiefly along the pith, leaving an open communication with the outside of the tree through which its globular woody excrements are discharged and which betray the active enemy within. A wire run up through the hole or stopping up the orifice with a peg are the safest means for destroying the insect, which otherwise is apt to take a horizontal turn in its progress and thereby to cut off the upper part of the tree. Its devastations are however insignificant compared with the "White Coffee-Borer". It is not usual to find more than one red borer in a tree. In its chrysalis state it is enveloped in a delicate silken cocoon. The moth measures about three-quarters of an inch across the wings which are pure white, and spotted with small dots of a bluish-black. The body is marked with a large black spot and the abdomen with rings of the same colour. The antennæ of the male are bipectinate to about their middle.

Still more destructive to young coffee plants is the

"*Ringer*", the larva of the moth *Agrotis Sagetum*, as identified by Dr. Bidie. At times it multiplies to such an extent, that many acres of young coffee are rapidly destroyed by it, unless checked in its devastating course. The "Ringer" gnaws off a circle of the bark just above the ground, stops the circulation of the sap, and thus of course kills the plant. The grub is an inch in length, of a greyish black colour and lives in the ground. Its agency for evil is active only at night time when its natural foes, the birds etc. are at roost, and vegetable gardens, especially when planted with beans and potatoes, are equally subject to its attacks, which are only checked by digging it up close to the destroyed plant, or by applying quicklime to the ground. The moth measures about one and three-quarters of an inch from wing to wing. The upper wings are of a clouded brown and the lower pair of a greyish or bluish white colour. The Charcoal tree (Sponia Wightii) is infested by the larva of the family *Hepialidæ*. It is a very lively creature from 3 to 4 inches long, pale red, with 8 pairs of feet. Its large burrow in the tree is easily detected by the protruding bag-like cover over the entrance, consisting of a texture of threads mixed up with powdered wood. The moth, when in repose, bends down its greyish brown wings which measure nearly 4 inches across.

Of the *Hemiptera* or halfwinged insects there are some brilliant but disagreeably odoriferous species. The white and the black bug have come to notice by their attacking coffee, but the brown or scaly bug (Lecanium Coffeæ, Walker) is the more dreaded species. The male as is usual with moths is innocuous save as the progenitor of evil, but the female after feeding on the sap of the tender shoots or bark, scatters its hundreds of eggs over the coffee tree, the branches of which are soon covered, and the foliage greatly suffers, while part of the berries turn black and fall off. The bug generally first appears in some sheltered damp ravine, but rapidly spreads over an estate and after 2 or 3 seasons disappears leaving the trees in an exhausted condition. Still it is not so much dreaded as the "White Borer"; for the bug-covered trees recover with propitious weather, and sometimes appear to compensate their owner for the temporary curtailment of produce by an unusually heavy crop.

Amongst the clamorous *Chirpers* the large Cicada or "Knife-grinder" is conspicuous for the tremendous noise which it creates on a sunny day in a bamboo-clump or in a grove on Báne land. It is nearly three inches in length.

The *Diptera* or two-winged insects are largely represented and some much dreaded, such as the Gadflies and Musquitoes (Culex irritans) which torment man and beast.

The Blue-bottle, like the vulture, makes its mysterious appearance, wherever animal substances are decaying. The common House-fly is at times very numerous, but its beneficient moisture absorbing services are hardly appreciated. Just before the monsoon Fleas (Pulex irritans), which are at large, seem to seek a sheltering abode in houses and become a great nuisance, but with the cold weather they make themselves scarce. Passing over the beautiful Dragon flies,

> "That flutter round the Jasmine stems,
> Like winged flowers or flying gems,"

our attention is arrested by the destructive Termite or White Ant, which also belongs to the order *Neuroptera* or nerve-winged insects. White ants are not so numerous in Coorg as on the coast, but buildings in the province are not free from their attacks, which they carry on in the light excluding mud-galleries which they construct on every exposed substance, they seek to consume. Their conical shaped mud-nests, which are sometimes 10 feet high, deserve the name of ant-hills, if compared with the tiny insect-architect. They are frequently seen in the dry Kanawé district, where the bark and alburnum of sandalwood trees seem to have great attractions for the white ant. The habits of the Termites have been exhaustively described by Kirby and Spence, Dr. Lardner and other naturalists.

The order *Orthoptera*, or straight winged insects, contains besides the familiar Cockroach, silvery grey Fish-insect or Lepisma, Cricket, Grasshopper and Locust, some singular looking creatures, namely: the "Walking-sticks", the "Leaf-insects", and "Mantis" which are not unfrequently found in Coorg. The "Walking-sticks" or spectres (Phasmidae) closely resemble a vivified twig. When at rest the two pairs of posterior legs lie close to the slender body and the two anterior legs are joint and projected, covering with the 5 inches long body a space of 10 inches, at least in the specimen now before me. It is but seldom provided with wings; the long legs are three jointed and the femurs armed with short spines. The "Leaf-insect" (Phyllium siccifolium) is nearly 5 inches in length and midway 2 inches broad; its bright green body is on both sides expanded like a leaf and on it rest the two reticulated green wings, joining their back-seams like the mid-rib of a natural leaf, from which the opposite side-ribs branch off at regular intervals. The first two joints of the 6 legs are likewise green and expanded like the petiolary stipules of the lime tree; the last joint is short and provided with claws. The head is rather large and depressed, the eyes protruding and yellow, and the antennæ very short. In the *Mantis* or praying insect, the front limbs are folded as in the attitude of prayer. With these sabre-like forelegs the reputedly sanctimonious mantis entraps and decapitates the small insects on which it feeds. When two "Mantis" are placed opposite each other, they will fight with extreme ferocity like a pair of game cocks. A most extraordinary species is the dry-leaf-mantis which seems to be a compound of the three before-mentioned insects. It has the forelegs of the "Mantis", the thorax and posterior legs of the "Walking-stick" and the wings of the "Leaf-insect", with some peculiarities of its own. The head, with its large elyptical protruding eyes, its horn-like appendage and filiform antennæ, has a formidable appearance, which is heightened by its erect position as it bends upright the expanded protorax and puts forth its powerful long forelegs; the torax is like a thin stick one inch long, and the wings which overlap each other and are bent downwards resemble a withered leaf. The long legs have at the extremities of the first joint a lateral expansion of the same colour as that of the whole insect, which is a light-brown.

Amongst the *Aptera* or wingless insects we need only mention the Centipedes and Millepedes which are rather numerous in Coorg, especially the "Scolopendra" the bite of which causes severe pain and the "Julus" which is frequently found under the bark of trees, coiled up like a watch spring. Other unpopular parasitic genera, comprised in this order and which are coextensive with man's habitation, are not wanting in Coorg, especially among the uncleanly low caste people.

The *Arachnidae* or Spiders and Scorpions have also their numerous representatives The "Coorg Spider" abounds in all parts of the province. Its central globular black body is supported by 8 hairlike 2½ inches long legs, which give it a ghastly appearace. These spiders are gregarious and haunt dark and damp places, where often thousands are crowded together forming one black mass, which, if disturbed, disentangles itself with astonishing rapidity and spreads in every direction.

The yellow banded spider is an interesting object for observation, as it spans its extensive curious web on sunny thoroughfares, watching in the centre for its prey and rushing at the least vibration along the disturbed thread, to catch the unfortunate intruder. The largest spider perhaps in existence is the "Mygale" which lives in the ground. The one in my possession is from a coffee estate. Its body is two inches and a half in length and one inch broad and the longest leg over 3 inches. The upper mandibles terminate in downward curved horny claws, with which it wounds its victims, the poison being conveyed through the perforated claws. It is of a greyish colour alternately marked along the legs with pale yellow and black bands. The creature is covered with grey bristles which are longest on the legs.

Scorpions (*Can.* Chélu), especially the large greenish black kind, are frequently met with on damp ground under large stones or near decaying trees, where they attain a size of over six inches in length. Their sting is very painful and the wound causes a considerable swelling of the injured limb that lasts for several days. The smaller greyish-yellow kind occurs chiefly in damp rooms and its sting is less painful.

The class *Crustacea* has its representatives in several kinds of Crabs (*Can.* Nalli), that live under stones, in streams (kallalli), in paddy-fields (hullalli) and on damp ground (mandalli), and are eagerly eaten by the natives. A mother of the Yeddavanád people will exhort her children with the proverb:

"Eat Kallalli and you will become a clever man;
Eat Hullalli and you will become brave as a tiger;
Eat Mandalli and you will become master of the house."

The land-crabs often do great mischief to cultivation, especially to coffee-nurseries in damp ravines.

Of the *Annelides* the "Coorg Leeches" (*Can.* jigini) impress themselves on the memory of every one who ventures during the monsoon into the jungles. They are from one to two inches in length, very slender and astonishingly swift in attacking their victims. Thousands of leeches seem to keep right and left watch for the approaching wanderer, walking along a jungle pathway, and should he stop for a moment, the bloodthirsty creatures make up to him in their peculiar doubling-up way of progress from every quarter, and woe to him, should they unobserved gain access to any bare part of his feet; they will bleed him unmercifully till he feels the blood trickling down. The wounds produce with some constitutions festering sores. A simple means for keeping them off is a little salt-bag round the ankle. The medicinal leech (*Can.* atte) is also found in tanks and made use of in the Hospital.

3. Meteorological and climatic conditions of Coorg.

Though Coorg is but a small country, yet its high mountain ridges and narrow valleys, its wood-clad hill slopes and open champaign tracts greatly influence the atmospheric conditions of the locality. Still the dry eastern or Kanawé district may in the mean present as constant a climate as the moist hilly tract along the Ghats or the Mercara plateau. We have to distinguish the hot, the rainy and the cold season, though throughout the year the atmosphere is not without humidity which is precipitated either in dense mists or in showers of rain. From the end of December to the end of March, rain, indeed, is scarce, but in the mornings and evenings the valleys are seldom free from fogs or dews. During these months the dry east wind prevails, which has long ceased to carry remains of north-east monsoon clouds to the Western Ghats. Towards the end of March the clouds begin to collect towards the south-west and the cooling sea breeze blows with more regularity over the Ghats. In April and May the sun increases in power, banks of massive clouds extend along the western horizon, and occasional thunderstorms and showers, indicating the approach of the monsoon, cool the atmosphere which is warm and moist. The thunderstorms during this season are even more impressive than in the low country. Mountains of clouds, in double and treble ranges, float against each other with the order of armies. The sound as of heavy cannon is heard from a distance; solitary discharges of the electric fluid shoot through the gloom. Now whole batteries seem to be in action; peals of thunder are heard at brief intervals, and the eye shuts involuntarily against the dazzling brilliancy of the lightning. Then the conflict seems to subside, the roar of thunder is heard at greater intervals, the flashes of lightning lose their intense and fearful glare and the rain pours down in torrents.

Towards the end of May the clouds take up a firm position in the western sky and grow in massiveness. In June the rapport between the western sea and the atmosphere of Coorg is fully established. Rain prevails, descending at times softly, but more frequently with great violence and heavy gusts of wind. In July the monsoon reaches its greatest vehemence. The clouds seem to be inexhaustible, the blasts of the wind irresistible! As much as 74 inches of rain have been registered within this month, and for several days in succession 5, 6 and 7 inches within 24 hours! The sun is often not seen for weeks, and existence in the province would be as dull and gloomy as the clouds overhead, did not the inhabitants adapt themselves to circumstances and learn to make light of the incessant downpour. But it is pardonable if one is sometimes tempted to envy those favoured few, who may bask all the while in the mild sunshine of pleasant Fraserpet, the monsoon-head-quarters of the Superintendent, 20 miles to the east of Mercara, where the roaring Kávéri river and an occasional shower from the fringe of the monsoon clouds are the only signs of the rainy season in the highlands. In August the rain is considerably less and a few days break with an open sunny sky, atones for all the past discomforts. The ancient Coorg hills send the floods controlled by steep river banks to the east and west and stand forth in renewed beauty. In September the sun breaks through the dense atmosphere. In October the north-east wind strong and cold, gains the ascendency and clears the sky; in November, however, it often carries heavy clouds from the eastern coast, which discharge themselves chiefly upon the east and south-east of Coorg. The greater part of December is foggy, but towards the end of the month the weather becomes delightful, clear and fresh, the thermometer falling to a minimum of 50°.

The meteorological observations in Coorg are almost confined to Mercara, the principal station. From the tables in the appendix which are based upon my observations for 7 years, the following facts may be deduced for the meteorological condition of Mercara, near the Central School. The mercurial barometer shows its maximum height during the hot weather months and reaches 26° 60′ and its minimum during the monsoon, when it falls to 26° 15′. The thermometer indicates a moderate temperature, owing not to the latitude, but only to the elevation of the country. During the cold months, from October to January inclusive, the daily average variation ranges over 24° Fahrenheit between the extremes, giving a daily mean of 65°; during the hot weather months, February to May inclusive, the daily mean temperature is 70°, deduced from the average extremes 57° and 82° which show a daily variation of 25°; during the monsoon, from June to September, the temperature is most equable, moving between the extremes 60° and 75° which leave only a daily variation of 15° and a daily mean of temperature of 65° for these months.

The prevailing winds are: west wind just before and during the monsoon; north-east wind directly after the monsoon; and east to south-east wind during the remaining season.

The percentage of humidity, as exhibited by Dr. Bidie in his "Report on the Ravages of the Borer", varies between 48 and 87, the minimum occurring in December and the maximum at the end of September; very gradually and steadily rising 10 cents from January until May, when with a bound it increases 10 cents in May, 5 cents in June, 5 cents in July, and after a decrease of 5 cents in August it reaches the maximum of 87 cents in September, falls 10 cents in October, 10 in November and 22 in December, when it attains its minimum.

The mean annual rainfall for the past 7 years amounts to 123·80 inches of which at a monthly average 1·90 inches fell during the hot, 26·43 inches during the monsoon and 2·64 inches during the cold season. According to the scientific theory of the south-west monsoon, the rainfall in Coorg would seem to be entirely dependent on the geographical position and geological configuration of the country, but practical experience attests the fact, which is also corroborated by the annexed pluvimetrical table, that the rainfall has for the last four years been steadily decreasing and the cause is attributed to the extensive denudation of forest-clad hills for coffee cultivation, contemporaneously with the natural decay of all the bamboos in Coorg. The same amount of vapours as in former years may be carried from the sea over the Ghats, but the local power of attracting the rain clouds has diminished with the disappearance of the forests. No one who has attentively watched the sailing of clouds over partially wooded hill-tops can have failed to observe their lingering hovering-over and descent upon the forests, whereas over the bare hills the clouds sweep past with unimpeded velocity. The rains are neither as heavy, regular or continuous, as they used to be, and since there is less rain sinking into the ground and the retaining qualities of the soil have been reduced by the extensive clearing of forests and jungles, there are fewer springs and shallower streams and the country in general has become drier. Were it not for the incidental droughts, injurious to coffee planting, and the increasing difficulty of rice cultivation in some parts of the country, the change might be hailed as a most welcome improvement in the Coorg climate, which for the sake of human health might be still less loaded with moisture.

On the whole the influence of the Coorg climate with its average temperature of 66° 6′ is salubrious. The nights are cool throughout the year and Europeans are able to take exercise in the open air at all hours. European children in particular enjoy excellent health and their fat rosy cheeks form a striking contrast to the thin pale faces of those in the low country.

The rarified, often cold and damp air of Mercara with the usually prevailing high winds, necessarily does not agree with asthmatic and bronchial affections, chronic disorders of the liver and dysenteric complaints, but Fraserpet, which is 1,000 feet lower than Mercara, affords a salutary change during the rainy season.

The native troops, especially new arrivals from the low country, suffer much from the cold and damp and are, during their first year of acclimatization, subject to fever and bowel complaints, but in time even they enjoy the bracing climate of Mercara.

The climate of the valleys, particularly during the hot months preceding the monsoon, when, as the natives say, the old and new waters are mixed, is far from being healthy. Fevers, agues and bowel complaints are then very frequent and protracted. For the rest of the year the natives of the country pronounce the climate to be excellent especially after the monsoon. Besides the dreaded Coorg fever, which appears in its worst form, especially to Europeans, in the vicinity of Atur in south-east Coorg and about Sampáji on the western boundary, small-pox has laid a fearful hold upon the natives though vaccination is much in vogue. Cholera but seldom makes its appearance; and yields readily to treatment. A peculiar ulcer-disease on the limbs has lately been rather prevalent about Virajpet, which is ascribed to impoverished blood, for want of nourishing animal diet.

The account which natives of Mysore or from the Western Coast give of the climate of Coorg is not favorable. They have experience on their side. Of the large number of people, whom Tippu sent from Mysore to replace the ancient inhabitants, or who during the various wars were carried off by the Coorg Rajahs from the neighbouring countries to cultivate their lands, but few survived the change. In our days the thousands of Mysore coolies who annually emigrate to work on the Government roads or on coffee estates stand the climate much better, care being bestowed upon them and a periodical return to their homes being rendered practicable.

4. Cultivation of the principal productions.

Native agriculture in Coorg, as elsewhere in India, is still carried on as it was centuries ago. A system of rural economy, formed at a remote period and transmitted for ages unchanged, is not likely to be disturbed by so conservative a people, as are the Coorgs.

Rice is the staple product of Coorg. The numerous valleys throughout the land have, from ancient times, yielded an unfailing supply every year for home consumption and for exportation to the Malabar Coast. The rice-valleys are most extensive in South-Coorg, in the neighbourhood of Virajpet and in Kiggatnád, where some fields are of considerable breadth and several miles in length; but owing to the surrounding low, deforested hills which yield little fertilizing detrition, the soil is of a quality inferior to those fields of the narrower valleys near the Ghats, where the ground is terraced at considerable pains, but every field large enough for the use of the plough. The lower and broader fields of a valley, having a rivulet running through them are called "Beilu-gadde," and those terraced up along the sides and chiefly depending on the rainfall are named "Maki-gadde."

The rice cultivated throughout Coorg and in general use is the large grained "Dodda-batta", which is also exported. A finer and more agreeable kind is the small rice "Sanna-batta" and a red variety the Késari; for parched rice they use the "Kalame".

Except in a few valleys in North-Coorg, there is annually but one rice crop, but its return is so rich, that the ryots may well be satisfied and allow their wretched cattle rest and their fields to lie fallow or to "sun themselves," as the natives say, for the remainder of the year. Whilst in the low country and also in some parts of North-Coorg the average return of one crop is from 10 to 25 fold, that in most parts of Coorg proper is from 40 to 60 fold, and in seasons of extraordinary fertility even from 80 to 100 fold, which exceeds by far the famous fertility of Egypt!

The agricultural implements are few and of the rudest kind. The plough, constructed by the ryot himself, consists of a Sampige-wood ploughshare, with an iron point, a handle of Pali-wood and a pole of palm wood for the yoke, and is so light, that the farmer carries it to the field on his shoulders. Its value hardly exceeds one rupee. The Tawe which answers to our English harrow is generally a simple board to which a split bamboo is fastened to connect it with the yoke. The driver standing on the board adds to the efficiency of the operation, be it for pulverizing dry ground, as in the Múdu-shîme or eastern district, or smoothing and levelling the wet fields. A strong sickle and a mamoti or hoe complete the stock of farming utensils. To cultivate 100 butties of land, which is equivalent to an area yielding 100 butties at 80 seers by measure of paddy, or rice in the husk, a farmer requires either a pair of bullocks, or a pair of buffaloes, one plough and two labourers. On Monday he does not plough with bullocks, but buffaloes only, considering Monday as the day of the bullock's creation.

Whatever of cattle manure and dry leaves has been collected during the year is in the dry season carried by the women to the fields in large baskets and deposited in little heaps which are there burnt and the ashes are subsequently strewn over the ground. With the first showers in April and May the ploughing commences. On a propitious day before sunrise the house-lamp—Táli-akki-balake (dish-rice-lamp)—which plays a conspicuous roll on all festive occasions, is lighted in the inner verandah, the housepeople assemble and invoke their ancestors and Kávéri Amma for a blessing; the young men make obeisance to their parents and elders and then drive a pair of bullocks into the paddy-fields, where they turn the heads of the beasts towards the east. The landlord now offers cocoanuts and plantains, rice and milk to the presiding deity of his Nád, and lifting up his hands in adoration to the rising sun invokes a blessing. The oxen are yoked and three furrows ploughed, when the work is finished for that morning. Of the turned earth they take a clod home to the store-house or granary praying Shiva to grant them a hundred-fold increase. This recognition of the source of material wellbeing, is followed by personal industry that should command success.

From 6 to 10 in the morning the ploughing is continued till all the fields are turned over 2 or 3 times. Then the borders are trimmed, the channels cleaned and the little banks between the fields repaired, to regulate the water.

By the end of May one part of the fields which commands a permanent water supply and which has been well manured, is prepared for a nursery by repeated ploughing and harrowing, whilst the whole field is submerged. For every hundred butties of land from 2 to 2½ butties of grain are required for seed. The seed paddy is heaped up on the north side of the house, watered for 3 days, then covered up with plantain leaves and stones, till it begins to sprout. The nursery ground has meanwhile again been ploughed and harrowed, and the water allowed to run off, so that the grain when sown is just imbedded in the soft mud. After 20 or 30 days the blades have attained a height of about one foot and the seedlings are ready for transplanting. Beautiful as are corn and clover fields in Europe, there is no vegetation there that surpasses in beauty the brilliant green of a rice nursery. The eye is irresistibly attracted to these bright spots and rests upon them with the utmost delight!

Regulated by the monsoon rain the rice-transplanting takes place during July and August. The women, covered with leaf-umbrellas, called Goragas, that rest on the head and protect the whole of the body, pull out the plants from the nursery, tie them in small bundles, which are collected in one spot. Meanwhile the submerged fields are repeatedly ploughed and levelled with the Tawe, "till the soil is soft as treacle, white as milk the foaming surface," when all the men of the house, placed in a line and standing almost knee deep in the muddy fields, begin the transplanting in which women are not expected to join. The bundles are conveniently deposited over the field; each man takes a handful of plants at a time into his left and with the right hand presses with great rapidity 6 or 8 seedlings together into the mud, keeping a regular distance of about 6 inches. Before the completion of the largest field an open space of about 10 feet wide is left throughout the whole length. This is the Coorgs' race-ground and offers right good sport which greatly exhilirates their monotonous task. All the men engaged in the work—and 15 are reckoned for a 100 butties of land—may run, but 4 or 5 only obtain a prize. Wearing merely a pair of short drawers, they are eager for the run, for which their powerful legs well qualify them. The sign is given and away they scramble and plunge and stagger in the deep mud and roars of laughter greet the unfortunate wight who tumbles into the mud. Having reached the opposite bank, they return the same way, and hard is their struggle close to the winning post. The first comer is rewarded with a piece of cloth, the second with a bunch of plantains, the third with a jack-fruit, the fourth with a basket of oranges and the fifth with parched rice. When all the fields are planted, a feast for the people is given by the landlord.

As a protection against the evil eye, some half burnt bamboos about 6 feet high are erected in a line throughout the middle of the fields. It is now the farmer's business, to regulate the water supply of each field and to fill up holes made by crabs in the embankments. Also the weeding is attended to and any failures are replanted. At the end of October, when the ears of the grain are fully out, huts on high posts are erected, one for every 100 butties, for the watchman who guards the crop against wild beasts and occasionally fires off a gun. In November or December the paddy gets ripe and the feast of first fruits or "Huttari" is celebrated, after which the paddy may be reaped. The water is drained off the fields, the paddy cut down with sickles close to the ground and spread out to dry; after 5 or 6 days it is bound up into sheaves and carried home and stacked in a heap, the ears turned inside. In January or February, chiefly in moonlight nights, the sheaves are taken down to the threshing floor, spread round a stone pillar, fixed in the middle, and trodden out by bullocks and buffaloes, when the paddy is winnowed, the best quality reserved for seed and the rest stored up in the granary, already described, for home consumption and for sale, the price varying from 2 to 4 Rs. a butty. A threshing machine, lately introduced by Lieut. Mackenzie, excited the astonishment and admiration of the natives; but the handlabour of two coolies for turning it appears to them too severe and impracticable for large quantities of paddy. A winnowing machine would find greater favour.

The cultivation of Cardamom is to a great number of Coorgs next in importance to that of rice, and the possession of a fine cardamom jungle is regarded as a mine of wealth. In the time of the Coorg Rajahs and for some time after, cardamoms were a Government monopoly, and the cultivators had to sell their produce at a fixed rate to the Sircar, receiving from 12 to 20 rupees per maund of 40 seers dry capsules. Now the jungles are held from the state on a lease of 10 years, at 3 lacs of rupees, but this revenue to Government has not yet reached the amount, cleared by the Rajahs which, owing to their monopoly of selling the spice, rose as high as 80,000 rupees per annum! Any jungles that are not disposed of at the lease-auction, are worked by the ryots for Government.

The Cardamom plant (Elettaria cardamomum *Kg.* yélaki) grows spontaneously in the evergreen forests or Males along the Ghat-line and its spurs at an elevation of from 3,000 to 5,000 feet. Still, nature requires a certain stimulus to produce the plant in greater abundance and this is effected by a singular process, but though perfectly empirical on the part of the natives, no doubt it is based on a natural law which holds good in many other instances, where seed is kept in the ground in a state of vitality for a long period, till such a change in the climatic condition is brought about, as will favour its germination and subsequent growth. Of many other instances besides the cardamom, I need only mention: the Mexican thistle (Argemone Mexicana), the white weed (Ageratum cordifolium) and the charcoal tree (Sponia Wightii), all of which spring up spontaneously on newly cleared or broken, but favourable soil.

The cardamom requires a rich, moist soil in a bracing hill-climate, accessible to sea breezes and favoured by deep shade and partial sunshine. A western or northern hill-slope offers the greatest advantage. A working party of about 10 men start for the forest in February or March; and the site for a garden being fixed, one of the largest trees is marked for felling; a temporary hut is built on a convenient spot and operations are commenced. The smaller trees and brushwood are cut down to some distance round the giant tree, that is to be felled, and a platform some 10 feet high built close to the tree on the upper slope. This part being completed, the party sets out early next morning with 4 good axes and, standing on the platform, a pair of cutters, generally Kudias or Yeravas, belabour the tree with all their might. When tired they are relieved by their comrades. Their work must be finished by noontide or they are unlucky. At noon the front part of the tree is cut and at last some strokes are given to the side facing the high ground; the tree now trembles bends over and topples down the side of the hill, with a thundering crash, carrying down in its precipitate fall a number of smaller trees. The thorough shaking of the ground is the essential object of this operation. A piece of ground thus prepared is called a garden and according to the size of the large trees the party may cut down more than one in a day and clear as many as four or five gardens.

Within 3 months after the felling of the tree, the young plants shoot up all over the ground, shaken by the fallen giant especially near its stem and roots, and reach a height of one foot with 8 or 10 leaves within the first year; in the third year they will be 4 feet high and require a little culling, whilst previously one annual weeding is all the necessary work. In April of the third year the fruit bearing racemes shoot forth from the ground; they are alternately covered with short-stalked, beautiful, pale-white, solitary flowers of a lion mouthed shape, marked with purple-violet stripes in the centre. The numerous angular black seeds are closely packed in oval trivalvular capsules of a yellowish white colour and, if bruised, have a pungent aromatic taste. On this account and for their cordial, stimulant properties they are much in use as an agreeable spice and as a cough and vomiting allaying medicine.

The capsules ripen in September or October, when the crop is gathered and being the first, is dedicated to the deity and called Déva-cottu (God's gift). A full harvest, however, is collected only in the fourth year and the plants may continue to yield a good crop for seven successive years, when on their decline they are reinvigorated by the felling of another tree on the top of them. According to the number of fruit-bearing racemes on one stem, which amount from one to four, the crop is estimated as a quarter, half, three quarters and a full crop. The perennial stem of the full grown plant is erect, jointed and from 6 to 9 feet high and enveloped in the sheaths of the 1 to 2 feet long lanceolate leaves.

The yearly gathering of the cardamoms is attended with much hardship, especially when the gardens are not in Umales, i. e. hills near the úru or village, but far away in the Gademales. The high and sharp edged hill-grass is in October infested by innumerable leeches and poisonous snakes.

The cardamom gatherers, consisting of a party of Coorgs with their coolies of the Páleya, Kudiya, Yerava and Kuraba caste, (the Holeyas are not permitted to set their foot on those grounds) first set up a camp near the garden. A hut thatched with the long hill-grass is erected. At night a fire is kindled and the men sleep around it. Early in the morning they are at their work. One party clears the ground of weeds, the other cuts the fruit branches. Each man gathers a good load into his leafy basket formed of the Netti-mara and returns to the hut before sunset. After a hearty meal, they pick the capsules from the branches, an operation that keeps them up till late at night. With the dawn of day the men set out again for the plantation. The master remains. At noon the women of the house arrive; the picked cardamoms are measured into bags which they carry home to the drying ground. In the Gade-males the cardamoms are dried on the spot on a bamboo mat in the open but near a sheltering hut in case of rain. They are thinly spread and require but 4 days' hot sun to dry; further exposure would cause the capsules to burst, which is avoided. Before the capsules are ready for the market, the fruit-stalks are rubbed off, and all impurities removed. When assorted according to size and colour, they are stored away in closed baskets in a dry room, to preserve their aroma. Mopla traders or their agents visit the Náds at this time with a stock of bright handkerchiefs and other attractive finery for the Coorg women and make many a good bargain.

Some Coorgs gather from 30 to 50 maunds in weight of dry cardamoms, one maund (equal to 1,100 rupees in weight) is worth from 50 to 65 rupees in Coorg. The average produce of one garden of a quarter of an acre in extent may be estimated at 10 seers of dry cardamom. The contingent expenditure is insignificant. With more systematic cultivation seedlings and roots might be transplanted, and by trenching, manuring and irrigation, the produce might be greatly increased in quantity; but the owners of cardamom jungles require to have them on a longer lease, to make such extra expenditure remunerative.

Coffee cultivation.—There are but few Europeans and natives in Coorg, who are not interested in coffee cultivation. As the rush to the Ceylon Coffee-districts before the memorable years of 1847 and 1848, so has been the influx of European settlers to Coorg for the last 8 years. Their number is now over fifty and the change already effected in the appearance of the country would surprise one who left Coorg 10 years ago. The capabilities of the province as a coffee-growing country have long been known to the natives, and it is a matter of surprise, that the European enterprise did not enter on the field till a much later date. It is conjectured that in the time of the Coorg Rajahs some Moplas, to whom they had given land near Nalknád, introduced the shrub from seed, which was brought from "Mocha" or perhaps second hand from Munzerabad. Its successful and profitable cultivation was at first concealed from the Coorgs, but these were shrewd enough to find out for themselves, that, whilst none of the fabled fatal consequences followed the cultivation of the shrub, there was a ready and lucrative sale for the produce. Through the exertions of the first British Superintendent, Captain Le Hardy, who took a deep interest in the material prosperity of the country, the coffee plant became almost universal, and now there is hardly a Coorg or any native house, that does not pride itself in a coffee-garden, comprising, it may be, a few trees or as many acres.

The native mode of cultivation was exceedingly simple. The plants, reared from seed in a nursery, were in the monsoon put out on a shady hill-slope, the underwood of which had been previously cleared away. An occasional weeding was all the attention bestowed upon the plants which in 3 or 4 years, according to the density of the covering shade, gave a promising crop, that was picked, dried and disposed of in the husk to the merchant, as they did with their cardamoms, the price of dry cherry coffee averaging from 7 to 10 rupees per batty of 80 seers measure.

When coffee cultivation was taken in hand by European skill and energy, the industry soon assumed greater importance. Mr. Fowler, the first European Planter, opened up the Mercara Estate in 1854, Mr. H. Mann became the pioneer on the Sampáji Ghat in 1855, Dr. Maxwell opened up the Perambadi Ghat estates in 1856, and in 1857 Mr. Kaundinya founded Anandapur village with a most promising plantation in the Bamboo district. Round these first centres of cultivation dozens of extensive estates sprang up within a short time. Every one who beheld a hill-side, covered with the rich, luxuriant coffee shrub was bewitched by its golden promises. Here seemed to have been discovered the Eldorado of honest industry in a delightful climate and home-like country! Natives too, enriched by the sale of forest land, followed the example of the European planter, and opened up large estates; private and public companies were formed to embark in the lucrative speculation; forest land was to be had either from Government for the mere asking or by purchase from native holders. Cooly labour flowed in plentifully. Thousands of acres of the finest forest land fell under the planter's axe. Every new settler was hailed as a lucky fellow, whose lot was cast in pleasant places. Lacs of rupees were spent in the expectation of a cent per cent return. With the approach of the looked for fabulous income, the excitement rose apace. Envy had fixed an eye upon the fortunate planter;—but never before stood he more in need of pity and sympathy than at that time. A succession of bad seasons disappointed his prospects year after year; then the "Bug" infested the finest estates on the Sampáji and Perambadi Ghat, and scarcely had it left, when the terrible "White Borer," whose acquaintance we have already made, threatened to destroy the very foundation of his prosperity. There are but few planters who have as yet escaped either of these dire calamities, and their success makes the loss of others all the more felt. There is however no cause for despair. The soil and climate of the country seem eminently suitable for coffee cultivation. Coffee may yet succeed in Coorg and the undaunted planter may yet have his reward, if the method of cultivation, best suited for each locality, is carefully adopted, and if with the increase of jungle vegetation, especially bamboos, better seasons may be expected to return and the "White Borer" to disappear.

The approved methods of coffee cultivation in Coorg are planting under shade and on the open ground, and an intelligent planter will be guided by his experience of the elevation, exposure, and amount of atmospheric humidity of his locality which method to apply. If shade-planting is decided upon, there is the choice between natural and artificial shade, and in either case due regard is paid to full light and free circulation of air. The former method is but the improved native way of planting already described. For artificial shade-planting the jungle trees are all removed and either burnt or—which seems to be better—piled up and allowed to rot, when of the spontaneous new growth, especially the Sponia Wightii or "Charcoal tree" which springs up like weeds, a sufficient number of trees is allowed to remain. More permanent shade-trees, however, are the jack tree, the Poinciana regia, Bauhinia, the mango tree etc., seeds of which are put down at regular distances on the plantation, and after 5 or 6 years the young trees offer already partial shade. Coffee trees on open ground, that require no shade owing to a moister atmosphere, are evidently in a more congenial habitat; they grow stronger, live longer and yield an earlier and successively more regular and larger crop than trees under shade. Some of the Sampáji Ghat-estates nearest Mercara are of this description and their present appearance leaves hardly anything to be desired in coffee planting.

The soil and elevation best suited for cardamoms is also best adapted for coffee cultivation, hence at first the desire to secure cardamom jungles for coffee plantations.

After a piece of land has been cleared and regularly pitted with holes 18 inches cube and at a distance of 5 or 6 feet from each other, the surface soil is filled in and a peg fixed in the centre. With the first burst of the monsoon, the sturdy seedlings of 3 or 4 pairs of leaves are removed from the nursery with a ball of earth attached to the roots and transplanted into the holes marked by the pegs. This is the surest and therefore cheapest mode of planting.

Weeding is the next operation to be carefully attended to, but where from the nature of the soil or of the lay of the land there is danger of loss of surface soil from heavy rain, no-hoe weeding is allowed during the monsoon; but only hand weeding or cutting with grass-knives and, after the monsoon, a breaking up of the soil, to turn the weeds down. Easy roads are laid out to bring every part of the estate within ready access and at the same time to be the means of an effectual drainage.

With the end of the first year's operations, the planter very likely builds for himself a simple cottage on a convenient spot, that commands a fine view and some Bungalows are most beautifully situated. With the third year the estate comes into flower and bearing. In March or April the snowy white of the blossoms, in their copiousness but slightly relieved by the dark green foliage, delights the eyes with its morning freshness and purity, wherever you look, and in their bridal glory the jessamine-like flowers fill the air with an agreeable aroma. Let us examine a three years' old tree of best growth. It is 4 feet high of a pyramidical shape with alternately opposite branches (primaries) of which the topmost are 8 inches and the lowest 3 feet long, which are subdivided by secondaries and tertiaries. The flowers are in appearance like jessamines on short stalks, in clusters round the branches and last but 2 days. The tree under examination numbers 20 pairs of branches, and 3 inches from the stem the clusters of flowers begin; the lowest branch contains 22, the middle 8 and the uppermost 2 clusters with an average of 12 blossoms each. These do not all set and produce mature berries, but give an idea of the fertility of the shrub. Gentle showers or heavy mists at this time greatly enhance the fecundity of the blossoming, hence the importance of spring rains. The leaves are oblong, lanceolate, dark green and glossy on the upper, paler on the lower side and form a striking contrast with the snowy flowers or red berries. After a fertile blossoming the ovaries, if favoured by a few showers, swell rapidly and the green berries resemble olives. In October they become hard, turn yellow and, when mature, red. They now resemble cherries. We open one. A sweet aromatic succulent pulp encloses 2 beans, which are surrounded by a parchment like skin, which, when dry, easily drops off. A thin silky skin called the "silver-skin" is the last coating of the bean which, if of good quality, is long, of a bluish green colour and of a peculiar aroma. In some cherries there is but one bean developed which fills up the whole space. It is round and called Peaberry, and fancy assigns to it a higher price in the market than to ordinary coffee.

The separation of the fresh pulp from the beans is effected on the estate by a machine called "pulper," after which the parchment coffee is washed and slightly fermented to remove all saccharine and gummy matter, carefully dried and sent to the Coast, where it is peeled, garbled, sized, packed and shipped for the market.

Considering that every crop takes a certain amount of nourishment out of the soil, it is clear, that something in the shape of manure must be given to it in return, and it is generally acknowledged, that according to the chemical analysis of the coffee bean, the Coorg soil wants phosphate of lime, carbonate of magnesia and potash as the principal ingredients of the requisite manure, and a mixture of superphosphate of lime and Peruvian guano or stable-manure. Lime and ashes may be the nearest approach to it. Experiments with different proportions of these materials on a number of trees of equal growth soon show which is the most effectual mixture for each locality.

Of almost equal importance with manuring is the pruning of the trees, whereby the extravagant elaboration of the sap is checked and the fertility of the soil economised. It is this operation which makes the planter most familiar with his trees and which impresses upon the appearance of an estate as decided a stamp, as the system of training characterizes a school. It is amusing to hear a planter call 'one's attention to this and that "dear little tree", which he has "brought round by pruning"; but these are often the men who do justice to a plantation and who eventually succeed!

The export of coffee for the last 12 years, as will be seen from the subjoined table, has with the exception of the last two years been steadily increasing.

Statement of exports of Coffee from Coorg

from 1857—1869 in maunds of which 4 are equal to 1 Cwt.

Year	Coffee in maunds	Avoirdupois weight			Value at Rs. 500 per ton
		Tons.	Cwts.	Qrs.	
1857—58	46,336	579	4	0	289,600
1858—59	66,862	835	15	2	417,850
1859—60	1,11,768	1,379	2	0	689,550
1860—61	1,28,412	1,605	3	0	802,550
1861—62	1,53,781	1,922	5	1	961,125
1862—63	1,40,113	1,751	8	1	875,700
1863—64	2,34,182	2,927	5	2	1,463,625
1864—65	2,40,000	3,000	0	0	1,500,000
1865—66	2,50,000	3,125	0	0	1,562,500
1866—67	2,60,000	3,250	0	0	1,625,000
1867—68	2,40,000	3,000	0	0	1,500,000
1868—69	2,20,700	2,758	15	0	1,379,375
	20,92,154	26,133	17	2	13,060,875

The extent of actual cultivation is difficult to estimate, owing to the survey being incomplete. The land under coffee cultivation on the 1st April 1870 was 5,222 acres less than on the same date in 1869, when 55,750 acres were held by Europeans and 29,930 acres by natives, or a total of 85,780 acres, yielding a landtax of Rs. 91,251 whilst the acreage in 1869-70 produced only Rs. 89,942. The assessment for each holder is, after an exemption for the first 4 years, from the fifth to the ninth year 1 rupee per acre and rupees 2 ever after whether cultivated or uncultivated land. The planters, however, hope that Government will reduce this landtax to 1 rupee per acre in consideration of the sore disappointments and losses from unforeseen causes, under the pressure of which 204 acres have already been resigned by planters and, to recover rupees 3,497 for assessment due, several estates amounting to 3,702 acres have been resumed and sold by Government.

Chinchona cultivation, has been initiated on a small scale by Government in 1863 in a favourable locality 3 miles to the east of Mercara. There are now several hundred trees in a thriving condition, that yield quantities of seed for distribution and for rearing new plants in the hothouse, which was erected for the purpose on the premises of the Central School. Plants have already been distributed to those taluq cutcherries, in the compounds of which they were thought likely to grow, and the experiment has to some extent proved successful. Seed and plants have also been given to private persons. On several coffee estates small patches have been planted with chinchonas for estate use; but the special cultivation on a large scale has not found favour with any planter, though there is little doubt, that, wherever in the open coffee grows, which belongs to the same natural order viz: Chinchonaceæ, the Chinchona will also thrive. There is some diffidence as to its success as a financial speculation, seeing that the Government plantations all over India are likely to supply every possible local want.

Of the many species of chinchona the most generally cultivated is the "Chinchona Succirubra" or "Genuine Red Bark," which grows to a lofty tree and is rich in Alkaloids; but Mr. Broughton, the Government Quinologist on the Nilagiris, has lately discovered a species, which yields more than 11 per cent Alkaloids, and of these 10 per cent Quinine, the largest amount ever obtained from the Peruvian bark.

Tea cultivation has received but little attention. To judge from the experiments already made by Mr. Mann, Dr. Macpherson and Mr. Roberts, there is however no doubt, that tea will grow in Coorg.

The cultivation of Sugarcane is a purely native enterprise and chiefly in the hands of settlers from Mysore, who sell it for raw consumption or use it for the manufacture of jagry, a kind of coarse sugar. It is propagated from cuttings put down in April and yields ripe canes the year after in September. It requires a moist rich soil, that can be brought under irrigation. Some coffee planters have begun to stock their swampy ravines with sugarcane; but, the produce not being large enough, it is doubtful, whether it answers as a pecuniary speculation.

Cotton of a fair description has long been under cultivation to a small extent by ryots in the north-eastern parts of Coorg, where the fibre is used for home-made fabrics and the seed for oil. New species: the Sea-Island, New Orleans, Egyptian and Hybrid Cotton have lately been introduced as experiments and they thrive very well, but the sudden depression in the cotton market discourages any further pursuit of the speculation.

The seed is sown in May on a well broken up rich soil, that is raised in long ridges 3 or 4 feet apart. The seedlings are sufficiently strong to withstand the heavy monsoon rains and the pods ripen in October or November, when the sunny weather favors the gathering; perennial plants yield however ripe cotton almost at all seasons; and the monsoon crop is of course lost. My own experience on a coffee plantation near Anandapur with all available kinds of cotton seed led me to the conclusion, that the Sea-Island and Berar-Hybrid would yield most satisfactory results. Egyptian cotton grown in 1865 by Captain Taylor on the Sampáji Ghat produced a fibre, which was pronounced by the Bombay Chamber of Commerce the best that had reached the Bombay market.

The Plantain (Musa paradisiaca) of which there is a wild kind in the hill-jungles, is common all over Coorg near native dwellings. The 10 to 12 feet high succulent stem consists of a number of fibrous sheaths that may be considered the continuation of the leaf-stalks and is at the base nearly one foot thick. The leaves forming a tuft on the apex of the stem are 6 or 8 feet long and 2 feet broad. In the centre of the stem is a white solid substance forming a cylinder throughout its length. It is used by the natives for curry, when broken across, it shows bundles of spiral vessels to great perfection. The continuation of this cylinder beyond the stem forms the flower-stalk, it is therefore evident that one tree can bear but once, after which it is cut down and a new shoot springs up from the root, by which means the plantain is chiefly propagated. The closely packed conical flower head is not unlike a red cabbage in appearance, and by its own weight inclines downward in a graceful curve. Each of the purple leathery leaves or involucres coated with a pale bloom of great delicacy, covers a double row of 9 or 12 elongate yellowish red flowers, extending in a spiral line over one-third of the circumference of the fleshy stalk. With the maturity of each successive row of flowers, the involucre reclines and falls off, and the fruit appears, which when ripe is from 3 to 6 inches long and from half an inch to 2 inches thick. In its spiral clustering round the stalk, it forms a large bunch numbering from 200 to 300 plantains. The fruit when divested of its skin may be eaten raw, roasted or baked, or when sliced and dried in the sun, reduced to a kind of flour which is considered very nourishing.

The fruit is supposed to have been the forbidden fruit of Paradise, hence the botanical name of the plant. There is a great variety of plantains, which differ in size, colour and the flavour of their fruit, but all the Coorg plantains seem to be particularly rich in saccharine matter and very nutritious.

The plant is highly esteemed by the natives as the emblem of plenty and fertility and is as such in constant requisition at their marriage and other festivals for ornamenting the entrance of houses and temples. Stumps of large trunks occupy also a conspicuous place in their games and amusements, for it is considered a feat of strength to cut one through at a blow with the famous Coorg knife.

The *Musa textilis* or "*Manilla Hemp*" Plantain has been introduced by Captain Cole, and I have successfully naturalized it in Mercara. Numbers of shoots have already been distributed for extensive cultivation for the sake of its valuable fibre for cloth and paper-manufacture. The fruit is like the common large plantain, but so full of seeds that it can hardly be eaten.

Along with this plant also *the Rhcea or Assam Nettle* (Boehmeria nivea) was introduced, and having successfully reared it in Mercara, I distributed a quantity of roots and cuttings amongst the planters all over Coorg, who find it thriving very well in their sheltered ravines without any further care, but do not yet see how to make the cultivation profitable, owing to the difficulty and expense in preparing the fibre. The plant is indigenous to south-eastern Asia and is known in China as Ma or Chuma and in Assam as Rheea. It is a herbaceous plant, with large, perennial, spreading and much divided roots, from which rise a number of straight, slender, slightly branching stems from the bark of which the fibre is extracted. The leaves resemble those of the nettle, are light green on the surface and silvery white below but are not stinging. The male and female flowers being separate and situated on different parts of the stem, the production of seed is uncertain.

From data, given in the December number of the Calcutta Review 1854, the "Rheea" is propagated either by dividing the roots or by cuttings. The plant is exceedingly hardy and thrives in almost any description of soil, but to have it grown to perfection, the land must be well manured and capable of irrigation. In planting a piece of ground, the roots or cuttings should be placed out in rows a foot or a foot and a half apart each way, so that the plants do not throw out too many lateral shoots which impairs the height of the stems. When once the roots have firmly struck, the plant grows vigorously, but more especially during the rainy season. The first principal shoots burst from the centre of the root, and are quickly followed by exterior ones. In two months generally may be expected, especially upon well manured land, the first cuttings, which must be taken off about one inch above the root. It is essential to mind, that the plant does not become covered with hard or woody bark, which is indicated by the former green coating turning brown, the discoloration commencing at the stem. A little browning strengthens the fibre, too much imposes additional costly labour. It requires a little experience to ascertain clearly the requisite time for cutting. There is another criterion by which the fitness of the plant for cutting may be known, by passing the hand down it from the top to the bottom; if the leaves break off crisply from where they are joined to the stem, it is a good indication that the plantation may be thinned out. If, on the contrary, the plant be not ready, the leaves, instead of breaking, tear off and strip the stem of the fibre. When all is ready for removing the stalks, cutting more than can be immediately attended to, should be avoided. When the sticks are cut, they should be stripped of the leaves on the ground, which is done by passing the hand down them from top to bottom, after which they are handed over to women or boys to be treated as follows:

The workers should be in couples, one to take off the bark or thin outer coat, the other to strip off the fibre. The barker being provided with some coir fibre and a wooden knife, proceeds with the former to rub the stick in one direction, from top to bottom, or vice versa, which, if the plant be fresh, is easily accomplished; if the bark be obstinate, she uses the wooden knife, scraping in one direction, when the fibre is thoroughly exposed. After removing the bark, she hands the stick to another cooly, who breaks it an inch or two at either end or in the middle by which a portion of fibre is separated and which enables him to lay hold of it and to strip off very carefully the entire fibre. Should any mucilaginous matter still adhere, it is scraped off with a blunt wooden knife and the clean fibre hung up in the sun for a day to dry, when it is ready for the market. Perhaps drying the cut sticks in the sun and exposing them to the dews for several days and then beating out the brittle herbaceous part with a wooden apparatus as they treat hemp in Germany, may be a cheaper and more expeditious mode of separating the fibre.

As to the return. 88 lbs. are calculated upon one acre for one crop, and if the field allows three annual cuttings, the yield is 264 lbs. or a little more than one-tenth of a ton, valued 80 rupees at £ 80 a ton, whilst an acre of coffee producing 5 cwt. would yield at 70 shillings per cwt. Rupees 175, all expenditure excluded in both cases.

The *Chocolate tree* or Theobroma Cacao has been successfully reared by me from seeds received from Sir Madava Row, the Deván of Travancore. The cultivation of this most useful tree, which requires a soil fit also for coffee, promises to prove a most welcome addition to Coorg exotics, as it produces fruit when 5 years old and requires but little care or labour. The plants are grown from seed, to be obtained in March, much in the same way as coffee seedlings, and after 15 months when they are about 18 inches high, they are transplanted in large pits about 12 feet apart and protected by shade.

The fact, that a wild species of Nutmeg grows plentifully in the Coorg forests induced me, to make an experiment with cultivating *the Nutmeg of commerce*, "Myristica officinalis," but the promised seed has not yet arrived. According to Dr. Bidie's instructions, the cultivation may be carried on on coffee-land and seems to offer no great difficulties.

Of *fruit trees* the *Coorg Oranges* are celebrated and as common as the plantain. There are several varieties, but the best is the sweet, luscious "Loose Jacket" so called because the rind of the ripe fruit is almost detached from the pulp. The Coorg Rajahs owned fine orange gardens in the most suitable localities of the country, but they have since been neglected. There are also varieties of Citrons and the Lime indispensable in Coorg etiquette is in abundance.

Apples and Pears do not succeed in Mercara, as the heavy monsoon does not favour their growth, but there is perhaps no reason, why they should not grow in warmer and more sheltered localities, as well as in Bangalore. Loquats, Peaches, Figs and Pomegranates thrive better and the Guava, which makes a most excellent jelly, would be the Coorg Pear, if it were not for the numerous hard little seeds and the peculiar flavor which is not always appreciated. Strawberries and Pine-apples grow to a large size. Grapes have been reared in sheltered places in Mercara, but the vine soon degenerates. The Brazil-cherry is very common, the fruit is the berry of a herbaceous plant and is made into excellent jam.

English Vegetables are satisfactorily grown by Mercara residents and still more so by some planters on their estates. Potatoes and Cabbage thrive remarkably well; also Peas, Beans, Knoll kohl, Salad, Beets, Turnips and Carrots of excellent quality are produced. The natives do now only attempt to cultivate these vegetables, but the markets are unsupplied with them.

Native Vegetables, which are reared on patches of paddy-fields after harvest time, or in small gardens, in the villages about Fraserpet, include: French Beans, Radishes, Pumpkins, Cucumbers, Indian Corn, Brinjals, Chillies, Coriander, Amaranthus and others, but even these are not plentiful in the Mercara market, and what there is comes chiefly from Fraserpet.

Dry grain, such as Ragy, Avary, Tavary, Huruli and others are chiefly grown in the open country of the Nanjarájpatna taluq lying along the western banks of the Kávéri. It is there also, that Tobacco is cultivated for sale, whilst in most of the Coorg farms little reserved patches of the narcotic is grown for home-consumption; but the Coorg tobacco is of an indifferent description, no particular care being bestowed upon its cultivation. The introduction of a new seed would have a beneficial influence. A few Hemp plants are here and there grown near native houses, but more for the use of smoking the intoxicating leaves, than for the sake of the fibre.

Similar to other hilly parts of India, there prevails a primitive mode of cultivation called "kumari," which is practised by the lowest classes of natives, the Kurumbas and Kudias, chiefly on the western slopes of the Ghats. They cut and burn a patch of jungle, and plant either the small reddish hill-rice, sown broadcast upon the slightly dug up land, or Ragy. The former yields a 10 fold, the latter a 200 to 300 fold return. Such fields are only once or twice cultivated, when they are abandoned in favour of a new piece of jungle and not resumed till after 5 or 6 years. This wanton jungle-waste has however been put a stop to by Government and brought within reasonable limits.

Bringing to a close the subject of Arbori-horti-culture in Coorg, it were ungrateful, did I omit to mention the many and beautiful exotic flowers and shrubs, that ornament the gardens of European residents and recall by their presence sweet remembrances of distant Home; I forbear however to enumerate any beyond the modest Violet, the fragrant Rose and the showy Dahlia, and leave it to the fancy of the reader to associate with these types of spring, summer and autumn the many other garden flowers, that are familiar to Europeans.

II. PART

The People of Coorg.

1. COMPOSITION AND DENSITY OF THE POPULATION OF COORG.

The country of Coorg has for ages been inhabited by various tribes, which, though not all of the same standing, are distinguished from other castes, that have immigrated at more recent periods from the surrounding countries.

The most ancient and important tribes, which for centuries have been in the relation of masters and slaves, are the Coorgs (Kodagas) and the Holeyas, who together form perhaps one-third of the whole population.

Classified according to their languages and relative rank, claimed by, or accorded to them in the present day, the following are the various tribes in Coorg:

A. Tribes who speak the peculiar Coorg language.

1. The *Coorgs* and *Amma Coorgs*, about whom more anon.

2. The *Eimbokalu* (contracted from eivattu-vokkalu i. e. 50 farmers). They are cultivators and in their mode of life, in dress, in superstition and festivals conform to the habits of the Coorgs, but the latter do not eat or intermarry with them. In bodily appearance and complexion they are not so well favoured as the Coorgs and are less spirited in manly pursuits. They came from Mysore in a body of 50, to settle down in Coorg, hence their name. In the Rajahs' time they worshipped

Kávéri-Amma, but under the British Government they reverted to their original sect, the Srívaishnavas, who have their Gurus in Talkád in Mysore and now think themselves superior to the Coorgs.

3. The *Hegadés* are independent cultivators, who immigrated from Malayálam and settled chiefly in Yedenalknád. Like the preceding tribe, they conform to Coorg customs, but are equally excluded from the community of the Coorgs, in whose presence they are allowed to sit only on the floor, whilst the former occupy a chair, or if these are seated on a mat, the Hegadés must not touch it. In bodily appearance and complexion they resemble the Coorgs.

4. The *Bínepadas*, formerly musical mendicants, now sober farmers, are also immigrants from Malabar, they do not dress in Coorg fashion, but wear jackets. On festive occasions they prepare the parched rice for the Coorgs, from whom they are quite distinct.

5. The *Airis* came also from Malayalam and are the carpenters and ironsmiths. They live and dress like the Coorgs, but have no closer connection with them. The *Badigés* are a similar tribe, but Canarese people.

6. The *Madivâlas* are found all over Coorg and, being descended from Malayalam washermen, they practise their hereditary trade in the Province.

7. The *Kávatis* are farmers who in a small number live in Yedenalknád taluq only. They resemble the Coorgs in dress, but are of darker complexion and less favoured in personal appearance. Their origin is traced to Malayalam.

8. The *Naindas* or Barbers are emigrants from the same country and resemble the washermen.

9. The *Koyuvas* or Potters are met with in every Nád, where they ply their trade.

10. The *Kudiyas* and *Témale-Kudiyas* live chiefly in the forests of the Western Ghats, where they cultivate their own

Kumari land, draw toddy from the Bainé-palm (**caryota urens**) for sale and work as labourers in cardamom gardens and on Coorg farms, when they live in the outhouses of the Coorgs and share their food.

11. The *Médas* live independently all over the country and subsist on the produce of their handicraft, umbrella making. They are the drummers at the Coorg festivals, and it is their privilege to receive annually at harvest time from each Coorg house of their district as much reaped paddy, as they can bind up with a rope 12 cubits in length. They dress like the Coorgs, only in a poorer style. Their religion is the worship of Káli and of demons. The Médas live on vegetable and animal diet, beef included; they are a quiet people, not robust in body and of a sallow brown complexion with black straight hair.

12. The *Holeyas* are found in the Coorg houses all over the country and do all the menial work for the Coorgs by whom, though theoretically freemen under the British Government, they were held as "glebæ adscripti" in a state of abject servitude until lately, when with the advent of European planters the slave-question was freely discussed and the "domestic institution" practically abolished. There are three kinds of Holeyas: the original Kémbati and the Máringi — from Malabar and the Canarese speaking Badaga-Holeyas from Mysore. They dress indifferently, are of dirty habits and eat whatever they can get, beef included. Their worship is addressed to Eiyappa-Dévaru and Chámundi or Káli goddess once every month; and once every year they sacrifice a hog or a fowl. They are a poor, ignorant people, generally of middle size and of a dark complexion.

B. Separate languages are spoken by:

1. The *Roman-Catholic Christians* at Virajpet, who are emigrants from North-Canara and belong to the Konkani

A Holeya and his wife.

Photog. by the Rev. [illegible] [illegible]

caste. They established the settlement in the time of Dodda-Virajender, when persecuted by Tippu-Sultan's cruel proselytism. Besides their own language, "Konkani," they speak also Canarese. They are cultivators and shopkeepers.

2. The *Shiváchárics* who are farmers and traders and scattered all over Coorg; they speak Canarese and came from Mysore. They eat no animal food.

3. The *Gaudas* or Vokkaligas who are farmers. Those that came from the Tulu-country, speak the language of that locality and live chiefly in Távunád; the remainder who emigrated from Mysore, live in the north-east of Coorg and speak Canarese.

4. The *Páles* or farm labourers that live principally in the western districts. They also speak Tulu and have immigrated from South-Canara. The Páles are of a more robust appearance than the Holeyas, of coarse features, middle sized stature and black straight hair which is wavy with the women. Some dress in Coorg—some in low-country-fashion. They have no idols, but like the Tulu people, they call upon their gods: Guliga, Khorti and Kalurti, whose names they pronounce over their food before eating. Their diet is like that of the Coorgs.

5. The *Maleyas*, a small wandering gipsy tribe from Malabar who speak Malayálam. They pretend to cure diseases and exact money from the ignorant; they also personate demons and the departed spirits of the ancestors of their dupes.

6. The *Kurubas* who are distinguished as Jénu and Betta-Kurubas, but are of the same type which is more Mongolian than Caucasian. Their cheekbones are rather high and prominent, their nose short and nearly flat; their lips large, their eyes small, dark and deep set; their hair curly, through neglect matted and almost woolly. In stature the Kurubas are middle sized, well proportioned and in habits nimble and

enduring. Their colour is dark. They have hair on the upper lip and chin but no whiskers.

The *Jénu-Kurubas* live in huts in the jungles of Coorg and wander from place to place in search of honey, whence their name. They worship the goddess Káli by pronouncing her name over their food, but once a year they sacrifice a fowl. They live on vegetable and animal food, but do not touch beef. They are skilled in the use of the sling and of the bow and arrow and are excellent climbers. Their language is peculiar, but allied to Canarese. They are a wild looking, but shy and harmless people.

The *Betta-Kurubas*, like the former, live chiefly in bamboo-forests, but have no social intercourse with the Jénu-Kurubas. Though they do not climb trees, they are excellent wood-cutters, but not reliable on account of their unsteady habits. They excel in making mats, baskets, umbrellas, boxes and cradles for which they chiefly use cane, Canarese: betta, hence their name or perhaps from the Tamil: vettu, to cut. In their scanty clothing and the woolly, top-knotted hair and broad features, their appearance is wild and repulsive, yet they are a good humoured, peaceable set of people and when employed are industrious at their work as long as it pleases them. They speak a language of their own, which is not understood by any other natives.

7. The *Adias*, a migratory tribe from Malabar who work as day labourers. They are like Pariahs and speak the Malayálam language.

8. The *Yeravas*, a wandering tribe originally from Wynád, where, like the Holeyas in Coorg, they were held in slavery by the Nairs. They speak their own language and live chiefly in Kiggatnád with the Coorgs to whose mode of life and worship they have conformed. Like them they eat no beef and therefore rank higher than the Holeyas and Médas. They are strong and diligent labourers and their frequent desertion

to coffee planters causes no little vexation and loss to their often hard task-masters. In features and complexion the Yeravas resemble the Kurubas; like them they are scantily dressed. At their weddings and at their Pándalata or demon feast they chant their peculiar songs and have dances, in which like in those of the Páleyas, women take part, an extraordinary practice amongst Hindus!

9. The *Káplas*, who live near Nalknád palace seem to be mixed descendants of the Siddis—the Coorg Rajahs' Ethiopian bodyguard—as their features resemble the Ethiopian type. They have landed property of their own near the palace, given by the Rajahs, and work also as day labourers with the Coorgs. Their number consists of only 15 families. One, Chátu, who is still alive but above 60 years old, was one of the execuioners of the late Rajah's family, and in February 1869 he pointed out to the Coorg Superintendent two pits, one containing 7 bodies of murdered men, the other 21 bodies, 7 of women and 14 of children! In 7 other pits 1,500 cannon balls were found.

Besides these tribes there are a few *Parsees* in Mercara, *Brahmins*, scantily spread all over Coorg in offices and in charge of temples, *Shetties* and *Mussulmans*, chiefly in Virajpet, Mercara and Fraserpet, *Moplas* in Padynalknád as farmers, a number of *Tamulians* in the service of European families, and thousands of Canarese *Coolies* from Mysore on the coffee plantations.

All these tribes and castes together with about 200 Europeans and 50 East-Indians make up the population of Coorg which on the 31st March 1870 is supposed to have amounted to 112,952 souls, but this number seems to be much under the mark as the more accurate census in 1871 will show.

Distributed over the 6 Taluqs or Districts and the 2 principal towns Mercara and Virajpet, the population stands thus:—

Localities.	Births in 1869-70	Deaths in 1869-70	Population on 31st March 1870
Mercara taluq . . .	200	263	11,697
Padinalknád taluq . .	598	460	20,303
Yedenalknád taluq . .	373	219	14,153
Kiggatnád taluq . . .	529	263	17,774
Nanjarájpatna taluq .	471	388	23,163
Yélusávirashíme taluq	392	348	18,979
Mahadeopet or Mercara	149	119	3,859
Virajenderpet	12	58	3,024
Total.	2,724	2,118	112,952

Separating the Coorgs from the Hindoos and classifying the remainder of the inhabitants according to their religion, the distribution of the above population stands thus:

Coorgs	24,585
Hindoos.	80,934
Mahomedans	5,774
Christians	1,659
Total.	112,952

It is said, that before the time of the tyrannical Mahomedan despots in Mysore, Coorg was much more densely inhabited. During 1760 and 1799 more than half of its population either perished or was carried away into captivity and after the fall of Seringapatam but a small part of the exculants returned to Coorg. This statement is corroborated by the fact, that in the Southeast of Coorg there are still many deserted farms grown over with dense jungle, and there are here and there traces of former villages and little towns. The Coorg tribe which in the time of the Rajahs scarcely numbered more than 5000 or 6000 armed men, has during the long period of peace and prosperity under the British Government considerably increased and may now be estimated at about 30,000 souls.

2. PERSONAL APPEARANCE, OCCUPATION AND GENERAL CHARACTER OF THE COORGS.

The Coorgs, or Kodagas as they are properly called, are the principal tribe of the country and from time immemorial the lords of the soil. For the last two centurics they are known as a compact body of mountaineers who resemble more a Scotch clan than a Hindu caste. In the Hindu scale they are Sudras and not pork-eating "Bastard Kchetrias," as some mocking Brahmins would have it; but it ought to be the pride of the Coorgs to discard the notion of caste altogether, which in fact does not apply to them, and to stand upon their own merits as "Kodagas", the remarkable mountain clan of Coorg. Reserving an enquiry into their origin for the historical part, I would only remark, that the Coorgs of the present day are as distinct from the Malayálam and Canarese people on the western coast, as they are from the Mysoreans in the north and east, though their peculiarities are to some extent allied to the habits of the one as well as to those of the other race, and even their language is but a mixture of the Dravidian tongues.

Look at a group of Coorgs of the better class by the side of some Mysoreans or people from the western coast. The difference is striking. The Coorgs are tall, muscular, broad chested, strong limbed and swift-footed. Men of 6 feet and above are not uncommon. Their features are regular, often distinguished by an aquiline nose and finely chiselled lips set off by a well trimmed mustache which in the "gala-mishe" terminates in a broad volute as worn by their Rajahs and men distinguished for bravery. Apparently anticipating the present military regulation, they shave their chin but sport mighty whiskers! The colour of the Coorgs is lighter than might be expected under this latitude. Their mode of life and pride of race impart to their whole bearing an air of manly independence and dignified self-assertion, well sustained by their peculiar and picturesque costume.

The principal Coorg dress is a long coat (kupasa) of white or blue cotton or dark coloured cloth and even velvet. It reaches below the knees, is open in front, has, if not white, short sleeves under which longer ones of a different colour extend to the waist, and is held together by a red or blue sash of cotton or silk which is several times wound round the waist and which holds the never failing Coorg knife, with ivory or silver handle and chains of the same metal. A red kerchief or the peculiarly fashioned turban, which is large and flat at the top and covers a portion of the back of the neck, forms the head-dress. The feet are bare or protected with light sandals. A necklace of the berry of Rúdrákshi (Elæocarpus ganitrus), silver or gold bracelets on the wrists, and silver and gold earrings with pearls or precious stones complete their festive costume. Those who are in possession of the Coorg-medal or the lunulate ornament called Kokaládi do not fail to suspend it round their neck, as may be seen on the front-illustration. Their every day dress is of course of a more simple nature. The Coorg warrior looks more imposing. His dress is of the same cut, but of coarser material and shorter. In addition to his handy waist-knife (Picha-katti), he wears on his back in a strong clasp of brass the curved, broad-bladed Coorg knife (Odu-katti) which is seen in the hand of the figure in our illustration. In a hand-to-hand fight it was a most formidable weapon and since the young Coorgs have no longer Mussulman or Nair antagonists to decapitate, they display at their feasts the strength of their arms and the sharp edge of their knives by beheading pigs or cutting at a blow through the trunk of thick plantain trees. The long matchlock gun is now more a weapon of curiosity than of practical use, except with the poorer Coorgs, the wealthier sportsmen having supplied themselves with English rifles of the best description. Their ancient arms and ornaments were manufactured with the most simple tools by natives of Coorg.

The Coorg Rajahs used to reward men distinguished for personal bravery with silver and gold bangles, or with an ornamented large knife bearing the Rajah's stamp ಲಿ upon the blade and these tokens are kept as sacred heirlooms and worn on grand occasions only.

The personal appearance of the Coorg women is not less striking than that of the men. They are remarkably fair, of goodly stature, well shaped and many are really handsome before the betel-chewing, which generally begins after marriage, disfigures their regular features, and blackens their otherwise brilliant teeth. Their festive costume—and the ordinary dress differs only in quality—is one of the most becoming that can be seen in India. A white or light blue cotton jacket with long sleeves fits tight and is closed up to the neck. A long piece of white muslin or blue cotton stuff forms the skirt, being several times wrapped round the waist and tied by means of a string, so as to make the skirt fall in graceful folds almost down to the ancles whilst one end of it covers the bosom and is knotted together on the right shoulder. To give fulness to the skirt the other end is arranged in folds, which, contrary to the fashion of other Hindu women are gathered behind, a sensible arrangement and most convenient for unobstructed activity in house and field. This peculiarity did not escape the notice of the prying Brahmins who of course accounted for it by a silly Purânic legend, which at the same time gives vent to their vexation at the intractability of these rude mountaineers.

The head with its raven-hair is covered by a white muslin or coloured kerchief, one end of which encircles the forehead and the two corners are joined together at the back, allowing the rest of the cloth to fall gracefully over the shoulders. The wealth of a Coorg family is displayed by the richness of the ornaments of the women. Glass, silver or gold bracelets of a simple description span their wrists; their neck is decked with chains of coral, pearls or gold from which are suspended old Portuguese gold coins. Even the nose and the outer rein of the ears are ornamented with pretty jewellery in gold, pearls and precious stones, and also silver rings are worn on the toes.

The white festive gowns of the men, as well as the kerchiefs of the women, are skilfully embroidered along the seams and in the corners with red marking cotton and the patterns of native design are often very elegant. The Coorg women esteem their own embroidery more than Berlin work, as the former unlike the latter shows the pattern equally well on both sides.

As for industry the Coorg women deserve high praise. They rise early and besides cooking and other domestic work, they bear a large share in the labours of the farm. The men plough the fields, transplant and reap the rice; the women carry manure, weed, fetch home and clean the paddy. The men do no menial work, they leave that to their women and to their servants, whilst they enjoy a dignified repose, discussing the affairs of the house and chewing betel, or stitching a piece of clothing in which art many are as expert as professional tailors, others, gun on shoulder, wander through the jungles in search of game, but the height of their ambition is to figure in the capacity of a Government Official in the administration of their country.

A Coorg woman is rarely idle, her busy hands find always some work to do, and no wonder, if we consider the life and bustle of a Coorg house with its 40, 60, or 80 and more inmates. Two or three generations, grandfather and grandmother, their sons and daughters-in-law and the children of these families all live and mess together. The labourers also belong to the household and look up to the mistress for food and orders. The fattening of the pigs, the milking of the cows, the water supply for the house, these and many other cares are under the immediate supervision of the mistress. Where peace and harmony exist, a Coorg house presents a patriarchal life indeed, but the idyllic picture is too often marred by discord occasioned by the harsh régime of an imperious mother-in-law, by the jealousy and heartburnings of married brothers, or the more material questions of family income and individual claims. The master or yejamána, who is always the senior male member of the house, has no easy position, especially in our days, when a tendency to break up these large houses clearly manifests itself. But Coorg women of a commanding spirit and superior character are often heard of who, like Abigail of old, with tact and wisdom subdue the unruly elements of this bustling human beehive and make the residents subservient to the common weal and honour of the family. Here is a story to the purpose:—"Six generations ago, there was a woman called Doddi Auwa—the great lady—who lived at Almanda house, in the village of Arméri, which belongs to Beppunádu. She was the mistress of the Almanda property, being the only child of rich parents. She was a woman of extraordinary size and strength of body. Nor was she less distinguished by qualities of mind and character. Throughout the country she was known as the wisest, the richest, the strongest of Coorg women. Independent owner of a Coorg estate, she was at liberty to choose a husband for herself. Her choice fell upon a man of the same clan. Utta-cha, a son of the Mánanda house. He was a good sort of a husband, but much inferior every way to his great wife. Perhaps she had chosen him for this very reason. His place in the house was rather that of head-servant, than of husband and master. Every year the people of Arméri used to send a caravan to Irkúr, in the low country, near Cannanore, to fetch salt. At other times caravars, carrying rice to the coast, would start from Arméri during the dry season. On such occasions Doddi Auwa would herself attend to every thing, put the cattle in readiness, prepare provisions, and at last accompay her husband and his oxen to the place of meeting, appointed for the whole train from the village. On parting, she would recommend her husband and his beasts to the kind offices of the best men in the caravan, and return home to her great house and her large business. Often, when husband or servants appeared too slow in loading the oxen, she would bid them step aside and taking the double sacks quietly with both hands, lay them softly and evenly upon the backs of the cattle. She was famed equally for wisdom and honesty.

Also Mudduráya who ruled Coorg in her time, respected and reverenced her, and often, on coming to Beppunádu, he stopped to have a talk with Doddi Auwa of Almanda house. In the course of time Doddi Auwa became mother of four daughters, but to her great grief no son was granted her, to succeed to the Almanda property. When the daughters came of age, she gave them in marriage to sons of neighbouring landholders. The eldest became the wife of a member of the Pálekanda family, the second married into the Púlanda house, the third was given to the Amnichanda family. The youngest, by a general agreement of the chiefs, was also given to the Pálekanda house, but, as heiress of the Almanda property, she had to give her sons, if she bore any, to her mother. This daughter, the youngest, bore 4 sons in succession. Of these, the two eldest were brought up by their grand-mother Doddi

Auwa at Almanda. The name of one was Timmaya, that of the other Máchu. Máchu had a son Ayappa whose son was Bollu, the father of Stephanas, the first Coorg Christian."

The culinary art of the Coorg women is not much appreciated by a European palate, which relishes less hot condiments and a more sparing use of oil and ghee. Meat, whether game, pork, mutton, fowl or fish is cut into small pieces irrespective of joints and made into a nourishing savoury curry, which, with a dish of boiled rice, seasoned with mango, lime, citron and Ambatti-pickle, makes to native taste an excellent meal. The Coorg women excel in preparing a great variety of pickle and chutney, also sweet preserves and sweetmeats. Their appams or níradóshe are relished even by Europeans. The kitchens of the Coorgs, which are inside the house, are remarkable for the cleanliness of the cooking-vessels in use.

The Coorgs generally take an early meal at 7 of rice-conjee seasoned with pickle or curds. At 10 they partake of a more substantial breakfast, consisting of boiled rice and curry. At 3 o'clock again conjee is taken as in the morning, and in the evening a hearty supper of boiled rice with vegetable or meat-curry and other condiments. Toddy of the Baine-mara (Caryota urens), also a kind of beer made of fermented rice, rice-brandy and arrack are the usual beverages, but lately the strongest European liquors have become only too familiar to the Coorgs at all hours of the day.

As is the custom with other Hindus, the Coorg women attend upon their lords and the male members of the house, before they sit down to their own separate meal. This selfish and unmanly custom greatly detracts from the charm of family life. The meals spread on brass plates, on low stools, are rather animal feeds than family gatherings round the social table.

The Coorgs are very hospitable; no beggar goes away empty from their houses. A visit from Europeans is looked upon as a great honour and on festive occasions they are frequently invited. Then great efforts are made to do honour to their guest, and in the more civilized houses a breakfast in almost English fashion is served on crockery and with knives and forks. But perhaps those receptions are more enjoyable where one comes unexpectedly and has to put up with little inconveniences which draw forth from the kind host all the greater concern for the comfort of his guest. At the unexpected arrival of a European visitor there is at once a great commotion amongst the fair Codagitis. Clean dresses are donned, ornaments put on and there is a running to and fro within the house. Soon the crackling of fire is heard and the aroma of roasted coffee indicates the coming treat. The coffee is brought in a spouted brass vessel or in a tumbler; it is highly sweetened, has also a bytaste of red pepper, as the coffee beans were broken in the mortar that serves for pounding spices, but you cannot resist to gratify the importunity of your kind host. To leave a Coorg house without having partaken of any offered refreshment, be it only a sip of milk or an orange, would be a grave offence against Coorg etiquette.

It has been said that "the Coorg women do not exercise the domestic virtue of cleanliness." Considering the nature of the work that falls to their share, it cannot be expected, that they should always appear in festive costume; but they bathe frequently and whenever they are seen in public the women are remarkable for their clean and tidy appearance. Coorg children show much affection for their parents and relations, and the little ones of whom there is generally a goodly number are great pets of the house. The visiting stranger is the object of their wonder, and if he succeeds to gain their confidence, he will be liked all the better by the whole family. The bearing of the young in the presence of the old is decorous, the latter being greeted by every junior member of the house or by a visiting neighbour whether male or female with great respect. The young man lays aside whatever burdens his hands, puts off his shoes and with folded hands first raised to the forehead, bows down and touches the feet of his senior, who lays his hand on the young man's head pronouncing a blessing, when the youth rises and repeats the ceremony to others.

The Coorgs are a hardy race and bear with fortitude a great deal of hardship, especially during the monsoon, whilst engaged with their rice cultivation. Exposed to wet and cold and often prostrate with fever, they soon regain their strength and old men and women of 70 or 80 years are not uncommon amongst them.

In the times of their Rajahs, during their wars with the Mysoreans and Malabars and in their marauding expeditions the Coorgs proved themselves brave soldiers and were dreaded for their fierce intrepidity; but their strength lay especially in their mountain fastnesses and behind the shelter of their native woods and the formidable breastworks extending for miles along the crests of hills. Since they have come under the rule of the British Government their warlike spirit has found no scope; but they are still a brave and manly race, who in time of need would doubtless stand by their new rulers with devoted loyalty. At the hunt of the tiger, the bison or the elephant no true Coorg shirks the dangerous sport; but with nerve and coolness and wary cunning he will dodge the advancing beast and with keen eye and steady hand fire at him at close quarters.

The intellectual and moral faculties of the Coorgs have for ages been neglected, and consequently up to the present day they are both ignorant and supersitious. The worship of demons and of departed spirits has usurped among them the worship of God. Charms and sorceries abound all over the country. Disease among men and cattle is readily ascribed to the curses and witchcrafts of enemies. The dead are supposed to trouble the living and to demand sacrifices and other atonements. Many of the Coorgs, though they may despise their old superstitions and neglect their idols, come to believe in nothing but money. The cruel despotism of their Rajahs engendered dissimulation, falsehood and treachery, and lying and deception, bribery and conspiracy are now often enough practised to ruin an opponent and to advance self-interest. The name of the Coorgs is still feared by their neighbours, who look upon them as proud, irritable and revengeful men, and such popular estimations of the character of a neighbouring race are seldom without some foundation. It still may happen, that the head of a Coorg house on his dying bed will solemnly charge his sons to reek vengeance on his personal enemies, a bequest which occasions calamitous feuds between succeeding generations.

The Coorgs have hitherto been an unlettered people. The Rajahs, themselves without education, did nothing for the instruction of their subjects. Even the English Government has for many years hardly attempted systematically to raise them in intelligence and character. Only lately most praiseworthy efforts have been made to satisfy the awakened popular desire for education in Coorg, and the provisions made have already borne good fruit in supplying Government with a body of well trained officials, though education is still in its first stage of development.

The public morality of the Coorgs is controlled by a council of elders called "Takka-mukyasteru", who are the moral censors and managers of social affairs, without however any magisterial power from Government. This institution dates from the Rajahs' time and is hereditary in certain families. The authority of the village Takkas extends over offences against social customs, attendance at public feasts and proper conduct during the same, drunkenness and adultery.

The offender has to appear before the council of the elders of the village, at the Ambala (a council-room on the village green), where the matter is investigated and discussed. The presiding Takka pronounces the sentence which may amount to a maximum fine of rupees 10. Should the offender refuse to pay, he will be excommunicated, when he may appeal to the "Nád-mukyasteru", that is the assembly of all the village Takkas of the district, and their decision is final. An outcast Coorg may after years be restored to his former status on paying the imposed fine. To the influence of these guardians of public morality the orderly conduct of the Coorgs in public is principally owing. It is, however, to be feared, that the increasing wealth and influence of many Coorg houses modify the strict control of the Takkas and make them more complaisant to the rich, which tendency will inevitably result in a decline of their authority and a greater laxity of public morality. Intemperance, which in the times of the Rajahs was rigorously repressed, is now rather encouraged by the numerous liquor shops, which are decidedly on the increase all over the country. It requires a new impulse on the part of the better type of Coorgs to combine in vigorous combat, especially during their festivities, against this ruinous enemy, and a victory gained on this field will be more glorious and beneficial to the Coorgs than their repeated triumphs over their Mahomedan antagonists of old. When the Coorgs have once embraced the truth of Christianity and placed themselves under the regenerating influence of the Gospel, they will become a noble race, probably not much inferior in bodily, moral and intellectual powers to their present European Rulers!

3. SOCIAL LIFE OF THE COORGS.

a. The Coorg house.

The Coorg houses are generally situated close to their paddy-fields on a sheltering slope of Báne land, surrounded by clumps of plantain trees, sago and betel-nut palms and other fruit-bearing trees. A coffee garden and a small plot for the growth of native vegetables are seldom absent, and, where the locality is favourable, a little tank well stocked with fish is not uncommon. The position, the style of building and the approaches of old Coorg houses strongly remind one of small fortifications, and tradition points back to a time of general feuds, when chief fought with chief, clan with clan. In the deep cadangas or ditches with high banks, we still see memorials of that warlike state of affairs. These war-ditches intersect the mountainous districts in every direction, and resisted not only many a furious attack of contending parties, but also the force of the annual monsoon.

A deeply cut passage, paved with rough stones and overgrown with shady trees, and the sloping side walls decked with a variety of luxuriant ferns, leads you in angular lines to the doorway, passing under an out-house. Over a paved courtyard, on three sides enclosed by stables, store-rooms and servants' quarters, you come to the front of the main building, which is a square of one story and raised about 3 feet above the ground. All the buildings are roofed with bamboos, and thatched with rice-straw. Considering that there is an open square hall in the centre of the house, called nadumaue there remain the four sides only for habitable quarters. The front side however is reserved for an open verandah—the reception hall. Near to the right end the principal door leads to the inner rooms, which are all dark, opening only by a small door into the inner square, which is lit by the sky-light formed by the junction of the four inner slopes of the roof, the dripping rain-water from which is collected in a masonry reservoir and drained off in an underground channel. On the side opposite to the verandah two doors communicate with the backyard of the house.

The front of the verandah is raised, and covered with a 2 feet broad wooden slab, so as to form a convenient seat; from it rise 3 or 4 wooden pillars, square and tapering and sometimes carved; the floor is of well beaten mud overlayed with cowdung; and the ceiling of wood arranged in small compartments. In some houses the verandah is separated from the inner hall merely by a wooden grating, in others by a solid earthwall with a sort of window, or lattice, made of wood. Like the principal door posts this aperture is often very handsomely carved in flowers and figures leaving small open spaces between, just enough to peep through without being seen, a contrivance chiefly for the benefit of the fair Kodagitis, who are as curious to see and observe visitors as their Mussulman sisters behind the Purdah or screen.

Entering through the principal door, the first compartment to the right is occupied by the master of the house and his wife. The next room is the kitchen from which the smoke issues and fills the whole house, coating and preserving the wood-work. While the European rubs his eyes and gasps for fresh air, the inmates of the house feel no inconvenience and only smile at his sensitiveness. The small compartments of the remaining two wings are tenanted by the married couples, and the unmarried women; the boys and young men sleep in the hall. From the ceiling are suspended matchlocks and rifles, the wooden bells and trappings for their pack-bullocks, and other domestic utensils, and the space under the roof, which is reached by a ladder, serves for storing bags, baskets, pads, pots, onions, salt, etc.

The house and yard are generally kept clean and orderly,

and the announcement of an approaching honored visitor sets at once the broom into activity and you may arrive just in time to see the retreating Coorg damsel and have to swallow the raised dust. However, the object is attained, you perceive what attention has been paid to you.

A stone built deep well is usually in the compound or the water is fetched from a hole sunk by the side of the paddy-fields, and near the well is the hut for hot bathing.

The low caste servants have their huts at some distance from the Coorg house; the meals given them they eat on plantain leaves apart from their masters.

As already remarked the Coorg house is the domicile of all the male relatives with their wives and children belonging to one parental stock. The landed property, or Jamma-púmi, is vested in the house and cannot be alienated from it, or divided amongst its members. The farm is cultivated by all the housepeople under the management of the master of the house, and the produce is divided amongst them after the Huttari feast. It often occurs, however, that an energetic member of the house or one in Government employment, acquires for himself some fields called Koppa, which are his own, and if sufficient for the support of his family, he may live there and establish a new house. Others own a small coffee plantation or cardamom-garden, and these individual enterprises seem to be the natural transition to an impending general social reform—the breaking up of the great houses, and the independent establishment of each married couple residing near their own paddy-fields, and eating the fruit of their own labour. The indolent will then have to work for their subsistence or sink into misery, the industrious and thrifty will prosper, and after a period of no little angry strife a happier life of personal freedom and domestic felicity will be the inheritance of future generations. The only danger to be apprehended is the tendency of the rich houses absorbing the poor ryots and reducing them to a state of servitude. A wise Government will, however, watch with solicitude the spontaneous development of the reform, and the more it is the work of the people themselves, the surer will be its successful accomplishment.

b. Prescriptive law of inheritance.

Sons, grandsons, brothers, brothers' sons, daughters, daughters' sons, cousins and adopted sons have the right of succession to inherit property successively in the order here mentioned. Property, in default of offspring, on the death of a man devolves on his widow; if he leaves a son under age, the widow is his guardian, and takes possession of the property. If the deceased leaves neither wife nor sons, but a grandson and a brother, or a brother's son, the property is divided, provided the family be undivided; but if it be divided the grandson takes possession of the whole property. The law of primogeniture, however, now prevails and division is strictly prohibited.

If the deceased leaves neither wife, nor children, nor grandsons, the property devolves on his brother or his brother's sons, if any, as the nearest relations. In cases where the deceased has left neither wife nor sons nor brothers, but a daughter not married, the relations of the family put her in possession of the property, and dispose of her in marriage, and on her death her husband or her sons inherit it. But if a man dies leaving a daughter not married, and a brother's son or a grandson, the family being undivided, the property used to be liable to a division. In failure of the preceding persons, the property used sometimes to descend to the cousins, and sometimes not, as the Government determined. In cases where the deceased leaves a son under age without relatives to protect him, the Government appoints the head of the village to act as guardian to the boy and to take charge of his patrimony, until he attains his majority, which ranges from 16 to 20 years, according to the maturity of judgment shewn by the individual, when he puts his ward in possession of it, and renders him an account of receipts and disbursements during the period of his nonage.

If the deceased has left no children, the widow adopts a child of her relations, if procurable, or otherwise of her tribe, and he succeeds to the property on his attainment of the proper age, provided he has been adopted formally and according to the usage of the clan.

c. Wedding and married life.

The marriage-customs of the present day present a curious mixture of old and new rites, fashions and notions.

In ancient times, it would seem, the marriage festivities had a peculiarly communal character. On some great day a family would call together the whole gráma (village), that is all the families of one of the rice-valleys, girt with farm-houses, to a feast. The youths would have their ears pierced by the carpenters for earrings, and the maidens had rice strewn upon their heads. This was in those days called the marriage feast. The whole community feasted together, and the young people were now at liberty to go in search of husbands and wives.

In the low country the piercing of the ear is generally performed by the goldsmith, except in out-of-the-way places, where a goldsmith is not to be found. In such a case another branch of the trade-fraternity, smith or carpenter, may act for the brother-goldsmith. In Coorg the carpenter has the exclusive privilege of piercing the ears for ornaments.

The girls have their ears pierced in early childhood. When they come of age, the ceremony of putting on their heads some corns of rice is a token of their being free to marry.

The present marriage rites of Coorg, especially in Kiggatnádu, where bride and bridegroom are welcomed together by the relatives and fellow-villagers of both parties, and sit together on the wedding-chair, closely resemble the common fashion of the Hindus, though they have not yet conformed altogether.

Young persons under sixteen years of age are not married in Coorg. Exceptions from this wholesome rule are very rare. It is to be hoped that the Coorgs will ever be preserved from the misery of child-marriages.

A young Coorg, when about to marry, has first to obtain the consent of his father or of the head of the family. This affair being settled, the Aruva of the house is taken into the marriage-council. He has to speak to the Aruva of the family, to whom the desired bride belongs. These Aruvas hold an important office among the Coorgs. They act as representatives, counsels, guardians of families and individuals on the great occasions of life. A particular friend of a neighbouring Coorg house becomes its Aruva, and a member of this house is naturally the Aruva of the other. On a certain day the Aruva of the intending bridegroom, accompained by his father or elder brother, goes to the house of the young woman, who is to be asked in marriage. They speak to the Aruva and to the head of the house. A favourable answer being returned, the whole house is carefully swept and a lamp is lit. Some families, affecting new fashions, at this time call in the astrologers to see whether the stars of the new couple will agree together or not. Where no horoscope has been taken, the astrologers, never at a loss, find the stars by the names of the parties! It is to be supposed, that the wise seers generally return acceptable answers. However, this part of the marriage-proceedings is evidently an innovation. The old fashion is to light a lamp in the newly swept house; when the two Aruvas, with the heads of the respective families, stand before it, (the bridegroom's Aruva and father, or elder brother, on one side, the bride's representatives on the other) and shake hands together, in token of an inviolable contract having been concluded, in the presence of the Divinity or sacred light of the house. Such engagements are rarely, if ever, broken. After the above preliminaries the time for the wedding is agreed upon. The nuptials are often postponed half a year, sometimes for a twelve-month, but generally the Coorg weddings come off during the months of April and May, when the rice-valleys are dry, and there is little work to be done. When the time approaches, the astrologer's counsel is asked for the choice of a propitious day. The relatives of the bride and the bridegroom are invited to the respective houses ten days before the wedding. Under the superintendence of the Aruvas they engage in the necessary preparations. The members of the respective families themselves are not expected to join in these labours. On the last day before the marriage all the families of the villages of the bride and bridegroom are summoned. Each house must send at least one male and one female representative. Now the wedding-sheds are finished; pigs are slaughtered and dressed; rice and vegetables are prepared. The whole company thus working together, join also in a good dinner provided for their guests by the principal parties interested. The Aruva of each house acts throughout as master of the ceremonies.

On the wedding day, at sun-rise, the two village communities, to which the bride and bridegroom belong, are in festive commotion. No house is permitted to absent itself from the general gathering. In the bridegroom's house the male guests, in the bride's house the female attendants, busy themselves with bathing, dressing and ornamenting the chief personage of the day, and in making every thing ready for a good Coorg-feast. The larger and fatter the pigs, the more abundant and strong the liquor, the greater will be the glory of the day. Ancient ballads are recited, extempore singers extol the names of the principal persons among the assembled relatives. Now the Muhúrta (the propitious hour) has come. At the same time both bride and bridegroom are conducted to the wedding-seat in their respective houses. The guests put themselves in order. One after the other approaches the bridegroom or the bride, strews some grains of rice upon his or her head, lifts a brass-vessel filled with milk from the ground, and pours some drops into his or her mouth, puts a piece of money, not less than three annas into his or her hand, and passes on. When the Muhúrta is over, the bridegroom or the bride retires into another room, where they continue to sit, sometimes for hours, until the last of the guests has come, and offered his salutation and gifts. At the end of the Muhúrta the wedding company apply themselves to the dinner prepared for them. The joy of the feast is heightened by the songs of the Coorg-bards, who sing of the glories of the relatives of the house, of the families belonging to the village community, and repeat the Palmé's (ancient songs) which they have learned from their fathers. I cannot refrain from entering here the humorous wedding-song translated by Mr. A. Graeter from the Coorg original:—

Wedding Song.

God Almighty, live and rule,
Rule as our Lord and God.
Rule as Sovereign, O King!
On the surface of the earth
Coorg is like a string of pearls,
Though one of the smallest kingdoms
In this land they count 12 valleys,
And the Náds are 35;
But in our Nád for ever,
Like a flow'r of paradise,
Blooms the name of Apparandra.

In this Apparandra house
Lived a man of reputation,
Mandanna the mighty hero;
When he offered a petition
To the ruler of the country
For a goodly jumma land,
He received it as a present.
For his money he now bought
Holeyas to be his servants,
And they laboured on his farm.
Bullocks too, his fields to plough,

He procured for heavy money,
And completed all his labours.
When he now lived comfortably,
Mandanna the mighty hero,
In his mind was meditating
And within himself he pondered
Constantly this one idea:
"I have rice and costly garments,
But no one to dress and nourish;
I have precious stones and jewels,
But where is the wife to wear them
In a household without children
Vain is all our toil and trouble;
No! there is not here on earth
Without wife bliss or enjoyment.
If a tank is without water,
Has it not been dug in vain?
And a garden without flowers,
Has it not in vain been planted?
Who would like to eat cold rice,
Void of curds and void of salt?
Sons must be in our houses,
And our rooms be full of children."
So he thought within himself,
And, one lovely Sunday morning,
When the silvery dew was sparkling,
Took a meal, and dressed himself,
Joined his hands in adoration
To the ancestors and God;
Sent a man to call his Ar'wa
To conduct him on the journey,
Took his stick adorned with silver,
And then started with his friend.
Where between the woody mountains
Thrones the lofty Kuṭṭamalé,
Wand'ring through the hilly country,
He went off to seek a wife,
Till his soles wore off with walking;
Pond'ring sat in all the Mandus,
Till his dress was torn by sitting;
Wandered in the scorching sun,
Till his head was hot and giddy;
Wandered till the walking stick
In his hand was growing shorter.
Mandanna the mighty hero
Sought a wife in ev'ry quarter,
But no house would suit his mind.
If he found the house was right,
Then the servants would not suit him;
If he found the servants right,
Then he did not like the cattle;
If he found the cattle right,
Then the fields were miserable;
If the paddy land was good,
Then the pasture ground was bad;
And if all these things were good,
Then the maiden did not please him.
While he thus was sorely troubled,
News arrived of consolation: —
In the Nalkunád there lived,
In the Pattamáda house,
Chinnawwa, a lovely maiden. —
When he heard this information,
Mandanna, the mighty hero,
Slowly with his friend proceeded
To the house, and there sat down
On the bench of the verandah.
Chinnawwa, the lovely maiden,
When she heard of their arrival,
Came and brought a jar of water,
Poured it in a silver pitcher,
Placed it on a glittering mat,
Spread another mat for him
In the seat of the verandah.
Pattamáda Chinnawwa
Modestly stood on the threshold,
And she asked him: "Why, my friend,
Did you not take any water,

COORGS

grandfather, father and grandsons

Use it and then call for more?"
So she asked, and he replied:
"Certainly I will, my dearest,
"If for ever you will bring me
"Water as to-day you brought it."
She replied: "You get the water
"If you come here ev'ry day."
Mandanna now took the water,
Washed his face and hands and feet,
Thought: I'll come for more tomorrow.
Mandanna, the wise and clever,
Took again the seat of honor
And began: "My pretty maiden,
"Tell me now, where is your father?"
She replied: "My father went
"To a meeting in the Mandu."
"And where is your mother then?"
"She went to the potters' village,
"Where they celebrate a wedding."
"And where is your brother then?"
"He went down the Ghat to Kóte
"With his bullocks, to get salt."—
When an hour or two were spent,
To his house returned the father.
Mandanna made his obeisance,
Bowed, and touched the old man's feet.
When an hour or two were spent,
To her house returned the mother.
Mandanna again saluted.
When an hour or two were spent,
To his house returned the brother.
Mandanna made his obeisance.
Then they had some conversation,
Talked about their friends and kindred.
Now they asked him: "Dearest cousin,
"Will you please to let us know,
"Why you undertook this journey?"
He replied: "My dearest father!
"I have heard, that in this house
"There are bullocks to be sold,
"And moreover that there lives
"In this house a lovely maiden,
"Whom you want to give in marriage."—
"All the bullocks have been sold
"In July," replied the father,
"And the daughter too has gone,
"In the month of May she left us."
Then gave Mandanna this answer:
"Those that went, let them be happy,
"Give me her who still remains."
Spoke again to him the landlord:
"Tell me, why you called me, 'Father'?"
Then spoke Mandanna the clever:
"I have seen your lovely daughter,
"That is why I call you 'Father.'
"Evermore with admiration
"You behold the stately palm-tree;
"If a tree is poor and crippled,
"You forget to look upon it."
Then the father spoke again:
"I will let you have the daughter,
"Give a pledge, that you will take her."—
"Shake then hands with me," replied
Mandanna, "and as a pledge
"Take from me this piece of money."
After this the father sent
For his Ar'va to assist him
In the wedding ceremony;
Women swept the house and chambers,
Filled the store-rooms with provisions
For the merry wedding feast.
Where the beauteous brazen lamp
From the ceiling is suspended,
Aruvas and near relations
Came together from both houses,
Stood and settled the engagement
And the lucky day of wedding.
Whereupon the happy bridegroom

from fallen nature; but we are not at liberty to record those solitary outbursts of evil passions as an established system or even custom; Hindus might as well regard the disclosures of our divorce-courts as the normal state of European matrimony. Whilst thus vindicating the honor of the married life of the Coorgs, I would not flatter their pride; but rather induce them to render and to maintain their family-hearths pure and honorable withal and to infuse also a better spirit into their public feasts, those popular schools of morality, from which all foul and indecent ribaldry should be banished for ever.

Polygamy is not prohibited amongst the Coorgs, but it seldom occurs and chiefly in cases, where the first marriage is not blessed with male issue. It also happens, that a young widow is taken to wife by another member of the same house, but this is a voluntary engagement on either part, and the woman loses all claim to her first husband's property, being now the wife of another.

The odd expression "*Sirkar wives*" refers to a tyrannical practice of the Rajahs, who, when severely punishing a Coorg house, exterminated all the men and reduced the women to a state of slavery, making them to work on the Sirkar farms or Panyas. Any low caste fellow, who applied for a wife to the Rajah, might then obtain one of these poor creatures, and such marriages may account for the comparatively fair and handsome appearance of many a low caste native of Coorg.

Divorce on account of unfaithfulness is a recognised institution and solemnly carried out by the Aruvas of the unhappy couple and by the Takkas of the village. The children remain in the father's house, the mother returns with all her belongings to the house of her parents. Should a reconciliation take place, the husband of a restored wife is looked down upon with contempt. No refutation of the alleged "communism of women" could be stronger than these facts.

d. Childbirth.

The birth of a child renders not only the mother of the new born babe, but the whole house unclean and every one who may come in contact with them. This ceremonial uncleanness (Sútaka) lasts for 7 days, be the babe male or female. The mother is confined for 2 months to the house and not expected to engage in any work, but to recover her strength and to devote herself entirely to her child. This singular custom no doubt greatly contributes to the general good health and vigour of the Coorg women. Daughters are not much valued. They must be brought up and yet are destined to be entirely alienated from the house by their marriage. Boys are the stay of families. As soon as a Coorg boy is born, a little bow of a castor-oil-plant stick with an arrow, made of a leafstalk of the same plant, is put into his little hands, and a gun fired at the same time in the yard. He is thus, at taking his first breath, introduced into the world as a future huntsman and warrior. This ceremony, however, has almost lost its meaning and ceases to be generally observed. On the 12th day after birth, the child is laid into the cradle by the mother or grandmother, who on this occasion gives the name, which in many instances is both well-sounding and significant: thus for boys—Belliappa (silver-father), Ponnappa (gold-father), Mandanna (the brother of the village-green); for girls—Púvakka (flower-sister), Muttakka (pearl-sister), Chinnawa (gold-mother).

The cradle, woven of slit bamboos and cane, and fitted to be hung up for swinging, requires but a little trimming to render it as tidy as any fashionable berceaunette; at all events the little Kodagu smiles and sleeps in it as happy as a prince; and as his mother bends over her darling with overflowing love and happiness and hums the Coorg lullaby:—

"Júwa, júwa, baby dear!
"When the baby's mother comes,
"She will give her darling milk.

"Júwa, júwa, baby dear!
"When the baby's father comes,
"He will bring you cocoanut,

"Júwa, júwa, baby dear!
"When the baby's brother comes,
"He will bring a little bird.

"Júwa, júwa, baby dear!
"When the baby's sister comes,
"She will bring a dish of rice."

Are we not reminded of our own familiar nursery-rhyme:—

"Baby, baby bunting, Father's gone a hunting,
"He's gone to get a rabbit's skin, to wrap my little baby in."

e. Death and funeral ceremonies.

A case of death defiles the house for seven days. The corpse is either burnt or buried. The bodies of the young, who die under 16 years of age and those of women are buried; those of other persons, especially of old people are burnt.

On the death of a member of a Coorg family, messengers are despatched to every house of the village-community. As on a wedding, each house must send at least one male and one female member to do service on the occasion. The Aruva of the family has again the direction of the ceremonies. Under his superintendence the corpse is washed and dressed by the men, who have followed the funeral summons, if the deceased is a man, but if a woman, by the women. It is remarkable, that the Coorgs see no defilement in the handling of a corpse by the funeral party. It is enough for them, to bathe and to change clothes on their return home. The preparations ended, the body is carried into the middle apartment (nadumane) of the house and laid upon a funeral bed, near to which a lighted lamp is placed. Instead of oil, those who can afford it, burn on this occasion clarified cow's butter in half a cocoanut placed on a handful of rice in a copper-dish. The whole company gathers round him and breaks out into loud wailing, beating the breast, tearing the hair, much in the usual Hindu style. Guns are also fired in honor of the dead. Towards evening the corpse is brought into the yard, a little water is poured into its mouth by the relatives, and a piece of money deposited in a copper-dish, containing a little cocoamilk, saffron, rice and well-water. Now the body is carried to the burial or burning ground. Each funeral guest approaches, dips his finger into the copper dish, moistens the lips of the corpse with a drop or two, and lays a piece of money into the plate. This collection goes to defray the expenses of the funeral. After all present have thus taken their last leave of the departed, the body is deprived of the ornaments, and laid in the grave or upon the pile, the contents of the funeral-lamp-dish are thrown upon it, and now the covering of the grave, or the burning of the pile, concludes the ceremony. Before this last scene, however, some relatives must be set apart for funeral observances until the Dhiti, the great ceremonial day, which is sometimes celebrated on the 28th day after the death of a person, i. e. at the end of the lunar month in which the decease has occurred, sometimes lator, as late as six months, when peculiar honor is intended to be done to the departed. In the interval the relatives, who offer themselves for this service, have to perform a lesser course of fasting. They forego the early and the second meal, at six and nine o'clock. At noon they bathe, prepare their own food, eat part of it themselves (it consists of rice and a little pickled vegetables), and give the rest to the crows, which consume it for the dead. When the Dhiti, the great day of the conclusion of funeral rites, arrives, the whole village community is again invited to a feast in honor of the departed and for the quiet of his soul, and thus the last end of a Coorg's earthly course has come.

The Coorg funeral song is most pathetic and touches a kindred chord in every sorrowing heart:—

Funeral Song.

Woe! my father, thou art gone!
Woe is me! For ever gone!
Gone with all thy soul of virtue!
Oh! how can I live my father!
Woe! thy days are now concluded,
And the share, assigned to thee
By the Lord, is now consumed
And no further portion granted.
Oh! thy wish was not to die,
But to stay among the living.
Surely, man came to this world
But to die; not one of us
Is exempted from this doom.
Onward! onward roll the years;
Oh! how soon were thine concluded!
Like the eagle in the sky
Thou wast roaming here on earth.
Woe! the string of choicest pearls
Round the neck of our children
Is for ever burst and scattered!
Woe! the clear and brilliant mirror,
Fallen out of our hand,
Fallen to the ground, and broken!
Woe! the wrath of God Almighty,
Floods of fiery indignation,
Beating on the lofty mountains,
Swept their summit to the ground!
Like the enemies at night,
Breaking into peaceful houses,

Slaying all the valiant men,
Even thus has God Almighty
Suddenly cut off thy days.
Like the top of Tumbemale
In the sultry days of summer,
When the sun is hot and burning,
And the grass is set on fire,
Thus, O father, was this house
Desolated by thy death!
As the raging storms in June
Break the fruitful plantain trees
In the garden round our house,
Thus wast thou cut off, O father!
When the floods destroy the shed,
Where the stores of wood were sheltered,
All the house is in distress.
When the meeting hall is ruined,
All the villagers lament.
If the temple is destroyed,
All the land is full of sorrow.
Thus is our house distressed
By thy sudden death, O father!
As they quench the shining flame
Of the beauteous golden lamp,
Thus has God destroyed thy life!
As the stately Banyan tree
In the lofty mountain forest,
Which the ax has never touched,
Is uprooted by the whirlwind;
Like the bright and shining leaf
Of the royal Sampigé,
Broken from the stem and withered;
Thus wast thou cut off, O father!
In the days of life thy hand
Had supported our house,
Thou hast planted our fields,
Thou hast laid the corner-stone,
And completed our mansion
To the roof, with costly timber.

Thou hast built the solid gate,
And the courts around the house.
Oh! my father; yesterday
Fallen on the bed of sickness,
And to-day before the feet
Of the Lord of earth and heaven,
And tomorrow, like the sun
Setting in the cloudy sky,
Thou shalt sink into the grave.
Woe! my father, thou art gone!
Woe! my father, gone for ever!

4. POPULAR FESTIVALS OF THE COORGS.

The festivals of the Coorgs are not numerous. A weekly day of rest is recognised as little by the Coorgs as by other Hindus.

The two great annual festivals take place in quick succession towards the end of the year. The *Kávéri-feast* in Tulámása i. e. the time of the sun's entering into the sign of Libra in October, and the *Huttari* or Harvest-feast in November or December.

Before the monsoon in April and may the *Bhagavati-festival* is observed all over Coorg and in August, generally at the first break of the monsoon, the *Keilmurta* or festival of arms, is celebrated by the youths and men of Coorg.

a. The Kávéri-feast.

About the middle of October all Coorg prepares for the grand festival of Kávéri. The sun has gained the ascendency over the monsoon clouds. A few passing showers only may still be expected. The rice valleys are clothed with rich paddy approaching maturity; the forests and grass hills resplendent with the freshness and beauty of spring. Every Coorg house sends one or two representatives to Tala-Kávéri. Also pilgrims from Malayálam, Tulu and Mysore repair to the sacred place by thousands. Distinguished amongst these are the Brahmini-widows—those sad figures, clothed with reddish brown garments, one end of which covers the shorn head. A bundle under one arm they trudge along, supported by a stick; perhaps they come by their own impulse, perhaps in the name and for the benefit of some sick relation. The nearer the pilgrims approach the end of their journey, the more frequent and the more numerous are the festive caravans of men, women and children in holiday-costume, who now rest in picturesque groups on the shady banks of streams, now proceed in gay defiles over the grassy hills. With the last ascent of a small elevation near the foot of the Tala-Kávéri-hill the view of the upper basin of the Kávéri valley, which is rather wide and flanked by steep hills, suddenly bursts upon us. The Bhágamandala temple with its copper roof is conspicuous in the middle of the valley and close to the Kávéri. A few rows of houses near it are changed into a busy mart. Thousands of people move to and fro, and the humming noise of the multitude sounds like the distant surf of the ocean. Hundreds are engaged in bathing in the sacred stream before they enter the temple, which forms a large square with an open centre like a Coorg house. Along the road pedlars are squatted behind their paltry wares which are spread under a flimsy awning. Mendicant Sanyásis with hollow sounding conch and brass gong in hand push, blowing and ringing, through the crowd. Hourly the multitude increases; new arrivals descend from all the neighbouring mountain pathways into the valley. Hundreds of people have already proceeded to reach the Kávéri source, in order to build for themselves and their expected friends sheltering booths against the cold damp night air. A pathway leads over paddy-fields through steep jungle and over rocky mountain ridges to the sacred spot. As they ascend, they shout "Náráyana, Oh!

Náráyana" and the echo is taken up by succeeding caravans. Near the summit there is an overhanging rock, called Bíma-kallu, which forms a sheltering abode for some fakirs during the festive season. The source of the river is enclosed by a stone basin, over which a small shrine of granite slabs is built. From this reservoir the pure water percolates into a tank of about 30 feet square, which by an outlet keeps the water to a level of 2¼ feet. On two sides there are rough stone terraces scooped out of the hill side and above the third terrace on a dip of the hill there is a small square temple dedicated to Ganapati with a few huts close by for the abode of the residing Brahmin-pújáris.

At the moment, fixed by the Astrologer, of the sun's entering into the sign of Libra, whether by day or by night, the pilgrim, who is anxious to experience the full power of the sin cleansing bath, must descend into the holy tank. With the approach of the hour an ever increasing multitude surrounds the tank, impatiently waiting for the propitious moment. Now the priest gives the sign and the living throng, old and young, men and women rush in wild confusion into the water, duck three times and drink as often of the water, and, on emerging, offer a small gift to the priests, who sit near the shrine, receive the money and pour some pure water over the devotee's head. Before leaving, most of the pilgrims fill a hollow reed (Wóte) with water from the sacred spring and carry it home for the benefit of their relatives and for purifying their wells. The effectual bathing season lasts for a whole month but with decreasing virtue. From 8 to 15,000 pilgrims may annually visit Tala-Kávéri, but the interest in the place seems to be on the decrease. The presiding Brahmins have secured some jungle for coffee cultivation in the neighbourhood of the temple, and the Coorgs complain, that the priests take greater care of their coffee gardens than of their religious duties, and only lately some valuable portions of the Tala-Kávéri shrine were stolen!

The Kávéri-day is celebrated also in the Coorg houses by those who remain at home, and is considered as a high holiday.

Before sunrise, the mistress of the house early leaves her bed, goes to the cooking-room, takes a brass-dish, throws into it a handful of rice, and having spread it over the whole plate, puts a common lamp, which has been in daily use, into the centre. The burning lamp is surrounded with flowers gathered from a garden or the jungle. To these a fresh, young cucumber is added. Then a red handkerchief is placed behind the lamp. Upon the handkerchief one jewel of gold or silver is laid. The mistress perhaps takes the necklace from her own person on the occasion, which is considered the luckiest choice. Then a good mat is spread on the ground, and a tripod, which serves the Coorgs for a dinner-table, placed upon the mat. Upon the tripod the woman sets the brass-plate with the rice, lamp, cloth and jewel. This done, she proceeds to bake little cakes from a dough of rice-flour and plantains, well kneaded together on the preceding night, upon a stone-mould well heated. Three of these little cakes are added to the contents of the plate. Then she calls the inmates of the house. They all rise instantly, go straight into the kitchen, and fold their hands before the tripod, as in adoration. One of the men takes three or five of the fresh cakes and carries them down to the rice-fields. There he puts the cakes upon one of the bamboo sticks, which have been placed in every field on the preceding day, crowned with a bundle of Keibala creepers. The field next to the house is chosen for this offering. When the cakes are duly laid upon the top of the creeper-crowned pole, the man gives three great shouts and returns to the house. It is now about five o'clock. (The cakes are afterwards gathered by the Holeyas, who live in the neighbourhood.) On the return of the man from the field, the whole family sit down in the kitchen and eat the cakes prepared by the mistress and the other females after their morning entrance into the cooking and dining-room. When the cakes are consumed, the ceremony of the Kávéri-day is over. In houses, where some one knows how to read, he takes the Góvina-pada book and recites *the Song of the Cow*, the rest of the family listening. The day is kept as a holiday; nobody is expected to work. But there is no further ceremony.

The substance of the lay of the cow is as follows:—One great herd of cattle was grazing in the forest, when a royal tiger appeared and in a few moments by three or four leaps threw himself into the midst of the poor, peaceful animals. The whole herd, affrighted, ran off in wild despair in all directions. One cow only stood still, and was seized by the savage beast. The cow, however, made bold to speak to her destroyer, and said: "You will kill and devour me. Do it. But give me a few moments' leave to go after my poor calf, to let it drink for the last time, and to commit it to the care of kind friends, before I die." The tiger, astonished and moved by the speech of his victim, causes the cow to swear, that, after performing her last duty, she will return and deliver herself to her hungry master. She swears and goes to seek her calf. Having found it, she gives it to drink, and then commits it to the care of her friends, entreating them to allow it to share their milk with their own calves, not to kick, when it comes from behind to drink, nor to turn their horns against it, when it comes in front. Having sworn, she would rather die, than break her word, she returns to the tiger, and begs his pardon for having detained him so long and increased his hunger. But the tiger in the presence of such truth and goodness, is seized with remorse. His heinous sins rise to his mind in dreadful array. The slayer of a thousand cows sinks under the burden of his wickedness.

"If I killed this pattern of righteousness, my sins could never be forgiven," he says to himself. He declares to the cow, that she may return in safety to her calf and her herd, takes a desperate leap high into the air, and falls down dead before the good cow. This is the Coorg lay of the cow, consisting of one hundred and odd verses.

b. The Huttari-feast.

The Huttari-feast is held in honor of the annual rice-harvest. The name is derived from the Malayálam Pudi-ari, new rice, and by the rules of Coorg grammar transformed into Huttari. The festival occurs in the month of Scorpio which succeeds Libra. The day of the Coorg-festival depends upon the day fixed by the Malayálam Astrologers for the celebration of the New-rice-festival in the month of Leo. The Malayálam festival takes place two months before that of Coorg, because the rice on the coast ripens two months earlier. If the Malayálam festival of the First-fruits fall upon the first day of the Simha-mása, that of Coorg is held on the first day of Vrishchika-mása; if the Malayálam festival be on the second day of that month, the Coorg holidays commence on the second day of this month, and so on. (Simha-mása corresponds to our September—October, Vrishchika-mása to our November—December.)

The Huttari is the great national festival of the Coorgs and of the Holeyas. It is a heathenish Christmas season, a sort of Saturnalia. The real holidays are only seven in number, but both Coorgs and Holeyas, who stand in an ancient and intimate relation to each other, generally add two or three more days of feasting and merry-making to the great week. On this occasion, as well as on the great Kávéri-day, Brahmins are in no way wanted. Nor could they well officiate in a Coorg kitchen on the Kávéri-day, or preside over the pork-and-brandy-feasts in the merry days of Huttari.

And it appears, that the people can do very well without them.

Six days before the chief festival of tasting the new rice, all the males from six to sixty years, assemble on one of the Mandus of the Gráma, after sunset. Mandu is the name of the open public place in which business is transacted or festive games carried on. Grámas have generally three Mandus, one called the Puncháyati-mandu for business; a second, Dévara-mandu, on which dances are performed in the name of Bhagavati during the after-Huttari-days; a third, Uru-mandu (i. e. the Mandu of the village) on which the Huttari performances take place.

The time of these national games and dances is from sunset till after ten o'clock. The whole male population of the Gráma, except little boys and old men, past sixty, has religiously to attend. The assembly gathers gradually between six and seven o'clock. When the assembly is full, a space is marked out for the performances of the party. At a little distance a band of musicians, two Holeya horn-blowers and two Méda-drummers, sit near a fire, which they have kindled for warming themselves and their instruments. The horns are large and of brass. The drums are a Pare (large drum) and a Kudike-pare (pot-drum of a smaller size).

Three Coorg-men step into the centre of the open space and call aloud three names: Ayappa! Mahádéva! Bhagavati! The men stand in a triangle, their faces towards the centre, their backs towards the company. Ayappa is the Coorg forest-god; Mahádéva, the Shiva of the Hindus, and Bhagavati, his wife.

The Chandukutti (ball-and-peg-play) now follows. The whole assembly takes part in it, the moon shedding a bright silver-light on the scene. A peg is driven into the centre of the chosen ground. A piece of rope is fastened to it by a loose loop. The people who make this preparation, seize some one, who must hold this rope. A piece of wood, generally of a creeper called Odi, is cut into seven parts, which are called Chandu, i. e. balls. The man holding the rope puts six of these balls in a circle round the peg at a distance of the rope's length, the seventh is deposited close by the peg. The whole company now endeavours to pick off the balls without being touched by their guardian. The player in the centre, always keeping the rope's end in one hand, turns round and round, and tries to touch some one of the aggressors. If he succeed, the person touched must take his place and the play recommences. When six balls are abstracted, the seventh must be moved to the distance of one foot from the peg. When this also is lost, the man has to run through the whole crowd and escape, without being caught, to the Musicians' place. If he reach this asylum in safety, the play is won and finished. If he be caught on his way, he is brought before the Nettle-man, an officer of the play-court, who has been waiting all the time, a long Angare-stick—a large fierce nettle—in his hand, for the victim. His hands and feet are well touched and the play ends. Now the assembly perform different kinds of plays and dances, representing the wars which in ancient times appear to have been waged between people of different districts. A man is wounded; a physician is called, who prescribes for him. Another wounded man dies, and Holeyas are called to invite his friends to the funeral. A scene of demoniacal possession is acted The funeral is performed. Now stories are told of incredibilities. "I saw the other day a little hare attacking a tiger and breaking its neck." Reply: "Did you? I saw a buffaloe flying over the mountains," etc. Three men invoke again Ayappa, Mahádéva and Bhagavati. Dances follow, accompanied by the beating of sticks keeping time with the music of the band outside. Feats of gymnastic strength and agility follow, and another invocation of the three deities concludes the performance. The Huttari takes place on the full moon. Early in the morning before dawn, a quantity of Ashvatha (ficus religiosa), Kumbali and Keku (wild trees) leaves, some hundred of each for great houses, together with a piece of a creeper, called Inyoli, and some fibrous bark called Achchi, are collected and deposited in a shady place for the use of the evening. During the day, the house is cleansed, brass vessels are scoured, and every thing wears the appearance of a great holiday. Beggars come and are dismissed with presents. The Méda brings the Huttari basket, the potter the little Huttari pot, the blacksmith a new sickle, the carpenter a new spoon, the Holeya a new mat. Each carries off his Huttari portion of rice and plantains. The astrologer follows, to communicate the exact time of the full moon, and claims his share of the Huttari bounty. The cattle are washed and scrubbed, for once; the menial servants have an extra allowance of rice; breakfast and dinner are served to the family. At sunset the whole house prepares for a hot bath. The precedence is given to the person whom the astrologer has chosen in the morning for the ceremony of cutting the first sheaves. On his return from bathing, he repairs to the threshing floor, spreads the Huttari mat, and, while the rest are engaged in their ablutions, cuts the Inyoli creeper into small pieces, rolls each piece into an Ashvatha, a Kumbali and a Keku leaf, in the fashion of a native cherroot, and ties up the little bundle with a bit of Achchi fibre. All the bundles are placed in the Huttari basket. Now the women take a large dish, strew it with rice, and place a lighted lamp in it. This done, the whole household march towards the fields; the dish with the lamp is carried in front; the sheaf-cutter follows with basket and sickle in one hand, and a bamboo bottle of fresh milk in the other. Arrived at the chosen spot, the young man binds one of the leaf scrolls from his basket to a bush of rice, and pours milk into it. He cuts an armful of rice in the neighbourhood and distributes two or three stalks to every one present. Some stalks are put into the milk-vessel. No one must touch the sheaf-cutter. All return to the threshing floor shouting as they walk on: "Poly, poly, Déva!" (increase, O God!) A bundle of leaves is adorned with a stalk of rice, and fastened to the post in the centre of the threshing floor. The company proceeds to the door of the house, where the mistress meets them, washes the feet of the sheaf-cutter, and presents to him, and after him to all the rest, a brass-vessel, filled with milk, honey and sugar, from which each takes a draught. They move into the kitchen. The Huttari mat is spread, the brass dish, the rice sheaf, and the basket with leaf scrolls, each with a stalk of rice, are placed on it. The young man distributes the bundles to the members of the family, who disperse to bind them to every thing in house and garden, doors, stools, roof, trees, etc. In the mean time he sits down to knead the Huttari dough of rice meal, plantains, milk and honey, seven new rice corns, seven pieces of cocoanut, seven small pebbles, seven pieces of dry ginger, seven cardamom seeds, and seven corns of sesamum are added. Every one receives a little of this dough upon an Ashvatha leaf, and eats it. The ceremony is over, and the sheaf-cutter mixes with the company. Supper follows, consisting of sugared rice and sweet potatoes, into which a handful of new rice is thrown, and of a substantial common repast of rice and curry. The Huttari chants follow now at every house during the night.

But the Coorgs have not yet done altogether, with their pleasant festival. Four after-Huttari-days are added to the holy week. On the eighth day the Urukólu, the village-stick-dance, collects the whole community. The women of two or three houses repair together to the Urumandu, a pair leading and a second pair following, all four beating cymbals and chanting ancient songs or impromptu verses. When they have arrived at the place of meeting, they sit down in groups with the children, and look at the dances performed by the men, who go through the evolutions of Coorg saltation, beating small rattans, of which they carry one in each hand, while they move to the time of a music, which proceeds from a group of Holeyas, stationed between the assembly of the Coorgs and that of their own people, who enjoy themselves, in the same fashion as their masters, at a little distance.

Theatrical performances are added. Brahmans, Moplas, Voddas (tank diggers from Orissa), Gadikas (snake dancers), Jógis (represented by little boys), play through the village.

After dinner, on the ninth day, the Nádukólu begins. This is an assembly of the whole district. Every thing is done as at the Urukólu, only on a larger scale. At these assemblies, while the monotonous music plays and the large circle of dancers moves in the measured stick-dance, a couple of men from different grámas and armed with a small shield and a long rattan, step from opposite sides into the ring with a shout of defiance and keeping time with the music, they approach and evade each other, swinging their rattans and dealing blows, aimed at the legs and with their shield warding them off, but often the players get so excited, that their single stick sham combat ends in a mutual severe flogging, which has to be stopped by the spectators. At five the parties from the different villages separate and go home.

In the afternoon of the tenth day, the Dévarakólu (stick-dance in honor of Bhagavati) takes place in every village. The entertainment is the same as on the two preceding days. Dinners are held at different houses of appointment, and terminate on the 11th day with a large public dinner that is given, on some open plain in the forest when the musicians, bards, drummers, Holeyas and Médas unite their exertions to give eclat to the festivity.

c. The Bhagavati-feast.

Of the two lesser annual festivals one, the Bhagavati-feast, has been introduced by Tulu Brahmans, or, if it was originally a Coorg observance, has been thoroughly brahmanized.

It takes place during the two months preceding the monsoon. Different localities differ in the time of its celebration. Two or three villages have one Bhagavati temple in common, and support it jointly. These temples are in charge of Brahmans entirely. Tulu Brahmans hold the livings; with them some Padárthis, a lower class of Brahmans, who wear no holy string, are associated as musicians to Bhagavati. The whole establishment is under the management of some Tantri-Brahmans in the Tulu country, who come every eighth or tenth year, to consecrate idols and to collect money. On these occasions large sums are offered by the superstitious. The Coorgs have an extraordinary dread of the power of these men. They say, that if one of the Tantri-Brahmans be offended and curse a man, he will lose his sight or hearing or even his life. It is enough, they believe, for one of these masters of the black art, to say to a man: "do you not see?" or "do you not hear?" and the poor fellow is doomed to blindness or deafness, or even death. Strange! It would appear, that the common worship of the great gods of the country was less degrading to the mind, and engendered a more cheerful kind of superstition, than this wild sort of idolatry, which has enslaved the poor Coorgs. The Tantries, on one of their visits, will gather some two or three hundred rupees from the money-loving Coorgs. Sometimes an idol of Bhagavati has lost its power, when they re-enliven it. Or the officiating Brahman, who has played the possessed on festival days, has died. The Tantri has to appoint his successor. These services are not performed gratuitously; the presiding Tantri receives every year one half of the profits of the establishment, through a curate whom he leaves in charge.

Some Coorg also is chosen as a subject for possession by Bhagavati. He likewise, and his successors, must be instituted by the ruling Tantri. They are selected from a small number of candidates presented by the community connected with the temple. The Tantri takes one of the men, pronounces some mantra and puts holy ashes upon his face, when immediately the individual commences to shake and to dance and to speak as one possessed.

Every house of the villages, connected with a temple, must pay an assessment in rice every year to the Brahmans employed, and money must be offered by every family, from 3 as. to one rupee, on the last day of the annual festival.

The Bhagavati-feast lasts nine days. During the first six days, every morning and evening, the idol is carried three times round the temple in procession, while the Tantri-curate, who is the chief authority in the place, performs púja, strewing rice and minced leaves of Calyptanthes Caryophyllifolia, mixed together, on the stones placed towards the eight regions of the heavens, and mumbling his mantras. One of the Tulu Brahmans carries the idol on his head; he is accompanied by the Pújári and the other officers of the shrine, followed by the band of Padárthis, playing the drum, cymbal and gong, and preceded by the Coorg-man performing a frantic dance in the ecstasy of demoniac possession. Many people come on these occasions to put questions to Bhagavati in behalf of sick persons, or for the discovery of thieves, etc. which are duly answered by the Coorg spokesman of the goddess.

On the evening of the sixth day things take a more excited aspect. Now the Brahman idol-carrier also is seized with the strange inspiration. He dances and trembles, and answers questions by making signs only. On the same afternoon a crowd of Holeyas, who have finished the Pannangalamma-feast (a corresponding Holeya festival) come to the open space before the temple, many of them possessed by devils of their own, which belong to the host of Pannangalamma, all of them jumping and dancing and beating their drums and gongs in the most approved fashion. Every one of them, man, woman and child, carries a long dry bamboo-stick. These bamboos are piled up in front of the temple, like soldiers' muskets, and set fire to at night, when the Holeyas dance round the flames until the pile breaks and falls to the ground. (If the pile fall towards the east, it is considered a lucky omen.) While these things take place outside, the temple-yard resounds with the voices of Coorgs, singing hymns in honor of Bhagavati, and the wild notes of many drums, through which the shrill words of the demoniac Coorg now and then pierce—a dismal scene!

On the seventh day, after the morning circumambulation of the temple, votive offerings are brought by the villagers of the parish. In each village the people collect at the house of some one, who has vowed a bullock-load of rice or cocoa-nuts, and take their breakfast. After breakfast, the whole company proceeds with the offering to the temple, singing and making music. The gift having been presented to the priest, the party returns to the village, to carry another contribution to the temple in the same manner. Thus the fore-noon is spent. Then the young men dance for some hours. Music heightens the joy of the entertainments, and all the rest of the community, women, girls, children and old men, sit round the temple-yard—admiring spectators. At four o'clock the idol is taken out and carried round the shrine, the whole assembly joining in the procession. The Brahman-carrier of Bhagavati is possessed by the goddess. He stretches out his hand during the strange dance, which he performs with the idol upon his head. Whoever can, puts some money into his open hand. He, conscious enough in this respect, casts every piece given to him into a copper vessel, held by the Tantri. With the setting sun the business of the day is concluded.

The morning of the eighth day is devoted to the delivery of votive presents, as on the preceding day. At ten o'clock dances are performed by the young men, as on the seventh day. This continues till two o'clock, when all the good shots assemble for shooting at a mark. A cocoanut is hung up in some tree between two plantain-bunch-tops as a mark. He who hits the nut, is rewarded with a present of three annas and the honor of the name of a good marksman. Then one of the Takkas, or the Coorg-dancer before Bhagavati, distributes a number of cocoanuts (of which there is an abundance, as every family must bring one or two) to the young men. One seizes a nut between his hands, others try to take it out of his grasp. In a few moments the whole ground is filled with parties struggling for cocoanuts. He who succeeds in forcing the nut out of the hands of the original possessor, carries it away as his prize. At three o'clock the idol-procession takes place again, after which all the men go with the idol to the river or the tank, to bathe the goddess and themselves.

Ninth day. From each house one person appears at the temple, bearing the yearly money-contribution, which is delivered to the Takkas. The collection being made, the salaries of the temple-officers and servants of the temple are paid. Then the Brahmans give a good, undefiled dinner of pure vegetable dishes, to their Coorg supporters, first, of course, eating themselves, and leaving the rest to their friends. This temple dinner is the last act in the Bhagavati festival.

d. The Keilmúrta festival.

The Keilmúrta festival is a very different affair, altogether a Coorg business. Early in the month of Leo (July—August) the Takka of the gráma calls some respectable men to accompany him to the house of the astrologer. They enquire of the wise man, what will be the most propitious day for the celebration of the Keilmúrta. By the sage's answer the day of joy for the village-youth is fixed. The hard labours of ploughing, sowing and rice-transplanting are over, there is a lull in the monsoon, and now and then a most lovely day spreads its bright light and sunny warmth over the hills and valleys, forests and fields of Coorg. The people have long been at labour in their fields and houses: a holiday is now most welcome. On the morning of the joyous day, the whole armoury of the house is collected in the verandah, gun and spear, bow and arrow, sword and knife. Some of the young men sit down to burnish the familiar weapons. When this is done, they are carried to some room or to the centre-place, the Nadumane, and there placed in a corner. They wait now for the muhúrta, the propitious time, assigned by the astrologer. At the right moment incense is burned before the weapons, sandalwood-paste is dotted upon them in profusion, and a show-offering of rice and other food (nevédya) is made to them, as to idols. As soon as this ceremony is over, a mat is placed before the weapons, and the whole house sits down to dinner. After the meal, the men take their arms and proceed to the Urumandu (village-green) to spend the afternoon in shooting at a mark, and in athletic exercises. When the cocoanut has been hit, some of the company jump over a rope extended four or five feet from the ground. After this exercise, plantain-trees are fixed upon the ground, standing three deep. Now the strength of arms and the goodness of knives are tried. He who succeeds in cutting through three plantain-trees at one stroke, carries away the palm. Then round, heavy stones, placed on the Mandu for the purpose, are lifted and thrown, or put as in Scotland, over the head by such as are strong enough. The evening has now set in, and the company disperses. On the following morning the youths assemble for a hunt in the forest, belonging to the village. Whatever game is brought down, is divided by the huntsmen in the following manner: the man who has killed the animal, receives a hind-quarter and the head, the rest belongs to the company. This day is followed by a great hunt of the whole Nádu, a repetition of the village-hunt, on a larger scale. The Keilmúrta, to the taste of young Coorg, is the most glorious of all the festivals.

5. RELIGIOUS OBSERVANCES AND POPULAR SUPERSTITION.

The previous description of familiar and popular Coorg life would be incomplete without an account of other *religious observances*, if such a name may be given to the lowest degree of superstitions, which take the place of the worship of God among this rude race.

a. The sanctuaries of a Coorg community.

Instead of a general description, a short sketch of the village "Arméri" in Beppunád, the centre of Coorg life, may serve as a specimen.

Arméri numbers only 25 Coorg houses, but is richly provided with idol shrines. First a Bhagavati temple in charge of Brahmans. In connection with this kind of worship there is a Mahádéva temple, and two Lingas in the jungle, which receive regular púja. Also two sanctuaries of Ayappa (the Shani, Saturn Pán? of Hindu mythology) have Brahmans for priests. Ayappa (Lord) is quite naturalized among the Coorgs. He is the great forest-god, a mighty hunter, to whom models in clay of dogs, horses and tigers are offered in abundance. In these observances the whole community joins under the superintendence of Brahmans. There are besides six places in which Chámundi or Raktéshvari (names for Párvati, Shiva's wife) is worshipped once a year, when pigs are sacrificed.— This is, of course, an abomination to the Brahmans.

b. Ancestral and Demon worship.

The principal place in Coorg-idolatry is held by the worship of the dead. Every family offers a sacrifice to its departed ancestors once a year, during the two months preceding the monsoon. A fowl, generally a cock, is killed upon a stone devoted to the Káranas, somewhere in the jungle-land belonging to the family estate. (Kárana is the name given to the heads of families whether living or dead.) Seven of the Arméri houses, however, have little temples where *Kóla* or *Bárani* is annually performed. Kóla is the name of a sacrifice connected with demoniacal dancing, Bárani, of a sacrifice to the dead without the dances. These temples consecrated to the worship of the dead are called *Keimada.* Mada is the Coorg word for Matha, a religious building. The meaning of the word "kei" may possibly stand for Kárana or simply denote: near, at hand, private. The Pújáris (officiating priests) employed in these ceremonies are Malayálas long since naturalized in Coorg, Panika, Maleya, Banna men, subordinate to the Kanyas, the hereditary Malayálam astrologers of Coorg. At the Kólas they beat drums and sing verses in commemoration of the ancestors. Those who are to be possessed by the spirits, wear masks and buckle on swords. As they sing of the deceased father, or grandfather, or other ancestor, his spirit seizes them and they speak as his mouthpieces. To each spirit a sacrifice is offered, a cock and a bottle of spirits, which his representative drinks, thus fortifying himself for future exertion during the night. The ceremony begins after sunset, in the presence of the whole village-community, and is continued until morning. About seven or eight o'clock in the morning pigs are sacrificed. The head of one of the pigs belongs to the performers, the rest is cooked in the house, to which the Keimada is attached, and is consumed by the whole community with a plentiful addition of liquor. At noon the ceremonies are completed. When Bárani only is performed, one of the strange priests does the whole work, but in the Kólas several are engaged. A peculiar kind of illumination is essential to both Kóla and Bárani. Some plantain trees are split into thin strips. These are placed on the ground in three or four layers, crossing at right angles, and forming a kind of network. Twenty-four or forty-eight or ninety-six such strips of split plantain-stems are used. Where they cross one another, spikes of a reed, called Wotté, are driven through them into the ground. At the upper end of these spikes, which are two or three feet high, pieces of cloth are fastened, twisted into wicks and well moistened with oil. When the whole net is thus arranged, two layers of strips are raised, one to near the top of the spikes, the other a foot lower. Between the crossings, plantain-leaf-pieces are placed, upon which quantities of rice, plain and fried, of arecanut, jaggory, etc. are put. When the ceremony begins, a few of the oiled wicks are lighted. At the pig-sacrifice all are kindled, and the whole square blazes up like a table of fire, without however consuming the offerings placed on the leaves, which are the perquisite of the performers.

Besides, every family has some spot on the estate, in a retired part of the jungle-land, where a sacrifice of a fowl is offered every year to the departed by the living members of the house. No strangers are permitted to attend on these occasions. A stone placed on a rough mound serves as altar.

On the day of *Sivarátri* a religious ceremony takes place in Mercara at the Rajahs' tombs, that of Dodda-Virájender being transformed into a temple, where the spirit of the hero is worshipped with the honors due to the saint or rather a god, for Virájender has been deified by the Lingaites. On the occasion a large concourse of people, chiefly Sivácháries, collect round the tombs, to pay their respects; or, at any rate, to participate in the liberal charity, dispensed at the time from the Government Treasury.

The people of Coorg have also great faith in a certain *Kaliatanda Ponnappa* or simply *Kaliat-Achchappa*, the spirit of a Malayálam man, who came to Coorg, many generations ago, was naturalized, married a Coorg-woman, and established himself at Nálknád. He was a great magician, and long the dread of the Coorgs. At last he was shot near the Cutchéri of Nálknád taluq. Since his death his spirit has possessed men, who give themselves to the strange arts that he practised. A similar worship is still maintained in honor of Achanaik in Chickamundúru in Kiggatnád.

Higher even than Kaliat-Achchappa, in the estimation of all Coorg, stands a certain female devil, at Kutta, called *Kuttadamma*. Kutta lies at the borders of the Wynád. Kuttadamma has no temple. The sanctuary is under a tree in the forest. The Pújári is a young man, the only person left of the family, which has engaged in this worship. Large sums of money are annually sent thither by people from all parts of Coorg. Many vows are paid to Kuttadamma in behalf of sick people or of the dead. And whether a sick person recover or die, the sum vowed for his recovery must be paid; or woe to the living! Liberal presents are also given to the man in charge of Kuttadamma, to engage her services against enemies, who, they say, are distressed or destroyed altogether by the demon, in answer to the prayers of her priest.

Each Báne (parcel of grass or forest-ground) has a presiding divinity, to which an annual sacrifice of pork and cakes is offered. If this sacrifice be not made, or not properly performed, the *Kádévaru* (the tending god, i. e. the god watching over the cattle) will withdraw his favour, and sickness and death among the cattle will ensue.

Besides the many groves set apart in each Nád for some object of worship, but chiefly for *Ayappa-dévaru*, there are some extensive forests, called *Dévara-kádu*, which are untrodden. by human foot and superstitiously reserved for the abodes or hunting grounds of deified heroic ancestors. These forests are: the *Iggudappa-dévara-kádu* in Pádinalknád, the *Chóma-male* in Katiednád and the *Iruli-báne* in Kuyingherinád.

Another annual sacrifice every house has to offer to a peculiar divinity called *Gulika*. This is an invisible constellation or star, belonging both to the order of planets and to that of the zodiacal stars (it is, as the people say, a son of Shani or Saturn). No mortal eye sees it. The astrologer only knows the Gulika and its power, especially over the sick. A stone is placed for the Gulika at the foot of some tree possessed of a milky juice. There the Coorg offers every year fowls, cocoanuts and a little brandy in a dish of plantain-leaves to his tutelary numem. In cases of frequent deaths in a family, a second Gulika, called *Mrityu-Gulika* (death-gulika) is worshipped.

Another object of solemn ceremonies are the *Nátas*, the spots on which cobra capellas have finished their course of terrestrial life. According to Coorg lore, the cobra capella lives a thousand years! When it has passed the meridian of its long life, its body begins to shrink and to brighten, till it shines like silver, and measures three feet or less at the age of six or seven hundred years. Still later, the reptile shines like gold, and is only one foot in length. At last it shrinks to the size of a finger. Then it will some day fly up high into the air, die and sink down upon the ground, where it disappears altogether. No man sees it, but, of course, the Kanya knows the important secret, which he will communicate for a consideration to the proprietor of the land. Should any human being, unawares, set foot upon the hallowed spot, incurable disease of the skin will break out upon his person, and the poor wretch will rot away by degrees. To prevent such disasters, the Náta place is marked by a little stone enclosure. During the month of Scorpio (November—December) a lamp is lighted every evening to the Náta, and cocoanuts are offered as oblations.

c. Astrology and Sorcery.

The ministers of Coorg superstition, the Kanyas, Panikas, Maleyas and Bannas make a handsome livelihood. The Kanyas find much work for the conjuring confraternity, dependent, in a great measure, upon their friendly patronage. The Kanya (astrologer) has complete mastery over the minds and, to a great extent, over the pockets of the credulous Coorgs. For a consideration in the shape of a purse of rupees, he writes the horoscope of the individuals who apply to him. Such is his cleverness, that he requires only to know the name of a person, in order to calculate the year, month, day and hour of his nativity. He is also the oracle of the Coorgs in cases of sorcery and witchcraft. It is believed by the Coorgs, that misfortunes, such as diseases of men or cattle, and deaths in the family or the herd, rarely come upon them in the natural order of things. The knowledge of an all-ruling Providence seems to have no place in their minds. Every severe affliction or great loss is ascribed to magic art or "an enemy hath done this." To find out the author of the mischief, and to induce or force him to keep the peace, is the only method that suggests itself to such people for obtaining deliverance from trouble. Application is made to some famous Kanya, who consults his books and caudies (little shells used for dice), and discovers the secret enemy's place, house, stature, age, etc. The man is called before a Pancháyat, and the case is discussed in the Parpatigára's Cutchéri. If things are not settled before this tribunal, the parties go to the Subadar, and frequently the quarrel is carried before the

Superintendent, who has to get out of the difficulty as best he may. By the Pancháyat's self-constituted authority the wizard, or the person who has employed sorcery against his enemy, must promise to abstain in future; and in many cases reparation of some kind or other is made. In the days of the Rajahs such crimes were often punished with death. The British Government cannot, of course, follow the precedent. By a matter of fact order (No. 32 of 1858) from the Honorable Court of Directors to the Government of India: "Such "an offence as sorcery ought not to be recognised by any "British tribunal. If a pretended sorcerer is accused of "really injurious practices against the person or property of "any one, he shall be tried for these practices and if found "guilty punished accordingly and not for sorcery. The pre-"tended exercise of supernatural powers should be in itself "an offence and should be punished as a form of Fraud."

d. Substitutes for human sacrifices and other peculiar rites.

As among other Dravidian mountain-tribes, so also in Coorg, tradition relates, that human sacrifices were offered in former times, to secure favour of their *Gráma-Dévatas: Máriamma*, *Durga* and *Bhadra-Káli*, the tutelary goddesses of the Sakti-line, who are supposed to protect the villages or náds from all evil influences. In Kirindádu and Koninchéri-gráma in Katiednád, once in three years, in December and June, a human sacrifice used to be brought to Bhadra-Káli and during the offering by the Pánikas the people exclaimed "Alamma!" (álu-amma i. e. a man oh mother!) Once a devotee shouted: "Alallamma, ádu!" i. e. "not a man, oh mother, a goat," and since that time a he-goat without blemish has been sacrificed. Similarly in Bellúr in Távaligherri-múrnád of Kiggatnád-taluq once a year by turns from each house a man was sacrificed by cutting off his head at the temple; but when the turn came to a certain house, the devoted victim made his escape into the jungle. The villagers, after an unsuccessful search, returned to the temple and said to the pújári: "Kalak-ádu" which has a double meaning viz. "Kalake," next year—"ádu," we will give, or "ádu", a goat: and thenceforth only scape-goats were offered. The devotees fast during the day. The he-goat is killed in the afternoon, the blood sprinkled upon a stone, and the flesh eaten. At night the Panikas dressed in red and white striped cotton cloths and their faces covered with metal or bark masks perform their demoniacal dances.

In Mercara-táluq in Ippanivolavádi and in Kádakéri in Hálerinád the villagers sacrifice a kóna or male-buffalo instead of a man. Tied to a tree in a gloomy grove near the temple, the beast is killed by a Méda who cuts off its head with a large knife, but no Coorgs are present at the time. The blood is spilled on a stone under a tree and the flesh eaten by the Médas.

In connection with this sacrifice there are peculiar dances performed by the Coorgs around the temple: the *Kombáta* or *horn-dance*, each man wearing the horns of a spotted deer or stag on his head; the *Piliáta* or *peacocks'-feather-dance*, the performers being ornamented with peacocks' feathers, and the *Chauriáta* or *yák-tail-dance*, during which the dancers, keeping time, swing yák tails. These ornaments belong to the temple, where they are kept.

In some cases where a particular curse is said by the Kanya to rest upon a house, stable or field, which can only be removed by an extraordinary sacrifice, the ceremony performed seems to be another relic of human sacrifices. The Kanya sends for some of his fraternity, the Panikas or Bannas, and they set to work. A pit is dug in the middle room of the house, or in the yard, or the stable, or the field, as the occasion may require. Into this one of the magicians descends. He sits down in Hindu fashion, muttering mantras. Pieces of wood are laid across the pit, and covered with earth a foot or two deep. Upon this platform a fire of jack-wood is kindled, into which butter, sugar, different kinds of grain, etc. are thrown. This sacrifice continues all night, the Panika sacrificer above, and his immured colleague below, repeating their incantations all the while. In the morning the pit is opened, and the man returns to the light of day. These sacrifices are called *Máranada bali* or *death-atonements*. They cost from 10 to 15 Rupees. Instead of a human being, a cock is sometimes shut up in the pit and killed afterwards.

In cases of sore afflictions befalling a whole gráma or nád such as small-pox, cholera or cattle-disease, the ryots combine to appease the wrath of *Mári-amma* by collecting contributions of pigs, fowls, rice, cocoanuts, bread, and plantains from the different houses, and depositing them at the Mandu; whence they are carried in a procession with tomtoms. In one basket there is some rice and the members of each house on coming out bring a little rice in the hand and, waving it round the head, throw it into the basket with the belief that the dreaded evil will depart with the rice. At last the offerings are put down on the nád boundary, the animals are killed, their blood is offered on a stone, the rice and basket are left, and the rest of the provisions consumed by the persons composing the procession. The people of the adjoining grámas or náds repeat the same ceremony and thus the epidemic is supposed to be banished from the country. In still greater calamities a flock of sheep is driven from nád to nád and at last expelled from the country.

e. Pilgrimages of the Coorgs within and outside their own country.

Besides the annual *Tale-Kávéri festival* in October and the *Kuttadamma-játre* in April there is a large concourse of people in February during *Sivarátri* at *Herumálu* in Kiggatnád and the day following at *Irpu* five miles further on where, at the foot of the "*Lakshmanatírtha fall*," thousands of pilgrims submit to the supposed sin-cleansing shower-bath. The way thither leads through a jungle, so that the landscape of Irpu, forming an open valley with a high wall of mountains at the back, bursts all at once upon the wanderer's view. The Lakshmanatírtha which, in its primordial course, descends in beautiful cascades over the almost perpendicular mountain wall lies before the eye and calmly meanders through the rice valley. On the right bank of it the Dévastána, an unsightly building, but adorned by a splendid specimen of the beautiful scarlet-flowered Asóge-tree, is situated. Near it and all along the banks of the stream pilgrims build their booths. The bathing place is 200 feet above the temple. The way is romantic, with steep rocks to the right, to the left the shallow winding stream, tumbling and foaming over large boulders, but during the monsoon swelling into a thundering torrent. All around the scene are the hundreds of pilgrims, Coorgs and Malayálam people. Every few steps a beggar is encountered exhibiting his deformities or sores. Here lies a fanatic as if dead with a wooden nail through his cheeks; there a boy with a lancet through his outstretched tongue and a smoking chatti on his stomach; here another man with a long knife across his throat, and a horrible corpse-like appearance. At the holy bath the stream high above breaks through a woody embrasure over a succession of rocky ledges till it spreads itself into a foaming shower-bath, received in a stony caldron formed by slippery sharp-edged rocks. Here the crowd of pilgrims finds its goal. The bathing multitude now forces its way under the falling spray. But few can, at the same time, make use of the sin-cleansing bath. See that old woman with bent head right under the spray, her body trembles from the shock, yet for several minutes she perseveres. There a father lifts his screaming child under the splashing water;

here with firm grasp a husband drags his timid spouse along the rock and into the caldron; and even the tender babe at his mother's breast is brought within the influence of the bath. Dripping and shivering the bathers force their way bacl through the new arrivals and seek a sunny spot to change their garments. The pressure is great, the path slippery, and the confusion and pressure alarming. According to Brahminical superstition the colour of the water in the caldron indicates the intensity of the guilt of the bathing pilgrim. The darker its hue the greater the guilt, and yet the phenomenon depends only on the accident, whether the falling water is intercepted by the bodies of the bathers or whether it reaches the basin directly, and by the force of its fall is beaten into foam.

After bathing the pilgrims assemble at about 4 o'clock in the temple, where a Brahmin dances before the idol shrine with a brass image of Isvara upon his head; another Brahmin with a plate receives the small money offerings, and a third distributes Prasáda i. e. flowers and globules of sandal. The native officials first make their obeisance, the most devoted amongst them even the Sáshtángam i. e. touching the ground with the 8 members of the body, and then offer their gift. This temple possesses 2,000 battics of rice-land and annually receives on this festive occasion Rupees 400 from Government! The origin of Irpu and Hérumálu-játre is based upon a common Brahminical legend:—One day when Ráma, with his followers, was living in this place, his younger brother Lakshmana in a fit of madness insulted him by returning the bow and arrows which Lakshmana some time before had received from Ráma. Repenting of his rashness, Lakshmana asked forgiveness, offering at the same time to throw himself into a large fire as an expiation for his crime. He shot an arrow against the foot of the Irpu rocks, when a large fire flared up into which he threw himself. In order to save his brother, Ráma immediately created a river, which up to the present day is called Lakshmanatírtha, but it was too late. Ráma afterwards desired to consecrate the spot and ordered Hanuman to bring a Linga from Kási (Benáres) within one hour and a half. During his absence Ráma, fearing that Hanuman would not be back in time, made a Linga himself of river-sand, in which operation he was surprised by Hanuman, who flew into a rage for having troubled himself in vain. He twisted his enormous tail round one of the neighbouring hills, *Hanumanbetta*, and attempted to upset it. Ráma, to comfort the furious monkey-god, assured him that Hanuman's Linga should become even more famous than his own. So the new Linga was set up at Hérumálu and the festive day of its worship precedes that of the Linga at Irpu!

In April and December there are játres to the *Iggudappakundu* in Padinálknád, where Tulu-Brahmins have a temple and receive the oblations of the Coorgs. It often happens, that a sick Coorg vows his weight in rice to that temple, and, no doubt, the heavier the man the more acceptable and effective the gift!

On the *Hattur hill* or *Kuntada-betta* in Betiednád there is an annual játre in honor of Isvara or Siva who has there a little stone-temple dedicated to him. In 1853 the dilapidated temple was rebuilt at the expense of the Takkas and headmen of Betiednád and their names are written on a stone slab in the temple, which is only 15 feet square, but substantially built with a Linga in front. It stands near the brink of the precipice which is about 500 feet deep and whence a beautiful view is obtained over Kiggatnád. There is also a remarkable stone on the very edge of the precipice about 2 feet broad and 5 feet long, where childless or unmarried people bring offerings of betel leaves, perform worship and turn three times round, believing that this ceremony will insure issue to the barren woman, or a suitable partner to the unmarried youth.

On the north side, a little below the temple, there is a small tank with perennial water, which is considered holy, but 100 years ago it is said to have been defiled by a Chándála woman bathing in it, when the spring ceased to flow for some time.

On the south-east ridge a cave is shown which, according to Brahminical discovery, offered an asylum to the exiled Pándus! After their departure the cave was occupied by a tiger, which with due respect for the játre quits his abode 7 days before the feast and afterwards returns.

On the precipitous side of the rock there are nests of vultures and several hundreds of beehives.

For seven days before the Tulásankramana in the village Mugutagéri at the foot of the hill, the ryots assemble one from each house at the Manda and sing Coorg chants in praise of Isvara. On the night of the 7th the inhabitants of the whole nád come together, disguising themselves in masks of 18 various descriptions, they then go to the Ambala and dance and sing to the sound of the tomtom. The day following a light hollow frame, representing a horse, made of cane-work, is decked out so as to hide the lower part of the man's body who carries it, making it appear as if he rode the horse. The multitude then ascend the hill in procession, headed by the horse and a band of musicians, dance round the temple and bring their offerings of water, fruit and money.

The *Pálúr játre* in Kuyingherinád in honor of Pálúrappa, brother of Iggudappa, is a similar affair, which takes place in the month of April. The temple was rebuilt only a few years ago at a considerable expense and chiefly by the exertions of a Coorg official whose zeal and devotion one could wish had been employed in a better cause, especially in the education of his ignorant and superstitious nád people!

Amongst the játres beyond this country those visited by the Coorgs are four: *Subramanya* on the northern frontier of Coorg, which, in December, attracts a great number of people, as with the feast there is connected a cattle-fair and the sale of superior metal vessels and idols; *Baitur* in Malabar to which in January chiefly the people of Beppunád and Yedenalknád proceed, they also send rice to the temple; *Payavur* also in Malabar, and especially supported and in February visited by the Katiednád-Coorgs, who send from one to ten butties of rice per house; *Nanchanagódu* in Mysore which comes off in December.

f. Dévastánas, Mattas and Musjids.

The Coorg Dévastánas or Pagodas are mostly of an insignificant character; none is distinguished for great antiquity or structural beauty; most of them are but rude village shrines of mud walls and thatched roofs within a gloomy grove and not calling for any particular description. A passing notice may be, perhaps, bestowed on the *Omkarésvara-dévastána* at Mercara, which stands in a hollow just below the Superintendent's Court and is built in the same style as the Rajahs' tombs, but with a small tank in the temple yard. From the centre of the tank a pretty little pavilion rises, which is connected with the land by a balustrated passage. The priests or pújáries of these places are chiefly Tulu, Havige and Karnátaka-Brahmins; the former are divided into 3 branches: the Kótu, Kandávara, and Shivalli-Brahmins, which latter are the most numerous in Coorg. The Havige-Brahmins are Smártaru, residing near Honore in North Canara whose native tongue is Canarese. They worship both Vishnu and Siva, and the marks on their foreheads are put horizontally. The Karnátaka-Brahmins are immigrants from Mysore.

There are altogether 863 pagodas or temples in Coorg and 57 Mattas or Jangams, of the total of which places 549 share a Government contribution of 13,800 Rupees annually in cash and 9,474 Rupees worth of remitted assessment from endowed landed property; 372 places only are maintained by private contributions. The lion's share of this large Government grant falls to the Mercara-Omkarésvara temple with Rupees 4,850, to the Bhágiamandala-dévastána with Rupees 3,956; to the Tale-Kávéri pagoda with Rupees 2,320 and to the Rajahs' tombs with Rupees 2,000 per annum—a total of Rupees 13,126! When the people once see the folly of their superstitious idolatry, what an amount of spiritual good for themselves and their children they may effect with these large sums, should Government continue its liberality!

The *Mattas* or *Jangams* are religious institutions, originated and endowed by the Coorg Rajahs, who were themselves Lingaites. They are now evidently of greater importance to the Siváchára-priests, who derive an easy living from the rich endowments, than of any practical use for the Coorg people, amongst whom this sect, in spite of its royal patronage, never struck any root. The Sivácháries are easily recognised by the silver capsule, enclosing the Linga, which they wear suspended round their necks. The 57 Mattas hold as endowments 31,457 batties of land, representing an annual revenue of 3,360 Rupees due to Government, if the land were held by ryots. Government, therefore, contributes not only that amount of revenue, but also the actual produce of the fields less the working expenditure.

The most richly endowed Mattas are the following:—

Bassava-hally	Matta in	Yedavanád with	4,105	batties of land,
Abbi	do.	do.	4,005	do.
Madapur	do.	Gadinád do.	2,643$\frac{3}{4}$	do.
Siddapur	do.	Horurnurocklenád	2,372$\frac{1}{2}$	do.
Thanady	do.	Amatnád with	1,485	do.
Chadadarally	do.	Horurnurocklenád	1,430	do.
Cheppada Katte	do.	Yedenálknád with	1,188$\frac{3}{4}$	do.
Thorenur	do.	Gadinád do.	1,100	do.
their endowments amounting to			18,330	batties of land.

Musjids.—There are but 5 small Musjids in Coorg, erected by the Mussulmans residing here, whose number does not much exceed one thousand. They are mostly poor people and live chiefly in Mercara, Virájpet and Fraserpet.

g. The Amma-Codagas.

In connection with the preceding subjects, it is natural, to enquire into the condition of the indigenous priesthood. It is clear, that the present intermixture of Hinduism with the more simple religious practices of the Coorgs points back to a time, when the encroaching Brahmins had to encounter popular superstition, upheld by an indigenous priesthood, whose direct descendants the present "Amma-Codagas" seem to be. In language, manners and costume they are hardly to be distinguished from other Coorgs, but are less favoured in appearance; many of them wear the brahminical cord, and all abstain from animal food and fermented liquor. They intermarry with their own people only, a custom which may perhaps hasten their gradual diminution and total extinction, as they constitute but a small portion of the whole population. There are altogether 42 Amma-Codaga houses with 281 inhabitants of whom 97 are men, 90 women and 94 children. They live chiefly in Kiggatnád and Padinálknád, 21 families in the former and 16 in the latter taluq. Like the other Coorgs they are agriculturists and only 3 are in Government service. Their name "Amma-Codaga" or Mother-Coorgs i. e. Coorgs belonging to Mother Kávéri denotes them as men devoted to Kávéri or as priests. With the rest of the Coorg tribe they celebrate in the same manner the great Kávéri and Huttari festivals, but of course as priests performing púja in their own houses, for they have nothing to do with the Kávéri temple. They have no sacred books or shastras, nor do they exercise any spiritual influence over the people. The history of the old Coorg-priests is shrouded in obscurity. They seem to have been of a rude character like the priests of ancient Britain and Germany, untractable and disinclined to adopt foreign culture. But the subtilty of the Brahmins gradually instilled into their minds some priestly notions which made them aspire after superior sanctity by adopting the sacred cord and a brahminical diet. It is said, that Timmappeyah, a Havige-Brahmin, and brother-in-law of the late Rajah, who died in 1868, as Karnika or Treasurer, gained such an influence over the Amma-Codagas, that many of them resolved upon laying aside the Coorg costume and imitating the Brahmins in dress and diet. There are even men amongst the Coorgs who under brahminical influence strive after some sort of sanctity by abstaining from the use of liquors and meat diet and by advancing brahminical interests. Brahminism in Coorg, which found no favour with the Rajahs, appears to be in the ascendency under the liberal patronage of the British Government. If it were not for the rich stipends, drawn from Government by the brahminical institutions in Mercara and Táwunád, their present existence would be more than doubtful. Left to the support of the Coorgs alone, they would long ago have succumbed to starvation, for the essential Coorg customs and religious practices can have little in common with Brahminism. There are old Coorgs who never once went to the Tale-Kávéri játre or had Brahmins perform any ceremony for them in their houses. All their lifetime they could do very well without them. Now the Brahmins find their staunchest supporters chiefly in Kiggatnád taluq and generally amongst the middle-aged Coorgs, and amongst such families whose reception by and assimilation with the Coorg-clan dates back to but recent generations. With them Brahmins are in requisition on many occasions. At the birth of a Coorg child, they ceremoniously purify the defiled house by sprinkling holy water within and without, for which they receive a gift in rice. At the Coorg wedding the Pújári of the village or nád offers Prasáda and whilst throwing a flower-garland over the bridegroom's neck, he mutters a blessing, for which pious act he afterwards receives a gift in money. In case of illness Brahmins are sent for, to implore the deity for recovery. In a place set apart in the compound they perform their ceremonies and, if the patient gets well, they are amply rewarded. At a housewarming (griha-pravésha) it has become the fashion among the Coorgs to invite Brahmins and to give them a good meal and presents. The expenses incurred amount from a small sum to upwards of a thousand Rupees. The Puróhita or officiating Brahmin kindles a fire of jackwood (hebalasu) in the middle room, throws ghee and rice into the flame and repeats some mantras as required for the occasion. Thus we see, that Brahminism invades every accessible opening in Coorg life, and pandering to the ignorance and pride of the Coorgs, it is more successful than the great truths of Christianity. It is, however, to be hoped, that education along with other civilizing influences will do its work, to dissipate the darkness of ignorance and superstition and help to free the Coorgs from the trammels of priestly imposition.

To acknowledge the indigenous Coorg priesthood and yet account for its degraded state as compared with the erudition of the twice-born, the Brahmins invented the following legend, which is not in harmony with the Kávéri-Purána:—The sage Kávéra as a reward for his austerities was blessed with a daughter Kávéri, whom he promised in marriage to Agastia another sage, who also resided on the Brahmagiris. Kávéri did not accept the proposal and assuming the shape of a river fled from the mountain. Agastia in hot persuit overtook her in Katiednád and persuaded her to submit their dispute to the arbitration of their friends. They called three families of Amma-Kodagas and six of Coorgs; the former took the part of Agastia, the latter that of Kávéri. The Amma-Codagas decided, that Kávéri should not be allowed to proceed; but the Coorgs declared, that a woman should not be forced to marry against her will. The enraged Agastia Muni pronounced a curse upon the Coorgs, that the generation of Coorgs should decrease, that their women should not tie their garments in front, that the sown rice should not grow and that their cows should not give milk. Kávéri Amma who was the patroness of the Coorgs counteracted the curse as well as she could in the following words: "the Coorg shall increase, but the Amma-Codagas decrease; the Coorg women shall tie their garments behind; the sown paddy shall be transplanted and the cows be milked after the calves have drunk." So saying she tried to escape, and on being held by Agastia by the border of her garment, she turned to the right and flowed rapidly away. Hence the place, where this occurred, was called Balamúri (turning to the right). A linga has been erected near the spot by the Brahmins and it is yearly visited in Tulámása at the time of the Kávéri feast by Coorgs and others, who bathe in the river. Dodda-Virájender built here also a rest-house, which, though over 60 years old, is still in tolerable preservation.

The only object this legend can have is, not to clear up the origin of the indigenous priesthood of Coorg, but to obscure and bury it under the rubbish of Puranic lore which eludes every historical investigation.

7. ARCHITECTURAL STRUCTURES AND ARCHÆOLOGICAL REMAINS IN COORG.

a. Palaces.

Besides the *Mercara-Palace*, there are two other Aramanes, one at *Nálknád* and the other in *Halerinád*, but neither is remarkable for extent or elegance. The palace at Nálknád was built by Dodda-Virájender in 1794 and formed in those days an almost inaccessible small mountain-fortress, defended by strong barriers along the steep approaches. Now it is partly turned into the nád Cutcherry and the upper rooms are reserved for visiting Government Officials. In front of the palace near the right corner stands in tolerable preservation a handsome little pavilion (Dáremandappa), which was erected for the celebration of Dodda-Virájender's second marriage with Mahadévamma in February 1796. Under proper management the land belonging to the palace might be turned into fertile and profitable vegetable gardens or other plantations. The palace at Halerinád is built after the plan of other Coorg houses on a larger scale only and secured by breast-works and barriers.

The Palace in Mercara, thoroughly repaired during the last two years and an iron roof put on at an expense of 80,000 Rupees, is a conspicuous building of modern date. According to an inscription on a metal plate in one of the palace-rooms it was commenced on the first day of the new moon of the Bhádrapada month (15th August—15th September) in 1735 of the Sáliváhana era i. e. in 1812 and completed in 2 years and 1 month by Lingarájendra Vodeya, the younger brother of Dodda-Virájender. The inscription concludes: "The pious, who praise Almighty God, by whose grace this "magnificent palace was constructed after the removal of the "rugged hill-top, shall enjoy eternal happiness in this world "and in the world to come."

The ground plan of the palace is that of a Coorg house with a superstructure in European fashion. It forms a large square of 200 feet with an open space in the centre, is 2 stories high and presents a fine front. A range of arches runs nearly along the whole extent of the bottom part, the upper having a contiguous row of windows shut in by glass sashes and venetian blinds, the centre window projecting into a small balcony supported by two upright horses formed of masonry. Along the ridge of the roof runs a balustrade of ornamental masonry. The other three sides of the building present nearly a blank space varied only by a few irregular apertures to admit air, for they can hardly be called windows. The rooms which have been adapted to European convenience as best they could, are tenanted by the officers of the Native Regiment, stationed at Mercara. The whole palace is built of brick and excellent mortar and altogether finished with solidity and elegance, such as characterise no other modern buildings in Coorg. In one of the lower rooms the strongly secured *Provincial Treasury* is located.

A reception house for English visitors to the late Rajahs formerly stood on the site of the present Government Central School, in the midst of a plantation of orange and other trees. It owed its existence to the gratitude of Dodda-Virájender who had a warm attachment for the English. It was a handsome building in the form of a square with four turrets at the angles and 2 stories high. Both as to architecture and furniture it was executed in European style, and nothing was forgotten, that could render it a comfortable abode to travellers, accustomed to the luxuries of civilized life. It is referred to with high praise in the Memoranda of English visitors in those days. With the advent of the British Government it fell into disuse which did not justify an expensive up-keep, and being abandoned it soon became a ruin, and was demolished, its stones being partly used in the erection of the Central School.

b. Mausoleums.

The most remarkable modern buildings in Coorg are the *Mausoleums* of *Dodda-Virájender* and *Lingarájender* and their favourite Queens. These edifices are exactly alike and stand close to one another. The first was erected shortly after Virájender's death in 1809 by Lingarájender, and the other by Virájender Vodeyar in 1821. By their side is a smaller tomb over the remains of an honored Guru of the Rajahs, Rudrappa, which was built by Devan Ponappa in 1834. The Mausoleums are situated at the northern extremity of the Mercara Petta (Mahadévapet) and enclosed by a high embankment. They are square buildings much in the style of Mahomedan edifices, with a handsome dome in the centre and four minaret-like turrets at the corners surmounted by Basavas. On the top of the dome is a gilded ball with a weathercock above it, and all the window frames are of handsomely sculptured sienite blocks with solid brass bars. A flight of stone steps, flanked on the top by 2 well carved pillars with representations of Siva, leads to an open platform all round the building. The inside consists of a covered verandah round one centre room in which two slightly raised slabs in the shape of a cross covered over with white cloth and daily renewed flowers indicate the sepulchres. A lamp burns continually and a Lingaite Pújári is in daily attendance upon the deified Dodda-Virájender.

In *Mádapúr* or *Jambúr* 10 miles north-east of Mercara, there is the ancient cemetery of the Coorg Rajahs' family. It is prettily situated on the banks of the Mádapúr river, but has no claim to architectural merit. The building is sorrounded by narrow out-houses which crowd too closely upon it. It is about 40 feet square and nearly the same height and stands on an elevated base. It consists of two stories, the bottom one inclosing the sepulchres in a central apartment; the one above is of the same size as the central apartment, leaving room for a passage and a low balustrade all round. The lower story is ornamented with a large figure of a Basava sculptured in sienite and similar images adorn the capital of four small pillars placed at the angles on the top of the building.

Near the Kávéri, at *Holesálhalli* there is the *tomb of*

Nanjunda Arasu, who had ruled over Periapatam. Shortly before his death, whilst on a visit to his nephew, the Coorg Rajah Dodda-Vírappa Vodeya, the fortress fell through treachery into the hands of the Mysoreans with the loss of all his remaining family. In his affliction he addressed the Coorg Rajah thus: "As old age had come upon us, we intended with your permission to have placed our son in the Government of Periapatam and, renouncing the desire of this world, to have given ourselves to constant adoration of Siva. At such time of old age the great God has shown us a misery, we ought never to have looked upon. Do you take possession of the country which has passed from our hands? Build and give us a house to live in till our life come to a close, and a temple for Vírabhadra, our household god. Besides, it is our mind, to consecrate a Linga in our name. For this purpose let a temple be built on the banks of the Kávéri river, in it a Linga be consecrated in our name after the close of our life, our grave be made in front of that temple, a stone portico be built over it and a Basavéshvara consecrated in it." In compliance with this request Dodda-Vírappa had a palace built near the river on the spot chosen by him at Holesálhalli, surrounding it with a ditch, settled him there and gave it the name Nanjaráyapattana. For his bodyguard he appointed 700 Coorgmen. He built also Vírabhadra's temple, erected another stone temple over the Linga, called Nanjundéshvara, and after Nanjunda's death he laid him in a grave constructed according to his wishes and made a grant of some lands for the perpetual performance of a religious service.

c. Antique Sepulchres or Cairns and Monumental Stones.

Cairns, those mysterious prehistoric tumuli, which are found all over the old world from Scandinavia to the far East and which puzzle alike the simple peasant and the astute archæologist, have lately been discovered also in Coorg and upon further investigation, their structure and contents prove to be of a character similar to that of the Cairns so widely distributed over Mysore, Coimbatore, Salem, Madura and other districts in Southern India. They are also remarkably like the ancient Allemanic tumuli, found in Southern Germany and Switzerland which contain similar pottery and implements.

The first discovery of them in Coorg in large numbers— for a solitary one had been opened at Almanda in Beppunád by Dr. H. Moegling in 1856—was made by Lieut. Mackenzie, Assistant Superintendent, in 1868 on Báne near Virájpet, but soon others were found and in better preservation near Fraserpet on the Mysore side of the Kávéri. The matter was taken up with great enthusiasm by Captain Cole the Superintendent of Coorg, and the excavations led to very satisfactory results. All of the Cairns found are either level with the ground or their tops crop just a little out of it. When laid bare, they present a stone chamber about 7 feet long, 4 feet wide and 4 feet high, composed of 4 upright granite slabs 7 or 8 inches thick and surmounted by a large slab that projects over the sides; the flooring is likewise of stone. The narrow front slab has an aperture of an irregular curve nearly 2 feet in diameter, broken out from the top and generally faces east. Sometimes a large compartment is by a partition stone divided into two chambers. These Cairns are either solitary or in groups, in some instances forming regular rows, so as to give the appearance of streets. Others are surrounded by a single or double circle of stones from 2 to 3 feet high. Many seem to have been tampered with by the natives for the sake of the stone-slabs or in the expectation of finding treasure. The relics found in them are peculiarly shaped pottery, buried in earth that nearly fills the chambers. The vessels contain earth, sand, bones, iron spear heads and beads. The pottery consists of chatties and urns of burnt clay and is of a red or black colour. Some resemble the ordinary native pots of various sizes; others are from 1 to 2 feet high narrow urns contracted towards the mouth and tapering towards the bottom, where 3 or 4 short legs give them support for standing upright. Some smaller ones shaped like Roman amphoras without handles, have no such supports. They are smooth and shining, but can hardly be said to be glazed. Ornaments there are none on the surface, except perhaps a line round the brim, but their forms are well proportioned and even elegant. Some of the vessels are in miniature like children's toys from 1½ to 2½ inches in diameter. The earth which fills the pots is the same as that within the chamber of the Cairn; bones, ashes and bits of charcoal are usually found at the bottom of the urns; grains of rági have also been found within the chambers, but it is likely, that some practical ryot or wandering Kuruba selected a Cairn for his granary, as it is the practice with natives to secure their grain in earth-holes. Beads of red cornelian of a cylindrical shape and longitudinally pierced and ornamented with straight or zigzag parallel lines, scratched into the stone and filled up with a white substance, are occasionally met with in the smaller pottery.

The iron implements, spears and arrowheads, are very much corroded, so that their shape is hardly distinguishable.

It would be vain to enter into the question of who were the builders of these Cairns. The Coorgs call them Pándupare (dwellings of the Pándus), but whatever is beyond their historical knowledge, they ascribe to the Pándus. It is certain, that the construction of these Cairns is quite disconnected from the life, customs and history of the present inhabitants of Coorg, nor can they have been the abodes of a legendary pigmy race; but were most likely the resting places of the earthly remains of a generation, that existed anterior to the historical records of the present local races.

Monumental Stones of a more recent date are the Kollekallu (from kollu, to kill—and kallu, stone) tombstones in honour of warriors slain in battle. They are found along the eastern districts of Coorg. One I saw in Tavalagheri-gráma in Kiggatnád, some in Kottecád, 6 miles to the east of Mercara, and many in Fraserpet and near the Sómawarpet; the same kind of monuments occur also frequently in the Mysore country, especially in Nuggur and as far north as Belgaum. In all these localities the stones show a similar character. A large collection of them may be seen in the town of Mysore in an open place opposite the Grave-yard. The slabs are of granite, with rough facings, about 6 feet high, 4 feet broad and 9 inches thick, and frequently the lower half is buried in the ground. The front side is generally divided into three compartments, each containing some figures in relief, the background being chiselled out, so that the figures are level with the frame of the compartments. The objects represented in the top frame are one, two or three central figures seated in various postures on low stools such as the Hindus still use, and two female figures standing by their sides with fans. The central figures are evidently the heroes, they sit sword in hand with consequential dignity. The second compartment is filled with a string of 3, 5 or 7 figures alternately males and females, the latter preponderating and in most lively attitudes, the male figures extending their arms and resting their hands on the shoulders of the females who support their partners' arms near the elbows. The extreme figures who are always females hold fans (or guitars?) in their hands. The third frame encloses a battle scene in which warriors on foot and armed with bows and arrows, swords and shields are engaged in combat, one man lying dead on the ground. In the right corner there is a warrior on horseback with sword in hand making gestures of command or encouragement and in the left corner one or two bulls are represented. The figures are in grotesque attitudes, but remarkably well grouped and closely resemble the sculptured reliefs of Halibeed.

In the top compartment there is occasionally a lamp and a Linga both on pedestals, and these insignia, together with the Basavas in the third frame, evidently denote the heroes as Linga worshippers and aliens from the present Coorgs, who know nothing about them; the Canarese Gaudas, in whose countries they are chiefly found, claim them as relics of their ancestors and annually present before these stones offerings of cakes and fruit. The dresses of all the figures represented are not in the Coorg but in the costume of Hindus of the scantiest clothing. Col. Wilks in his *History of Mysore* Vol. I. p. 15. explains the sculptured representations in the three compartments thus: "The lowest describes the battle in which the hero was slain; the centre compartment represents him in the act of being conveyed to heaven between two celestial nymphs: in the uppermost he has arrived at the regions of bliss and is delineated as seated before the peculiar emblem of his religion—generally the lingum—for the practice of erecting monuments seems chiefly to belong to the sect of Siva."

In north and north-east Coorg similar stones, but with simple and coarse sculptural figures are still erected by relations of influential men who met with a violent death or were carried away by small-pox and cholera.

With the Coorgs it is the custom, to keep images of men and women in Coorg costume chased in silver-plates in the *Keimatta*, which is a small square building near the house, in remembrance of their ancestors whose departed spirits are there annually worshipped. These plates which are of little artistic merit are made by the country goldsmiths. Near the *Kannana house*, on that fine hill slope opposite the Central School in Mercara, there is a stone-slab with a picture in relief of a Coorg warrior. The stone is erected in the paddy fields in remembrance of the (Dalavai) military chief *Kannana Doddeya*, who fell in an engagement with the forces of Hyder Ali near Kájúr-Bágalu in North Coorg in 1767. Before setting out on this expedition he said to the king Muddarájah: "I have twice returned from defeating the Ma-"homedans and made Salam to the Rájah, but this time I shall "not return." The celebrated Coorg hero Appachoo Mandana fell in the same battle. When, after the death of Hyder Ali, Tippu Sultan invaded Coorg, he burnt Kannana's house and hanged 24 members of his family, and the ruins are still visible. A silver plate 3 inches by 2 inches large, with a relief picture similar to that on the stone is preserved by the family in honour of their renowned ancestor.

Shásana-kallu. In some localities viz. in the temple yard at Bhágamandala, in the dévastána at Pálúr, in the ruined temple in Nallúr in Hatgatnád of Kiggatnád-taluq and at the Central School in Mercara (brought from Fraserpet) there are large stone-slabs of granite with inscriptions in peculiar characters that resemble the oldest forms of the Dravidian alphabets, but have not yet been deciphered. They are supposed to be *Shásana-kallu* i. e. memorial stones or records of Government grants. Their inscriptions might perhaps throw some light on the early history of the places in which the stones have been found. In the Mercara Treasury there are three copper plates 8 inches by 3 each, held together by a copper ring, the ends of which are united by a seal representing an elephant about one inch in length from head to tail. The 2 outer plates are inscribed on one side only, the inner plate on both sides. The inscription which numbers 1304 letters seems to be "old Kanada, but many of the letters strikingly resembling Lat and old Pali forms," acccording to a statement by the Bombay Asiatic Society. The text is said to relate to a grant of land to certain Mysore Brahmins in the villages of Uyambal and Badaneguppe. The date corresponds to A. D. 1006 and the charter concludes with the solemn de nunciation "whoever takes away this land which he or others have given, shall for sixty thousand years be born as a worm."

d. The Coorg Cadangas and other remains of defensive works.

In the April number (1855) of the "Fortnightly Review" in the article: "Were the Ancient Britons Savages?" by W. Walker Wilkins, there occurs a passage which has a most appropriate bearing upon the Coorg Cadangas: "Probably "no country in the world possesses so many ancient earth-"works, certainly none upon such a stupendous scale as our "own.—They are extremely difficult of access from the steep-"ness of the mountain height on which they were formed. "This difficulty the primitive engineer greatly increased by "the most simple and natural means. He sunk one or more "deep trenches round the summit of the hill and raised lofty "banks with the excavated soil. Undoubtedly this is the "most ancient species of rampart known; it existed ages be-"fore the use of mural fortifications and originated in all pro-"bability with the nations in the East. But be that as it may, "the examples above indicated incontestably prove, that the "realization of vast works was as familiar to the mind of the "British regulus or chieftain, as to that of any oriental prince "his contemporary. The organization of labour necessary "for carrying them out evinces besides a condition of society "here in prehistoric times, utterly incompatible with the pre-"vailing notions on the subject."

The description here given literally applies to the Coorg breast-works called *Cadangas*, which are seen in almost every part of this country and which testify to the indefatigable perseverance with which these highlanders toiled to secure the possession of their Hills. They are of a very remote age, for in the time of Dodda Vírappa Vodeya who ruled for 49 years (from 1687-1736) war-trenches (Cadangas) already existed to which he added new ones, as the passage in the Rájéndranáma states: "He caused ditches and trenches, etc. "to be dug all over the Coorg kingdom; erected frontier "gates, etc. repaired all the *war-trenches* within the country and "thus fortified the Principality of Coorg."

These Cadangas stretch over hills, woods and comparatively flat countries for miles and miles, at some places branching off in various directions or encircling hill tops. In the Méndalanád they show a great conformity and are broad and deep, the lower side of the ditch facing the open country, but in Kiggatnád they are of smaller dimensions. As stated in the preceding quotation they were "*war-trenches*," but it is more than probable, that at the same time they formed at least to some extent also the boundaries between different náds. In their conflicts with Hyder Ali and Tippu Sultan, the Coorg Rájas strengthened these works, established Ukadas or guard-houses wherever a road or pathway intersected them, every opening being faced with rough stone-walls and even in the last campaign at the taking of Coorg in 1834 the Cadangas proved no contemptible obstacle to the advance of the English troops.

Other remains of defensive works in Coorg are the *Fort at Mercara*, the *Fort ruins at Fraserpet*, *Beppunád*, *Bhágamandala* and *Palupáre*.

Mercara Fort is still in pretty good preservation, but of little strategical valuc, as it is commanded by hills all round within short range of cannon. The Fortress was originally built by Muddarája Vodeya in 1680 or thereabout, and then consisted probably of mud walls, but it was rebuilt with stone by Tippu Sultan, who called it "Jaffarabad," and it was held by his generals till 1790, when Jaffar Ali Beg evacuated the place and left it with all its guns and ammunition to the Rája, Dodda-Virájender. It simply consists of a rampart

8 feet thick and outside from 15 to 20 feet high with parapets 2 feet thick and 5 feet high. The fortress is an irregular hexagon and nearly conforms to the shape of the hill top, leaving enough space for a ditch all round and on the north side for a glacis. At its 6 corners there are bastions and the whole is built of strong masonry. The entrance on the east is intricate and circuitous and guarded by 3 successive gates, which close in the space, that is now occupied by public buildings the Jail, the Taluq-Subadar's, the Assistant Superintendent's and the Superintendent's Courts with the local Treasury. On the left side of the third gate there is a shrine erected against the wall, dedicated to Ganapati, the lord of hosts, whose image is daily worshipped by a Brahmin and who gets the first offerings, flowers and cocoanuts by Hindu devotees, because all who wish to prosper should begin their undertaking in Ganésha's name, and in former days it was not so dangerless for a Coorg to present himself before the Rája, as it is now before the British Superintendent! The fantastic superstructure has been added about 20 years ago by a devoted maistry who had been engaged in the building of the Fraserpet-Bridge, and who must have made large profits, to spend his money so lavishingly. Within the fort itself there is in the centre the palace, to the left and in front of i the English Church, to the right the Quarter-guard and armoury and behind the palace the powder magazine. The English Church stands near the place which was formerly occupied by a temple dedicated to Vírabhadra and which was demolished in 1855 to make room for the Church. The latter was built by the Rev. A. Fennell in 1856-57 by private subscriptions, the Church Building Society and Government assistance and consecrated in April 1858 by Bishop Dealtry. It is a remarkably neat structure in plain Gothic style, having a tower surmounted with a low spire. From its position and elevation it is a conspicuous object from whatever side Mercara

is viewed. Its interior is light and chaste, the fittings,—chiefly the handiwork of the Rev. Mr. Fennell—in remarkably good taste and the whole much set off by ground glass windows, with apex and borders of coloured glass, that at the east end being of larger size, of a more elaborate design and extremely elegant. The interior contains also an ornamental monument in white marble by Westmacott to the memory of the late Major Frank Vardon and a circular tablet in memory of Mrs. Barclay, the wife of Dr. Chr. Barclay.

The *Fort at Kushálanagara* (Fraserpet) built by Tippu Sultan was taken by the Coorgs in June 1789 under Dodda-Virájender, who sacked and burnt the place. When in 1846-1848 the fine bridge over the Kávéri was constructed, the ruins of the Fort supplied excellent building material.

The *Fortress at Arméri* in Beppunád was razed to the ground in August 1789.

Bhágamandala Fort, where Tippu seized some 5,000 Coorgs with their families whom he sent into Mysore in 1785 and forcibly made Mussulmans, was invested by Dodda-Virájender in 1790 and taken after 5 days' siege. The Rája himself fired the first cannon from the hill of Mumbáratu. During the bombardment 3 copper tiles of the Dévastána were destroyed by a cannon shot, but Dodda-Virájender replaced them by 4 tiles made of silver.

The *Pápáre Fort*, (Pálu-páre) on the Kire river, a tributary of the Lakshmanatírtha, in Hatgatnád in Kiggatnád taluq, in which there are also the ruins of a temple, is said to have been built by *Kolli-Ninga* and *Benne-Krishna* of the Bedaru or hunter-tribe. It was destroyed by Tippu Sultan's armies and its ruins are extensive.

8. THE COORG LANGUAGE AND ITS LITERATURE.

The prevalent and official language in Coorg is Canarese, but this small mountain clan, the Coorgs, with their former slaves, the Holeyas, have a language of their own, which is intelligible to themselves only. Upon closer examination, however, it is apparent, that the Kodagu tongue is but a dialect more or less related to the 5 principal Dravidian languages—the Telugu, Tamil, Malayálam, Tulu and Canarese—but eminently so to the older forms of these languages. The old Coorg chants (Palamé) have been written for ages past with Canarese letters, and the first attempt in printing a Coorg Grammar has likewise been carried out in Canarese type, also the Canarese numerical figures are used by the Coorgs. The Kodagu language is shorter, more simple, but less refined than the Canarese and a convenient medium for conversation; by its contracted, rounded forms with abrupt terminations in half vowels, it does not require a great exertion of the organs of speech and admits of chewing betel and retaining the precious juice, whilst the flow of conversation is uninterruptedly carried on. Indeed a beginner should practise the pronunciation with his mouth half full of water, till he can speak without spilling any. The Kodagu language has not the force and expressiveness of the Canarese, but it glides more readily over the lips. It is rich in words and forms and, as the Coorg chants attest, admirably suited for expressing easy flowing poetry of a humorous or solemn strain.

Of the 51 letters that constitute the new Canarese alphabet - old Canarese has only 47—the Kodagu language appropriates but 33, viz. 12 vowels, 1 half consonant, 16 classified and 4 unclassified consonants, for it rejects all aspirated consonants.

The vowels are: the short and long a ಅ, ಆ, e ಎ, ಏ, i ಇ, ಈ, o ಒ, ಓ, u ಉ, ಊ, and the diphthongs ei ಐ and ou ಔ.

The half consonant or medium between vowel and consonant is ಂ which sounds like m, n, or ng, according to position.

The 16 classified consonants are: the

Gutturals:	ಕ **ka**		ಗ **ga**		ಙ **gna**		
Palatals:	ಚ **cha**		ಜ **ja**		ಞ **nya**		
Cerebrals:	ಟ **ṭa**		ಡ **ḍa**		ಣ **ṇa**		(ಳ **ḷa**)
Dentals:	ತ **ta**		ದ **da**		ನ **na**		
Labials:	ಪ **pa**		ಬ **ba**		ಮ **ma**		

The 4 unclassified consonants are the Liquids:

ಯ **ya** ರ **ra** ಲ **la** ವ **wa**

It would lead me too far, to enter upon the method of changing this simple system of letters into their various combinations; this may be found in the Rev. Thos. Hodson's Canarese Grammar or in Captain Cole's Elementary Coorg Grammar, which in its etymological part is based upon the former. I may only remark, that in writing Kodagu with the Canarese alphabet there is a frequent use of half letters which are denoted by a peculiar flourish above the respective consonants, to preclude, as it were, the ordinarily used definite final vowel; Ex. ಮ್ = **mō**, ದ್ = **dō** instead of ಮ **ma** and ದ **da**. Yet these half letters are not mute consonants, but are followed by either of the two peculiar short and dull vowels *ŏ* and *ŭ* which frequently occur in German and French. The former (*ŏ*) is pronounced like *e* in the French relative pronoun "que", or the *ö* in the German "Götter", the latter (*ŭ*) sounds like the French *u* in "vertu" or the *ü* in the German "Mütter". As a general rule in the Kodagu language every half letter at the end of a syllable, whether mediate or final, is pronounced with the consounding short nasal vowel *ŏ*, where in new Canarese the same syllable would terminate in **anu** and in old Canarese in **am.** Ex. Can. **kurubanu.** Kg. **kurumbō** = a shepherd. But where the half letter in Kodagu implies the vowel *u* in Canarese, it is pronounced *ŭ*; Ex. Can. **idu**, Kg. **idŭ** = this.

It is remarkable that a similar system of half letters obtains also in Tulu, Tamil and Malayálam; it would appear, that both Tulu and Kodagu are in a medium and transition stage between the comparatively vowelless old Canarese and the sonorous new Canarese.

The Canarese short and long *i* before cerebrals and the terminal *u* are in Kodagu pronounced *ü;* Ex. Can. iḍu, Kg. üḍü = to put.

The Canarese short and long *e* is before cerebrals pronounced *ö*, but before a double cerebral the short *e* in Canarese is changed into *o*; e. g. Can. ēḷu, Kg. öḷü = seven; Can. peṭṭige, Kg. poṭṭi = box.

A slight nasal sound occurs at the end of the word avang instead of the Canarese avanu = he.

Soft and hard consonants are often interchanged and single consonants doubled; e. g. Kg. unḍu for Can. unṭu = are, Kg. ikka for Can. iga = now.

Compound consonants are separated; e. g. Can. chandra Kg. chaṇṇurō = moon; Can. yentha Kg. yennatō. The letter ಶ (sha) becomes ಜ (ja); e. g. Can. désha, Kg. dḗja = country; ಸ (sa) becomes ಚ (cha); e. g. Can. súrya, Kg. chúriyō. The Canarese letter ಹ (ha) at the beginning of a word retains the old Canarese form ಪ (pa); e. g. Can. ಹಿಡಿ hiḍi, Kg. ಪೂಡಿ pūḍi = to seize.

The noun and verbal roots are in Kodagu chiefly mono- and dissyllables, that may be traced back to old Canarese or to the common Dravidian stock; there are however also many Sanscrit words, which as Tadbhavas are by Coorg pronunciation tortured into queer forms. The intercourse of the Coorgs with the Mussulmans has naturally enriched their language also with Hindustáni expressions.

Taking now a rapid glance over the grammatical forms of the Kodagu language, I would refer for further instruction to Captain Cole's Elementary Coorg Grammar, which gives a great deal of valuable information, though as a first attempt it is somewhat defective and requires critical sifting.

Regarding the *noun* there are in Kodagu simple and compound nouns; the combination of the latter follows more the convenience of pronunciation than grammatical rules, for the Kodagu language in its present form is anterior to Kodagu grammar. There are, as in Canarese, 3 genders, but as in the other Dravidian languages the principle of distinction is the separation between the divine, the human and the below human; only the nouns relating to the former beings partake of the distinction of male and female sex, all other words are neuter. As to number there is a singular and plural form. Following the usage of other grammars of the Dravidian tongues, the declension of Kodagu nouns may be represented with 7 or 8 cases, but several of them being but the result of affixed particles, the cases might well be reduced to 5 viz. the Nominative, Objective, Genitive, Dative and Vocative. According to the terminations of the nouns there are 3 declensions, viz. of nouns ending in *a*, in *i* or *e* and in *u*. Examples will make this clear.

First declension of Nouns ending in a.

Masculine form "rájŏ," the king.

	Singular.			*Plural.*		
Nom.	rájŏ (1.)		the king.	rája (2.)		the kings.
Obj.	rájana		"	rájara		"
Gen.	rájanḍa	of	"	rájanḍa	of	"
Dat.	rájangü	to	"	rájakü	to	"
Inst.	rájanagonḍu	by	"	rájaragonḍu	by	"
Loc.	rájandapakka	in	"	rájandapakka	in	"
Voc.	rájané		Oh king.	rájaré		Oh kings.

1. Though corrupted at the end of a word the *a* takes again its full sound as soon as new syllables are added.

2. The plural sometimes adds *anga* similar to the old Canarese *angal*, e. g. Kg. *rájanga*, old Can. *rájangal.*

Feminine form "móva," daughter.

To the crude form the objective singular adds ḷa and the plural ḷia.

	Singular.			*Plural.*		
Nom.	móva		daughter.	móḷia		daughters.
Obj.	móvaḷa		"	móḷiaḷa		"
Gen.	móvaḍa	of	"	móḷiaḍa	of	"
Dat.	móvakkü	to	"	móḷiakkü	to	"
Voc.	móvaḷé	Oh	"	móḷiaḷé	Oh	"

Neuter nouns have no particular form for the plural number.

Second declension of Nouns ending in i and e.

Masculine form "dore," the master.

The plural is formed by adding: ya.

	Singular.			*Plural.*		
Nom.	dore		master.	doreya		masters.
Obj.	dorena		"	doreyaḷa		"
Gen.	dorera	of	"	doreyara	of	"
Dat.	dorekkü	to	"	doreyakkü	to	"
Voc.	doreyé	Oh	"	doreyaḷé	Oh	"

Feminine nouns are declined like the foregoing.

Neuter noun "poṭṭi," the box.

Nom. poṭṭi, *Obj.* poṭṭina, *Gen.* poṭṭira, *Dat.* poṭṭikkü, *Instr.* poṭṭinji, *Loc.* poṭṭilü.

Third declension of Nouns ending in u.

Masculine form "guru," the priest.

The plural is formed by adding: va.

	Singular.	*Plural.*
Nom.	guru	guruva
Obj.	guruna	guruvaḷa
Gen.	guruḍa	guruvaḍa
Dat.	gurukkü	guruvakkü
Voc.	guruvé	guruvaḷé

Feminine nouns are declined in the same manner.

Neuter form "puḷu," the worm.

Nom. puḷu,* *Obj.* puḷuna, *Gen.* puḷuḍa, *Dat.* puḷukkŭ, *Instr.* puḷuvinji, *Loc.* puḷuvalŭ.*

Adjectives precede the nouns which they qualify. As in Canarese their number is not very great, but many are formed from nouns by affixing the irregular participles ánŏ having become, and uḷḷŏ being, possessing: e. g. chái beauty, cháiánŏ beautiful; paṇa money, paṇauḷḷŏ rich. The relative participles also are frequently used as adjectives: e. g. páḍuvŏ pakki, the singing bird; bandŏ guru, the priest who came. For expressing the comparative and superlative the adjective remains unchanged, but the notion of degree is produced by a peculiar construction of the sentence viz. the comparative by a construction like this: than your book his book useful, i. e. his book is more useful than yours; the superlative: among all books his book useful, i. e. his book is most useful.

The numerical Adjective, this criterion of the origin of a language, is, as may be expected, in the Drávida languages very much alike, but entirely different from other tongues. The neutral numerals in Kodagu from 1-12 are: ondŭ, danḍŭ, múndŭ, nálŭ, anji, árŭ, yeḷŭ, yeṭṭŭ, oyimbadŭ, pattŭ, pannondŭ, paneranḍŭ; from 13 to 19 the units are added to the crude form of pattŭ, viz. padu-múndŭ, etc. 20 is iruvadu, to which after changing the d into tt, the units are added for 21-29.

In all compound numbers for danḍŭ, 2, ranḍŭ is substituted, which resembles the Canarese yeraḍu. 30 is muppadŭ, 40 nápadŭ, 50 eimbadŭ, 60 aruvadŭ, 70 eḷuvadŭ, 80 embadŭ, 90 tonúrŭ, 100 núrŭ; 101 núyittondŭ etc.; 200 innúrŭ, 300 munnúrŭ, etc., 800 eṭṭunúrŭ, 900 ombeinúrŭ, 1,000 áyira, which is borrowed from Sanscrit.

For the formation of ordinals the affix ne is added to the

* If the crude noun is long, or consists of several syllables, the final u disappears in the Instr. and Loc. e. g. nádŭ, *Instr.* náḍinji, *Loc.* náḍŭlŭ.

crude form of the cardinals; e. g. **ondane, dandane, múndane, etc.** the first, second, third, etc.

Only the numbers one and two have three genders, all the rest are neuter.

obbō	**one man.**	**ibbō**	**two men.**
obba	**" woman.**	**ibba**	**" women.**
ondü	**" thing.**	**dandü**	**" things.**

As in Canarese doubling a number renders it a distributive; e. g. **ondondü, dandandü, etc.** every one, two, etc.

Of fractions, which even in Canarese form but a limited system, the Coorg stock is still smaller and refers only to concrete terms viz: $\frac{1}{2}$ **åre̊**, $\frac{1}{4}$ **kálü**, $\frac{3}{4}$ **mukkálü**, which help to divide the **Maṇa** of 40 seers and the **Baṭṭi** of 80 seers of capacity-measure and the Rupee.

The Coorgs have no idea of abstract reckoning and fractional arithmetic is a most difficult subject for native teachers.

The *pronouns* in Kodagu greatly resemble those in Canarese.

The personal pronouns are declined in the following manner:—

First person: ná = I.

	Singular.		*Plural.*	
Nom.	**ná or nánü,**	**I.**	**enga, nanga,**	**we.**
Obj.	**enna,**	**me.**	**engḷa, nangaḷa,**	**us.**
Gen.	**ennaḍa, éḍa,**	**of me.**	**engaḍa, nangaḍa,**	**of us.**
Dat.	**enakü, nángü,**	**to me.**	**engakü, nangakü,**	**to us.**

Second person: ní = thou.

Nom.	**ninü,**	**thou.**	**ninga,**	**you.**
Obj.	**ninna,**	**thee.**	**ningaḷa,**	**you.**
Gen.	**ninaḍa, niḍa,**	**of thee.**	**ningaḍa,**	**of you.**
Dat.	**ninnakü, ningü,**	**to thee.**	**ningakü,**	**to you.**

Third Person: **Ivang, avăng,** he; **iva, ava,** she.

(The proximate and the remote forms are declined alike.)

	Singular.				*Plural.*	
Nom.	avăng,	he.	ava,	she.	avu,	they.
Obj.	avana,	him.	avaḷa,	her.	ayana,	them.
Gen.	avanḍa,	of him, his.	avaḍa,	of her.	ayanḍa,	of them.
Dat.	avangü,	to him.	avakü,	to her.	ayangü,	to them.

idü, adü—it.

Nom. adü, it; *Obj.* adüna, it; *Gen.* adanḍa, of it; *Dat.* adangü, to it; *Instr.* adatinji, from it; *Loc.* adülü, in it.

Tánü, himself; *Obj.* tanna is declined, like nánü, I.

The following are the interrogative, demonstrative and indefinite pronouns:

yé, yévö, yéva, yédü, which; árü, dárü, who.
i, ivang, iva, idü, this; ivü, these.
á, avang, ava, adü, that; avu, those.
ennata, what kind? innata, annata, such.
echakü, how much? ichakü, achakü, so much.

It will be remarked, that the idea of nearness and remoteness in the pronouns is finely distinguished by the use of the two vowels *i* and *a*.

Of *verbs* there are two conjugations in the Kodagu dialect; one of verbs ending in *u* and the other with the termination *i*, *e*, and *a*. The verbs ending in *u* add to their root the affix vö in the present and nö in the past relative participle; e. g. root: páḍü, sing; pr. rel. part. páḍüvö, who sings; past rel. part. páḍünö, who sang. Verbs ending in *e* add pö and tö; e. g. root: nene think; pres. relat. part. nenepö, who thinks; past rel. part. nenetö, who thought. The various inflections of the verb are formed from the root, the present relat. part. and the past relat. participle.

I. Conjugation. Verbs ending in u.

Root "páḍū," sing.

Infinitive Mood: **páḍūvákū, to sing:**

Present Gerund or verbal Adjective: **páḍiandū, singing.**

Past do. **páḍitū, having sung.** *Old Can.* **páḍdu.**

Negative Gerund **páḍatte, not singing.**

Relative Particip': Present: **páḍūvō, who sings.**

Do. Past: **páḍūnō, „ sang.**

Do. Negative: **páḍattō, „ does not sing.**

Present Tense.

Singular.	*Plural.*
nánū páḍuvi, páḍuvaḷe.	**enga páḍuva, páḍuvaḷa, we sing.**
ninū páḍuvia.	**ninga páḍuvira.**
aváng, ava, adū páḍuva, páḍuvaḷa.	**avu páḍuva, páḍuvaḷa.**

Past Tense.

nánū páḍūne, I sang.	**enga páḍichi.**
ninū páḍia.	**ninga páḍira.**
aváng páḍichi.	**avu páḍichi.**

Future Tense.

nánū páḍuvō, I shall sing.	**enga páḍu.**
ninū páḍuvia.	**ninga páḍuvira.**
aváng páḍu.	**avu páḍu.**

Neg. Mood Present Tense: **nánū, ninū, &c. páḍule, I do not sing.**

Past „ **páḍille, did not sing.**

Imperative Mood: **páḍū, sing; páḍi, sing ye; nánū, &c. páḍaḍū, let me sing; enga páḍanga, let us sing.**

II. Conjugation. Verbs ending in e, a and i.

Root: "nene," think.

Infinitive Mood: **nenepākū, to think.**

Gerund or Adjective Participle Present: **nenatāndū, thinking.**

Gerund or Adjective Participle Past:	nenetittŭ, having thought.
Do. Negative:	neneyatte, not thinking.
Relative Participle Present:	nenepō, who thinks.
Do. Past:	nenetō, who thought.
Do. Negative:	neneyatte, who does not think.

Present Tense.

Singular.	*Plural.*
nánŭ nenepi, nenepaḷe, I think.	enga nenepa, nenapaḷa.
ninŭ nenepiya.	ninga nenepira.
avaᵘng nenepa, nenapaḷa.	avu nenepa, nenapaḷa.

Past Tense.

nánŭ nenete,	I thought.	enga nenettätŭ.
ninŭ nenetiya.		ninga nenettira.
avaᵘng nenettätŭ.		avu nenettätŭ.

Future Tense.

nánŭ nenepō,	I shall think.	enga nenekku.
ninŭ nenepiya.		ninga nenepira.
avaᵘng nenekku.		avu nenekku.

Neg. Mood Present:	nánŭ nenepile, I do not think.
Neg. Mood Past:	nánŭ nenetille, I did not think.
Imperative Mood:	nene, think; neneyire, think ye.
	nánŭ neneyattŭ, let me think.
	enga neneka, let us think.

Some verbs ending in *e* and *a* form their participles in the following manner:—

Root:	kaḍa,	*part.*	kaḍanḍō, kaḍapō.
„	naḍa,	„	naḍanḍō, naḍapō.
„	pare,	„	parandō, parevō.
„	bóḷe,	„	bóḷandō, bóḷevō.

Verbs ending in i:—

Root:	**kani,**	*Part.*	**kaniohō, kanipō.**
"	**kuri,**	"	**kuriohō, kuripō.**
"	**kei,**	"	**keichō, keipō.**
"	**kodi,**	"	**kodiohō, kodipō.**
"	**ohadi,**	"	**ohadiohō, ohadipō.**

Conjugation of the auxiliary verb irū, *be.*

Infinitive Mood: ippōkkū, to be.

Gerunds or Adj. Participle Present: injanḍū, being.

Do. Past: injittū, having been.

Do. Negative: iratte, not being.

Relative Participle Present: ippō, who is.

Do. Past: injō, who was.

Do. Negative: irattō, who is not.

Present Tense.

Singular.		*Plural.*
nánū ippi,	I am.	enga ippa, we were.
ninū ippia.		ninga ippira.
avǎng ippa.		avu ippa.

Past Tense.

nánū inje,	I was.	enga injattū.
ninū injiya.		ninga injira.
avǎng injattū.		avu injattū.

Future Tense.

nánū ippō,	I shall be.	enga ikkū.
ninū ippiya.		ninga ippira.
avǎng ikku.		avu ikku.

Negative Mood Present: nánū ippile, I am not; *Past:* nánū injile, I was not.

Imperative Mood: irū, be; irri, be ye.

nánū iradū, let me be.

nangō ikka, let us be.

Conjugation of the auxiliary verb áu, *become.*

Infinitive Mood:	ápŏkkŭ, to become.
Gerund or Adj. Participle Present:	áyanḍŭ, becoming.
Do. Past:	áyitŭ, having become.
Do. Negative:	átte, not becoming.

Pr. R. P.: ápŏ, who becomes; *Past*: ánŏ, who became. *Neg.*: áttŏ, who does not become.

Present Tense.

Singular.		*Plural.*
nánŭ ápi,	I become.	enga ápa, we become.
ninŭ ápia.		ninga ápira.
avaͧng ápa.		avu ápa.

Past Tense.

nánŭ áne,	I became.	enga áchi, we became.
ninŭ ániya.		ninga ánira.
avaͧng áchi.		avu áchi.

Future Tense.

nánŭ ápŏ,	I shall become.	enga áku.
ninŭ ápiya.		ninga ápira.
avaͧng áku.		avu áku.

Negative Mood Present:	nánŭ ápile, I do not become.
Do. Past:	„ áyile, I did not become.
Imperative Mood:	áu, become; áyiri, become ye.
	nánŭ áḍŭ, let me become.
	nanga ákka, let us become.

The irregular verb "póŭ" to go, is conjugated in the same manner.

I may remark, that as in Canarese the affirmative ahudu haudu is an old form of the future tense of águ, become, so in Kodagu akku, yes, corresponds with the 3rd person singular, future tense áku, it shall become, which is the same form as the old Canarese akkum. The fine distinction between irü, be, and áu, become, extends even to the derivative negations ille and alla, not, the first negativing existence, the second, the state of existence.

There is no passive voice in Kodagu; a little change in the construction of a sentence renders it superfluous.

A medial or reciprocal form is obtained as in Canarese by adding to the past participle: koṇḍa (Can. koḷḷu) which properly means, take, but in this connection: "relating to oneself." e. g. dárü máḍi koṇḍandötü, who made it?

To express causal verbs in Kodagu, the affix chirü is added, e. g. maḍu-chirü, cause to do.

List of Irregular Verbs.

English.	Canarese Root.	Kodagu Root.	Present relat. Participle.	Past relat. Participle.
Know	ari	ari	ariwö	arinjö
Become	águ	áu	ápö	anö
Choose	áyu	áyu	áyuvö	áñjö
Put	iḍu	iḍü	iḍüvö	iṭṭö
Fall		iḍi	iḍiyuvö	iḍinjö
Be	iru	irü	ippö	injö
Descend	iḷi	iḷi	iḷiyuvö	iḷinjö
Eat	uṇṇu	uṇṇü	umbö	unḍö
Plough	uḷu	úḷü	uppö	uttö
Rise	yéḷu	yéḷü	yévö	yeddö
See	káṇu	káṇü	kámbö	kanḍö
Be hot	káyu	káyi	káyuvö	káñjö
Wait	káyu	káu	kápö	katö
Spoil	keḍu	keḍü	keḍüvö	keṭṭö
Make		keyü	keyuvö	kejja
Cut	koiyu	koiyü	koyuvö	kojjö

English	Canarese Root.	Kodagu Root.	Present relat. Participle.	Past relat. Participle.
Hear	kéḷu	kéḷü	képö	kéṭṭö
Kill	kollu	kollü	kolluvö	kondö
Take	koḷḷu	koṇḍa	kowwö	koṇḍandö
Win	gellu	gellü	gelluvö	geddö
Die	sá	cháü	chávö	chattö
Boil	suḍu	chuḍiü	chuḍüvö	chuṭṭö
Give	tá	* tá	tappö	tandö
Sink		távü	távö	tándö
End	tiru	tüüḷü	tüüpö	tüütö
Pay	teru	terü	terüvö	tettö
Wear off		téyu	téyuvö	ténjö
Touch		toḍü	toḍuvö	toṭṭö
Fold		tou	toppö	tottö
Plant	neḍu	naḍü	naḍuvö	naṭṭö
Stop	nillu	nillü	nippö	nindö
Blame		paḷi	paḷiuvö	paḷiṇjö
Increase		pere	peröpö	perötö
Bring forth	heru	perü	peruvö	pettö
Beat	hoḍiyu	poyi	poyuvö	pojjö
Make		poraḍü	poradüvö	poratö
Go	hógu	póu	pópö	pónö
Stitch	holi	pollü	pollüvö	pondö
Fight	hóru	póḷü	poppö	pottö
Come	bá	* bá	bappa	bandö
Live	báḷu	báḷü	bávö	bándö
Leave	biḍu	büḍü	büḍüvö	buṭṭö
Fall	biḷu	búḷü	búvö	buddö
Put		beyi	beppö	bechchö
Boil	bé	bé	bévö	benjö

* Tátü, he gave; bátü, he came.

As in Canarese *adverbs* are in Kodagu formed of nouns by adding the affixes áyitŭ, áyi (Can. ági), e. g. chamáyi (Can. samavági) according to.

The most common adverbs of time and place are the following:—

yekkŏ	when,	ikkŏ	now,	akkŏ	then.
yendŭ	which day,	indŭ	this day,	andŭ	that day.
yelli	where,	illi	here,	alli	there.

By the usual affixes these adverbs undergo like nouns of the neuter gender a kind of declension, in which the instr. case indicates motion from and the dative motion to a place; e. g.

Instr.	yellinji	whence,	illinji	hence,	allinji	thence.
Dat.	yellikkŭ	whither,	illikkŭ	hither,	allikkŭ	thither.

Most of the adverbs, however, do not admit of declension.

To advert in a few lines to the Kodagu syntax, it may be remarked, that it is quite in harmony with that of the Dravida languages. A Kodagu or Canarese compound sentence, though it presents a complete reversion of our European structure of sentences, is to the accustomed ear as perfect and harmonious as a Greek period, which is perhaps equally involved by participial constructions. The principal verb (verbum finitum) invariably is placed last in the sentence and as a general rule every complement to the subject, object and predicate, whether expressed by a word, a phrase or a clause, precedes the word complemented.

Literature. Strictly speaking there is no literature in the Kodagu language, as a few indigenous songs of a very limited range of subjects comprise the whole catalogue. These songs are known in every Coorg house, and, commemorating as they do the chief events of social life, marriage, death, and festivities, and the warfare with the Mussulman power in Mysore, they are likely to continue to be popular.

The people learn them by heart or by writing, using, as already observed, the Canarese alphabet. Some of them, as the Harvest and the Wedding Chant, which show the Kodagu dialect in all its peculiarities, seem to be very old and their authors are unknown. The latter mentions the country as being divided into 35 Náds or districts, and consequently must have existed previous to the events related in the Rájendranáme, in which the country is differently divided and which begins with the year 1633. Others are of a more recent date and contain numerous modern Canarese expressions. In fact with slight modifications the set poetical phrases of the old stock serve the Coorg bard on any occasion for new compositions; but these are usually local and trivial and obtain no circulation. The author of the epic song on the war with Hyder Ali and Tippu Sultan, which, however, has no poetical merit, is Boppanda Mádeya who died in 1868; and the Queen's Song, which testifies to the loyalty of the Coorgs, was composed by Chókandra Appeya in 1839. Of these songs little was known until my late Assistant, Mr. Graeter, took up the subject and after his study of the Kodagu dialect made them accessible to the English reader in the translation given.

Reflecting the Coorg mind in its own language, and uninfluenced by European culture, these songs are highly interesting ana in their simple beauty often evince considerable poetical merit, whilst others please by the vein of hearty good humour, that runs through their lines.

The rules of Hindu versification do not apply to the Coorg songs; these are cast in a less artistic mould and have something of the free mountain air about them. It is true, they move not in the gay, iambic foot; the more dignified trochaic measure suits the Coorg mind better; each line contains 7 or 8 syllables, but the accent is not carefully observed, nor is there either rhyme or alliteration. In its simple form the

Coorg measure may be best compared to that of English or German blank verse. Songs somewhat resembling those of the Coorgs are also found among the Badagas on the Nílagiris.

The following lines, taken from the beginning of almost every Coorg song, may give an idea of the construction of the Kodagu language and its resemblance to Canarese, in which language, as well as in English, a literal translation is given:—

1. *Kodagu.*	Nóṭi nóṭi kámbakkŏ
2. *Canarese.*	Nóḍi nóḍi káṇuvága
3. *English.*	Having seen, having seen, when one looks
1. *Kg.*	Bümikelloyandadü
2. *Can.*	Bhúmige yella unnatavádadu
3. *Engl.*	Than the earth all high
1. *Kg.*	Mahamméru parvata
2. *Can.*	Mahamméru parvata
3. *Engl.*	Mahaméru mountain
1. *Kg.*	Pú marakkoyandadü
2. *Can.*	Húvu maragaḷige unnatavádadu
3. *Engl.*	Than the flower-trees high
1. *Kg.*	Mánjappeya púmara
2. *Can.*	Mahá sampigea húvu mara
3. *Engl.*	The great Sampige flower-tree
1. *Kg.*	Déjakelloyandadŭ
2. *Can.*	Déshagaḷige, yella, unnatavádadu
3. *Engl.*	Than the countries all high
1. *Kg.*	Pommále Koḍavápa
2. *Can.*	Honnu mále Koḍagu águttade
3. *Engl.*	Gold necklace Coorg is

FREE TRANSLATION:

"High above the lofty hills
"Thrones the snowy Mahaméru;
"And among the flowering trees
"Is the Sampigé the finest;
"Thus is Coorg, a string of pearls,
"Far surpassing other countries."

The "*Harvest Song*", being rather long and adding no new information to what has already been given in the description of rice cultivation, is here omitted.

The Queen's Song.

God Almighty live and rule,
Rule as our Lord and God!
Rule, O glorious Sun and Moon,
In the sky as king and queen!
Land of our fathers, thrive!
Land of houses and of farms!
In the ancient times, they say,
Kunti, mother of the Pándus,
Ruled the six and fifty countries
Of the mighty Jambudwípa,
Famous from the earth to heaven,
To the borders of the ocean.
But in our days there rules
By the grace of God Almighty
On the glorious throne of England
Our gracious noble Queen,
Beauteous like a string of pearls,
Like the sweet and fragrant jasmin.
And the Lord and General *
Of her great and valiant armies,
Raised in ev'ry land the banner
Of his Queen and Sovereign;
And, the sword in mighty hand,

* The Duke of Wellington.

Conquered kingdom after kingdom,
Conquered our happy land,
Like the bright and starry heaven
Full of villages and houses,
Houses full of blooming children
Like a garden full of flowers;
And the young men fine and stately
Like the royal Sampigé;
Like a string of choicest pearls
Like the flower of the forest
Are the wives, and all their childre
Like the sweet and fragrant jasmin
Happily they live, and prosper.
And their cattle are increasing
Like the game in mighty jungles.
Rice and paddy are abundant
Like the sand along the Kávéri.
By the grace of our Queen
All the people of this country
Suffer neither want nor hardship.
Happily they live, and prosper,
Free from terror and from danger;
Like the deer in holy forests,
Where the gun is never fired,
Nor the hounds attack and slaughter.
Thus our gracious noble Queen
Guards this country and defends it
In the shadow of her wings.
Thus the Governor of India,
Thus the English rule this country
By the grace of God the Highest.
May God bless the noble Queen,
Ruling our happy country;
May He keep her and defend her.
May she gather mighty armies,
Terrible to all her foes,
To her friends a kind protector,
May she govern all the earth!
On the fiery steed of battle,

Riding forth the world to conquer,
The commander of her armies
Vanquished all her enemies;
Sitting on the throne of judgment
Executed right and justice.
As you shoot the ruddy samber,
So he slew his adversaries.
When the great and valiant hero
Had destroyed the royal tiger, *
All the flocks lived free and happy.
Fearless all the nations dwell
Near and far in the dominions
Of our gracious Queen and Ruler.
Long live our noble Queen
By the grace of God Almighty
To protect this happy Coorg-land!

The chanting of these songs is very simple and varies only within a range of 3 notes which are intoned with a slow tremulous and rather melancholy utterance, especially when accompanied by the rude native instruments, the monotony of which, however exciting to a crowd, is grievous to a musical ear. The Coorg instruments are: the *Pare* and *Kudikepare*, a large and small wooden drum, the *Dudi*, a metal drum, the *Kombu* or brass horn and the *Tála* or cymbal.

It may be expected, that the Coorgs, who are a shrewd and good-humoured people indulge also in racy proverbs, with which they spice their conversations during their idle hours, or when convened in solemn meetings in the Ambala of the village-green. The following are a few specimens:—

1. Paṭṭama pádekága, pireke karikága
Beppeneke beohaka pireke karikáku
Poppaneke pottaka paṭṭama paḍekáku.

Brahmins are worthless for fighting, the pirike fruit (Colocynth) useless for curry, but if the pirike is properly dressed, it may be

* Tippu Sultan.

used for curry. With proper management even Brahmins may fight.

2. **Peiyu kartaka, pálu kartadá?**
If the cow is black, will the milk be black?

3. **Andü maḍapavana kanḍü naḍakanḍu.**
Him who holds sway we must obey.

4. **Andü portavangü áche porpokü keiyá?**
Have we endured for one year, and can we not endure for a day?

5. **Kettuvökü bandavang totaka buḍuvá?**
He who is doomed to loose his head, will he be freed for making Salám?

6. **Kóndale keichaka kóime naḍaku.**
He who can spend money is accounted an honorable man.

7. **Kumbiyeṭṭu kakudi adirallariyu.**
He who indulges in toddy in the fine season will find out his mistake in the monsoon.

III. PART.

The History of Coorg.

1. THE LEGENDARY PERIOD OF THE KĀVÉRI-PURĀNA.

The ancient annals of Coorg history are the Kávéri-Purána which forms an episode in 4 chapters (11—14) of the Skanda- or Kártikéya-Purána; but in a brahminical legend we must not look for the simple record of a popular tradition. The Brahmins, the creative minds of the old Indian literature, had it in their power to mould any original tradition into whatever shape they pleased for the furtherance of their own interests.

It has ever been their policy, as gods terrestrial, to lay claim to the whole Indian world, their great champion Parshuráma having presented to their Patriarch Kashiyappa as a gift the conquered earth, the Jambudwípa, after the defeat of the Kshetrias and the destruction of their 18 tribes. The primitive gods of the nations of Jambudwípa or India were either turned into Avatáras of Vishnu or incorporated as Demons with the host of Siva, the high mountains were peopled with celebrated Rishis or hermits, and the mightiest and most fertilizing rivers brought into relationship with the principal brahminical deities. Ganga and Kávéri fell to the lot of Siva; Krishna and Gódáveri were sacred to Vishnu.

The Kávéri-Purána or Kávéri-Mahátmya (glorification of Kávéri) describes the sacred river from its source to its union with the sea and enumerates the holy bathing places and the temples on its banks. The Purána had naturally to treat also of Coorg, where the Kávéri rises, and accomplished the task as it would best suit brahminical interests. This was no easy matter. We have seen, how ill the tough materials of the wild world of Coorg suited brahminical taste; how these illiterate and untamable hunters seem to have ever had an instinctive antipathy to, and thorough contempt for, the sanctities and pretensions of the smooth and crafty Brahmins and that these were not slow in returning the compliment has been described in former pages.

The author of the Kávéri-Mahátmya, of which a Canarese translation has been made in 1864 by Srínivásеyengar at the desire and expense of the late Head Sheristadar, Biddianda Nanchappa, does not appear to have been very skilful; for anticipating no serious criticism he allowed his fancy to run away with his better judgment.

The story of the invisible river Sujyóti, joining the Kánake and Kávéri is a lame imitation of the northern tale, that Sarasvati, a stream of great renown among the Brahmins, is not lost, as it seems, in the desert sands, but joins the Ganges and the Jumna (Yamuna), unseen, at Prayága. The holy Sarasvati must have an end worthy of its sanctity. But here in the Kávéri-Purána the third, altogether invisible, stream Sujyóti is an idle fable introduced only to complete a southern trinity of holy rivers. The extraordinary anachronism of Párvati's blessing given to Chandravarma, the founder of the Coorg people, who is thereby rendered victorious over the Mlechas or Turks, who made their first appearance about 500 years ago, transgresses even the thoughtless audacity of a Purána; for the Purána belongs according to its own account to the age of the Rishis, who were long extinct, when the Turks appeared. The numerous passages, inculcating the duty of the valiant Coorgs, to offer to the Brahmins the honors and gifts due to them, have met with singularly bad success. The Coorgs, it would appear, never troubled themselves much about the contents and the admonitions of the Kávéri book, and, though the translation of it was designed to make it accessible to them, it is so highly spiced with Sanscrit and old Canarese expressions, that few do understand it.

The Kávéri-Purána seeks to glorify the holy river. Its divine origin, its connection with the Rishi Agastya, (the settler of the Vindhya-mountain-range, the great son of both Mitra and Varuna), and its course through the eastern country into the sea in obedience to the counsel of Agastya, all conspire to give it a character of surpassing sanctity.

The seizure of the Amrita, the produce of the ocean-churning by the Asuras, spread consternation and despair among the hosts of the gods. They invoked the great Vishnu, the lord of all. He had compassion on them. From him Móhini emanated,—Lakshmi at the same time sending forth Lópámudre (a form of Párvati),—charmed the Asuras by her transcendent beauty, and restored the drink of immortality to the gods. After having delivered the gods, she retired to Brahmagiri—where the sources of the Kávéri now are—and was changed into a rocky cave.' Lópámudre was given to Brahma, who brought her up as his daughter. Thus ends the first act, the scene (true Purána fashion) being laid in the heavens. The second act passes to the earth. Kavéra Muni retires to Brahmagiri, there to give himself wholly to meditation on Brahma. He asks Brahma for children. Brahma—how could he refuse the prayer of his devout Rishi?—gives him Lópámudre for a daughter. She, in order to procure beatitude for her new father, resolves on becoming a river, pouring out blessings on the earth, and all the merits arising from this course of devoted goodness, are to be appropriated to Kavéra Muni. For this purpose she resorts to one of the heights of Brahmagiri and invokes Brahma, to give her the privilege, when turned into a river, of absolving all people bathing in the holy waters, from every sin they may have committed. Brahma, of course, grants this blessing to his daughter. Now another person appears upon the stage, who is to control the future course of Kavéra Muni's daughter. While Kávéri is still absorbed in her devotions, the great Rishi Agastya espies her, and forthwith asks her to become his wife. Though longing after the fulfilment of her vow, she consents to live with Agastya, under the condition, however, that she shall be at liberty to forsake him, whenever she is left alone. One day Agastya went to bathe in the river Kánake, leaving Kávéri near his own holy tank, guarded by his disciples. Thus deserted by Agastya against his promise, she plunged into the holy tank and flowed forth from it a beautiful river. The disciples tried to stay her course. She went under ground. At Bhágandakshétra she appeared again, and flowed on towards Valamburi. When Agastya, on his return, saw what had happened, he ran after Kávéri, begged her pardon, and entreated her to return and to remain with him. Unwilling to change her mind, yet loth to grieve Agastya, Kávéri divided herself, one half flowing off a river, the other half staying with the Rishi. Agastya then explained to the River-half, which road to take to the eastern sea, enumerating all the holy places lying in the way of the new stream.

Previous to this origin of the Kávéri river, a Brahmin, Suyajna, performed great devotions to Vishnu at Dhátripura, a spot near the fountain of the Kávéri. Vishnu appeared to him. Suyajna asked the god, to give him Mukti, (beatitude i. e. in the Hindu sense, loss of consciousness, even of self; individuality being the source of sin and misery) and to render him a benefactor of the world. Vishnu gave him Sujyóti for a daughter, and told him, "*she* will be a benefactress of the world, and *her* merit shall be thine. Go to the Agni Hill.

Kánake, a servant of Dévéndra, lives there. Into her charge give Sujyóti, and do thou attend to thy devotions". Suyajna fulfilled the command of Vishnu. Sujyóti joined Kánake in her meditations. After a while Dévéndra came on a visit, and asked Sujyóti to become his wife. She promised to obey; but secretly she opened her mind to Kánake and told her, what grief she felt at having to be Dévéndra's wife instead of becoming a river. Both of them set off immediately as two streams, Kánake and Sujyóti. Dévéndra finding himself cheated, cursed Sujyóti, and said: let thy waters disappear. Whereupon Sujyóti begged his forgiveness, when Dévéndra, pitying her, said: when Kávéri will appear, you and Kánake may join her and in her company go to the great sea. This word of Dévéndra was fulfilled, when Kávéri flowed forth from the holy tank of Agastya.

(There are only two streams, let it be remembered, which join at Bhágamandala. The Kávéri runs under ground for some distance, which is accounted for in the Purána by the interference of Agastya's disciples.)

Now follows a glowing description of all the holy country. In the eleventh chapter Sanaka and the other Rishis ask Sútapuránika about the country, in which the sources of the river Kávéri are. What name has it? they inquire; and what is the origin of the name? What are the frontiers of the country, its customs, its tribes?

To these questions Sútapuránika replies by repeating the account given in times of old to the king Dharmavarma by the Rishi Dalbhya. The frontiers of the country are these:— it lies to the west of Rámanáthapura; (thither the earth in the form of a cow went to implore Shiva's help against the Rákshasas, who destroyed her; her stony form is still to be seen there, says the bard. There Ráma, to atone for his murder of the Brahma-descended Rávana, consecrated in Shiva's name the holy Linga), to the north of the renowned Parshuráma's

Kshétra (holy land); three gávuda (6 leagues) to the east of the western sea; to the south of Kanva Rishi's habitation. From east to west it measures 6 yójana (72 miles), from north to south 3 yójana (36 miles).

The country has three names: the first, *Brahmakshétra*; the second, *Matsyadésha*; the third, *Kródadésha*. The origin of these names is as follows:—

a. When Brahma performed his pilgrimage over the world, i. e. India, he came to Sahyádri, where he saw a strange sight. A Nelli tree (Phyllanthus emblica) stood before him spreading a hundred boughs. As he looked at the tree, he beheld the form of Vishnu with shell, discus and club. The next moment, when he fixed his eye upon it, he saw nothing but a bare tree. Upon this Brahma worshipped Vishnu many days, pouring upon the tree out of his holy vessel water from the Virajá river. (This river is not to be found in modern geography; it runs beyond the seven seas, which surround the world). On this account the country, from which the holy river Kávéri springs, has been named Brahmakshétra.

b. Of the second name two accounts are given. There is a mountain called Halfmoon in this country, the bard says. Near it there is a holy spring. In it Vishnu took the form of a fish and worshipped Shiva. Shiva blessed the fish with immortality, and Vishnu gave the country the name of the Fish-country (Matsyadésha). The second account contains the root of Coorg tradition. Siddhártha the king of the renowned Matsyadésha, had four sons. They were learned, heroic, strong in battle. The first of them longed to rule his father's kingdom. The second was addicted to pleasure, and served his elder brother. The third had a turn for philosophy. The fourth, the most talented of the four, gave himself to ascetic exercises and visited all the Tírthas (places of holy water washing away sin), but he felt also a strong desire after dominion, and was fond of worldly pleasure. His name was

Chandravarma. In due time he took leave of his father and set out to seek his fortune. He was accompanied by a goodly army. He visited in turn many of the holy places, Jagannáth, Tirupati, Kanchi (Conjeveram), Chidambara. At Shríranga he worshipped Ranganátha. At Dhanushkóti he bathed according to the precepts of the Shástras. Thence to Rámésh-vara, to Anantashayana (Cochin), at last to Brahmádri. Here he dismissed his army and devoted himself to the worship of Párvati. Pleased with the fervent worshipper, the goddess appeared to him, and permitted him to ask a boon. Chandravarma replied: "I desire a kingdom, better than my father's. I desire a wife of my own caste and a fruitful mother of children. I desire victory over mine enemies, I desire entrance into Shiva's heaven after death." Párvati replied: "all your desires shall be fulfilled, except the second. On account of the sins of a former life, you cannot obtain children born of a wife of your own caste. This wish you must forego in this life, in another life it may be fulfilled. You shall, however, have a wife of your own caste, and be enabled to fulfill every holy rite. But, besides her, you shall have a Shúdra wife." Saying this, she created a Shúdra woman, twelve years old, adorned with every charm, and gave her to Chandravarma. He received her at the hand of Párvati, "but," said he full of sorrow, "what will be the use to me of Shúdra children? I shall not have a real full-born son, and shall be debarred from heaven. What then is a kingdom to me? What is to me enjoyment? What then shall I do with this girl? Take back this woman, O Párvati!" Párvati says: "give up your sorrow, O Chandravarma. Through my grace thou shalt be happy in this life and in the life to come. Hear my word! Eleven sons shall be born unto thee. They will not be Shúdras. Being children of a Kshetriya father and a Shúdra mother, they will be called Ugra (fierce men). They will be valiant men, worshippers of myself and Shiva, righteous, true and faithful, devoted to the Brahmins, fit to rule, honored by kings, in every respect, except the possession of the four Védas and six Angas, equal to the Kshetriyas. They will be thy joy in this life and in the next. In this holy country I will appear, in due time, a river rich in blessings, the daughter of Brahma, the daughter of Kavéra Muni, the wife of Agastya. From the sacred tank of the Rishi, near the roots of the holy Nelli tree, in the month of Tulá, I will flow forth and give many blessings to thy sons from love to thee. The country is dear to me as mine eye. Mlénchhas have now rule over it, enemies of gods and Brahmins, destroyers of elephants and other living things, subverters of the law, sword-handed, wrathful, of terrific valour, with frightful bodies, a burden of the earth, the offspring of drunkenness. By my grace go forth to conquer them. Do thou become the king of this land, uphold the laws and establish holy Brahmins." Párvati gave him a victorious sword, a white horse, quick as wind, and an army, and sent him against the Mlénchhas (Turks). Upon this Párvati disappeared. Chandravarma, by Párvati's blessing, overcame the Mlénchhas. Then he collected his army, all the Rishis and all the Brahmins, to celebrate his marriage with a woman of his own caste, according to the Shástras. Both the king and the queen were crowned by the Rishis and Brahmins. Chandravarma now gave houses and lands to the Brahmins, and called also other tribes to settle in his kingdom. The country was called Matsyadésha, because a son of the king of Matsyadésha was its first king.

c. The third name of the country is Kródadésha. The following account is given of its origin. Chandravarma was the best of kings. His Kshetriya queen was barren, but his Shúdra wife bore him eleven sons. The first-born of them was Dévakánta. He and all his brothers were brought up according to the word of Párvati. Like Kshetriyas they received the name, the holy cord and the tonsure, with due ceremonies. When they arrived at maturity, Chandravarma was anxious to obtain for them wives worthy of such princes. He heard, that the king of Vidarbhadésha had a hundred daughters born of Shúdra mothers. Ambassadors were sent to Vidarbha Ráya, who cheerfully agreed to give his daughters in marriage to the valiant sons of Chandravarma. He himself accompanied them to the mountains of the Matsya country and to the palace of Chandravarma. A great royal marriage-feast ensued. Dévakánta, the first-born of Chandravarma, received twenty of Vidarbha Ráya's daughters in marriage. The second son sixteen, the third twelve, the fourth ten, the fifth and sixth each eight, the seventh and eighth princes received each seven of the princesses, and to each of the three youngest sons of Chandravarma four of the daughters of Vidarbha Ráya were given. When all the festivities were concluded, Vidarbha Ráya returned to his own country, but a good number of his people stayed with his daughters in the country of their adoption. Chandravarma's family multiplied greatly. Vidarbha Ráya's daughters became, by the blessing of Párvati, fruitful mothers. When age came upon Chandravarma, he grew tired of the world and of his kingdom. He called his sons together, placed the crown on Dévakánta's head, exhorted his sons to love and union, and retired with his two wives to the Himálaya, there to spend the rest of his days in the worship of Párvati and self-mortifying exercises. Before his departure, he told his sons and grandsons, that Párvati would soon be born in their country as the holy river Kávéri; "and you will be happy," he added, "as long as you abide in the worship of Brahmins, of Shiva and of Párvati."

Dévakánta was now king. All the houses of Chandravarma's sons abounded in children. Each of them had more than a hundred sons. They were all mighty men of valour, strong of arm and foot. Their nails resembled the fangs of boars. Ere long there was not room enough for them. The produce of their fields did not suffice to feed them. But they righted themselves soon. They went out to prepare new fields for themselves. With the nails of their strong hands and feet they tore up the ground and levelled the slopes of the hills with the valleys in a circumference of five yójanas. Then they settled themselves anew in the country, the face of which they had changed by the strength of their own arms. Around them they planted houses and families of Brahmins and other castes. Because this re-establishment of the country resembled the renowned deeds of the Varáhávatára (the boar-incarnation of Vishnu), the country of Chandravarma's sons was henceforth called Kródadésha, and its inhabitants Króda people. This word Króda is said to have been changed and corrupted by degrees into Kodagu, which is the present, and probably was the original, name of the country.

From the time of the departure and prophecy of Chandravarma, his sons and their people waited for the appearance of the holy river Kávéri. Two days before Tulásankramana (the time of the sun entering the sign of Libra) Párvati appeared in a dream to king Dévakánta, and ordered him to assemble his whole people in a place, called Valamburi. There she would appear to them. Accordingly the whole tribe assembled at Valamburi. The river came rushing down the valley, and the assembled Coorgs bathed in the fresh flood. The violence of the stream turned off the knots of the women's dresses round to their backs, and the Coorg women (says the Purána) wear their gowns in this fashion until this day, in remembrance of the first bathing of the Coorgs in the water of the Kávéri at Valamburi. In the middle of the stream, Párvati appeared in person. "Ask a boon of me," she cried. The Coorgs asked for fecundity, for dominion, for riches and for a priest. Párvati answered: "well; a priest you will find near the fountain of the Kávéri, a friend of my father Kavéraráya, who has for three lives worshipped me" ('three lives' does not here mean, father, son and grandson, but three actual lives of the same person, who worshipped Párvati until his death, and, when he was born again according to Hindu theory, spent his second life, and after that his third life, in the service of the goddess.) The Coorgs went and found him at the sources of the Kávéri. He taught them during a whole month, which they spent there, how to prepare food for their ancestors, and other holy rites. Since that day all the Coorgs assemble each year in the month of Tulá (October—November) to celebrate the great festival of their tribe in honour of Kávéri.

2. POPULAR TRADITION.

Disappointed by the extravagant brahminical legends regarding the origin and early history of the Coorgs, we naturally expect, that the Coorg bards, who in their Palamés so graphically and with truthful simplicity depict the domestic and social events of Coorg life, would with equal artlessness have preserved the early pages of their country's history; but Coorg shares in the general fate of primitive Indian history—the dark ages are left with hardly a ray of reassuring light. Coorg tradition has been supplanted by Brahminism and what information one is able to obtain is in most cases but a faint echo of the legends of the Kávéri Purána or some other brahminical imposition. There is, however, one story free from this imputation, and it is of considerable value as it throws light on the origin of some of the Coorg deities, who are not the creations of brahminical fancy, though their shrines are now presided over by Brahmins. The story is taken from oral tradition, and runs thus:—In ancient times there lived in the Malabar country six brothers and a sister.

Five of them, accompanied by their sister, Ponnangálatamma, went to Coorg by the Páditoraghát. While they were on the road, four of them said: "How is it that our sister comes with us; the people will say, that she is our wife?" One of them replied: "If she comes with us, we will spoil her caste.' When they came to the Chouripadé-hill near the Kakabé river they felt hungry. Then Iguttappa said to his sister: "Prepare us some food." She replied: "There is no fire nor rice." Iguttappa said: "I will give you rice, but you must boil it without fire." She replied: "I will boil it without fire, but you must eat it without salt." To this the brothers agreed. Then Ponnangálatamma, seeing a cow, which belonged to the Paradandra house went and milked her, letting the milk fall into a chatty full of rice, and while the brothers were sleeping in the shade of a tree, went to the bank of the river and buried the pot in the sand, where it began to boil. Then she called her brothers to eat the rice which she had prepared. When they had eaten enough, Iguttappa took some rice, threw it up into the air and exclaimed: "See how the hail is descending from the sky." Ponnangálatamma, angry at this, took a wooden ladle, gave him a heavy blow on his back and said: "See how the thunder breaks in the monsoon." Then the brothers all laughed at him. Afterwards, while they were sitting together and chewing betel, Pálúrappa said: "Let us see whose betel is the reddest." Then they all spat out the betel into their hands, looked at it, and the brothers threw the betel behind their heads, pretending that they were throwing it again into their mouth and chewing. The sister, deluded by this, threw the betel into her mouth again, and went on chewing. They now said that she had lost her caste. Their brother in Malabar too, to whom they appealed, confirmed their decision. Ponnangálatamma was excessively grieved, and wept bitterly. Iguttappa afterwards threw an arrow from the Iguttappabetta and ordered his sister to go with the arrow and stay where it fell. The arrow struck into a mango tree at Ponnangála in the village of Yawakkapádi. Ponnangálatamma, assuming the shape of a crane, flew towards Ponnangála. Near the Karatandra house some Holeyas were working in the paddy fields. Ponnangálatamma flew upon one of them, who became possessed with a devil, and ran towards the tree, in which the arrow was sticking. The brothers afterwards separated into different villages, where they settled. The whole family were afterwards worshipped as gods. Beytúrappa has a temple at Beytur in Malabar, the second in Taliparambu in Malabar, the third in the Maletambira forest in the Chómamale in Coorg, the fourth on the Iguttappa-hill near Kunjila, the fifth at Pálúr in Kuyangérinád, the sixth, Tirnalli-Timmeya at Tirnally in the Wynád. A temple was also built for Ponnangálatamma round the tree, where the arrow had stuck. At her annual feast, in April, Ponnangálatamma weeps, and is worshipped by the Holeyas. The arrow is, up to the present day, seen sticking in the wild mango tree.

Regarding the ancient government of Coorg the popular tradition states, that the country was divided into 12 Kómbus (districts) and 35 Náds (subdivisions) ruled over by petty chiefs, called Náyakas who lived in constant feuds amongst themselves and gradually succumbed to the wily encroachments of the Háleri-Polygars about whom more anon.

3. CONJECTURES REGARDING THE ORIGIN AND EARLY HISTORY OF THE COORGS.

In the absence of any reliable records prior to the Mussulman historian Ferishta who at the end of the 16th century casually mentions, that Coorg was governed by its own princes, our conjectures regarding its history anterior to this period are but guesses at the truth, based upon collateral circumstances, the nucleus of brahminical legends and Coorg traditions.

The name "Coorg", which is a corruption of the native name "Kodagu" needs not the elaborate and forced derivation of the Kávéri-Purána however well it may have served its purpose to mystify the natives. "Kodi" means in the Coorg dialect a top or peak, and Kodagu in Canarese signifies the same, so that "Kodagu" is emphatically the *Mountainous country*.

We have seen that the Coorg language and the antebrahminical demon- and ancestor-worship are rooted in the Dravidian stock; we need therefore not go beyond the Dravidian family, to seek the origin of the Coorgs. They are certainly not the offspring of the Kshetria Pándus, as some brahminised Coorgs would have it, for the Pándus had perished in the snows of the Himalayas centuries before the Coorgs through the Mahá Bhárata even heard of their existence. It is however not unlikely, that the Coorgs were somehow connected with the Pándya kingdom which flourished in the south of India perhaps in the fifth century before Christ; but the Mahá Bhárata Pándus have nothing to do with this Pándyan kingdom, whose rulers were not Kshetrias, but belonged to the agricultural class. Like the Nairs in Malabar, the Bants and Tulu Gaudas in Canara and the Vokkaligas and Gaudas of Nagara, the Coorgs are—in the brahminical scale—Súdras. The original inhabitants of Coorg were very likely a branch of the cognate South-Indian tribes, and their number may have been augmented by immigrants from the countries just named, who settled at various periods, perhaps under the pressure of national calamities, or attracted by the sheltering forests and fertile soil of Coorg. The now ruined fort Pálpáre five miles to the east of Ponapét in Kiggatnád, is said to have been built by the Béda- or huntertribe; the tradition of the Padinalknád Coorgs already narrated, as well as Malayálam influence on Coorg superstition, points to a settlement of Malayálam immigrants, and it is not unlikely, that in the days of the formidable Bellála dynasty, which was, or pretended to be, of the Zádu branch of the Rájputs, a military settlement was effected in Coorg, as the Bellála Rájahs held sway over the whole of Karnata together with Malabar, the Tamil country and part of Telingana. When this kingdom was subverted by the Mlénchhas or Mussulmans about A. D. 1310 or 11, under Káfur, the western provinces and Coorg amongst them seem to have escaped the ravages of the conquerors, but ten years later Khusru was sent to complete the work of destruction; it is, however, supposed that the expedition extended only to Coorg (vide Elphinstone's and Marshman's Histories of India). This Mussulman conquest in the Deccan was of short duration. In 1336 already their possessions passed into the hands of the Vijayanagara kingdom and there can be little doubt, but that Coorg was included amongst its dominions, perhaps as an outlying neglected and wild jungle district, at least there are no records whatever in token of an early state of civilization. Col. Wilks in his History of Mysore Vol. II. p. 103 states, that the Coorgs are conjectured "to be descended from the conquering army of the Cadumba kings," whose capital was Banawási, in the southeast corner of the present Soonda or Sóde district of North-Canara. On what evidence this conjecture is based, he does not explain. It points, however, to the same conclusion, that a military settlement of some branch of the neighbouring ruling dynasties was effected in Coorg and this opinion is also supported by the Kávéri-Purána in its account of *Matsyadésha*, the puránic name of Coorg, as already stated. After the battle of Tálicóta in January 1565, the monarchy of Vijayanagara and with it the Hindu power of Southern India were broken and the country fell into the hands of petty princes or of those insurgent officers of the old government since so well known as Zemindars or Polygars.

Up to this time the little Coorg country seems to have been of no political importance. Its chiefs, called Náyakas, ruled over their small Kómbus (districts), levied taxes within their dominions, which they guarded by boundary and defensive ditches (the Cadangas) and to assert and maintain their self-constituted importance they engaged in frequent feuds amongst themselves. The Keimatta or ancestral monument of the Achu-Náyaka of Anjigheri-nád in Kiggatnád taluq is still in good preservation. The family was exterminated about 60 years ago. Of the Beppunád chiefs the name of Utta Náyaka of the Arméri house is still in popular remembrance. In Padinalknád the name of Karanembáu, the chief at Bhágamandala is mentioned with veneration. There may have been more Náyakas, and very likely one over each of the 12 Kómbus or districts, but the names of their houses are no longer known.

According to the Ráya Paddhati in Dr. Francis Buchanan's "Journey from Madras through Mysore etc." vol. III. p. 125, one of the chief Polygars, who on the decline of Vijayanagara assumed independence, was Sadásiva, the son of the Gauda of Kilidi or Ikeri. Being endowed with a government comprising Guty, Bárakuru, and Mangalúru, his name was changed into Sadásiva-Ráya-Náyaka and he and his descendants, who were styled Rájas of Kilidi or Ikeri, possessed the government for 203 years (from 1559-60 to 1762-63 A. D.)

From intelligent Coorgs I have learnt, that during the reign of this neighbouring dynasty an Ikeri prince came to Coorg, and settled in Hálerinád. At first he assumed the pious garb of a Jangam or Lingaite priest and as such gained a considerable influence over the people of the surrounding Náds. When feeling sure of his position, he imposed upon his followers instead of the voluntary Dhúli-batta (dusty-grain) a regular tax of one and a half butty of rice and nine annas eight pies in cash per house per annum. His next step was to call upon the people, in alternate parties to guard his dwelling on the Háleri farm. These watchmen were called *Chaudigara*, a name ever afterwards retained for the Coorg Rájahs' troops. Having openly declared himself and being acknowledged by his adherents ruler of Háleri and of the surrounding Náds, the Padinalknád Karanembáu Náyaka also submitted and so did the others under the condition, that they should receive three-fourths of the revenue and pay one-fourth to the Háleri chief. His increasing power soon threatened the safety of the Coorg Náyakas, who at last were put to death and the whole country brought under the Háleri government.

That the Coorg Rájahs were aliens to the country is evident from the fact, that they were Lingaites, whilst the Coorgs maintained their own crude form of demon- and ancestor-worship and rarely joined the Shiváchóries. These are most numerous in north-east Coorg where the people are closely allied with the Mysoreans, and where the influence of the Rájahs was naturally greatest. Again in Padinalknád the Malayálam element seems to be predominant, whilst in Táwunád, Benganád and Surlabimuttanád the Tulu Gaudas and Bants make their influence felt. If a further proof were required to show that the Coorgs are a mixed race, I need only mention, that besides the striking difference in features and colour of the Coorgs, varying between the Caucasian and Mongolian physiognomy and between a fair and dark skin, the house-names also of many Coorg families clearly point to Mysore, Tamil, Malayálam or Tulu origin. Even within the memory of the present generation strangers were received by and incorporated with the Coorgs. There is now a dispute pending about six families in Kiggatnád, who ten years ago were, by the Head-Sheristadar Nanchappa, received as Coorgs, but after his death were expelled from the clan by the rest of the Coorg people. The settlement of the dispute will perhaps be only a matter of time, but not of intrinsic caste spirit which as such is inconsistent with the notorious Coorg practice of assimilating cognate tribes into one clan, and with the fact, that during the Seringapatam captivity of thousands of Coorg families by Tippu Sultan, most of them were forcibly made Mussulmans and, though on the return to their country, they abjured Islam, the very process of circumcision deprived them of their previous caste—in a brahminical sense—and rendered that of their descendents defective. The renown of the Coorgs lies certainly not in the purity and antiquity of their genealogy, but in the union and strength of so many discordant elements into one compact body or clan, that bravely fought on every occasion of danger for the honour and safety of their adopted country, whether under the leadership of their own Náyakas or their alien Rájahs, and there can be no doubt that they would in time of need, with equal loyalty rally round the standard of their English Rulers!

To the question, how such a conglomerate of divers tribes could have been formed into an almost homogenous body, I would reply, that what might perhaps have been impossible amongst a civilized and politically powerful state, was a comparatively easy process in a small uncivilized and secluded hill-country, which, seldom influenced by the politics of its more powerful neighbours, and in blissful ignorance undisturbed by subtle religious disputes, vented its savage strength in intestine feuds, till the despotic hand of the alien usurper subjected the turbulent chiefs, and united them and their adherents in deadly combat against common foes or for marauding expeditions. Their defeats as well as their achievements originated and strengthened national sympathies which time matured into a healthy spirit of clanship, that asserted itself the stronger, the narrower its local limits were confined, and the less it came into civilizing contact with surrounding nations. With the ascendancy of the Ikeri princes in Coorg, who spoke Canarese, this language became the written official medium and counteracted the Malayálam influence; but, however great the latter may have been through the intellectual superiority of the Malayálam people over the savage Coorg mountaineers, who dreaded their supposed supernatural powers, it never laid a beneficial hold on the Coorg mind by imparting the means of acquiring knowledge in the Malayálam tongue. It is true the horoscopes which the Kanyas wrote and still write for the Coorgs are in the Malayálam language, but they are unintelligible to the Coorgs. Thus it was left to the Coorg Rájahs of the Ikeri house to mould or rather to disfigure the Coorg mind into the character in which the English found it on their assumption of the Government in 1834; that it was of the most pitiable description, we have enough evidence to adduce: Lieut. Connor describes thus the condition of the people under Lingarája—and the picture applies equally well to the times of his predecessor and of the late Rájah—: "The chief of Codagu exercises an authority, that knows no restraint. He shares in common with the gods, the homage of the people and a more than ordinary portion of eastern humiliation is observed towards him; he is approached with a reverence due alone to the deity and addressed with all the servility fear could yield, or despotism claim; in his presence, in which no subject dare be seated or indeed within the precincts of his fort, the subject clasps his hands as in the act of prayer—the last sign of slavish vassalage—; and he is accosted in a language quite correspondent with this suppliant attitude; his subjects know no duty more imperious than attending to his mandates, which received with veneration are executed with singular precision, and his projects of whatever nature seconded without enquiry; nor would the most presumptuous hazard an opinion as to the propriety of his commands or actions; but fear alone produces this instantaneous compliance with his will, however capricious; and obedience is maintained by an exemplary severity that, however it may command submission, cannot create affection.

"The rigorous exercise of such unbounded power will of course be tempered by customs and usages, which having the force of law and sanctity of religion, must challenge some respect, but the real situation of the people is complete slavery; under so arbitrary a sway safety of person and permanency of property must depend on the precarious will of the ruler; political freedom forms no part of the elements of an Asiatic system of government, nor perhaps is it desirable it should; but the inhabitants of this little state are interdicted from almost any share of that practical liberty which their neighbours enjoy."

Col. Fraser, in his despatches to the Supreme Government dated 7th April 1834 states: "The whole and entire power of the country and almost the very faculty of thinking, seem to be concentrated in the Rájah himself, and we shall continue to know little or nothing of the disposition and wishes of the people of Coorg until the utter and permanent abolition of the power of the Rájah shall emancipate them from their present slavish fear."

Again under date 12th April 1834: "Their minds are so abject and enslaved, that they (the Coorgs) dare not speak against their late Rájah or they have not a motive for doing so."

Again in a letter dated 14th July 1834: "If we could succeed in dispelling the moral gloom, that has weighed upon the spirits and faculties of the people, as a consequence of the wretched system of government under which they were placed, an effect that, I am happy to say, is becoming daily more perceptible, I think the small district of Coorg will be found in its ameliorated condition a year or two hence, to possess many advantages denied to other parts of India."

4. HISTORY OF THE COORG RAJAHS AS DELINEATED IN THE RĀJENDRANĀME AND FROM OTHER DOCUMENTARY SOURCES.

From 1633 to 1807.

PREFATORY REMARKS.

The Rájendranáme (account of Rájendra, the king of heroes) is the work of Dodda-Virájendra Vodeya, the hero of Coorg History and the beau ideal of the Coorgs of a warrior king, and comprises, from 1633 to 1807, a period of 175 years 2 months and 7 days.

A manuscript copy of the Canarese original was found in the Archives at Mercara in 1834, and, with the original English translation obtained from the records of the Chief Commissioner's Office at Bangalore, was edited by Dr. Moegling and printed for the Madras Government in the Mangalore Mission Press in 1857. The subjoined seal of the Coorg Rájahs ornaments the front page. The names of the Rájah and of his ancestors as well as those of English Governor Generals, Governors and other high functionaries are written with red ink throughout the book. The chronicle is very well written. It gives the history of Coorg, especially the account of the Rájah's exploits and of his intercourse with the officers of the East India Company in simple language. Not one foolish story, not one improper expression, disfigures this Canarese

book. The language is strongly impregnated with Hindustani words, yet it retains its Canarese character thoroughly, and far surpasses both in composition and idiom the bombastic, would-be classical Canarese translation of the Kávéri-Purána.

The *English translation*, made by Lieut. R. Abercromby in 1808 at Mangalore, renders accurately the contents of Dodda-Virájendra's original, and very likely remained untouched by the Rájah's successors who were unacquainted with the English language. But the *Canarese original* has undoubtedly been destroyed after the preparation of spurious copies one of which remained in the Mercara Archives. A long passage relating to the intrigues of Appájirája, in which the name of Channavíra another relative of the Rájah's is mixed up, does not appear in the English translation by Robert Abercromby, and is probably an interpolation made by the late Rájah after the murder of Channavíra and his family, some time before the year 1825. The two last pages of the English translation, on the other hand, are not to be found in the Canarese original. They were probably expunged by Lingarája or his son, because they contained the last will of Dodda-Virájendra, the suppression of which lay in their interest. The translator, who could have had no motive to deviate from his original, finished the translation almost a year before the death of Virarája. Víravája's guilty successors have dabbled with other documents, forged some and destroyed others. The above conjecture seems, therefore, to be legitimate enough.

As for the trustworthiness of Víarája's history, there is no reason to doubt the veracity of its statements, but it is very far from giving the whole truth. Three principal omissions deserve to be noticed:—

By commencing the history of his family at so late a date, Vírarája escapes the disagreeable necessity of disclosing two circumstances, without a knowledge of which Coorg affairs contain much that is unintelligible, namely the dependence of the Coorg Rájahs on the Ikeri royal family of Shivappa-náyaka, from which probably they descended, and the fact, that they belonged, with the Ikeri family, to the sect of the Lingaites, while the Coorgs themselves are unconnected with any of the general religious systems of India. Hyder and Tippu, after having absorbed the kingdom of Ikeri, claimed the allegiance of the Coorg Rájahs as a matter of course, and knew how to enforce their rights of sovereignty as long as their day of prosperity lasted.

The second point is indicated, indeed, but in the slightest possible manner, that the Coorgs in their plundering expeditions into Mysore, the provinces on the Western Coast and the districts to the north of Coorg, pillaged without mercy the unfortunate towns, villages and farm-houses, which fell into their hands. Remnants of the spoils of the low countries may yet be treasured up among the hoards of the wealthy families of Coorg. Noses, ears and hands were cut off by the Coorg banditti, they deserve no better name, without ceremony, for the sake of the jewels attached to them. The Coorgs became proverbial for wanton cruelty and sensuality in all the surrounding districts, to which they extended their ravages.

Lastly, the Rájah is most careful not even to hint at the system of terror by which he ruled his country. Human life seems to have had very little value indeed in his sight. He had been trained in a bad school. Hyder had cut off one whole branch of the family of the Coorg Rájahs. Víraréja's nearest relatives died in prison at Periapatna, the victims of hunger and disease. At Kurchi, his own wives and children were cut off in one night by the robbers sent from Kóte and led by a traitor, a Brahmin. Amidst bloodshed and rapine he had grown up. No wonder, that he would not spare those who were, or whom he conceived to be, his enemies among his subjects. But the Rájendranáme is studiously silent on these subjects. The book was written for the use of his friends and patrons. For this purpose the English translation was made, at the request of Víraraja by Mr. Abercromby, and Hindustani translations distributed as remembrances among the higher officers in the Company's service. Víraraja was anxious, more anxious than appears to have been natural in a person of his situation, to bear a fair character in the eyes of the English Sirkar. He seems to have been conscious, that to his own people he was an object of terror, probably of hatred, and that he had no friend on earth, but the English Government, whose gratitude he had indeed fully deserved.

The English translation of the Rájendranáme being available for further particulars, a succinct summary may suffice our present purpose.

A. PRINCES OF COLLATERAL LINES.

1633—1780.

a. Muddurája and his descendents.

The chronicle commences with the reign of Muddurája who is introduced as the son of Appájirája and the grandson of Víraraja. He reigned at Haléri in 1633, but subsequently established himself at Mercara, where he built the Fort and a Palace in 1681. He had three sons: Dodda-Vírappa, Appájirája and Nandarája. After a long reign of 54 years Muddurája died and his eldest son Dodda-Vírappa succeeded him. The second son was settled at Haléri and the third at Horamale.

Dodda-Vírappa, with the harelip, had a son Appájirája who married and had a son, whose name was Chikka-Vírappa Vodeya.

Appáji of Haléri had five sons of whom three died in early life. The eldest Muddaya had a son Appájirája; the second

Lingarája married Dévambikegamma, who bore him a son at the full moon of June 1763, Vírarájendra Vodeya, the author and hero of the Rájendranáme. His two brothers were Lingarája and Appáji.

Of the Horamale branch Nandarája had a son Muddaya whose son was Mallaya.

The relationship of the descendents of the different lines will appear more clearly from the annexed

Genealogical Tree.

Virarája.

Appájirája.

Muddurája.

- *Dodda-Virappa*, at Mercara, born 1657 + 1736.
  - *Appájirája*, born 1680 (?) + 1729.
    - *Chikka-Virappa*, + 1766.
- *Appájirája*, at Haléri, born 1670 (?) + 1737.
  - *Muddaya*, born 1700 + 1770.
    - *Appájirája.*
  - *Lingarája*, born 1710 (?) + 1780.
    - *Virájender Vodeya*, born 1763 + 1809.
    - *Lingarája*, + 1820.
      - *Virarája*, deposed 1834 + 1862.
    - *Appáji*, + 1808.
- *Nandarája*, at Horamale, + about 1738
  - *Muddaya.*
    - *Mallaya.*
      - *Dévapparája*, + 1774.

Such was the state of things in Coorg, when Chikkadéva Vodeya of Mysore, Dodda Channamáji, the mother of Sómashékara Náyaka of Ikeri, Dodda-Sadáshivarája of Sóde, Venkatádri Náyaka of Bélur, Víravasurája of Chirakal lived and ruled their respective principalities. The country of Periapatna and of Coorg were then one. The frontier of

Mysore and Coorg passed between Uddur in Coorg and Kattemálalavádi in Mysore.

b. *Dodda-Vírappa.*

In the reign of Dodda-Vírappa of Mercara, Nanjunda, his kinsman, was Rájah of Periapatna. Some of his officials opened a treasonable correspondence with Chikkadéva Vodeya of Mysore whom they invited to come and rule over them. Nanjarája, perceiving the threatened danger, went to Mercara to implore the assistance of his relative, who espousing his cause, marched immediately to support him, but on reaching Siddapur he had the mortification to learn, that Periapatna had fallen and that Vírarája, the son of Nanjunda, who had been entrusted with the command of the capital, seeing his situation desperate, had gallantly fallen in its defence, having previously in compliance with the sanguinary dictates of honor, put to death his wives and children to preserve them from polution.

(In Col. Wilk's "History of Mysore" this event is placed in the reign of Canty Reva Narsa Rájah in 1644 and Lieut. Connor in his "Memoir of the Codagu Survey" mentions "Immadi" as the Rájah of Mysore who attacked Periapatna, but he was only 20 years old, when in 1637 he succeeded Cham Ráj and as he was poisoned in 1639, it is not likely, that he attempted the conquest about 50 years later!)

Encouraged by his success the Mysore Rájah, Chikkadéva Vodeya, prepared for the conquest of Coorg. His army advanced but a short way beyond Bálele in Coorg and encamped on the plain of Palupáre, when they were met by the Coorgs. Before daybreak Dodda-Vírappa attacked them and slew 15,000 men with 77 officers, the rest fled back into Mysore. Immediately after this event the Coorg Rájah marched to Tómara, to oppose an invasion of the Rájah of Kotangadi, who with an army of 5,000 Nairs had ascended the Ghats and in a fortified camp at Tómara awaited the issue of the Mysorean campaign.

Dodda-Vírappa had previously detached a body of fifteen hundred men in advance, and the decisive victory gained soon enabled him to follow with a larger force. He made a spirited attack, forced the entrenched camp of Víravarma and destroyed the Rájah and his army at one blow.

After some time Chikkadéva Vodeya invaded Bélur, the country of Venkatadri Náyaka. Dodda-Vírappa, desirous of obtaining a share of the spoil for himself, sent a force northward and seized upon the Yélusávira district. The Mysore Rájah, having occupied most of the country, demanded that district as a part of its territory; but little disposed to restore, what he could claim with as good a right as Chikkadéva, he declined compliance and a predatory warfare ensued which, however, after a short time ended in a compromise: Coorg retaining the district in dispute, but Mysore receiving a portion of the revenue arising from it. On this account the Yélusávira district received the name of Harige Shíme i. e. country belonging to two parties.

Dodda-Vírappa had enjoyed but a short repose, when the Rájah of Chirakal implored his aid against the arms of Sómashékara Náyaka of Ikéri who had already made rapid strides towards the conquest of his territory. The Coorg chief exerted his influence to avert the impending fate; the Náyaka, however, refused to listen to his proposals, pleading the expense of the war in money and men. At last he yielded so far, as to agree to evacuate the country on payment of 18 lacs of Rupees, which Víravarma promised to pay and begged Dodda-Vírappa to become security for him. On Sómashékara's return to Ikéri, he halted some days at Subramanya, where the Coorg Rájah paid him a visit of state. Nine lacs of Rupees had been unhesitatingly paid by Víravarma, but when the second deputation from Coorg came and demanded the balance, he treated them most insolently. Dodda-Vírappa forthwith despatched a force of 5000 Coorgs under his general Jógi Muttana, to ensure a more strict observance of the convention. Payment was delayed, however, from day to day. Muttana at length threatened; whereupon the Malayálam debtor formed a scheme to destroy the whole force, which had come to dun him so disagreeably. Intelligence of this design reaching Muttana, he marched directly to Cannanore, defeating a body of Chirakal troops who opposed his passage, and by means of boats the Coorg force reached Kumbla, a port near Mangalore, and empty handed returned to Coorg through Tulunád. Dodda-Vírappa seems to have taken no revenge on the treacherous Víravarma, but paid the remaining nine lacs to Sómashékara, who presented his kinsman with a number of villages in the Tulu country contiguous to Coorg to supply him with milk (Amrita). Dodda-Vírappa took this opportunity for purchasing the district Sulya with money taken from the Talekávéri temple-treasury, in order to secure a regular supply of cocoanuts for the goddess. The whole district was called *Amara-Sulya* and became a part of the territory of the Coorg Rájahs.

Dodda-Vírappa evinced throughout his long and vigorous reign an unconquerable spirit and, though surrounded by powerful neighbours, neither the number nor strength of his enemies seem to have relaxed his courage or damped his enterprise. He died in 1736, 78 years old. Two of his wives ascended the funeral pile with the dead body of the Rájah.

c. *Chikka-Vírappa.*

On the death of his grandfather Chikka-Vírappa, who in 1730 already had been anointed successor, assumed authority. His early years were clouded by misfortune; having lived in prison from his childhood, he was sickly and subject to nervous complaints. Appájirája, his father, and the only son of the late Rájah, incurring the suspicion of having caused the destruction of his wife at the instigation of a favourite mistress, had been thrown into prison, where he languished for twelve years until his death, when his son who had shared his misfortunes, was released and, like many oriental despots, quitted a prison to seat himself on a throne.

During his weak reign a change, ominous to the destinies of Southern India, took place in the government of Mysore. The restless ambition of an adventurer had succeeded to the peaceful and indolent rule of a Hindu prince, and Mysore, now under the vigorous government of Hyder Ali threatened destruction to the smaller states in its vicinity. He seems early to have turned his thoughts towards Coorg. When Hyder took Ikéri, which was thenceforth called Hydernagara (Nuggur) and incorporated the kingdom with his growing territory, he considered himself the liege-lord of Coorg and, though foiled for a long while in his assertion of suzerainty, at last he succeeded by dint of fraud and force, in coercing the refractory hill-chiefs into a state of vassalage. As a preliminary step he urged the claim on the Yélusávira district, which had been relinquished by a former government. Chikka-Vírappa, unwilling to provoke so powerful an opponent, yielded to the demand; but Hyder, not satisfied with this concession and fertile in expedients, found soon a pretext for breaking with the prince. In 1765 he sent an army under Fazul Ulla Khan against Coorg. On its north-eastern frontier many battles were fought between the two countries. At last the Mysoreans were defeated and Hyder offered to the Rájah of Coorg eternal peace and the Uchingi district, contiguous to the northern frontier of Coorg, for 300,000 pagodas. Chikka-Vírappa acceeded to the proposal. He paid a portion of the sum and sent hostages for the remainder; the stipulations on the part of the Mahomedan commander were as yet unexecuted, when the Rájah died. Having no children, the family of Dodda-Vírappa became extinguished and in its stead the representatives of the Haléri- and Horamale-family, Muddurájah and Muddaya ruled Coorg together in good harmony. They immediately demanded the execution of the treaty, but Hyder, under various pretexts, eluded its fulfilment. After protracted fruitless negotiations, the Rájahs recommenced hostilities. Lingarája, the younger brother of Muddurája, attacked Fyzul Ulla Khan near the Yélusávira district and defeated him. Attempting to retire towards Mangalore by the Bissly Ghaut, his Coorg opponent outmarched and faced him again, and completely routed his army. The whole camp, treasure, guns and ammunition fell into the hands of the Coorgs. Hyder proposed peace. In lieu of the Uchingi country he gave the districts of Panje and Belláre for the sum of 75,000 Rupees already paid to his general and fixed the boundary between Mysore and Coorg at the river Sarve. Thus peace was for a while established in 1768.

d. *Dévapparája and Lingarája.*

In 1770 both Rájahs died, Muddaya and Muddurája. Lingarája of Haléri wished to see his nephew, Muddurája's son, on the throne. On the part of the Horamale family, Malleya the son of Muddaya proposed his own son Dévapparája as successor to the throne of Coorg. A fatal family dispute arose, that led the way to foreign subjection. Lingarája, being unable to force his claims, fled with his son Vírarája and his nephew Appájirája, to seek the powerful aid of Hyder, who at this period exercised supreme control in Mysore. Wolf Hyder was delighted to be chosen umpire between the quarrelling jungle-sheep of Coorg, and promised every assistance to his new clients, whom he kept as his guests at Seringapatam. The irruption of Triyambaka Máva (uncle or father-in-law to Shrímant Peshwa of Poona) which occurred at this juncture,

(1771) gave full employment to Hyder's arms and obliged him, reluctantly to postpone any attempts at improving a circumstance so congenial to his designs.

After the departure of the Mahrattas, a severe famine prostrated the whole of Mysore. Lingarája suggested an expedition into Coorg, where plenty of grain would be found. Hyder Ali took his advice and in 1773 he marched his army into Coorg by way of Arkalgúdu and Bettikanave, but was repulsed with loss in Yedavanád. Intrigue, however, removed the obstacles which force could not overcome. The seed of discord was sown amongst the adherents of the ruling prince and the Mysore troops on again passing the frontier at Bálele, in Kiggatnád, were joined by a large body of Coorgs and marched without opposition straight to the capital, Mercara. Dévappárája sought refuge with the Rájah of Kóte, but true to the character of his house, Víravarma gave the fugitive Coorg an inhospitable reception saying: "Your ancestor, Dodda-Vírappa, took the life of my ancestor Víravarma at Tómara. Your head shall now atone, unless you redeem yourself with a round sum." The hapless refugee paid to his treacherous friend Rs. 1,666; but feeling still insecure, he fled in disguise with only four attendants; but was seized by Hyder's people at Harihar and carried to Seringapatam, where his family lay already in prison, and was murdered together with them. Thus the Horamale branch of the Coorg family was cut off by the sword of Hyder Ali.

The Nawab now offered to restore Coorg to Lingarája, if he paid the expense of the expedition. But the resources of the country being exhausted, he consented to receive a yearly tribute of Rs. 24,000; he also sanctioned the Coorg family to take possession of a part of Wynád, said to have been wrested from them at some remote period; but, apparently repenting of his moderation, he after a few months demanded and obtained, though with constrained assent, the cession of Amara-

Sulya, Panje, Belláre and Yélusávira. With a force of 3,000 Coorgs Lingarája invaded Wynád and erected a wooden fort at Kalpavati, by means of which and a force of 2000 men he kept the district for five years.

When Appájirája died in 1775, Lingarája himself succeeded to the throne, setting aside the claims of his two nephews, whom, however, he brought up together with his own son Vírarája Vodeya. In 1779 the Wynád garrison was obliged to retire, being short of provisions and closely pressed by the Rájah of Kóte. Upon this disagreeable news, Lingarája despatched a body of 2000 Coorgs, headed by his two nephews. On the way this force was intercepted by the Rájah of Kóte and defeated; amongst the slain was one of the princes and the other, being taken prisoner, was soon after put to death.

B. COORG UNDER DODDA-VĪRARĀJENDRA VODEYA.

1780—1807.

a. Virarájendra in Mysore captivity.

Lingarája died in the beginning of 1780. His sons, Vírarájendra Vodeya and Lingarája were of tender age, the eldest being only about 16. Hyder, conceiving it a favourable moment to complete the spoliation, he had so successfully begun, assumed entire possession of Coorg, under the pretence of being guardian to the princes until they would come of age. Meanwhile they were to reside in the fort of Garúru. A Brahmin, Subarasaya, formerly Káranika (Treasurer) of the Coorg Rájah was appointed Commissioner of Coorg by the usurper, and a Mussulman garrison held Mercara fort, which Hyder caused to be strengthened.

Enraged at the abduction of their princes from their country and the Brahmin's lording it over them, the Coorgs broke out in open rebellion in June 1782. On hearing that

Hyder had marched for the Carnatic, to oppose the British army under Sir Eyre Coote, they drove the Mussulmans out of the country and proclaimed their independance.

The death of Hyder prevented an immediate retribution; but Tippu Sultan, his son, was fully determined on the re-conquest of Coorg. He first sent the family of the Coorg Rájahs to Periapatna and after having treacherously seized General Mathews and his officers at Nuggur and reduced Mangalore in 1784, he marched through Coorg on his way to Seringapatam, when he compounded matters with the insurgents. On this occasion, according to Col. Wilk's account, Tippu is said to have harangued the Coorgs on the subject of their moral and political sins in the following words: "If six brothers dwell together in one house, and the elder brother marries, his wife becomes equally the wife of the other five, and the intercourse so far from being disgraceful, is familiarly considered as a national rite; not a man in the country knows his father, and the ascendancy of women and bastardy of your children, is your common attribute. From the period of my father's conquest of the country, you have rebelled seven times and caused the death of thousands of our troops; I forgive you once more; but if rebellion be ever repeated, I have made a vow to God, to honour every man of the country with Islam; I will make you aliens of your home and establish you in a distant land, and thus at once extinguish rebellion and plurality of husbands and initiate you in the more honorable practice of Islam!" But scarcely had Tippu left, when the Coorgs, stirred by the apprehension of incurring his vengeance, again took up arms, and repossessed themselves of their native hills in 1785.

To suppress this revolt, Tippu despatched a force of 15,000 men under Janulabdin. At Ulagulli, in Múdugeri-nád, the Mussulmans were opposed by a body of 4,000 Coorgs, who after a sharp encounter forced them to retire to Bettadapur with the loss of their baggage. The ill success of his general induced Tippu, to take the command in person, and having collected another army, he entered Coorg by the same route and reached Mercara with but little loss, where he effected an amicable settlement. Under pretence of peaceful intentions and conciliatory measures, Tippu allured most of the Coorgs to Talekávéri (in 1785), and when they felt most secure, he seized them suddenly with their families about 85,000 souls, sent them to Seringapatam and, carrying out his former threat, had them forcibly circumcised. On the same auspicious day, when he added so great a number to Islam, he assumed the royal dignity and declared himself independent of Delhi.

Into depopulated Coorg he sent Mussulman landlords and gave to them the lands and slaves of the exiles, besides a supply of labourers from Adwáni in the Bellary district and armed them with a degree of cruel proscription:

"The country is given to you in Jaghir, improve it and be happy; the extermination of those mountaineers being determined on, you are required as an imperious duty, to search for and to slay all who may have escaped our just vengeance; their wives and children will become your slaves." A Brahmin Nágappaya, a nephew of Subarasaya, was charged with the government of Coorg; but was soon convicted of embezzlement and condemned to the gallows, when he fled to the Kóte Rájah in Malabar.

b. Vírarájendra at liberty.

Conflicts with Kóte and Mysore.

Such was the state of affairs, when in December 1788 Vírarájendra (also written Vírarája) Vodeya, accompanied by his wife and his two brothers, Lingarája and Appáji, the principal survivors of the Coorg family, effected his escape from Periapatna after a confinement of six years. Leaving his family in a secure retreat at Kurchi in Kiggatnád, Víra-rája was inveigled beyond the frontier by Nágappaya and fell into the power of Víravarma, the Kóte Rájah, who availed himself of his misfortunes and obliged him after some detention to cede, as an atonement for the death of his ancestor who was slain at Tómara, the site of a fort at that place and to give up for ever three valuable and extensive districts viz. Kiggatnád, Amatnád and Yedenalknád. Complying under the pressure of circumstances, Vírarája thus purchased his freedom and returned to Coorg. A fortnight after Víravarma ascended the Ghats to take possession of the ceded districts. Now came Vírarája's turn. With a number of Coorgs, who had rallied round their chief, he surrounded the camp of the Kóte Rájah, and forced him, not only to return the document, extorted from him at Arala, but to renounce also on his part every claim to the Wynád country.

Vírarája now sallied forth at the head of his Coorgs to fight the Mussulmans. In a short time he had cleared the country of the usurpers from Bissly Ghat to Manantody. Successful plundering expeditions into the Mysore were carried on at the same time and large supplies of cattle and grain carried away into Coorg, where they were divided among the adherents of the Rájah. During this season, full of daring and successful exploits, the gallant Vírarája once, on his return from an expedition into Mysore, found the residence of his family at Kurchi a heap of ruins and ashes. Every soul of his family had been destroyed and all the old family treasures carried off. The runaway Nágappaya had shown the way to a troop of Nair banditti and Mullukurubas, despatched upon this errand of treachery and blood by the fiendish foe of the Coorg Rájahs, the Kóte Arasu.

Tippu Sultan, irritated by these daring incursions, determined on retribution. He ordered a large force into Coorg under the command of Golam Ali, who carried fire and sword all over the country.

Víraája must soon have succumbed to the superiority in numbers and discipline of the Mysoreans, had not a revolt of the Malayálam Rájahs compelled Tippu to order Golam Ali with his army to the Western Coast. The latter was, however, not permitted to leave Coorg unmolested. On his march he was fiercely attacked at the Kodantur-pass and suffered severe losses. Thereupon Tippu sent a considerable reinforcement under four captains, amongst them a Frenchman. Víraája lay in wait for them at the Heggala-pass. The Mysoreans left 800 men dead on the ground and 400 wounded. Their baggage and stores fell into the hands of the hill-men; the whole force might have been destroyed, had not the Coorgs preferred plundering to fighting. The booty came most seasonable. The prisoners were sent back into Mysore.

Tippu was alarmed, and despatched in 1790 Buran-u-din, his own brother-in-law, with a strong army and large supplies to secure Coorg by strengthening the four forts Kushálnagara (Fraserpet) Mercara, Beppunád and Bhágamandala. On his way to Mercara he was attacked and beaten by Víraája, but escaped thither with the loss of one-half of his military stores. Without having seen the other forts, Buran-u-din returned to Seringapatam and concerted with Tippu another campaign for the same purpose; but Víraája anticipated their design by storming and dismantling the several forts. At the head of 1500 Coorgs Víraája marched in June 1789 against Kushálnagara on the banks of the Kávéri. A sally from it checked his advance guard, but coming up with the main body to their support, after an obstinate encounter, he captured the place having closely followed the enemy as they fled in at the gate. The garrison endeavoured to escape by swimming the river, but was pursued with such success, that 500 out of 700 were killed. The Killadár's head was laid at the feet of the

Rájah, Kushálnagara was sacked and the Fort burnt. In August Víraája attacked the Fort of Beppunád. The garrison capitulated and obtained a free passage through Coorg. The Fort was destroyed. By dint of extraordinary exertions Buran-u-din, dividing his army into three columns, succeeded in throwing supplies into the Fort of Bhágamandala, but was repeatedly attacked and beaten on the march and had to fall back on Seringapatam. The capture of the Fort, which was of some strength, speedily followed. Víraája planted his guns on the hill of Mumbáratu and pointed them with his own hand against the Fort which was well defended. After five days the place fell. Three copper-tiles of the temple at Bhágamandala had been destroyed by the Rájah's cannon balls, they were replaced by tiles of silver. After this achievement Víraája sent a detachment into the Tulu country to take possession of Amara-Sulya which Lingarája had ceded to Hyder. There was now only Mercara left in the hands of the Mussulmans, under Ali Beg, but he was cut off from all communication with Mysore and in fact a harmless prisoner.

A few remarks on the military force of Coorg at that time may prove of interest.

The Jamma-Coorgs holding their land by a military tenure in return for the immunities which they enjoyed, all able bodied men of this active and warlike peasantry constituted the Rájahs' military force, which, though irregular in its organization, was kept in constant practice of its duties. These personal services of the Choudigaras or Coorg soldiers as guards for a period of fifteen days at a time, enjoined by the Rájahs and admitted by the ryots, were rendered with cheerful obedience.

Under the chief command of the Rájah, the force, numbering at times from six to ten thousand Coorgs was subdivided into bodies of various strength, the smallest numbering from ten to hundred men under a Jemindar, any larger and more indefinite number was commanded by the Káriagára, who again acted under a Sarva-káriagára or General; both were distinguished by a gold banded scarlet head-dress, the kombu toppi.

As the Coorg force was not a standing army, it received no pay. Whilst on active duty as guards or during warfare, the soldiers were maintained at the public expense, and being remarkable for their predatory habits, they largely shared with the Rájahs in the spoil. Without discipline and organization, the Coorgs displayed their strength chiefly behind their stockades and Cadangas. In the open field they rarely faced the attacks of regular troops.

c. *Víraràja an ally of the East-Indian Company.*

Conclusion of the alliance.

About this period the first connection between the English and the Coorgs took place. Desirous of gaining the friendship of so able a partizan and foreseeing the strategical value of Coorg in the impending struggle with Tippu, the Government of the Company eagerly seized the proffered hand of Víraràja who dreaded and hated Tippu, from whom he could expect no mercy and whose assurances and promises, he knew, he could never trust. His hopes depended on his success in gaining the support of a powerful ally. His eyes were directed towards the rising star of the Company. The union with Tippu's enemies was therefore effected without difficulty. After the receipt of orders from Bombay to conclude in the name of the British Government an offensive and defensive alliance with the Rájah of Coorg, Robert Taylor, the English Chief at Tellicherry invited the Rájah to a conference. Accompanied by Capt. Brown, who had been sent to conduct him to the head-quarters of the Campany on the Western Coast, Víraràja repaired thither in October 1790.

A formal treaty was concluded with the following stipulations:—

1. While the sun and moon endure, the faith of the contracting parties shall be kept inviolate.
2. Tippu and his allies are to be treated as common enemies. The Rájah will do all in his power to assist the English to injure Tippu.
3. The Rájah will furnish for fair payment all the supplies his country affords, and have no connection with other "topiwalahs" (viz. the French).
4. The Company guarantee the independence of Coorg, and the maintenance of the Rájah's interests in the case of a peace with Tippu.
5. An asylum and every hospitality is offered to the Rájah and his family at Tellicherry until the establishment of peace.

God, sun, moon and earth be witnesses!

Signed: *Robert Taylor Esq.* on behalf of the Governments of Madras, Bombay and Bengal.

Vírarájendra Vodeya, Rájah of Coorg.

When Sir Robert Abercromby, the Governor of Bombay, arrived at the coast, the Rájah was invited to an interview and was escorted by an officer and a company of sepoys. He on this occasion, interceded with his new friend, Sir Robert Abercromby for the poor Bibi of Cannanorê and her son. She had made an attempt at decoying to Cannanore and betray into the hands of the Mussulman army the English detachment at Tellicherry; and Sir Abercromby had resolved on deposing her and sending her with her son to Bombay. Vírarájendra effected a reconciliation and thus requited the service, which the Bibi's ancestor, Ali, had rendered to his ancestor, Dodda-Vírappa with the harelip, by delivering his Captain from the hands of the Chirakal Rájah.

First war of the allies with Tippu.

Meanwhile the Mussulman garrison at Mercara had consumed all its provisions. Tippu, afraid of losing his last stronghold in Coorg, despatched a convoy with a considerable force under Káder Khan. On its reaching Mullusóge (near Fraserpet) Víraája attacked and repulsed it with a loss of 500 men on the side of the Mysoreans. Encamped upon a little hill near the battle ground, with the provision bags piled up for defence, the beaten troops expected a new attack, for which the Coorgs longed with impatience; but Víraája forbore. Recognising in the commander of the Mussulmans, Káder Khan, an old acquaintance, who had befriended him during his captivity at Periapatna and protected the honour of his sister, Víraája resolved to spare his life, and, when subsequently informed by Káder Khan, that unless he could accomplish his object, he was sure to be destroyed with his family by Tippu, the Rájah ordered his men to escort the convoy to Mercara and to invite Jaffar Ali Beg to capitulate, which he did after the new provisions were consumed. These extraordinary proceedings could not fail to raise a suspicion of treachery in the mind of General Abercromby, that the Rájah was leagued with Tippu against the English. Víraája satisfactorily explained his motives, and however the General might disapprove of his acts, he was equally assured of his sincerity, as struck with his romantic generosity. On the evacuation of the Fort of Mercara, all its guns, ammunition and treasure were delivered to the Coorgs and the Rájah, who had come over from Nalknád, liberally supplied the wants of the captured garrison and permitted them to withdraw in safety across the frontier. He was now for the first time undisturbed master of his ancient patrimony, but the repeated devastations, of which it had been the theatre, left it little better than a vast wild. No wonder, therefore, that Víraája, who had undertaken to provision the English force, determined on retaliating by raids into the enemy's country the injuries he had so long experienced and the spoil of 1500 heads of cattle and vast stores of grain evinced the success with which he replenished his resources.

The period had now approached, when Tippu was to encounter the most formidable combination, he had yet met, and the capture of Bangalore gave hope of success. Lord Cornwallis advanced towards the capital from Madras and General Abercromby was to meet him for support. A passage was prepared through Coorg for the Bombay army. The route of the Heggala-pass was chosen. Víraríja waited upon the General and made over to the English Officers a great quantity of grain in addition to upwards of a thousand draught cattle previously supplied. Víraríja accompanied Sir Robert before Seringapatam. Operations had commenced with every prospect of an immediate and successful termination, when the severity of the monsoon of 1791 suspended active military operations and obliged both armies to fall back, Lord Cornwallis to Bangalore, Sir Robert to Bombay. The artillery stores and ammunition, belonging to the Bombay army, were left in charge of the Rájah, who, during the rainy season was engaged in purchasing all the grain he could from his own people and from the Pindári contractors of Tippu. Aware of the great advantages, that would attend the friendship of the Coorg chief at this juncture, Tippu now condescended, to send a confidential officer, Káder Khan, the friend of Vírarája, with an autograph letter from Tippu, and letters from Mír Sáduk, his Prime minister, and Purneah, the minister of Finance, soliciting Vírarája's forgiveness and friendship and offering as the price for his co-operation against the English, to cede the districts on his eastern frontier: Heggānadévana-Kóte, Periapatna, Bettadapur, Konanur and Arkalgudu, and to enlarge his western boundary by the addition of certain districts, dependent on Cannanore. Víraraja shewed these letters to Sir Robert, who at the end of the monsoon had returned, and after consulting with him, replied to the Sultan's overtures in these words: "By similar fair speeches and promises you have formerly deceived and ruined Coorg. God has given me one tongue, with which I have pledged fidelity to the English. I have not two tongues like you." Mussulman violence and treachery had now their reward. Víraraja remained faithful to the Company and the Bombay army had a safe road through a friendly territory into the heart of Mysore. Leaving part of his military stores, not immediately required at Heggola in charge of a regiment commanded by Col. Finch, who was to draw his supplies from the Coorgs, Sir Robert marched with the main body of the Bombay troops to Siddapur, where he received large supplies of grain, stored up in Kiggatnád. The success of the first operations by Lord Cornwallis, having driven the Mysore troops during two night attacks to seek shelter under the walls of Seringapatam, about 5,000 Coorgs, who had been carried away by Tippu, with their wives and children, altogether about 12,000 souls, made their escape in the confusion that ensued and returned to their native country. The Coorgs being better adapted to an active guerrilla warfare, than to the tedious operations of a siege, Víraraja was desired to intercept a valuable convoy, proceeding from Nuggur to Seringapatam by the Astáreghat. This service was effected with his usual address, and a warrant to plunder the neighbouring country coming within the limits of his commission, gave a wide license to the predatory habits of his followers. Part of the booty he distributed amongst the returned exiles, whom he had reinstated into their hereditary possessions; he also had houses built for them and provisions supplied for two months.

Lord Cornwallis made peace with Tippu under the walls of Seringapatam, on severe, but still too easy terms. Tippu had to pay three crores of Rupees and to cede one half of his dominions to the Company and to its allies, the Nizam and Peishwa, "from the countries adjacent, according to their situation." Coorg was in danger of being overlooked and sacrificed. It required the zealous intercession of Sir Robert Abercromby, to induce the Governor General to make an after demand for the cession of Coorg, though not adjacent to the Company's torritory, in order to keep faith with Víra-rája and to save him from the fangs of Tippu, whose first move after the peace would, no doubt, have been to wreak his vengeance upon his former vassal. The rage of Tippu was unbounded. "To which of the English possessions," he cried, "is Coorg adjacent? Why do they not ask for the key of Seringapatam?" The treaty was in danger of being broken off; but Lord Cornwallis remained firm. English guns, which had already been sent away, were ordered back, and Tippu began to prepare for defence. At the last moment he gave an unwilling assent to the demand and, admitting the stipulation, which guaranteed the independence of the Coorg principality from Mysore, he transferred his claims of allegiance and the tribute of Rs. 24,000 annually from the Rájah to the English and peace was concluded (March 1792).

An armed peace.

Sir Robert Abercromby on meeting Vírarája at Heggala in April 1792 informed him of the terms of the treaty and requested him to give back the districts, which he had lately wrested from Tippu and informed him, that he was expected in future to pay his tribute to the English Government. Vírarája was indignant at both these propositions, for he had expected some better reward for his important services. Sir Robert did all in his power, to pacify the brave ally, who had served him so well, but, of course, the Mysore territory had to be restored and the Rájah's dream of "an independant principality of Coorg" could not be realized. Sir Robert appeased, however, Víraája by promising him an English Engineer to rectify the boundaries, which proved the more desirable, since Tippu extended his claims also to Amara-Sulya, besides the districts of Panje and Belláre. The two latter the Rájah yielded, the former remained in his possession.

At his last meeting with Víraája at Cannanore in March 1793, when proceeding from Bombay to Calcutta to take up his appointment as Commander-in-Chief of Bengal, Sir Robert honoured the Rájah by drawing up a new agreement, to satisfy the gallant ally and to bind him still closer to the interests of the Company. The terms of the document are these:

1. The Rájah of Coorg has himself recovered his hereditary principality from Tippu Sultan. The Company have in no wise assisted him in this struggle. When hostilities between Tippu and the Company commenced, the Rájah, of his own accord, attached himself to the Company and concluded a treaty, the documents of which are preserved in the archives at Tellicherry.

2. The Rájah freely opened his country to the Bombay forces, which marched from Tellicherry to Mysore, and was most zealous in providing the Company's troops with every thing he could procure for them in Coorg and Mysore. Without his friendly assistance the Bombay army would have met with great difficulties. Of his own accord, the Rájah refuses to receive payment for his supplies of grain, cattle, etc.

3. Tippu repeatedly tried to shake the fidelity of the Rájah, but the latter never swerved from his allegiance to the Company.

4. In March last, when the treaty was concluded at Seringapatam, Lord Cornwallis, in order to free the Rájah of Coorg entirely from the power of Tippu, desired to take him under the special protection of the Company. Tippu

raised the most violent opposition, but in vain. Upon that he falsely stated, that Coorg had paid him a yearly tribute of Rs. 24,000, which he would transfer to the Company.

5. In opposition to this falsehood the Rájah of Coorg asserts, that he has never paid such a tribute; but he is quite willing to pay of his own free will the sum of 8000 Pagodas (24,000 Rs.) to the Company every year for their friendship and protection.

6. The Company on the other hand, engages, to give no molestation to the Rájah and in no wise to interfere with the government of Coorg; for the Rájah is quite competent, to take care of his own affairs.

Cannanore, 31st March 1793. Signed: *Robert Abercromby.*

P. S. The above 8000 Pagodas, 3 Rupees being an equivalent for 1 Pagoda, are to be paid annually at Tellicherry

From this time to the end his life, Vírarája remained th trusty friend of the Company and his affairs prospered.

On the place where he had first met with General Abercromby on his march to Seringapatam in 1791 the Rájah founded the town Víraréjendrapet in 1792. In April 1795 Vírarája took up his residence in the new palace built at Nalknád. Meanwhile Tippu, maddened with revenge against the Chief, who had so long alarmed his fears and so successfully defied his power and resisted his arms, resolved on his destruction by the basest means, gaining over Lingrája, a relative of Víraréjendra, and some Coorgs to undertake the foul plot of shooting the Rájah at a favourable spot in the jungle on his way to Mercara. The first attempt failed; but Tippu, little controlled by feelings of compunction, concerted with Lingarája more effective measures to accomplish his design. Two of his best marksmen were to lie in ambush in some place belonging to Lingarája, to shoot the Rájah, when he would come from his new palace at Nalknád, to attend the Shivarátri festival at Mercara. The conspiracy, however, was betrayed, the assassins seized, and during the night-scuffle Lingarája and his family were killed. The two would-be-murderers were kept alive at Vírájendrapet as manifest witnesses of Tippu's treachery, but each had one leg cut off to prevent their flight. Letters of congratulation on his providential escape were received by the Rájah from Sir John Shore, the Governor General, and from Mr. Duncan, the Governor of Bombay.

Vírarája having no sons, he resolved to marry a second time in 1796. In front of the palace at Nalknád a fine pavilion, which may still be seen (1870), was erected for the occasion. Honored by a deputation from the English Commissioner at Malabar and a company of sepoys, and amidst a large concourse of people from Coorg and the adjacent provinces, the ceremony took place and Mahádévamma was declared Ráni and her children were to succeed to the throne of Coorg.

To show more clearly the personal character of Vírarája and the tenor of his intercourse with the British Officials, a few hitherto unpublished letters of the Coorg Chief, written in 1798 may find here a convenient place.

He therein apprises his friends of the movements of his arch-enemy, Tippu, whom he constantly watched, and who, since the hurried treaty of Lord Cornwallis, was secretly preparing for a new war with the Company.

To

CHRISTIAN PEILE Esq.

Commissioner of Malabar.

From

VĪRARĀJENDRA

of Haleri in Coorg,

14th February 1798.

Salam!

Until now I am well and hope frequently to hear also of your well-being.

The news from the east are these: Tippu purposes by way of Coorg to come to you, and he has hitherto collected troops in the north, especially cavalry. Several Regiments are stationed in Sakunipuram under Purneah and Mír Sahib. Besides there are 15,000 men at Mangalore and in the Fort of Belláre. On the 16th February he is to leave his capital with his whole army to march upon my country; at least so he gives out. It is said, he also sent word to the Kóte Rájah, that the English at Tellicherry would probably came to the assistance of the Coorg Rájah; he should prevent them from ascending the Ghats. For this purpose, the Rájah should, under pretence of performing some funeral rites, proceed to Tiranelli (in Wynád) and there hold a conference with Tippu. Since the conclusion of the peace in 1792 Tippu never made such vast preparations as now, collecting powder, shot, cannons, provisions and draught cattle, in order to attack three points at once. If he comes this way, I shall give him a warm reception. But this time, it may turn out a more serious matter. I must think of fighting him as well, as of protecting women and children. To send them to Tellicherry during hostilities, may be attended with difficulties, since I cannot trust those Nairs and Parias. Of this I wish to inform you; but I may assure you, that I shall boldly oppose him. I will try to find an asylum for my family with my friends in Chirakal, for which purpose I should thank you for a Captain with three companies of sepoys, to keep aloof the rebellious Nairs. You will thus have the honor, to be the saviour of my family. Then I shall rush to arms and hope, as a gallant soldier, to secure your approbation. Please let me know, whether I may count upon your assistance. In the event of your inability I shall try my utmost, and in the extreme case kill wife and child and perish in the fight. What I desire in this life is, the mercy of the great God and the favor of the Company. Besides this I seek neither friendship nor help. The Company is my mother, her officers my brothers; therefore their cause and mine are *one*. This is the cause of Tippu's hatred. Pray, send me a speedy reply. Every news I send without delay, be it by day or by night. One thing more. Report says, the French came to Mangalore."

In Mr. Peile's reply the receipt of two letters is anounced, but concerning the principal question he has to wait for the decision of the Commissioner; but the Rájah may count upon his own friendship and support.

On the 23rd February 1798 Víraréjendra writes again to Mr. Peile: "I am well and wish often to hear of your welfare. On the 14th I informed you, how Tippu was collecting all his strength. My officials are on the look-out for every news and how could I keep it from my friends? The Tulu men whom I sent into the Tulu country estimate the assembled troops there at four thousand. In Subramanya there are thousand Canarese. Measures are first to be taken against the Rájah of Kumbla (20 miles to the south of Mangalore) who, after his return from Bombay, showed a rebellious spirit. There are also some troops in Békal (36 miles) south of Mangalore and a few Moplas in Mangalore. During the impending monsoon all the forts in the Tulu country are to be thoroughly repaired. My scout from Mysore reports, that Tippu was concentrating his troops, that he had left Wallagulla and was then encamped at Pallammurikád, where the Kóte Rájah had met him and was present on horseback at a revue; that Tippu had presented the Rájah with a pálky, two bracelets, two fans and two horses, after which he returned to Wynád with 60 Nairs. These men were unmistakably Nairs, for they wore the forelock and no turbans. The Rájah was called the 'Kóte Rájah'; whether he was the Rájah himself or only a member of his family, or an ambassador, the scout could not say. There arrived also 20 Moplas with loads, which, it was said, contained presents from Cannanore. On the day of the Rájah's departure, 3000 sepoys and 1000 Canarese men proceeded to Nanchanapura, to secure for him Wynád. Some say, Tippu will return to Seringapatam; others, that he will make a raid into Coorg; others that he will descend the Tamarajeri-ghat into Malabar."

To

JAMES STEVENS Esq.

It is already three months, that I ordered my confidential agent at Mahé, to pay the tribute to the Company. As Capt. Mahoney is now with us and the Karanika Subbaya has to travel with him, there will be some delay. Immediately after his return, I shall settle the whole amount, pray send me then a receipt as usual. I am very glad, that you are now first Magistrate in Tellicherry. May you be on as friendly terms with me as Mr. Taylor was and look upon my weal and woe as upon yours."

Second war with Tippu.

Tippu, whom no treaty could bind, nor any ties of faith or morality control, was preparing amidst the most amicable professions, to violate those treaties, which he pretended so much to respect. The English Government, apprised of the offensive alliance which he had entered into with the French, adopted the means of early crushing so formidable a confederacy. Actuated by a still stronger resentment Víraája hastened to their standard and in all the warm of sincerity declared, "that his exertions should be increased tenfold." A depot was immediately formed at Víráajendrapet, and measures taken, to accumulate whatever his little state could afford. In conformity to the military preparations determined on, Generals Stuart and Hartly at the head of the Bombay army ascended the Heggala-ghat (20th February 1799) and experienced the most prompt and effectual assistance with coolies, draught cattle, elephants, grain and sheep, an aid the more grateful, as proving the fidelity of the Chief. His first exploit was in saving a large portion of the baggage, which had been seized by a body of Moplas at the foot of the pass. Instigated by Tippu and incited by the prospect of plunder, a body of Nairs was to invade Coorg, as soon as the army proceeded to the eastward. To repel such an attack, and to secure the rear, especially the hospital which was erected at Víráajendrapet for the sick of the Bombay army, whom General Stuart left in Coorg, when he marched against Seringapatam, Víraája, who had offered to accompany the English army into Mysore, was politely requested to stay behind with his Coorgs, who were rather troublesome auxiliaries to a regular army, as bad as the Mahrattas, if not worse. Capt. Mahoney, who had been appointed Resident of Víraája a short time previous to the commencement of the last war with Tippu, communicated to the Rájah the Earl of Mornington's proclamation of war, dated Fort St. George 22nd February 1799, and asked him in the name of the Company's Government, to exert himself to the utmost of his power, as he would necessarily share the fate of the English, if Tippu were victorious.

In the early part of March Tippu moved with a large force towards the frontier of Coorg, to oppose the Bombay army. He encamped near Pariapátna. The battle of Siddeshwara ensued, when three native battalions under Colonel Montresor and Major Disney held their ground from 9 A. M. until 2 P. M. against the whole army of Tippu, and the two flank companies of His Majesty's 75th and the whole of the 77th under Lieut. Colonel Dunlop, led by General Stuart to their assistance, broke Tippu's line within half an hour and obtained a complete victory at a comparatively small loss, whilst that of Tippu was severe, numbering amongst the slain, the famous Benki-Navab—or "Fire-prince," one of Tippu's best generals.

The Rájah of Coorg personally accompanied General Stuart and witnessed for the first time the conduct of European troops in the presence of an enemy. There is a chivalrous air in all that proceeded from this extraordinary man, and some passages of his letter to the Governor General, giving an account of the operations of this day are tinged with his peculiar character.

"General Stuart," he writes, "marched with two regiments of Europeans, keeping the remainder of the army in the plain of Kanidygúdu; on approaching, he ordered the two regiments to attack the enemy. A severe action ensued, in which I was present. To describe the battle, which General Stuart faught with these two regiments of Europeans, the discipline, valour, strength and magnanimity of the troops, the courageous attack upon the army of Tippu, surpasses all example in this world. In our Shástras and Puránas, the battles fought by Allaret and Maharut have been much celebrated; but they are unequal to this battle; it exceeds my ability to describe this action at length to your Lordship."

While Seringapatam was besieged, Víraája sent an expedition of Coorgs under Subbaya and Bopu into the Tulu country, the greater part of which was wrested from the Mussulmans and plundered in Coorg style. His efforts in Mysore were not less vigorous or less successful. Baswanpatam, Arkalgúdu and other smaller towns were captured and the

Coorgs indulged themselves in the full gratification of every military appetite.

On the 4th of May Seringapatam was stormed and Tippu himself killed in the fray. On the 23rd of May General Harris, the Commander-in-Chief, sent a letter of thanks to Víraája, accompanied by a present of one of Tippu's own horses, one of his pálkis and one of his howdas. The promise was also given, that the country of Coorg would be restored to the Rájah.

Víraája's relation to the Company after the war.

Purneah, the Brahman minister of Finance under Tippu, was placed at the head of the government of Mysore, which the Company restored to a descendant, then a child of six years, of the ancient Rájahs. The Governor General informed the Coorg Rájah of the new order of things and begged him to refer in future any difference, that might arise between himself and the Mysore Government, to the decision of the Company. Víraájender had a mean opinion of the new Rájah, who was "a mere orphan child" and thought, names only had been changed. The Brahmins, his old foes had held power under Tippu and they held it now. They would not fail to do their utmost to embroil him with the Company's Government. Víraája had to restore to Mysore the districts he had occupied during the season of hostilities and Karanika Subbaya had to evacuate the Tulu country. Víraája had expected to be put in possession of Periapatna and the contiguous districts, but he was not to have any part of the Mysore country for political reasons, connected with the relation of the recently established government of Mysore to the government of the Company. Suggesting this course of action in a letter to Lord Clive (Governor of Madras and son of the great Clive), dated Seringapatam 1st January 1803 (v. Dispatches Vol. I. p. 320, 321) the Duke of Wellington further states:

"The services of the Rájah of Coorg still deserve remuneration. It appears by Capt. Mahoney's accounts, that he expended sums of money and furnished supplies of cattle and provisions, in the late war against Tippu Sultan, of a value amounting on the whole to about four lacs of Rupees. If he had consented to be reimbursed this expenditure, he would have received bonds of the Bombay Government for this sum of money, bearing interest at 12 per cent. per annum, in the beginning of the year 1799 and in this manner could have added nearly two lacs of Rupees to the sum above mentioned. It may therefore be fairly concluded, that, by the liberality of the Rájah, the Company's treasury is richer at this moment no less than six lacs of Rupees, than it would have been, if he had taken payment of the money expended and for the supplies furnished by him. In this view of the question, I do not take into consideration the nature of his services or the time at which they were rendered, but I have stated particularly, what the supplies, furnished by him, would have cost the Company, if they had been furnished by any other person, as I found thereon the amount of remuneration which I intend to recommend to your Lordship to grant him.

"When the arrangements of the territory of the late Tippu Sultan were made, in the year 1799, the Rájah of Coorg was desirous, to have the districts of Panje and Bellåre, to which he conceived he had a right, as they had belonged heretofore to his family and were connected with Marka and Subra in the same province. It is supposed, that these districts are worth about 6000 canterai pagodas per annum and they might form part of the proposed remuneration to the Rájah of Coorg.

"The districts in Mysore, to which the Rájah of Coorg in like manner stated a claim, are Periapatna, Bettadapur and Arkalgúdu, the value of which by the schedule appears to be 17,500 canterai pagodas. It will not be proper, to give the Rájah those districts, and I recommend to your Lordship, that others, of equal value, connected with Panje, Belláre and the Bantwál river, in the province of Canara, be ceded to him.

"Under this arrangement, he will have nearly 24,000 canterai pagodas per annum, which is about the value of the sum which the Company have annually saved by his frobearing to demand payment of the money due to him: he will have two districts in Canara to which he conceived he had a claim and certain other districts in the same province, connecting him with the Bantwál river, of the same value with districts in Mysore, which he is desirous to possess, but which, under existing circumstances, it is not possible to grant him."

Víraràja did not consider himself well treated and was mortified by the withdrawal of the Resident, Capt. Mahoney, and the request addressed to him, that he should for the future put himself in correspondence with Col. Close, the Resident at Seringapatam, who does not seem to have ingratiated himself with the Rájah, as may be seen from the following letters:

Seringapatam, 16th November 1799.

Col. WARREN CLOSE

To

THE RĀJAH OF COORG.

"Lord Mornington has transferred me to Seringapatam as Commissioner of Mysore, of which *you** may be aware. A report reaches me from the Manjerabad frontier, that five days after the fall of Seringapatam your people have made a predatory incursion into the Maharájadurga district and plundered of 17 villages women and children, cows and calves, gold and silver, rice and seed grain, and carried the spoil beyond the frontier. I enclose a list of the plundered articles.

* The word used for "you" in the original, is the uncourteous Canarese form, in which no person of rank is addressed. This was very likely intentionally done by the Brahman writer, but unknown to Col. Close.

From the day of the capture of the capital Mysore belongs to the Company, but Maharájadurga belongs to Mysore; there is therefore no difference between Mysore and the Company. But you are an ally of the Company. You are therefore requested, without delay to return every article contained in the list.

"I am told, you wish to see Seringapatam; as the army will return to this town within a few days, you should inform me of your resolution."

List of articles, plundered by the Coorgs in the Maharája-durg district:—"67 women, 34 men, 11 boys, 10 girls, 1383 cows, 574 buffaloes, 834 oxen, 121 calves; 729 canterai pagodas, 82 silver ornaments, 36 silver bracelets, 27 coral-necklaces, 63 silver girdles, 54 pairs of golden earrings, 215 brass plates, 93 copper vessels, 67 guns, 6 horses, 155 sheep, 95 knives, 96 sickles, 90 axes, 5 brass pans, 7 iron chains, 72 bundles of clothes."

This affair seems to have been settled not without considerable difficulties in which the Rájah implored the good services of his personal friends amongst the English, as we gather from the following letter, dated 16th December 1799:—

To

JAMES STEVENS Esq.

"Since the English have commenced war with Tippu, I have twice assisted the Bombay army, first under General Sir R. Abercromby and then under Generals Stuart and Hartley; I have tried my utmost to carry out the orders of the British Government and served the Company with my own body, as you well know. What I have accomplished, I did with no view to self-interest—honor excepted.

"As to Purneah, he is and remains a Brahmin. His and my caste dislike each other. In the time of Tippu he has blackened my name and persecuted me and now he is master in the country; therefore he distributes the offices in the districts amongst his friends and relations, calumniates me through his district-officers and other caste-fellows with the English Government and even submits a complaint against me, with a list of booty which my people are accused of having made in the north. Upon this Col. Close wrote to me, enclosing the list, and demanded that I should accordingly pay compensation.

"This Col. Close has never seen me and does not know my history, nor does he understand Canarese. Thus he wrote me a letter through a Brahmin as if addressed to a slave. I enclose the letter of Col. Close and a copy of the list of booty. Upon the perusal of these papers you will understand all.

"Convinced in my mind, that all the enemies of the English would succumb, that the English Government would be victorious, and that the British flag would float triumphantly in all the four quarters of the world, I served the Company from the beginning of the war in the hope to have to deal with friends like you and to be treated honorably. According to my wishes, the enemy has been defeated and the power of the Company has risen greatly. This I saw with my own eyes and greatly rejoiced, as I believed to obtain the more honor myself. But this Purneah lodges a complaint against me as if I had offended against the Company. Being thus dishonored, I have no wish to live any longer. You know all my acts. I write to you with deep sorrow, that all my services have been requited with such dishonor from the Company.

"The facts of the case are these: On the 6th March, when Tippu advanced upon Siddeshwara, to commence the war, Generals Stuart and Hartley and Capt. Mahoney told me: 'Peace is at an end; now fall upon Tippu's people.' Ten days after the fall of Seringapatam, on the 14th May Capt. Mahoney told me: 'Now give orders to stop fighting. What hitherto has been done during the war, is done.'

"If after this time my people have anywhere plundered or committed damages, I will give compensation. Upon enquiry, my people said: 'when according to your orders we commenced war, the Mysoreans seemed to have carried away all their goods into safety. From those who fell, we took their arms and other valuables; but of other booty there was little, except perhaps bullocks, goats and sheep, as your Highness well knows.' When the Coorgs enter upon a compaign, no care is taken for provisions, as with the Company; but their women and children pound rice and bring it to the camp; this you know. As many sheep as my men could plunder, they brought to me and I gave them to the Company. All the wants of my 6000 or 7000 Coorgs, their provisions, clothes, powder and lead I provided myself, and cared for the wounded and the relatives of the dead.

"The territory of Mangalore I have conquered, but surrendered it to Col. Wiseman whom the General sent. Is it then not the duty of Government to treat me honorably? But the complaint with the list of booty is the reward for what I have done amiss towards the Government!

"If I am desired to pay, the question is, whence to take the money? What my ancestors and myself accumulated, was spent, when I twice faithfully supported the Bombay army. What after the peace of 1792 I obtained from my country, I annually made over to the Company. If anything remained, I expended it on the assistance to General Stuart. But in case I should have to pay according to this list, I must earnestly request, that, as a compensation for my services, at least my honor remains intact. However, I am quite unable to pay. In Bombay I have one lac of Rupees deposited with the Company; this money I will send for and pay. If it does not suffice, I beg you and the officers of the Bombay army to be my brothers. My honor is yours. If matters reach extremities, I come to you and all the officers together will perhaps give me the rest of the sum and leave to me only my honor. What you do for me, I will certainly repay. If you cannot help me, I must turn elsewhere to save my honor.

"Take these matters into due consideration, and kindly let me know what more I have to do."

Regarding the alleged poverty of Víraŕja, it should be observed, that on his death in 1809 he left in the treasury forty lacs of Rupees including his deposits with the English Government. He was in the habit of laying aside annually a large sum of money and the booty of his plunderous expedition before the fall of Seringapatam greatly replenished his exchequer!

General Stuart, who sailed for Madras and Europe, promised the Rájah on parting, to send him from Europe a sword with the arms of the East-Indian Company and a portrait of Lord Mornington and himself. After the departure of the General from Cannanore Víraŕja returned to Coorg.

Soon after he received a letter from the Governor General in which his services rendered to the British Government during the last and in former wars were gratefully acknowledged, and as a compensation of the same the tribute which the Rájah hitherto paid, was remitted. Mr. Duncan, the Governor of Bombay, was to inform the Rájah, what annual present in lieu of the tribute would be acceptable to the British Government.

Before Capt. Mahoney left, it was settled that the Rájah of Coorg should every year send an elephant to the Company in lieu of the former tribute of Rs. 24,000. A paper to this effect was given to the Rájah by Capt. Mahoney at Virájpet on the 13th October 1799.

Another certificate also, dated 12th October 1799, was given by Capt. Mahoney. It was as follows:

1. The Rájah has exerted himself to the utmost in the service of the Company.

2. He has collected large supplies of rice and forwarded them to Seringapatam, thus saving the troops from famine.

3. He has furnished 1,000 coolies to the army and for the conveyance of the ammunition to Seringapatam 2000 men without receiving remuneration.

4. He has furnished the Bombay army with more than 3000 bullocks, 5 elephants, 3000 sheep and 40,000 batties of rice.

5. For all this trouble and expense he has accepted of no payment or reward.

6. The Rájah's conduct has afforded great satisfaction to the men and officers of the Bombay army, many of whom have experienced his friendship".

In 1801 Víraája contracted a matrimonial alliance between his daughter Rájammáji, by his first Ráni, and Basavalinga the Rájah of Sóde, who resided in the Goa territories. Víraája wrote to the Governor General, to apprize him of the intended marriage and to procure for the Sóde Rájah three months' leave from the Portuguese Government. He also wished to settle one lac of Rupees of the property, held by him in the Bombay Government paper, upon the Sóde Rájah who was poor, as Rájammáji's portion. The wedding took place in December 1801 at Nalknád in the presence of Capt. Marriot from Mysore, and Capts. D. Foulis and Ashbourner from Malabar, and before the monsoon 1802 the Sóde Rájah returned home.

In 1804, Capt. Mahoney arrived at Mercara with a letter from the Governor General, informing Víraája, that six Máganes of the province of Canara would be transferred to him by Mr. Ravenshaw, the Collector of Mangalore, in return for the supplies, he had furnished, and the services he had rendered to the British Government during the late wars. The districts, thus added to Coorg on the western frontier, yielded 24,897 pagodas.

In the same year, at the suggestion of Major Mark·Wilks, then Acting Resident at the Mysore Durbar, the boundary between Coorg and Mysore on the Subramanya side was finally adjusted by Mr. Peile and Major Mackenzie to the Rájah's entire satisfaction. 190 stones were ordered to be erected with the Company's mark on the top, that of Mysore on one side and that of Coorg on the other.

Before the end of 1805 Rájammáji, the Ráni of Sóde was delivered of a son, who received the name of Sadáshivarája.

Vírarája was now left in the free and full possession of his principality; he lived on the most friendly terms with the Mysore Residents, the Madras Governors, Sir George Barlow and Lord William Bentinck, and the Governor General, the Marquis of Wellesley, from whom he received a splendid sword of honor. About the time his first grandson was born to him at Sóde he was fondly attached to his new wife, Mahadévaráni, who had born him two daughters, and might have lived and died a happy man, if he had had a son and heir, if he had not distrusted his nearest relatives and if his violent temper had not often carried him beyond the bounds of humanity. He lived in constant dread of poison and it is difficult to say, whether the frenzy which seemed at times to seize him was not caused by drugs administered to him in spite of all his caution.

The Rájendranáme, in its conclusion affords a glimpse of the alternations of hope and fear, which agitated the poor Rájah's heart.

Vírarájendra's last will.

The English translation by Lieut. Abercromby, made from the Canarese original of the Rájendranáme in 1808, at Mangalore brings in two additional pages the last will of Vírarájender, which is not contained in the extant copy, that was found in the Mercara archives in 1834, and the suspicion lies near, that the Canarese original was destroyed and the Testament omitted in the copy by Vírarájender's successors.

His last words are:—"On the 7th of the Pushya month (Dec.—Jan.) Ractáxi year (1805) Capt. Mahoney brought the sword, sent by Marquis Wellesley from Bengal and fastened it round the Rájah's waist. In the Mágha month (Jan.—Feb.) 1806 Víraràja told Capt. Mahoney for the information of the Governor General, that on the day of his second marriage when he sat on the throne with his Ráni, he had determined that any son of his by this wife should be his successor; that his wife had born him two daughters. If any son be hereafter born of her, he would be the heir; but if it was the will of God, that she should bear no son, then the three sons of his concubine, called Rájashékarappa, Shishushékappa and Chandrashékarappa should succeed to the throne. Since the above date, two more daughters, in all four, have been born by Mahadévaráni who died at 3 o'clock on Sunday the 7th day of the month Jéshta (May—June) 4909 Prabhava year (1807). As by her death the Rájah's hopes of having a son by her were blunted, and he was afraid, lest, if the succession devolved on the sons of another mother, they would create trouble to the four daughters of his lawful queen, the Rájah determined, that of the four daughters, who are named: Dévammáji, Muddammáji, Rájammáji and Mahádévammáji, the eldest should be married and whatever son she might have, he should be named Víréjendra, receive the Rájah's seal and the sword which was presented to him by Marquis Wellesley and be the successor to the throne. If she should, however, have no son, the son of either of her younger sisters according to seniority should be the successor and so long as the line of any of his four above named daughters continued, none of the heirs of the other mother should succeed to the throne; but, upon the family of his four daughters being extinct, the fittest of the above three sons or their posterity should succeed. The Rájah, sensible of the instability of human life and all other things, has thought proper now to determine and record this matter, in order that no wrong may hereafter occur; and he requests, that the English Sirkar will be the guardian of his family and see the execution of the above written will attended to.

"In order that the Rájah's heirs may be acquainted with his resolution, he has written a copy thereof, to which he has affixed his seal and signature and which is lodged in the palace treasury."

Here ends the Rájendranáme.

5. THE LAST YEARS OF THE INDEPENDENCE OF COORG 1807—1834.

A. DODDA-VĪRĀJENDRA'S MELANCHOLY END. 1807—1809.

With the death of Mahádévaráni commenced the last act, full of blood and horrors of the drama of poor Vírájendra's life. With her his hopes of a son and heir were buried. He had loved her, it appears, passionately. She may have turned and softened the savage nature of the wild Border-Chief. Her loss almost drove him mad. When the paroxysm of his grief had passed, he was alone in the world. There was no one to love him, no one in whom he could confide.

Mahádévaráni had left him four daughters, the eldest of whom was eight years old, when the mother died. They succeeded to whatever remained of human affection and sympathy in the breast of the woe stricken father. He had formerly intended to choose for his successor one of his sons by another wife, if Mahádévaráni had no male issue. Now he changed his mind. One of Mahádévaráni's daughters, if they lived to woman's state, might have a son. That son was to succeed him. The eldest of them, Dévammáji, was betrothed to a Coorg, of the name of Mallappa, when she was about nine years old. The Rájah, who was possessed of immense wealth, gave to her one lac of pagodas in gold and jewels, and costly shawls and dresses in profusion. The death of his favourite wife had not only rendered him unhappy, but had soured his temper, and, to judge from Coorg analogy, he could scarcely avoid the cruel suspicion, that some traitors had conspired against the life of Mahádévaráni and destroyed her by charms and incantations. He himself began to live in dread of secret enemies. No doubt, but he had such, for he detested Hindus in general and Coorgs in particular. He had killed hundreds of his own people on some idle suspicion or malicious denunciation, or on the mere impluse of a sudden gust of passion. But now his cruelty and his dark fears rose higher and higher. At last matters came to a crisis.

The Rájah had surrounded himself with an African body-guard, and eunuchs from Mysore had charge of his Harem. But the guards of the palace and all the military officers with very few exceptions were Coorgs. No longer able to bear the iron yoke, they conspired against the Rájah's life. The day and the hour were fixed. All the Coorg guards, who held the gates of the fort and the entrances of the palace, being of one accord, his destruction seemed to be certain. But a few minutes before the signal was given, the secret was betrayed to Víraája. He was roused by the impending danger. With great presence of mind he imitated Hyder Ali, who had in similar circumstances gained time, by placing a bundle of clothes on his bed covered with a blanket. The Coorgs rushed in and cut the form, which they mistook for the sleeping Rájah, in pieces. Next moment they discovered, that the Rájah had fled, that he had, at the last moment, been warned. They were paralyzed. Víraája in the mean time had run out and summoned his Africans. The Fort gates were shut. Some three hundred Coorgs had assembled in the palace yard. The Africans received orders to cut them down to a man. The Rájah himself took his post at a window and fired upon the terror stricken conspirators. They allowed themselves to be slaughtered like sheep. Vírarája himself boasted of having shot twenty-five of them. The rest fell without resistance, under the swords of the Siddis, who waded ankle deep in blood. An old Jemadar, who had been eyewitness of the dreadful scene, said, that the blood ran out of the palace yard as the rain in a heavy monsoon day. Three-hundred Coorgs, by his account, fell that morning in front of the palace. Coorg tradition says eight-hundred. Both accounts are probably correct, for Víraràja would, as a matter of course, destroy many of the families of the fallen conspirators, ordering the men to be killed and distributing the women among the slaves. Such was Coorg Rájah fashion. This massacre took place in the end of 1807 or early in 1808. The Rájah reported his suppression of a dangerous conspiracy to the Governor of Madras and the Governor General. The Rájah's account was not credited at Madras. It was rather thought, that he had acted on some sudden impulse of passion; for his cruelty and sanguinary temper were sufficiently known. Yet the Government did not consider it their duty to interfere, partly from regard to their faithful ally, partly from ignorance of the extent of the fearful slaughter.

On the 7th October 1807 Vírarájendra addressed a long letter to the Governor General, Lord Minto. He informed him of the death of his principal Ráni, who had left him four daughters and of his will regarding the succession after his death, as already stated. Vírarájendra appears to have expected, perhaps longed for, his own death, after the loss of his beloved wife. A deep melancholy settled upon him, from which he was roused from time to time by rumours of conspiracies and dreams of rebellion among his treacherous subjects, when he would start like a lion from his lair and kill and tear whatever objects first met his fury, until he was satiated with blood and his paroxysm subsided. Dr. Ingledew, who was sent early in 1809 by Mr. Cole, the Resident in Mysore, to attend upon the Rájah, heard some vague rumours of several thousand people having been destroyed "after the late disturbances," that is, the conspiracy above related. Víraréjendra had long to wait for an answer from the Governor General to his petition of October 1807. He had requested, that the concurrence of the Governor General with his settlement of the succession might be registered in the books of the Supreme Government and a copy sent him of the registry, which he would wear about his body as an amulet.

During the year 1808 fits of madness seized the unfortunate Rájah. They rarely passed without some victims of his incontrollable fury, falling by his bullet or under the knives of his African executioners. Some time in October or November 1808 Víraréja was seized with forebodings of his own death and terrible fears for the safety of his daughters in case of his decease before the Governor General had concurred in his plan of securing to Dévammáji the throne of Coorg, and before his sanction insured her succession and, it might be, the preservation of her life. His melancholy warned him of his approaching death. And if he was carried off on a sudden, who would be the friend and guardian of his daughter? Appáji, his proud brother, who had never loved him, and who had long kept sullenly at a distance, or even the dull mean-spirited Lingarája might covet the wealth and power of the throne, murder the helpless children and seize the great prize. But no! He was yet alive and omnipotent in Coorg, he could yet defend his beloved Dévammáji and her sisters. The executioners are called. A party is despatched to Appagalla, a second party to Háleri, to bring the heads of the brothers, Appáji and Lingarája. They prostrate themselves and depart on their dark errand. Víraája is left alone. Now at last the dear children will be safe. There will be none alive to molest them. The Governor General will sanction the last will of the faithful friend of the Company. Dévammáji will sit on the throne of Coorg like the former Ráni of Ikkeri. She will have a son. The grandson will bear the grandfather's name and inherit his wealth and his glory. Such dreams must have floated on the mind of the unfortunate prince, when he had hurried away the ministers of his wrath, to slay his brothers. Within an hour, however, the excitement subsided, reason and humanity gained the mastery and suddenly messengers of grace were sent after the murderers. They were bid to run as for their lives. The decree of death was revoked. The brothers were to live. Alas, the messengers who ran down to Appagalla, were met by the executioners carrying Appáji's head. The distance to Háleri was greater, and perhaps Lingarája had had a friendly warning. He had not been found by the executioners on their first arrival, and, before he was discovered, his pardon arrived. Appáji's head was brought before Vírarája according to his orders. The men dared not deviate from the command of the Rájah, though they knew, that he had changed his mind.

Vírarája was horror struck at his own deed. The dead could not be restored to life. What was done could not be undone. But Vírarája would do what he could to make amends. Lingarája was ordered to take charge of his brother's family and of their property. The Jaghir of Appáji, worth 600 kanterai pagodas, was added to the Háleri Jaghir of Lingarája, valued at 200 kanterai pagodas per annum. Still Lingarája remained confined to his village, as he had been for the last ten years. Vírarája utterly despised him as a stupid spiritless farmer. It was the conviction of his perfect insignificance and harmlessness that gave him security, not brotherly affection.

In the beginning of the year 1809 Mr. Cole, the Resident of Mysore, received a message from Mercara, that the Rájah was insane, and that the assistance of an English physician might be granted. Dr. Ingledew was despatched without a moment's delay. He found the Rájah in a dangerous state. His madness came upon him in fits, which were succeeded by the darkest melancholy. The presence of an English gentleman was a relief to him. There was one man now near him, whom he could trust. On the other hand he was distracted by fears, lest Dr. Ingledew might learn the true state of the country, and receive information of the atrocities he had committed, especially during the last year. If he reported the truth to the Company's Government, Víraraja dreaded loss of character, deposition and ignominy. He took all possible care to keep the Doctor in ignorance. But towards the end of February the black clouds again gathered around him; the evil spirit prevailed. His passion rose one day against four of his principal officers. He ordered them to be assassinated. The executioners went and cut them down. Next morning he sent for one of them. He was dead, it was reported. He called for another, and the third, and the fourth. His attendants trembling declared, that they had been killed according to the orders of the Rájah. Víraraja was seized with an agony of remorse and despair. He bit his arm, that the blood gushed out, and went into his chamber, where he shut himself up, refusing to see any one, or to taste food. He was not fit to live. He would die. His torments were increased by dreadful pains in his shoulder, which he had dislocated by a fall, sometime before the Doctor's arrival, and which had been unskilfully treated by a native quack.

The mind of the man was unhinged under circumstances such as these. Yet even now, the Coorg did not forget his cunning. The murder of the four chief officers could not be hid from Dr. Ingledew. He would surely report to Mr. Cole, and Mr. Cole would report to the Governor General, (Mr. Cole, indeed did report on the 4th of March) and he would be disgraced for ever in the eyes of the Company. There was one way of escape. If it appeared undoubtedly, that his acts of atrocity had been committed in moments of insanity, if, on recovering his consciousness, he felt such utter despair, as to find life intolerable, the English authorities must hold him excused and feel inclined, rather to pity than to degrade him. As for his distress of mind and the stings of conscience, driving him almost to despair, he did not require to simulate. He felt as wretched as man could feel, but words would not satisfy the Company. Appearances of deepest grief might be suspected. He resolved, therefore, to make some attempt at suicide sufficient to convince Dr. Ingledew of the reality of his despair. Accordingly he cut his throat sufficiently deep, to inflict a serious wound, but not deep enough to endanger life. The Doctor was called in. He stayed the blood and bandaged the throat. On enquiring into the motives for such an act of despondency, he was informed by the Rájah, that he had no desire to live. The murder of his trusty servants, ordered in a fit of insanity and executed by slavish dependents, preyed upon his mind. He could not bear the thought of having disgraced himself for ever in the eyes of the Governor General and all his English friends. Dr. Ingledew tried to reassure him and to soothe his apprehensions, declaring, that acts committed in a state of insanity, and so much grieved for afterwards, would not be laid to his charge. But the Rájah would not be comforted. Shortly after, Doctor Ingledew was called again. The Rájah had swallowed a large dose of corrosive sublimate dissolved in water, which he had been advised to use as a lotion. He had called his eldest daughter, Dévammáji, and desired her to give him the deadly draught. The poor girl did not understand what she was doing. Doctor Ingledew instantly administered an emetic, but had no hope of the Rájah's recovery, though his medicine acted freely. However, to his astonishment he was soon enabled to report to Mr. Cole, with whom he was in daily communication, that Vírarája was in a convalescent state. The scheme was completely successful. Dr. Ingledew had not the slightest suspicion of Vírarája's acting a part before him. Mr. Cole, the Resident, on Dr. Ingledew's report, hastened in person to Mercara. He found the Rájah oppressed by the darkest melancholy, full of sad forebodings of the displeasure of the Governor General, but improving in health. He assured him of his own sympathy, and begged him to confide in the continuance of the friendship and regard of the British Government. Acts committed during a state of insanity would be considered as a misfortune worthy of commiseration, not as crimes deserving of blame or punishment. He would, on his own responsibility, promise the Rájah amnesty for all that had passed. These assurances had the desired effect. Vírarája recovered. Favorable letters arrived from the Governor of Madras, congratulating him on his recovery. A despatch from the Governor General, in answer to the Rájah's letter of 1807, concurred in the wishes of the Company's faithful ally, though not as perfectly as Vírarája had hoped. The bequest of the large legacy of money to his favorite daughter was sanctioned, and the Resident of Mysore was directed to take charge of the treasure, to be invested in the name of Dévammáji, Víraréjendra's daughter, in the Company's funds at Madras. As to the succession, the reply was couched in general terms and the Rájah was desired to confer with Mr. Cole, who had private instructions to make due investigation as to the consistency with Coorg law and custom of the succession in the female line, before he gave the sanction of the British Government to the arrangement proposed by Víraája. Another letter from the Governor General soon followed full of kindness and regard. The Rájah was most affectionately assured of the uninterrupted friendship of the British Government and of the Governor General's undiminished regard. Whatever the Rájah might have done in moments, when his reason was clouded,—and his subsequent deep contrition expressed, that he had not been guilty of deliberate cruelties,—should be forgiven and forgotten. Whereupon Vírarája wrote his last letter to the Governor General. He offered his thanks for the sanction, accorded by the Supreme Government to his testamentary disposal of his hereditary principality, "settling the succession in favor of the male child, which may hereafter be born of one of my daughters by my principal Ráni, to the throne of my dominions, conformably to the mode prescribed by me in my letter to your Lordship. I consider the line of succession to be now settled under the sanction of the British Government, which circumstance has conferred honour upon me, and is beneficent to the interests of my Government. I desire to show forth the daily increasing ardour of my devotion to the service of the British Government, and that my children after me may successfully emulate the example of their father."

Under the 16th March Mr. Cole had already reported to Government, that "the Rájah had despatched to the Presidency Treasury the sum of about 170,000 pagodas, which was invested in the Company's funds under the name of his eldest daughter. I have had the honour to be introduced to this Princess and her sisters, whom his Highness recommended through me, in a very affecting manner to the protection of Honorable Government." In fact the Rájah under the idea of obtaining a kind of adoption by the Honorable the East India Company for his daughters, begged the Hon. Mr. Cole to embrace the four girls in the name of the Governor General. Mr. Cole was deeply moved, and returned a most cordial answer to the hapless Prince. A receipt was given to the Rájah soon after for Star-pagodas 186,000, to be invested in the Company's funds as the property of Dévammáji, his eldest daughter.

This was the state of affairs in April 1809. Mr. Cole had returned to Mysore. Dr. Ingledew soon followed. His place was supplied by Mr. Clarke, a physician recommended by Dr. Ingledew. The Rájah had passed through the worst dangers. The confidence of the British Government had been only more firmly re-established. He believed that the Governor General had sanctioned, and thereby guaranteed the succession to Dévammáji and her future son and heir. The Company had taken charge of her rich legacy, to which he had added with the sanction of the Supreme Government other three lacs of Rupees in the Bombay funds. His daughter had been, as it were, adopted by the Company. All his wishes were realized. He might now set his soul at rest. Alas, no. He had buried his very life in the grave of Mahádévaráni. The dead, the victims of his suspicious cruelty, troubled him. He knew himself to be hated by the living, and believed, that traitors had administered to him maddening drugs. Appáji his brother was slain, his most faithful servants were slain. Wherever he went some memorial of a dark deed of cruelty met him. His sleep was disturbed. The blood of thousands was upon him.

Under the 24th May 1809 Mr. Cole reported to the Chief Secretary of the Government of Fort St. George, that the Rájah of Coorg was again labouring under insanity, and showed a most sanguinary disposition; that the people of Mercara were in constant terror; that Dr. Clarke also entertained fears for his own personal safety, and that he himself would probably find it difficult to deal with him, as his ancient jealousy and hatred of Mysore and every person connected with the Government had been reawakened. Dr. Ingledew, who possessed the confidence of Vírarája, was again sent to Mercara. In the mean time, Mr. Clarke was enjoined to prevent, as far as it lay in his power, any re-enactment of former scenes of sanguinary violence. It was proposed that Captain Mahoney, the former Resident, should return, take charge, if necessary, of the administration of affairs, and settle the question of the succession in case of the decease of the Rájah. Mr. Cole himself offered to proceed in person to Mercara. When Dr. Ingledew arrived, the end of Vírarája was at hand. It does not appear from the records, that Dr. Ingledew had an interview, or, if he had, that he was recognized by the dying Rájah. During his last days he seems to have been more favorably inclined, than formerly, towards the Sóde Rájah, who was appointed to transact business for him, and whom he desired, it was said, to act as Devan during the minority of Dévammáji. On the 9th June 1809 the unhappy prince called his beloved daughter to his bedside, gave his seal into her hands, and shortly afterwards breathed his last. He lies buried in one of the Mausoleums, which grace the hill overlooking the town of Mercara.

A sad spectacle! A noble vessel, after having gallantly weathered the storms of Mussulman domination and conquest, is torn from its moorings by the swell of wild grief and passion, and drifts into the breakers of sanguinary phrensy and suicidal despair, to perish there a miserable wreck, with many to look on, but none to help!

And how awfully has the Righteous Ruler of the whole earth executed judgment upon the guilty prince and the objects of his love and hope! The forlorn Rájah lived ages of anguish from the day of the death of his beloved wife, 17th May 1807, to the date of his own decease, 9th June 1809. His idolized daughter was married and had four children, two sons and two daughters. She was deprived of the throne and of her father's legacy, and lived in obscurity. Before the end of 1833 her husband was murdered in the palace, she herself carried a prisoner to Mercara, her property seized by her cousin, the late Rájah, (one lac of pagodas at one sweep,) and shortly after she herself was murdered at Mercara, and her three children (one boy appears to have died a natural death), at Nalknád, by orders of her relative, and their corpses thrown into pits.

B. LINGARĀJENDRA.

1809—1820.

1. *Lingarájendra's Intrigues.*

Dr. Ingledew, on the sudden death of Víraràja, had to fulfil the duties of a British Agent quite ex-improviso. He acted, it is true, with considerable tact and prudence and with perfect honesty; but he was not equal to the deep play of the Coorg parties, and was not sharp sighted enough to discern the principal mover in the scenes acted before him. Thus he failed in the task, devolved upon him by a most unforeseen combination of circumstances and persons upon a ground he had scarcely explored. He ought to have carried out the wishes of the late Rájah, as far as they had received the approbation and sanction of the British Government. But it happened otherwise.

When Víraràjendra died, there seemed to be a good prospect of peace and prosperity for Coorg. A short time before his decease, Víraràja permitted the Sóde Rájah to act for him as principal Devan, and expressed a desire, that his son-in-law should have the regency of Coorg, during the minority of Dévammáji, in conjunction with an Agent of the East India Company to be appointed by the Governor General. He had once given to Dr. Ingledew a testamentary document, expressive of these wishes, but had afterwards recalled and never returned it. As soon as the Rájah had expired, his daughter Dévammáji was acknowledged as Ráni of Coorg, by the assembled chiefs. The Sóde Rájah continued to perform the duties of principal Devan, or rather of Regent, and all people seemed to be happy and contented. Dr. Ingledew wrote to Mr. Cole, the Mysore Resident; "owing to the many acts of cruelty, committed by the late Rájah, the Coorg people would be satisfied with any tolerable Government, but more particularly with one like the present promises to be, where the life of the subject is more secure and more regarded, than it has been for the last two years, or, I believe, at almost any period of the late reign." Some of the eunuchs gave themselves airs, and commenced to intrigue with different parties. But upon the complaint of Umbala Náyaka, one of the Devans, who threatened to resign, unless these men were removed, they were ordered to retire to their villages, and placed under surveillance. The first serious disturbance was occasioned by a rumour, that the Sóde Rájah had forged the last will of the Rájah. Dr. Ingledew inquired into the charge, and found, that the copy of the will, produced by the Sóde Rájah, had a signature not attached to it by Víraràja himself, but by a farrier, who had been in his favour. However, the alterations in the will itself were of no great consequence, and were in perfect harmony with Víraràjendra's wishes shortly before his death. Yet, to quiet the minds of the Coorg chiefs the spurious, though honest, document was cancelled. The Sóde Rájah retained his position. But soon affairs began to take a new turn.

Lingarája, then 34 years old, appears to have had many interviews with Dr. Ingledew, and impressed him with a strong conviction of his honesty, simplicity and humility. Lingarája confessed, indeed, that he was somewhat disappointed at being entirely superseded. But his elder brother, he said, having recovered the country by force of arms, had a perfect right to dispose of the succession. He had therefore no cause, nor any inclination to complain. He would ever cheerfully submit to whatever arrangements were sanctioned by the

Governor General. Dr. Ingledew was quite charmed with the man, and recommended him strongly to the favour of Government, as he had well deserved of the country. He had asked for an increase of his pension, which now consisted of two hundred kanterai pagodas for himself and six hundred pagodas a year for the family of his brother Appáji, who had been murdered eight months ago, and the Doctor zealously pleaded for the good, peaceable man. This recommendation is dated 4th July 1809. The peaceable Lingarája, however, was not quite as unworldly minded as he appeared to the honest Doctor. He was much at the palace, and was busy among the principal Coorgs. They certainly did not much approve of the rule of a foreigner, like the Sóde Rájah, but they seem to have had no particular predilection for the late Rájah's brother. One day there had been a large gathering of the chiefs, of which Dr. Ingledew knew nothing, at the palace. It was proposed to displace the Sóde Rájah by Lingarája, but the proposition was thrown out. Lingarája mounted his horse and rode away, in the direction of Háleri, his own residence. As he rode through the market street of Mercara, in deep despondency and actually weeping like a child, Kshauryakere Appanna, one of the Devans, met him, on his way to the palace. "Why do you cry, Lingarája?" he inquired. "I have been rejected by the Coorg Pancháyat. All is lost," was the reply. "Come with me, Lingarája," said Appanna, "I will set you on the throne of Coorg." With these words he seized the bridle of Lingarája's poney, and set off with him to the Fort. He pleaded there for his helpless client before the assembled chiefs. Being a man of known integrity and considerable influence, he prevailed. The Coorgs changed their minds and Lingarája was preferred to the Rájah of Sóde.

Dr. Ingledew knew nothing of all these things, and was therefore not a little astonished, when on the 9th July, five weeks after the death of Víraréjendra, during which period his reports had been full of Lingarája's praises, the little Ráni sent for him, and told him, that she had reason to be dissatisfied with the conduct of the Rájah of Sóde, and wished to have Lingarája, her uncle, for her guardian. Immediately afterwards, the Sóde Rájah came to him and asked his leave to return to his own country, as he had convinced himself, that he had to deal with a formidable opposition, and considered it prudent to withdraw from a situation of imminent danger. Dr. Ingledew objected strongly to so hasty a step. He was waiting for orders from Government, and before the Governor General had signified his will, he wished, that no change should be made in the arrangements, which had been in operation before Vírarájendra's death. But the Sóde Rájah informed him, that Lingarája had already taken possession of the government of the principality. A similar announcement was made by Lingarája himself. Dr. Ingledew now saw, that he had been duped. He protested against Lingarája's usurpation and resolved on withdrawing immediately from Coorg. However, the little Ráni interposed and begged him to stay, whereupon he consented to remain at Mercara, until the arrival of orders from Government, but refused to transact business with Lingarája. The worthy Doctor had now the unpleasant task of reporting to the Resident of Mysore, that he had been made a fool of by the peaceable, humble, simple-minded Coorg; but he acquitted himself of it very honestly. He had been outwitted, he wrote on the 13th July, in an extraordinary manner, and would offer no other excuse but the fact, that he had followed in the footsteps of the late Vírarájendra, who had possessed a good discernment of character, and yet spared the life of Lingarája, his only surviving brother, because he considered him a perfectly harmless creature. No wonder, if the deep cunning, which had succeeded in baffling the keen eye of a tyrant brother, and the vigilancy of Coorg espionage, got the better of a stranger like himself. Mr. Cole forwarded Dr. Ingledew's reports to Madras and Calcutta. He had, before the death of Víraréjendra, in anticipation of the approaching difficulties, under the 7th of June fully entered upon the Coorg question in a paper, which reported the temporary assumption of the government of Coorg by the Rájah of Sóde. His idea was, that Lingarája was successor to the throne of Coorg de jure, or as Mr. Cole expresses himself, by the doctrine of the shástras (as if the Coorgs had any shàstra, or had any thing to do with Hindu Shástras; as if there had been any law in Coorg, different from the will and whim of the Rájah). After Lingarája, his son, it appeared to the Resident, had a right to succeed. If Lingarája had no son, a son of the Rájah of Sóde would be the next heir. Female succession was excluded altogether. However, Mr. Cole acknowledged, that he could not speak positively as to local usage. (Female succession was law in the Ikkeri family, from which the Coorg Rájahs had sprung, of which circumstance Mr. Cole seems to have been ignorant). He wished to receive instructions from Government, how the Agent at Mercara ought to be directed to act. Was he to adhere to the doctrine of the Shástras? or to local usage? or to the personal wishes of the Rájah? Opposition, in the three cases mentioned, was to be expected from the Sóde Rájah, who was now the actual ruler, but had no right to the succession.

On the 15th June Mr. Cole reported to the Chief Secretary to the Government of Fort St. George, as an amendment to his last despatch, that the principal men among the Coorgs seemed unanimously well inclined to the Sóde Rájah, wherefore he would rather purpose, that Government should acknowledge him. On the 16th June he writes to the same authority again, that all Coorg was in favour of the Sóde Rájah, and that it would, therefore, be expedient to acknowledge him without delay. On the 18th June he sent the additional intelligence, that Lingarája also had declared himself in favour of the Sóde Rájah, and on the 4th July he reported fully on the excellent conduct of the brother of the late Rájah, Lingarája, and recommended, that a decent, yea liberal provision should be made for him in consideration of his meritorious exertions during the critical period succeeding the death of his brother. Mr. Cole relied most fully on the reports sent almost daily by Dr. Ingledew. When this last letter arrived at Madras, Lingarája had seized the reins. Dr. Ingledew was indignant. But nothing could disturb the tranquillity of Mr. Cole. Since Lingarája was now actually in possession of Coorg, he advised Government to countenance him as long as he would respect the rights of the little Ráni. In his innocency he thought, that such a declaration of Government was sufficient to secure the safety and happiness of the princess, whose guardianship he had solemnly undertaken in the name of the paramount power during his last visit to Vírarájendra. The Governor of Madras, under the 10th July, informed Mr. Cole, that he reprobated the conduct of Lingarája, yet he did not see, why the Company should, and how they could, interfere in the internal affairs of a country so inaccessible, and that therefore Lingarája, if he had made himself guardian of the little Ráni and regent of Coorg, must be acknowledged. Even if he should aspire to absolute power, it was not for the Company's Government, to thwart his plans. This was a very easy way of keeping faith with the faithful ally of the English Government, poor Vírarájendra. But he was now dead. In the course of July a bracelet arrived from the Governor General for Vírarájendra, in token of his sympathy with his grievous affliction and of his undiminished regard and friendship. The Governor of Madras directed Mr. Cole to present the bracelet, intended for her father, to the little Ráni. This was done accordingly.

In October Mr. Cole had some disagreeable correspondence with Lingarája about the seizure of a British subject, Parsi Byramji, who had been cast into prison under a fictitious charge of having forged papers for the Rájah of Sóde. In the same month the Resident reported to Madras, that he had presented the bracelet to the little Ráni; that Lingarája was not likely to give up the reins; that the Sóde Rájah claimed one lac of Rupees of the money in the Bombay funds and a Jaghir of the value of 4000 or 5000 pagodas according to a promise made him by Vírarájendra; that Lingarája objected to this demand, and that Mr. Cole wished to know how he should act. The Rájah of Sóde afterwards consented to receive one lac of Rupees in specie, and four thousand Rupees for travelling expenses, in full for all his claims, when the money was paid him and he retired to his own country. Lingarája sent a deputation to Madras, consisting of Ayya Ponnappa, Muttanna, and Hírji, a Parsi, who had to deliver to the Governor a picture of the late Vírarájendra. The present was graciously received, the deputation dismissed with suitable gifts, and a letter written to Lingarája, which was calculated to satisfy him fully. He was thanked for the picture, praised for having taken under his immediate care the children of his late brother, commended for having taken the guardianship of Dévammáji and the regency of Coorg at the desire of his niece, and for having made a liberal provision for the Sóde Rájah, and, lastly, his professions of fidelity and attachment to the British Government were acknowledged and reciprocated with expressions of favour and friendship. The letter was addressed to Lingarájendra Vodeya, Regent of Coorg, and bore the date of 28th February 1810. Under the same date a letter was addressed by the Governor General, the Marquis of Hastings, to Dévammáji, Ráni of Coorg. The Governor General said, that he had received the acknowledgement of his letter of 3rd April 1809 to Vírarájendra, which had unfortunately came too late; and that he wished the daughter to keep the Amulet (sic!!) of favour and protection, which had been intended for her lamented father. "The arrangement which has been made for the administration of the country during your minority, has my entire approbation. As your uncle and guardian, Lingarájendra Vodeya was justly the object of your choice, while from his respectable character he possesses in a great degree the confidence and affections of the people, I am satisfied, that an administration conducted by his virtues and abilities, is calculated to promote the prosperity of your country and the happiness of your subjects, and that in his parental care and guardianship you will experience the utmost attainable compensation for the loss of your respected father."

Lingarája was now acknowledged guardian of the young Ráni and regent of Coorg. The next step was, to make his helpless ward sign a paper, in which she abdicated her sovereignty in favour of her excellent and loving uncle. The document was duly transmitted to Mr. Cole, who was requested to forward it to the Governor of Madras and to the Supreme Government. This was done in the summer of 1810. On the 14th December the Marquis of Hastings signed a despatch to the Government of Fort St. George on the subject of Coorg. The document of abdication, signed by the little Ráni, appeared to him to be of no value whatever. Being a child, she could not be considered as capable of judging correctly and acting for herself. It was no doubt altogether a scheme and a fraud of Lingarája. However, the Governor General was of opinion, that it was unnecessary to take any steps now. It would be time enough, when the young Ráni attained her majority, to inquire, if she was really resolved on abandoning her claim to the throne of Coorg. In the beginning of 1811 Lingarája announced to the Government of Fort St. George, that he had permanently assumed the Government of Coorg, whereupon the Governor in Council addressed a letter to the Resident, desiring him to make inquiry into the claims of Lingarája to the sovereignty of Coorg according to Coorg law and usage, and suggesting, that the end might be best attained by a personal visit to Coorg. This plan, however, was not executed, nor would it have been of the slightest use to conduct an inquiry in Coorg, where no one, who cared for his life, could speak the truth in an affair connected with the Rájah.

One thing remained to be accomplished. Lingarája had taken possession of Coorg, supplanted his niece and obtained the sanction or at least the connivance of the Government of the East India Company, but there were three lacs of Rupees in the Bombay funds and upwards of five and an half lacs of Rupees in the Madras funds, both sums standing in the name of Dévammáji. His heart was fully set on the money, and throughout the year 1811 he was busy in smoothing the way for the appropriation of the treasure. Some deputies were sent to Madras with instructions from the Rájah of Coorg, to demand the interest of the sum deposited in the Company's treasury by Vírarájendra. The Accountant General first demurred to the payment of interest into the hands of any other person but an accredited agent of the owner of the bonds, Dévammáji, the daughter of Vírarájendra. Lingarája represented, that Vírarája had left this large legacy to his daughter, because he intended her to succeed to the sovereignty. But since he himself was now charged with the government of the country, he must protest against any private member of the family being considered proprietor of so considerable a portion of the public funds. At the same time an attempt was made to appropriate the three lacs in the Bombay funds. The Company at that period reduced the interest on the public loan. Creditors, disinclined to submit to the contemplated reduction, were to receive payment for their bonds. Lingarája took the opportunity of selling the three lacs of Víraŗájendra to Messrs. Forbes and Co., who demanded cash payment from Government. Here also the treasury objected, because the bonds were not in Lingarája's name. References were made from Bombay and Madras to the Supreme Government on the subject of the Coorg bonds. Instructions were requested.

The Governor General, however, declared, that he reserved the settlement of the question for the future. It was not absolutely necessary now to solve the difficulty. When Dévammáji attained her majority, it would be time enough to see, whose the property in the Madras funds was. In the mean time Lingarája might draw the interest as guardian of Dévammáji and regent of Coorg. As to the Bombay bonds, it was Lingarája's business to prove in a court of law, that he was the proprietor, when the principal should without any demur be placed in the hands of his agents. Lingarája disliked the idea of a judicial investigation, but succeeded afterwards in appropriating the bonds to himself. At Madras, Messrs. Binny & Co. drew the interest every year for the Rájah of Coorg, first in Dévammáji's name, and afterwards in the name of Lingarája and his son, Vírarája, themselves How the change in the wording of the bonds was effected cannot now be discovered.

Before the end of 1812 Lingarája had succeeded to his full satisfaction in all his plans. He had taken possession of the inheritance of his brother Vírarájendra, Coorg was his, and he was almost formally acknowledged as Rájah by the paramount power. The large legacy, left to Dévammáji by her father, was as good as his own, because the Company, who had taken charge of the money from Vírarájendra for his daughter, permitted him to draw the interest, although not recognizing the claim, which he had endeavoured to set up, saying, that there could not be a transfer from a Rájah of Coorg of large property, by way of bequest, to a private member of his family, since the property of the Rájahs was always considered as state property. It was, indeed, of no great consequence, whether Lingarája's plea was allowed, or disallowed, by the Supreme Government, as long as they winked at his robbing his niece of the interest of her bonds. Yet Lingarája felt uneasy from time to time. He distrusted the disposition of the English Government, though it was perfectly friendly to a fault. He had a higher opinion of the good faith of the Company to Vírarájendra and his daughter, than they had themselves of their duty to keep their word pledged to the fulfilment of their devoted ally's last will.

It may be seen from the following extracts, that the Coorg Rájah as early as 1811 was subject to fits of fear, lest the Company should execute judgment upon him, which induced him secretly to fortify his country.

2. *General Welsh's visits to Lingarája.*

The extracts, embodied in the following pages, are taken from a work, entitled "Military Reminiscences extracted from a journal of nearly forty years' active service in the East Indies, by Colonel (now General) James Welsh." General Welsh's somewhat loosely connected, but truthful, though now and then romance-like, sketches give a perfectly correct account of Lingarája, and show also to very life the character of the relations then existing between the Government of the East India Company and the Rájah of Coorg. The Rájah was on friendly terms with the Company's Government, yet dreaded it. He was dependent upon them, yet affected a semblance of independence. He courted the favour of English Officers and invited them frequently into his country, yet guarded with the greatest jealousy their intercourse with his people. He prided himself on his European manners and character, and pretended to be adored by his subjects, while he kept them in the most abject bondage and crushed their spirit by a system of savage cruelty. He was permitted to do what he liked with his own people. The Company's Government took their responsibilities as the paramount power of India easy, and forgot, that they had pledged themselves to the fulfilment of Víraráјendra's last will.

The 10th chapter of the Reminiscences treats on Coorg; we read there:—"In the days of Hyder's successful usurpation of the Musnud of Mysore, the reigning Rájah of Coorg was defeated and taken prisoner by this Mussulman Prince and carried to Mysore, where he was kindly treated from policy, and persuaded the usurper, that if he would send him back to his own country, he would prevail on all his subjects to submit to the Mussulman yoke; they having previously betaken themselves to their hills and fastnesses, from whence he could neither drive nor recall them. He proved himself an able statesman, if such a term be applicable to a mountain chief, since he improved the natural fortifications of his kingdom, built towns, formed an armed militia, and successfully defied his former conqueror. He was succeeded by the boy, whom his blindness had spared, and left him immense wealth, as well as most absolute power over all his subjects and every kind of property in his little kingdom, indeed, I blush to write it, the absolute deity of his ignorant and misguided people. Such, in March 1811, was Lingarájendra Vodeyaru, to whom I carried an introduction from the Honorable Arthur Cole, Resident in Mysore, who was also nominal Resident in Coorg."

In the above extract General Welsh, though no doubt unintentionally, makes several mis-statements. Amongst the English Officers and Officials, then stationed in Mysore, such may have been the current talk about the Rájah of Coorg. But, as already shown in a former part of the history, it is a fact, that Lingarája, the father of Víraája was allured to Mysore by Hyder Ali and there detained, ostensibly as a guest, but in reality as a prisoner, until by stratagem he returned to Coorg. Víraŕája, however, lived for several years as a prisoner in the Fort of Periapatna, until he escaped over the frontier into his mountain home and asserted his independence. General Welsh confounds father and son. Again Lingarája was no longer a "boy" when his brother Víraŕája died, but a man of 34 years of age. Finally the Coorgs as little worshipped their Rájahs as Gods, as did the Romans their Cæsars, when they burnt incense before their images!

"On the 19th of the same month, having heard much in praise of the sport in Coorg, and being at leisure for such a trip, I set out from Bangalore, in company with Lieut. W. Williamson, a young man of my own corps, both a keen and hardy sportsman as well as a very agreeable companion. We travelled post, in palanquin, to Víraŕájendrapet, a distance of one hundred and fifty miles. On the 22nd of March after a hearty breakfast, provided for us by the Rájah's people, *gratis*, we mounted two large elephants, at daybreak, and proceeded over hills and through vales, up and down, zigzag, now at the bottom of deep ravines, then at the top of precipices, till, at last, after eight hours' fagging, we reached the palace built for the accommodation of Europeans outside the stonefort of Mercara, the capital.

"This place is delightfully situated on an eminence, near the summit of a range of lofty and difficult mountains. The pass up these mountains being fortified and defended, however, would make it a very strong place, for it completely commands every approach on the other side. The distance we estimated at twenty-four miles. The Rájah's own palace is inside the fort; but his horse and elephant stables are outside on the slope of the glacis. The town is remarkably clean and well built, about half a mile off by an excellent high road, and at the farther extremity there is a rising ground, with a strong mud barrier, after entering which, you come upon a small plain with a magnificent tomb, erected by the present Rájah to the memory of his late brother and his wife. It is much in the style of Mahommedan edifices, being a wide square with a handsome dome in the centre and four turrets at the angles. On the top of the dome is a gold ball, with a weathercock above it, and all the window bars are made of solid brass.

"On this spot, by appointment, we met the Mahá Swámi, at half past three in the evening. He was dressed in a Major-general's uniform, appeared to be about thirty years of age, with very handsome features, and a person in which were joined both activity and strength. He immediately shook hands with us, and desired us to be seated, after a short conversation in Hindustáni, which he at first addressed to an interpreter, until he found that I could speak and understand him in that language; he then produced several rifles, ready loaded, ordered cocoanuts to be hoisted on the tops of spears, fifty yards off, and then desired us to fire. Suffice it to say, he beat us both most completely, splitting every nut he fired at in the centre, while we either struck the sides or missed entirely. After this, he asked us to take a ride with him; a beautiful English horse was brought to me, an Arabian to Lieutenant Williamson, and he himself also rode a very fine Arabian. We rattled about in the square for half an hour, when he desired us to alight and rest ourselves; and taking a long spear, performed several feats with it still on horseback, with great grace and dexterity. Our horses being brought again, we remounted, and proceeded with him to the fort; the Rájah insisting on our riding one on each side of him all the way. On entering his palace, we were amused by a set of dancing girls, keeping time to reels and country dances, played on two fiddles; and the Mahá Swámi shewed us various portraits of himself, the King, the Prince of Wales, General Wellesley, &c. He then took us into another apartment, and shewed us a dozen of highly finished single and double rifles, by Manton and Jover; fowling-pieces, pistols, &c., then an air gun, which he desired us to try. It was now seven P. M., and torchlight had succeeded the daylight in his courtyard; we took aim out of the window, at various things, and hit them, and I even knocked down a lime, a species of small lemon, off the top of a cocoanut, so uncommonly true did it carry. His son and several relations were next introduced to us, all fine looking boys; and the heir apparent, being about seven or eight years old, dressed in a General's uniform, with a sword by his side, put me in mind of some old French prints, in which the girls are dressed in hoops and farthingales, and the boys with bag wigs and small swords. Ram-fights, &c. were going on all this time in the yard, as it were to amuse the attendants; and two of the rams had four horns each. Then a lion made his appearance, led by a dozen men, with a strong rope. He appeared very tame, played with his leaders, and suffered me to go up to him and pat him on the back. Next came a large royal tiger and two panthers, the former having his claws pared, but very savage, trying every instant to break loose. We took leave at half past seven, quite pleased with the kind and affable treatment of this Prince, who, I am inclined to believe, is adored by his people.

"I must now describe our own habitation, built on a small island, surrounded by paddy ground, now dry, for the sole accommodation of Europeans. It is a large square, having a hall in the centre, a large covered-in verandah all round it, and four bed-rooms projecting at the angles of the verandah, all on an upper story, the lower rooms serving for the guard, attendants, store-rooms, etc. It stands on a square of seventy feet, the verandah having thirty-eight glass windows, with Venetian blinds outside. The bed-rooms have sixteen windows, and the hall eight glass doors; every part being neatly furnished, in the English style, with beds, tables, card-tables, writing boxes, chairs, chandeliers, settees, etc. etc. And there is an old butler of my early Vellore friend, Colonel Ridgway Mealay, and a dozen active servants, who very speedily produce an English breakfast or dinner, served up on handsome Queen's ware, with every kind of European liquor; and what is even still more extraordinary, the cook bakes good bread!

"After all our exertions of this day, it may readily be supposed we slept soundly; and on the morning of the 23rd rose betimes an usual, a custom which I most strenuously recommend to all young men doomed to spend any time in the East, and went to visit the Rájah's stud and elephants; and amongst the latter found a young white one, about two years old, most perfectly formed, with flaxen hair, light eyes, and fair skin. Of these animals, as his country abounds in them, he has great abundance. After breakfast, we were astonished by a visit from the Mahá Swámi, in state. No longer disguised in an European dress, he appeared in his native robes, richly decorated with jewels; and *certes*, in my eyes, he appeared a much handsomer man. He sat a few minutes, and then told us that he had received intelligence of a wild elephant, and would, if we pleased, accompany us to go and shoot him. To us, this was the most acceptable offer he could have made. We retired to prepare ourselves, and our shooting apparatus; and, on our return from our own rooms, found his Highness ready, with elephants and attendants. Away we set, the Rájah himself driving the one I rode, sitting across its neck, with a hook in the right hand and a knife in the other, to cut down any small branches of trees likely to incommode me in the excursion. 'Such a man,' thought I, 'at the head of his followers, must be invincible.' So perfectly different from the effeminate grandeur of most eastern potentates.* Arrived at the spot, which was only about a mile off, we dismounted, and, while the people were preparing seats on trees for our reception, amused ourselves shooting arrows at a mark, in which, as usual, the Rájah beat us hollow. When all was ready, each climbed his own tree, the Rájah between us, and sat in a snug little wicker-box with three guns of the Rájah's each, and two of his eunuchs to load our pieces. The Rájah had a single rifle carrying a twelve ounce ball, and two double ones, of one ounce each....The creature rolled over instantaneously, carrying away several small trees, as he extended his enormous bulk upon the ground....It stood ten feet high, and was in excellent condition; the tusks were two feet outside, and nearly three feet long when extracted; and the length of the body was very nearly the same as its height.....Here, supposing our day's work was concluded, we proposed to take leave, but we were yet to learn something further of the kind attentions of this excellent Prince. He told us, that having kept us so long from our own tiffin, it being then three o'clock, he had ordered a dinner to be brought out for us; and, to our surprise, we found a small house built of leaves, a table and chairs, a dinner, consisting of pillawe, mutton cutlets, curry, &c. all ready for us. Nor was this all: the Rájah followed us in, and begged us to excuse him, as he was not very well; but left his servants with guns, powder, shot, &c. and four elephants, desiring us to amuse ourselves after dinner as we pleased. We accordingly dined, and then beat a thick jungle for game, though without success, it being the dry season, when they retire into the most inaccessible parts of the mountains. At five P. M., we returned to our palace, well satisfied with the adventures of the day.....On the 25th of March, we

* Sorry shall I be, in the sequel, to reverse this most delightful, though airy vision; but truth, with me, is the first maxim, and it will force me to dispel the delightful romance which was here intruded on us by the most plausible appearances.

paid our parting visit to the Mahá Swámi, and received from him the following presents: two gold-handled Coorg knives, two panther-skin caps, two sandalwood sticks, one royal tiger- and two panther-skins, and parted from him with mutual expressions of esteem and regard. The Rájah informed us, that the present indifferent state of his health, and not being certain of finding game immediately, had alone prevented his taking us into the country to shoot, but promised, if we would return at the same season next year, we should be amply gratified with field sports. Thus ended my first trip to Coorg.... I shall anticipate a period of my Journal, and extract the next trip at once. Accompanied by Lieutenant Meredith, I set out on the 17th of October 1812, and reached Siddhéshvara, the first village in his country; after which my Diary regularly proceeds as follows:—

"Here we were regaled with curry and rice, by the Coorg Rájah's guards, who refused any pecuniary remuneration. The stockade seems newly finished. We had some very unpleasant heavy rain in the evening, and saw many wild fowl in the tank. The whole road from Periapatna is extremely bad, and would require much repair to fit it for the passage of guns. There was more rain in the night, succeeded by a fog.

"On the 18th of October we set forward, still in our palanquins, in a dense fog.....The road the whole way was very bad. The last four miles, in particular, through swamps and paddy ground, intersected by deep water-courses.

"We arrived at Vírarájendrapett at twenty minutes past three P. M., and took a walk to look at a Christian church building at the western extremity of the village; it is about half finished, and will be a grand edifice for the Romish Christians to erect in a Pagan country. It is built from the foundation of a porous stone, called soap-stone on the Malabar Coast, cemented with light clay, very thick; and from a distance resembles on old Gothic ruin in England. The Rájah's Subadar gave us a curry, rice, fruit, vegetables, &c. and even sent us two China plates and one copper spoon. He had previously furnished us with a table and two chairs. On the 19th we set out at three A. M., and proceeded to the Kávéri, which we reached at seven A. M., and crossed in boats, the stream being about six feet deep. The banks are exceedingly high and steep, and a strong barrier is placed on the left bank, called Angree.....We found the fort of Mercara completely repaired, and, passing it, took up our abode in the old place, at a quarter-past twelve, having been nine hours and a quarter on the road; the last five on elephants. We then had our breakfast and took a sleep, after which mounted two fine horses, and paid our respects to the Mahá Swámi. He received us in his usual manner, in his palace, having sent off his camp equipage, &c. to give us a shooting party in the interior. No general officer's uniform this time; but he looked well, and was very kind and attentive. He shewed us two lions, two tigers, two wild buffaloes, and a royal tiger-cub; then a gun, completely made, and highly finished, by his own smith; and I really never saw a more elegant fowling-piece. After sitting nearly two hours with him we took our leave; and when our dinner was served up, two of his fiddlers made their appearance and regaled us with English tunes! In short, every thing apes England in this most extraordinary place. We, two plain soldiers, sat down to a roasted goose, and twenty other dishes, and drank a bottle of English claret between us; rejecting, to the amazement of the beholders, Madeira, beer, hock, &c. all of which they expected us to swallow.

"On the 20th of October we rose with the lark, and took a walk, first to the Mausoleum, and afterwards to the horse and elephant stables. The little white elephant had grown considerably, but his skin was getting darker, and he appeared to be in bad health. Lieutenant Davies joined us here from

Mysore, at half-past ten; and having to start early, we dined at noon. At one P. M., the Rájah arrived in his military uniform, on horseback. He dismounted and sat with us some time, shewing us some of his guns, and then inviting us to mount our horses and proceed, he accompanied us to the top of the hill, when, wishing us good sport, he returned, and we pursued our journey. We found six tents pitched in a clean compound, about five miles off.....On the 21st of October, after breakfast, we mounted our elephants, at seven A. M., and proceeded over nullahs, swamps, hills, &c. about five miles further, where we found our trees prepared, and all the jungle beset by some thousands of beaters; when we forthwith climbed our respective ladders, to wicker litters, in the centre of a deep jungle.....

"On the 22nd we set out a little after six A. M.; it was impossible to tell the direction, but through rivers, jungles, &c. and latterly, ascending a steep and very high mountain covered with wood, our elephants groping and kneeling, while our empty palanquins could not even be carried up from the bottom, we gained a beautiful plain on the summit, covered with trees and deep jungle all round it; the distance about eight miles: it is called Perumboo Kaud, on a range designated Pannimatta Kundu.....And here, at nine A. M., we set to work in the old way. I saw six elks, and fired at three; Lieuts. Davies and Meredith saw only three, the former did not fire, the latter fired twice.....On the 23rd we started at half-past six. I have remarked that all the Coorg pike-men, instead of trailing or sloping their pike, when they come to trees and other obstacles, always carry it in the left hand, and advancing the right to support it, 'charge pikes,' and push on. This is evidently descipline, and may be taught for their own safety, in advancing among wild beasts. We passed the mountain we were on yesterday, and dismounting at the bottom of one a mile further, ascended on foot to the summit. Our sport did not commence till eleven A. M., the jungle being amazingly thick and game rather scarce. I fired and wounded an elk, which Meredith killed, and I killed a jungloe buckrah, or wood-goat, with a single ball, while running like the wind; it was a very curious animal, with a body the same colour and size of a deer, having exceedingly short legs, and therefore its swiftness must proceed from the length and strength of its body; it had short branching antlers, and was so extraordinary an animal altogether, that I preserved the head and antlers.....It was the only animal of the kind, I ever saw in my life. A panther was started, but he escaped, from the density of the jungle. We got into our palanquins at sunset, and moving in great state, with every one of our three thousand beaters carrying a lighted fire-stick, arrived at our pavilion at half-past eight P. M., actually illuminating all the country through which we passed. Our total game killed this day was one wild hog, seven elks, and one junglee buckrah. It matters not to what distance we ramble, the Rájah's attention and kindness extend all over his dominions. We never sit down to a meal, but in pops a large basket of fruit, or some sweetmeats from his own table, and his people are the most orderly, obliging, willing creatures I have ever met in my life. And all this without the slightest hope of reward, which in general will go a great way with the natives of India; but these people reject, with apparent horror, every proffered present, even when alone. There is certainly something very uncommon, indeed unfathomable, in this.

"On the 24th of October we tried another spot, a little out of our way to Mercara, but had no sport, killing one elk only and returned home in the evening. I have observed, that every square league, or mile occasionally, is marked out into a kind of fortification; having a high bank, deep ditch, hedge, and barrier. This renders the country extremely strong in a military point of view, every man being a good marksman, and famous for sporting; because two thousand men can do more in such enclosures, than ten, or even twenty thousand, in equally thick jungle, without these advantages. I remarked also, this evening, from my bed-room window, an immense concourse of people, seemingly labourers, winding through a distant road, and mentioning the circumstance at dinner, I observed it threw a damp on the countenances of the attendants, amongst whom, in spite of all my entreaties to the contrary, I saw the native officer of our honorary guard. No one would satisfy my curiosity. I therefore changed the subject, and speaking to my old friend the butler, asked him how he came to be so sickly since I last saw him, and what had become of four fat Bengalees, who amused me with their civilities, when I was last there? A part of their duty being to run after us, if we only went into the garden for a moment; one carrying a chair, another a juglet of water, a third a bottle and tumbler, as if an European could not exist a minute without such accompaniments. He turned pale, and trembled; told me he had had a fever, but was now better, and that the other men were gone away. I rallied him on his grave appearance, and inquired if he was not happy. He immediately replied, "Happy! he must be happy in such a service; that every one, under the Mahá Swámi, enjoyed happiness." I immediately launched forth in his praise, and I observed this gave Mahomed pleasure; little did I dream, that every word he or I uttered, would be instantly repeated to the Rájah; yet, fortunately every thing I then had to say, was favourable. On retiring to rest, and sitting down to bring up my Journal, the occurrences of the day passing in review, I began to ruminate particularly on the workmen I had seen, and all the repairs I had witnessed in the fort and barriers. It immediately struck me that the Rájah, mistaking a late prohibition of Europeans passing through his country, issued in consequence of the gross misconduct of two officers, both since dismissed from the King's and Company's service, had imagined the British were going to declare war against him, and was consequently fortifying his country; and I supposed the work-people were employed on some strong place in the neighbourhood. Having obtained special permission for myself and companions, I determined that I would immediately undeceive him, as an act of kindness to both parties.

Rising very early on the 25th, we took a quiet walk in the garden, and returning up-stairs, were followed by Mahomed Sahib, the butler, who entreated to speak with me in private, and to request Lieutenant Meredith to remain in the verandah, to prevent any one from listening. This we acquiesced in; and no sooner were we alone in the bed-chamber, than he threw himself at my feet, and entreated me, by the memory of his old master, to save his life. I was perfectly thunderstruck; raised him up, and desired him to explain himself; when he told me a tale which harrowed my soul. The four Bengalees, whom I had left fat and happy, had become dissatisfied with promises, and wages protracted and never paid; they had demanded their dismissal, and had, in consequence, been inhumanly murdered. He himself had applied for leave, and was immediately mulcted of all he had, and his thumbs squeezed in screws, made on purpose, and used in native courts; his body flagellated, and a threat held out, that the next offence would be punished with death. That the Rájah being acknowledged as the God of the country, exercised the supposed right without remorse and without control. That, for instance, if a poor fellow, standing in his presence, with both hands joined in adoration as of the Supreme, incessantly calling out Mahá Swámi! or Great God! should be suddenly bit by a musquito, and loosen his hands to scratch; a sign too well known, would instantly be made by this *soidisant* Deity, and the poor wretch be a head shorter in a twinkling. This, he told me, had been the fate of the fine-looking Parsee interpreter, whom I had seen at my last visit, who, having built a house, and amassed some wealth, was beheaded, and his property seized for the state; and this, he also assured me, was the fate of every man who entered the country, if he ever attempted to quit it again: and the Rájah, admitting his troops to a share in the plunder, bound them to his interests by chains of adamant. He entreated me to take him with me out of the country, which, he said could be easily accomplished, because he must accompany me to the barrier; but I could not listen to such a proposal, and at once told him so. To connive at the escape of one of the Rájah's servants, while I was his guest, would have been a direct breach of hospitality, which I could not consent to practice. But learning on some further conversation, that the native officer, under the appearance of an honorary guard was placed there as a spy over every word and action of every gentleman who lived in that palace, I proposed to enter into such conversation with him, in Hindustáni as being reported, might induce the Rájah to grant him leave. He also told me, that the Rájah fearing some attack from the English, was building new forts, and repairing all the old ones, and then retired, I believe, unobserved. The signal being made for breakfast, we sat down, attended as usual. I entered into conversation with Mahomed Sahib, talked of his mistress now at Madras, and his late master's will, and asked him if he had received the thousand pagoda legacy his master had left him. He replied, it was the first he had heard of it. I had, however, actually heard something of the kind, and advised him to get four months' leave of absence, to go and see his old mistress, before she embarked for England. He told me, he certainly should like to go and see her, but he could not bear to leave so good, so kind a master as the Mahá Swámi; to which I replied, that I was sure the Rájah would allow him to go with pleasure, and said, I would immediately ask his Highness; but he begged me not, as he was sure the Rájah would allow him to go, if it were really for his advantage; here the conversation dropped, and being reported, it had a capital effect.

This forenoon we took our leave of the Rájah, who received us in his palace, where he was amusing himself shooting blunt, but very heavy headed arrows, at different men, armed with spear and shield; whose business was to guard themselves, and receive the blow on their shields. He afterwards fired at marks, rode several horses in a ring, and lastly, managed two elephants, one of which he requested me to mount, and drove me about for a short time, and then dismounted. I had been informed, that in consequence of my increased rank, since I was last there, he had prepared an elephant as a present. I then imagined this was the one, but I was mistaken. He gave Meredith a bird's head, called Malliárapah, a gold-mounted Coorg knife, and sandalwood stick; and to me, two spears, a gold-mounted knife, sandal-stick, and bird's head, and wished us a pleasant journey. With all this kindness, I could not help remarking, that his Highness had lost some of his affability, so easily are we led by circumstances, or by previous opinion, to fancy what, perhaps, has no existence. His conduct to us throughout had been kind and condescending, beyond that of any native Prince I ever knew, and was never equalled, in after times, but by the Rájah of Népaunee. He was particularly fond of the flower of the Calderah, called in Hindustáni, Kewrah, the odour of which is generally too strong for English organs, but sweet beyond any flower in the East. No man in his dominions dare use it, all being the property of the Mahá Swámi; as the finest flowers of their gardens are appropriated solely to the decoration of their temples, by all the other natives of India.

The sequel may as well be anticipated here, to connect the whole in one. A few months after, when in my own house at Bangalore, I was surprised by the sudden appearance of Mahomed Sahib, extremely emaciated, ill-dressed, and with a picture in his hand. He threw himself at my feet, and told me I have saved his life, that the Rájah had given him four months' leave, and desired him to carry his picture to me, in proof thereof. I refused it, however, when he told me he had returned a beggar, being stripped of every thing at the last barrier; but that he never would return. I saw him in a good place, shortly afterwards, well and happy. The Rájah, Lingrájender Wodeer died in the year 1820, and was succeeded on the Musnud by his son, whom I had seen an infant in 1810. I have heard of no cruelties committed by the present Mahá Swámi, who is described as a mild, inoffensive young man. The English have had, however, little or no intercourse with that country, since 1811, a road being opened through Wynád to the Malabar coast, and a capital ghaut made by our own pioneers. I have omitted to mention, that as this country abounds with royal tigers, it is absolutely necessary that they should be hunted every season, and the former Rájah seldom killed fewer than there were days in the year; and invariably gave a gold bangle to the first man who should touch the tiger, after he had fired, which must make brave soldiers."

The above extracts give a tolerably correct idea of Lingarájah's character and of the state of Coorg from the death of Vírarájendra to the deposition of the present ex-rájah in 1834. Vírarájendra was impelled to deeds of blood by a naturally savage temperament, hardened by habits of internecine warfare in which he was engaged almost throughout life, and inflamed towards the end of his career by paroxysms of the darkest suspicions, and a melancholy ever hovering on the brink of insanity. His brother, Lingarája, had none of his redeeming qualities. His cruelty was without excuse. He had some ambition to shine as a poet. Some of his pieces, addressed to one of his wives, are still preserved. They have no merit, and were perhaps made for him. However, he may have been a Nero in a small way. Cruelty seems to have been his sport. He liked to kill his victims with his own hand, with gun, bow or knife. For small offences people had their ears cropped, their noses cut, or their tongues clipped. For an impertinent answer men or women had their mouths rinsed, that was the phrase, i. e. their lips were cut off all round their mouths, and they were left to perish without food or drink. Others were thrown down a precipice on the hill side, near the "Rájah's seat" in Mercara. Many seem to have been destroyed merely for the purpose of confiscating their property, for Lingarája had as great a passion for gold as for blood.

During the first years of his reign he was restrained from giving full vent to his atrocious propensities by the influence of his Devan, Kshauryakere Appanna, who seems to have been a man of character and independence, bold enough to lecture the tyrant whom he had placed on the throne in preference to the rule of a stranger, the Rájah of Sóde. But by degrees Lingarája became impatient of the control of a subject. Appanna, relying on the Rájah's gratitude, continued to exhort, to warn and, at times, to resist his master. He had mistaken his man. One day the Devan was seized and carried before the Rájah. He was charged with treason. He knew, that he was doomed. The Rájah himself conducted the investigation. "Confess your guilt," he cried. "I am guilty indeed," replied the intrepid minister, "of one crime, of having made a wretch like you, Rájah of Coorg." Lingarája was mad with rage. Appanna, with several other so called accomplices, was carried out into the jungle to a distance of some miles. There they were nailed to some large trees, the Rájah feasting his eyes on the torments of his helpless victims, who died with curses on their lips. A large number of people, the families, relations and friends of the condemned men, were slaughtered on the occasion. Some say, that the Devan had entered into a conspiracy against the Rájah's life, and that on a hunting excursion a shot, aimed at Lingarája, passed close by him, whereupon he seized the traitors and exterminated them and their party; but this may only be an invention of the Rájah, calculated to throw a veil over a crime of a dye too dark even for Coorg. In 1820 the miserable tyrant died. He believed that he was destroyed through magic arts and demoniac influences employed by secret enemies. He had held possession of Coorg for eleven long years. The complete ignorance of his subjects, whom he managed to isolate entirely from the surrounding countries, subject to the East India Company, combined with the terror of his arm, kept up by frequent executions, and a system of treacherous espionage, fostered by the Rájah among his terrified slaves, laid the Coorgs prostrate at the feet of their rapacious and blood-thirsty master. He died forty-five years of age amidst the gloom of dread superstitions. His queen, who preferred death to the fate which, she thought, awaited her from the hatred of the young Rájah, swallowed diamond powder, and was buried with Lingarája in a splendid sepulchre near the tomb of Víragájendra.

3. Lingarája's character.

Of Lingarája's personal character, Lieut. Connor who made his acquaintance gives us the following graphic picture:—

"The late Chief, anxious to prevent his brothers from acquiring any influence, retained them in a species of exile; Appáji Sáib, the elder, is represented as having been of a violent temper and impatient of control; this turbulent spirit hurried him to a premature end, and Lingarája had nearly shared the same fate, but seems to have owed his safety to his insignificance. Having passed the early part of his life in occupations but little removed from those of the ordinary husbandman, his abilities are not above mediocrity, nor does he possess docility to compensate for the absence of genius. Weak, frivolous, and puerile, he is naturally swayed by those around him, but overbearing, irascible and sometimes cruel, he is represented as being controlled by no compunctions of morality or conscience in quieting those apprehensions to which a jealous and distrustful disposition give birth; but a suspicion easy to be provoked and difficult to be appeased, suggests the belief, that he feels all those terrors which he inspires. Authority in Codagu would seem always to have been maintained by the sword, and though circumstances will not allow of a proof of what they indicate, they warrant the conclusion, that he is at least equal to any of his predecessors in the liberal use of it. He is said to be disliked by his subjects, many of whom have fallen victims to his caprices. Of his acquirements but little can be said; his means of observation have been too limited, to admit of an extended knowledge of other countries, indeed both his ideas and information are confined within the narrow limits of his own little territory.

"A courteous dissimulation disguises under a polite deportment, a temper naturally imperious and relentless, and a suspicious and vindictive disposition is concealed by a mild and specious address; to Europeans he is remarkable for a prepossessing affability and condescension; feeling only the servility of others, and in a situation where none can resist, few dissuade, our wonder should be more excited by the suavity of manners for which he is remarkable, than the severity of disposition that characterises him.

"The nature of his education has given him a propensity to active exercises, much of his time is occupied in field sports; they are on an extensive scale and embrace a wide circle of slaughter, game without distinction or number being killed on these occasions. He is a good marksman, uses his spear with dexterity, is an excellent mahout and skilful rider; it is difficult to say, whether he takes an active personal share in the administration of his affairs—I am led to think not—nor is it easy to state what are his usual occupations or the ordinary distribution of his time, when not exposed to public view; much of it, however, is devoted to frivolous and childish pursuits.

"Lingarája is now in his forty-fourth year, about the middle size and actively formed, but in no way remarkable for any particular symmetry of features; he is rather dark complexioned and the general expression of his countenance is not disagreeable, though not indicating the habit of peremptory authority and acknowledged command; he is plain in his dress, being usually habited in a loose gown, reaching to his ancles; to this is added a black silk cape, and a cap of similar materials substitutes the place of a turban; on great occasions, however, this simplicity of dress gives way to the splendour of an English general's uniform; a string of pearls to which some jewels are affixed suspended round his neck forms the only ornament of his person, a Codagu sword is always placed on the table before him (it appears one of the ensigns of his authority) or carried with him, when he moves.

"The forms of his court exhibit but little pagentry, presenting nothing of that cumbrous and barbaric pomp in which Native Princes of whatsoever rank so much delight; indeed it is remarkable that he seems always surrounded by menials rather than men of rank. There is, however, an appearance of permanent regularity and economy, the reverse of that gorgeous improvidence for which they are remarkable. About 90 elephants and half as many horses together with some troops of dancing girls—without which Hindu greatness would be incomplete—serve to maintain the rustic splendour of his court; the few troops that garrison his town are also his guards."

Dr. Moegling pithily characterises Lingarája thus: "He was the incarnation of the worst elements of the Coorg spirit. Greediness after gold, no matter how obtained, a bottomless depth of cunning, the most brazen hypocrisy, cowardice as abject as cruel and a strong dosé of sensuality were united in his character."

In a Shásana-stone deposited in the Mercara Onkáreshvara dévastána, which was built by him, he is however, by his native admirer praised as:—"The illustrious Lingarája Wadeer, son of Lingarája and grandson of Appájirája, of the Lunar race, pure as the milky sea, worshipped with the fragrance of the Párijáta flower, of the family of Bháradwája, follower of the Ashwaláyana Sútra of Rig Véda, a zealous and learned worshipper of Shiva, sitting on the illustrious throne of Coorg in the centre of the milky city, adorned with precious jewels, of unequalled beauty and bravery, smiling like the sun in unparalleled glory, famous to the end of the world, generous and brave.—"

C. VĪRARĀJA.
1820—1834.

1. *Vírarája's tyranny.*

With the death of Lingarája affairs in Coorg did not improve. The unfortunate people had only changed masters. As soon as the young Vírarája, who was about 20 years old, had taken possession of his father's throne and treasure, he destroyed the people, who had displeased or thwarted him during the life of his father. Many members of the family of the Coorg Rájahs seem to have fallen at that time. One, Channa Víra, escaped with his family across the Mysore frontier. But to no purpose; his relative knew how to turn to account his connection with the British Government. Letters and messages were despatched to Mr. Cole, the Resident in Mysore, requesting him to order the seizure of a refractory farmer, who had made his escape from Coorg after having committed a crime, and the delivery of the criminal to the servants of the Rájah. Mr. Cole had the man apprehended near Periapatna, and sent him back to Coorg with a letter to the Rájah, requesting information as to the guilt of and the punishment awarded to the refugee. No answer was given to the Resident. Channa Víra was carried to Kántamúrnád, where he was massacred with his whole family, twenty-two souls on one day. In 1826 Mr. Casamajor, the successor of Mr. Cole, despatched a Captain Monk to Mercara and charged him, among other things, to enquire after the fate of Channa Víra. Captain Monk was told by Vírarája, that there had been much sickness in the country during the last season, and that Channa Víra with his whole family had been swept away by cholera. After this inaugural bloodshed, the new Rájah seems to have shown less cruelty than his father or uncle. An intelligent Brahman, who is intimately acquainted with Coorg affairs, told me one day, that he estimated the victims of Dodda-Vírarája's reign at about five thousand; Lingarája, he thought, had not killed more than three thousand, or perhaps three thousand five hundred; and the late Rájah had not destroyed more than fifteen hundred lives, if so many. Still, the last man was a greater curse upon Coorg, than his predecessors. Less cruel he appears to have been. (The above estimate of Coorg murders is no doubt greatly exaggerated, but the proportion assigned to the three Rájahs agrees perfectly with the general tradition of the country.) But, if less cruel, Vírarája, young as he was at his accession to the government of Coorg, became a monster of sensuality. He kept the youngest of his father's wives for his use and increased his establishment of concubines to about one hundred. A number of other women, of the best families, were summoned to Mercara after accouchements, and kept in a house near the palace during the period when they gave milk to their babes. Part of their milk was daily taken for the Rájah, to be used as a medicinal ingredient of his food which according to some superstitious notion became thereby more wholesome and nourishing. To refuse compliance with the demands of the master of Coorg was certain death, not to the recusant party only, but probably to the whole family. The wretch was free to riot as he pleased. He actually demanded to have the choice of all unmarried girls in the country. When hearing of this outrageous resolution, the Coorgs at once—it is said in one night—married all their grown up daughters. The Rájah was furious. Many of the unfortunate parents, who thus saved the honor of their children, were dreadfully flogged or had their ears cropped, or were thrown into prison. Rumours of these doings reached Mr. Casamajor. He reported to Government. But no reliable information was procurable. Coorg was kept hermetically sealed. Only a few passes were open. These were guarded by strong posts. Travellers were often detained. Without a passport no one could enter the country. On slight pretences persons were fined, maltreated, imprisoned. Some, who had gone to Coorg, disappeared altogether. Manuel Pereira, a British subject, was kept in custody by the Rájah; so was a Jew of the name of Samuel Joseph. Apprehensions were entertained for the safety of Dévammáji, the daughter and heiress of Dodda-Vírarája.

Mr. Casamajor went in person to Mercara, about the middle of November 1826, to make inquiries on the spot. He was too polite, and was completely baffled by the Rájah. The representative of the British Government was surrounded by guards and spies. No inhabitant of Coorg dared to answer his questions. The Rájah met his interrogations and admonitions with the most barefaced lies. Mr. Casamajor had to report: "I have not been able to obtain any satisfactory information from the Rájah respecting his family. Having heard, that he had a brother, eight years of age, a son five years old, and a daughter a year and an half old, I mentioned to him, that I had heard so. He said, it was a mistake; that he was quite alone, and the only male of the family." "'I am the only male, the rest are females. I have said so.'" "Dévammáji and Mahádévammáji, Dodda-Víraréjendra's daughters, were not, he said, in the palace, but in distant villages." Mr. Casamajor did not even succeed in obtaining a sight of Manuel Pereira. He returned to Mysore little satisfied; still his account of the Rájah was, on the whole, rather favorable. "He appeared anxious to please the British Government, was inquisitive, showed a good deal of intelligence, and there was some hope of improvement, as he was a young man."

Rumours of frequent executions continued to reach Mysore, and Mr. Casamajor received instructions to demand of the Rájah a regular report of every case of capital punishment ordered by him. Some correspondence ensued; Víraréja protested against this demand, but his protest was of no avail: the order was repeated. However, the Rájah never complied with it, and matters went asleep again. News came, that Víraréja had raised a regiment of female cavalry, who accompanied the Rájah on his rides, and who were drilled like soldiers. Mr. Casamajor thought, that the Rájah must be mad. He was confirmed in his opinion by the report that a Coorg, of the name of Nága, having fled the country, had been shot in effigy at Mercara. This took place in 1832.

2. *Channa Basava and Dévammáji's flight. Muddaya's murder.*

1832.

On the 17th September 1832, I. A. Casamajor, Resident in Mysore, reported to the Chief Secretary to the Government of Fort St. George, that a Coorg of the name of Channa Basava and his wife, Dévammáji, sister to the Rájah of Coorg, had taken refuge at the Residency. They had fled their country to save their honor and their lives, and implored the protection of the British Government. Dévammáji had long been kept from her husband. After an engagement of eight years, she had been permitted to join him. Of late the Rájah had made incestuous proposals to her through an old woman-servant, and had threatened to kill her husband, if she refused compliance, on the following Shivarátri festival. In this extremity they had drugged the guard of honor, who watched them, and set off from Appagalla, their residence, at nightfall. During the night they reached Beppunád, passed Amadnád in the morning and were drawing near the Mysore frontier, when they were stopped by the Coorg frontier guard. Being fired at, their party returned fire. Channa Basava placed his wife behind him on his horse, and made his way into Mysore, followed by a few of his attendants. The rest fell into the hands of the Coorgs and were carried to Mercara. Also the child of Channa Basava, a boy of a year and a half, was seized and delivered to the Rájah, his uncle. This is the substance of the reports of the Resident. That Channa Basava would have been murdered, if he had not run for his life, is probable enough. He was a scheming fellow and had drawn upon himself the Rájah's suspicions. But the charge made against Vírarája by his sister may have been unfounded, and only brought forward in order to strengthen their claim on British sympathy and protection.

The Rájah demanded, that the fugitives should be delivered to him. Mr. Casamajor demurred and referred the matter to Government. The Supreme Government decided under the 18th January 1833, that the Coorg refugees should not be restored to Víraája. In the mean time the Rájah formed mad schemes for the recovery of his relatives. They all came to nothing. Channa Basava and his wife were removed to Bangalore. There they were to have been assassinated. But every thing failed. The fugitives had dreadful stories to tell. Accusations accumulated against the Rájah of Coorg. A Parsee from Bombay had been killed at Mercara. Probably Manuel Pereira also had been destroyed. A man from the north of Coorg deposed: that he saw Víraája, on a hunting excursion, shooting at Náráyana Náyaka, Hoblidára, first with blunt arrows, then with a sharp arrow which killed him, in presence of all his retinue. Besides, numbers of people, men and women, Coorgs and slaves, relatives of the Rájah's family and others, who were believed to have been privy to the plans of Channa Basava, or to have assisted him in his escape, were killed, or mutilated, or starved to death, or thrown into prison.

Among the first victims of the Rájah's wrath was Muddaya, a brother of Channa Basava, Munshi to the Rájah, and a favourite. Víraája himself beat him cruelly; afterwards he was executed by Kunta Basava, an upstart favourite of Lingarája, who having been both the tool and the prompter of the father, kept his position and influence with the son. He was first dog-boy, then soldier, then Jemadar; then he rose to the post of Commander; at last he became principal Devan. He was a vicious, overbearing, slavish, unprincipled man. By killing Muddaya, he got rid of a rival. Muddaya had been a clever and respectable man, and was perfectly ignorant of Channa Basava's plans. Every body knew, that the poor man had been destroyed without cause. The Rájah himself, hardened as he was, had terrible fits of remorse. Muddaya would not let him sleep. As soon as he sunk into slumber, Muddaya would stand over him with a drawn sword, and Vírarája awake, crying: murder! Muddaya! seize him! After some days a conjurer showed the Rájah how to obtain rest. If he had a picture of the dead man painted on a fresh wall, and looked at it every twenty-four minutes during the day, his nightly frights would abate. The Rájah took the wise man's advice, had a likeness of Muddaya painted on a new wall, and walked up to it every now and then, saying: I slew him, because he was a traitor. By degrees his sleep returned.

3. *Complications with the British Government.*

These cruelties of Vírarája accelerated his downfall. On the 18th January 1833, Sir Fred. Adam, Governor of Madras, addressed a long letter to the Rájah of Coorg, giving him a sound lecture on the principles of good Government, warning him most earnestly and positively demanding compliance, in future, with the order of Government, communicated to the Rájah in 1827, to report all capital punishments taking place in Coorg. Sir Fred. Adam informed the Rájah, that Mr. Casamajor was desired to proceed to Coorg in order to have a personal conference with the Rájah, and that Government demanded free passage for any person, who might desire to accompany Mr. Casamajor on his return out of Coorg. The interview between the Rájah and Mr. Casamajor took place before the end of January 1833, at Mercara. Seven years, Mr. Casamajor observed, had produced a marked change in the Rájah. The Resident wondered; for he had not, could not have, an idea of the extreme profligacy of the man, nor of the strength of his murderous propensities, that had steeped him deep in blood during the interval between 1826 and 1833. The Rájah looked uneasy, seemed to be subject to sudden alarms and very unsteady of purpose. The presence of an English gentleman and a representative of the great Sirkár, to which he owed allegiance, must have been very distressing to the abandoned, guilty man, whom folly, passion and a maddened conscience were now hurrying onward to ruin.

While Mr. Casamajor was at Mercara, Víraája was deep in intrigues. He had lately entertained the bedmaker of the Rájah of Mysore, who had come on a secret mission of treason against the Company. He had endeavoured to engage the services of a merchant of Mysore, Nun Lál Barti, for the murder of Channa Basava, and for opening a communication with Ranjit Sing, whom he was led to believe to be a secret enemy of the English. He succeeded in finding out a Sikh man, a native of Lahore, called Lahore Sing, and persuaded him to go on an embassy to the Sikh-ruler, undeterred by the shrewd remark of the stranger, that Lahore being so far from Mercara, it would be difficult for Ranjit Sing to avail himself of the friendly offices of the Mahárájah of Coorg. He had secretly encouraged a rebellious Polygar of Nagar, of the name of Súryappa, who had given considerable trouble to the English authorities. And now he had to confront Mr. Casamajor. He could not but look embarrassed, alarmed, unsteady. The Resident solemnly warned the Rájah to abstain in future from his cruelties, and advised him to relax the rigour with which he had shut up his people from communication with their neighbours under the rule of the Company. Víraája contended, that he could not do away with, nor even relax, ancient observances without losing his authority. When Mr. Casamajor hinted, that he knew more, than he chose to say, of the Rájah's disaffection, and that further disobedience might be punished with deposition, the Rájah used the language of calumniated innocence, and made the strongest professions of obedience to the Company. Formerly, when very young, he might have been too severe, he admitted; but now he was more considerate. As for a change of system, however, he was most reluctant, and when Mr. Casamajor pressed the point, he turned round and asserted, that he would do as he pleased, Coorg was an independent country, etc. Mr. Casamajor replied, that Coorg had been subject to Tippu, and was now subject to the Company, as was proved by the annual tribute of an elephant, in lieu of the former payment of Rs. 24,000. When the Resident requested the Rájah, to treat Dévammáji and the other members of his family kindly, he answered, that he required no such admonitions; but as for Dévammáji and her family, they were all dead, long since. This was the most barefaced lie. Dévammáji indeed, and her sister Mahádévammáji had been murdered, probably before the end of 1832, a month or two before Mr. Casamajor's visit, but her three children were still alive, and were murdered at Nalkanád, when the British troops crossed the frontiers of Coorg.

4. *Assassination of the Rájah's family.*

The end of the two daughters of Dodda-Víraréjender was most miserable and surpasses in horror all the other abominations of this monster tyrant. Shortly after the flight of Channa Basava and his wife, Dévammáji, her sister Mahádévammáji and their children, were taken by the Rájah's orders and by his sepoys to the Appagalla Panya, one of the private farms belonging to the Rájah, about four miles distant from Mercara. After some days, the Devan Basava and an eunuch, named Mandaya, a Jemadar of the palace, came there one morning early, conveyed Dévammáji and her sister Mahádévammáji, to the fort at Mercara, and confined them in the store-room in rear of the palace, placing a strong guard over them. The same morning, before noon, the Devan with the same eunuch came to the store-room, and in presence of some of the guard, compelled the prisoners to put their hands into boiling ghee. They left them shut up till about 2 o'clock P. M.;

when the Devan and the eunuch came again, and ordered one of the Jemadars on guard to bring two ropes. When brought, the Devan himself adjusted them round Dévammáji's neck, who made great resistance and implored to be taken before the Rájah, whilst the Jemadar and some of the guards held her hands, and pulled at the rope, which was thrown over a beam in the roof. In this manner both sisters then and there were put to death. As soon as life was extinct, they were taken down, wrapped up in matting and placed just outside the store-room beneath a small plantation of sugarcane. In the meantime orders had been sent by the Devan to the guard of Válekárs, Pariahs, at the Kumblagiri barrier, about a mile from the fort, to dig a hole for two bodies in a secluded part of the jungle, and for some of the said guard, to be in attendance in the evening at the Sallyport, (a secret passage, leading under the ramparts) by 7 P. M. Several of them attended and, with the help of some of the men from the store-room-guard, conveyed the two bodies to the hole already prepared; the Devan accompanying the party and witnessing the interment.

Perhaps Dévammáji had revealed the place, where she had deposited her wealth, on a promise that her life would be spared, and therefore, in her anguish, desired to be brought before the Rájah. Certain it is, that the Rájah learned from her the exact spot, where her jewels had been immured; for he despatched a Munshi of his, a Yedavanád man, of the name of Kálingaya, in company with the Devan Basava to Dévammáji's house, some time after her removal from it, and instructed the Devan to break the wall of the room adjoining Dévammáji's bedroom, a little above the floor, where he would find the treasure. "On our digging," Kálingaya says, "a brass vessel of a size holding one and an half seer of water, with the mouth properly closed, was discovered. It could have been lifted with one hand. We did not open the mouth of the vessel, but brought it to Mercara, and the Devan Basava delivered it to the Rájah. It was not opened in my presence. I am not aware, what description of coins or jewelry or precious stones it contained. The vessel was not full, as on taking it up in the hands the contents were shaking about." Dévammáji probably had given her treasure to the Rájah as a ransom for her life; but by this very surrender of her wealth she sealed her doom. Dévammáji is described as a person of a commanding figure, fair complexion and round face. Her sister Mahádévammáji was short and slender, but also fair. Thus ended two daughters of Dodda-Vírarájendra and of his beloved Ráni.

The grand-children of Dodda-Víraája and the remaining members of Appáji's and Lingarája's families, the nearest relatives of the Rájah, were carried to Nalkanád palace, when he himself retired to that secluded spot, in March 1834. Their removal to Nalkanád boded no good. They were kept in a couple of garden houses, under strict watch. General Fraser states:—

"One day subsequent to our troops entering the country, orders were given in the morning by the Devan, to dig a pit for a dozen persons, and in the dusk of the evening five women were put into one house and seven children into another, and the Kaplas (a jungle-tribe residing in the Nalkanád forest) and some of the Yedavanád men (Kunta Basava's especial followers), who had assisted in the murder of Dévammáji and Mahádévammáji, were sent into both houses with ropes, and then and there strangled every one of them, and afterwards tied them up in mats, the Devan Basavappa standing outside and accompanying the party, when the bodies were interred. The Rájah, also on this occasion, was close by the scene of murder, though not present. On the following morning, when walking with the Devan in front of the Nalkanád palace, on observing the Kaplas, he said to the Devan, that as they, the

Kaplas, had executed the murders, they had better be put to death also. But the Devan interceded for them. They are old servants, he said, who have come from a foreign country (the Malayalam). He suggested, that they might be sent out of the country, and a present given to them, which was done accordingly. But instead of quitting the country, they proceeded with their families some miles distance into the jungle, where they remained about a month; and when all was quiet, they returned to Nalkanád."

This account shows that, sometimes at least, the Devan was more humane than his master.

5. *The war and the Rájah's surrender.*

The personal conference of Mr. Casamajor with the Rájah in the beginning of 1833 having proved fruitless, the Resident returned to Mysore. The accounts from Coorg continued as bad as ever. The Rájah harboured rebels, intrigued with Mysore and scarcely cared for appearances. Mr. Casamajor recommended the quartering of a native Regiment in the neighbourhood of Mercara, to keep the Rájah in check and to protect his subjects, but the Government were still loath to go to extremities. Since the Rájah had taken a personal dislike to Mr. Casamajor, Mr. Graeme, the Resident at Nagpore, then residing for the benefit of his health at Bangalore, was requested to proceed to Coorg and charged to make a last attempt at an amicable settlement. However, the Rájah was unwilling again to meet an English representative, seized and kept in durance two native envoys of Mr. Graeme viz. Daraset, a Parsee merchant of Tellicherry and Kulputty Karnikára Manoon, a Sheristadar of the Collector of Malabar, who had gone to Coorg furnished with passports from Mr. Graeme. The former the Rájah allowed to return to Tellicherry, but the latter he refused to set at liberty until the Rájah's relatives were given up to him by the Government. Having an extraordinary idea of his power and the strength of his country, he resolved on war. He addressed the most insolent letters to Sir Fr. Adam, Governor of Madras, and to Lord W. Bentinck, the Governor General. Now the patience of the most peace-loving Governor General was at an end, and a British force was organised to march into Coorg and depose the Rájah. As it drew near his frontiers the Rájah published the following outrageous proclamation:

Proclamation of Vírarája.

Proclamation published for the information and guidance of the Hindoos Mussulmans, Poligars, public servants, Ryots, Chetty Merchants, and people of other castes in Hindoostan.

1. It is well known that the Kaffers, Nasara (Christians), low Pheringhies, with the view of converting people of other religions to their dirty faith, have, ill intentionally, polluted the Dévastánams, Muszeede, and other temples at Bangalore, Cuddapah, Mussulibunder, Nagpoor, Ramocpet and several other countries, sent out their Padres and ruined them. This circumstance being certainly too well impressed on the mind of every one, what more need be said?

2. Those who have from time to time strenuously attempted to convert, by force, people of other religions to their faith, have by the commands of God, perished—but set this aside, an instance in proof of this may be given. Tippoo Sultan attempted to force all the other religions, to embrace his religion; and with this view ruined a great number of people, destroyed the Hindoo temples and committed various sorts of oppressions; which acts not being acceptable to God, he was destroyed. This fact is well known to all of you. Now, the Kaffers, Nasara, low Pheringhies have in like manner commenced to destroy the religion observed by people of different castes, and to introduce their own religion. When evil comes, people lose their senses. When death comes, medicine avails naught; thus then their end is fast approaching. There is no doubt of it. The Hindoos and Mussulmans having respectively consulted their Shástcrs have found, that, if for the protection of their religions, these Kaffer, Nasara, Pheringhies be now fought with, God will help us, and make us successful. There is no doubt of this, so let all be fully convinced of it.

3. These Kaffers, Nasara, low Pheringhies have now wickedly determined to wage war with the Halery Samsthánam, and have accordingly

collected some black people of Hindoostan, whom they are going to send in front, that they may all be cut down, and the race thus annihilated in some degree, thinking that by these means they will be able easily to convert the rest to their faith. It is, therefore, to protect people of all castes against such invasion, the Halery Samsthánam have determined to meet with arms those Kaffers, Pheringhies, Nasaras. Accordingly, if all of you will join the army of the Halery Samsthánam, you will not only be defended, but you will also render the devastation of those Kaffers, Pheringhies, quite easy; after this is done, you will be protected and enabled to live happy and contented, following the religion of your respective castes unmolested. Do not think, that another such opportunity will offer itself again.

4. To avert the evil which threatens you now, we have taken all this trouble and published this proclamation. Should any of you pay no attention to it, but keep yourself neutral, you will at last find yourselves under the yoke of the Pheringhies, lose your caste, and experience the greatest misery to the end of your lives, and after death you will not be admitted before God, for having thus sinned against him. Do not doubt this. Therefore, if ye, people of all countries, join the Halery Samsthán and help it, you will meet with every kind of protection from it, and be able to live happy. Accordingly it is expected, that all of you will come forward and help the Halery Samsthánam.

5. P. S. It is further hereby commanded. Those Nasaras, Kaffers, Pheringhies will, in order to get possession of the Halery Samsthán, spare no pains to gain you over. They will even give ten, where one would be enough. Let not this allure you and make you swerve from your real intention or lead you to entangle yourselves; for, after they attain their object, they will oppress you, and violate your religion. Be sure of this.

(True Copy and Translation.)

(Signed:) F. CLEMENTSON,

Pl. Collector.

(Abstract translation of the proclamation published by the Coorg Rájah, received from the Officer commanding in Wynaad with his letter of the 31st March 1834.)

The Governor General through his Political Agent Col. Fraser issued the following proclamation:—

The conduct of the Rájah of Coorg has, for a long time past, been of such a nature as to render him unworthy of the friendship and protection of the British Government.

Unmindful of his duty as a ruler, and regardless of his obligations as a dependent ally of the East India Company, he has been guilty of the greatest oppression and cruelty towards the people subject to his government, and he has evinced the most wanton disrespect of the authority of, and the most hostile disposition towards the former, from whom he and his ancestors have invariably received every degree of kindness and protection.

It would be needless to enumerate the several instances of his misconduct, but it is sufficient to state that, in consequence of an asylum having been afforded in the British Territories to his own sister Dévammáji ana her husband, Channa Basavappa, who to preserve their lives had fled from his oppression, the Rájah has presumed, to address letters replete with the most insulting expressions to the Governor of Fort St. George and the Governor General of India, that he has assumed an attitude of hostility and defiance towards the British Government, that he has received and encouraged the proclaimed enemies of that Government, and that he has unjustifiably placed under restraint an old and faithful servant of the Company, named Kulputty Karnikára Manoon, who had been formally deputed by the British representative for the purpose of opening a friendly negotiation, thus committing a gross outrage, not only upon the authority by whom the above named individual was deputed, but upon the established rules of all civilized nations, by whom the persons of accredited agents are invariably held sacred.

The ancient alliance and the firm friendship, which had so happily subsisted between the predecessors of the present Rájah and the Honorable Company, have caused his errors to be treated uniformly with indulgence. The most earnest remonstrances have been in vain tried, to bring him to a sense of his obligations, and it is not until further forbearance would be culpable, that His Excellency the Right Honorable the Governor General, at the suggestion and with the concurrence of the Right Honorable the Governor in Council of Fort St. George, has resolved on employing the only means left of vindicating the dignity of the sovereign state and of securing to the inhabitants of Coorg the blessings of a just and equitable Government.

It is accordingly hereby notified, that a British army is about to invade the Coorg territory, that Vîrarájendra Vodeyar is no longer to be considered as Rájah of Coorg, that the persons and property of all those who conduct themselves peaceably or in aid of the operations of the British troops, shall be respected, and that such a system of Government shall be established, as may seem best calculated to secure the happiness of the people.

It is also hereby made known to all British subjects, who may have entered the service of Vírarájendra Vodeyar, that they are required to place themselves under the protection of the British authorities, by whom they will be kindly received, and their rights and privileges respected, and that such of them, as may in any way render assistance to the enemy, will be considered as traitors and punished accordingly.

This proclamation will be carefully made known in Chittledroog, Raidroog, Mysore, Bellary, Malabar, Canara, in order that the relatives of such persons as have taken service in Coorg from those places or adjoining districts, may adopt the earliest means of communicating its purport to the parties in whose safety they are interested.

(Signed:) J. S. FRASER, *Leut. Col. and Political Agent of H. E. the Right Hon. the Governor General.*

Issued at Bangalore this 15th day of March 1834.

Upon this Vírarája published the following:

Counter Proclamation.

The explanation of a proclamation, issued for the knowledge of the bad English people, who are mean slaves and servants of the auspicious feet of the Halery Samsthán Mahárája.

In answer to a proclamation of the bad Englishman, son of a whore, who in a state of forgetting Mahádéva (God) and through pride had written on a paper whatever occurred to his mind, for the purpose of giving information to the inhabitants of Halery Samsthán, and fastened the same near the boundary, I, the slave of my Master's Majesty, let you know as follows, that the proclamation (containing the evil subjects) which was fastened in the boundary by the wicked Englishman, the son of a slave, is not at all possible even to be seen with our eyes or hear with our ears, and in the very time of tying the said proclamations, which are replete with indecent subjects, the hearts of all of us, who are the servants of the king's feet, were inflamed as the fire through wind. The wicked Christian European, the son of a slave, who resolved to prepare this, should be beheaded, and his head thrown out, the hands, mouth and head of the person, who wrote this, should be cut off, and the generation of the low caste, blasphemer and bad European should be burnt down. These hopes are to be soon effected. All the above subjects are certain. All the wicked Europeans, the sons of whores, have evil intentions. Very well, very well, we will fill up all your bellies according to your wishes. Be this known to you, written on Sunday, 6th decreasing Moon of the month of Phálguna, of the year Vijaya, corresponding with 30th March 1834.

The invading force numbered six thousand men and was placed under Brigadier Lindsay in whom was vested the supreme command of the expedition, whilst Col. Fraser was to accompany him in the capacity of Political Agent of the Governor General for Coorg affairs.

The force was divided into four columns which operated in the following manner:—

The *Eastern Column* under Col. Lindsay and composed of one Company of Foot Artillery from Bangalore—three 12 Pr. Howitzers, two 5½ inch heavy Howitzers, two do. mortars, one 6 Pr. gun—400 Rank and File and Head-Quarters of H. M. 39th Regiment of Foot, 4th, 35th, 36th, 48th Regiment, and the Rifle Company of the 5th Regiment Native Infantry and 300 Sappers and Miners with Head-Quarters, marched on the 2nd April from Bettadapur upon Sulacottu and reached the Kávéri opposite Hebbale, where on the Coorg side a barrier was thrown up, consisting of a rude wall of mud and stone with a range of loopholes near its upper part and defended by a few men armed in various ways. Before the force was ordered to advance, Col. Fraser with a white handkerchief in his hand attempted to cross the Kávéri as a messenger of peace, when a Ginjal was fired from the opposite side, followed by two more in quick succession. It was then necessary to reply in kind, and two Howitzers fired a few rounds of grape and ball, under cover of which the advanced guard crossed with Cols. Lindsay and Fraser; but before they reached the opposite bank, the enemy was seen retiring towards Rámaswámy Kanave. Commanded by a Coorg Káryagár, it numbered but 100 Mussulmans, of whom about 60 were armed with matchlocks and the remainder with swords, a very few Coorgs provided with firearms and having also the management of the Ginjals, and about 50 ryots armed with bows and arrows. The strong position at the fortified Pagoda near Rámaswámy Kanave offered but a feeble resistance and was carried in about a quarter of an hour and likewise a rough breastwork and barrier near Haringi, at the sacrifice of a few men wounded and on the side of the enemy, who mustered 350 men, chiefly Coorgs, half a dozen killed. On the 4th April the force advanced only five miles on account of the difficulty of the road which had been obstructed by large trees felled across it. But a flag of truce having been sent into camp from the Rájah, accompanied by one of his four Deváns, named Laksminárâyana, another person, Mahomed Taker Khan, who called himself the Rájah's friend and four of their attendants, there was no further resistance to the advancing force except by the obstacles of the road. Of the two preliminary conditions for an armistice, one had been complied with. Kulputty Karnikára Manoon had been delivered by the Rájah to the British camp, but the Rájah had not yet placed himself at the unconditional disposal of the British Government. On the 5th April another Deván, Apparanda Bopu, with a party of 400 Coorgs, went to meet Col. Fraser, surrendered to him and offered to conduct the Company's troops to the capital. At 4 P. M. on the 6th April they entered the Fort of Mercara; the Rájah's flag, which was flying in one of the bastions, was lowered and the British colours hoisted in its stead under a salute of twenty-one guns. A company of the M. 39th Regiment remained within the Fort, the remainder of the troops encamped on the heights around.

On the 11th Col. Fraser published the following Proclamation:—

Whereas the rule and dominion of Rájah Vírarájender Vodeya over the country of Coorg have now definitively and for ever ceased, it is hereby proclaimed and directed, that the whole civil administration of the country shall be conducted as heretofore by the Gaudas, Shánabhogas, Hoblidárs, Parpadigárs, Subadars, Deváns and Karnik, as at present employed in their respective stations, with the privilege of immediate and direct appeal from every native of Coorg of whatever rank or degree to Lieut. Col. Fraser, the Political Agent of His Excellency the Right Honorable the Governor General, until the permanent establishment of a form of Government which will be determined under the authority of the Governor General and upon the model best calculated to secure the future wellbeing and happiness of the people of the country.

It is hereby further distinctly explained, that the administration of justice will be exercised by the authorities above enumerated only to that extent and degree with which they have been hitherto individually charged to the entire exclusion of that superior power and jurisdiction which have been heretofore exercised by the Rájah Vírarájender Vodeya alone. No punishment therefore extending to life or limb or more severe than simple imprisonment will on any account whatever take place without a reference to Col. Fraser and the sanction of the British Government.

(Signed:) J. S. FRASER,

Mercara, 11th April 1834. *Lieut Col. and Political Agent.*

Vírarája, at the commencement of the war, had removed to his palace at Nalkanád, a place almost inaccessible to an army. He had taken with him his women, his band, his treasures and what remained of the Coorg Rájah's families. that he might destroy them all, if necessary, in order to render it impossible for the English Government to transfer the principality, or the property of the murdered Dévammáji to any other heir of Dodda-Vírarájendra, and thus secure his wealth and his country to himself.

The leaders of the Coorgs who in their ignorance had boasted before the Rájah, that they would sally forth and exterminate the English, were true enough to their words and took up their posts at the different passes, where they might have defended themselves most effectually and caused great loss to the Company's troops, had the Rájah like his great uncle, Dodda-Víraréjendra, headed his Coorgs and vigorously directed the defence. But his spirit showed no spark of heroic courage. Incited partly by hope, that a reconciliation was yet possible, partly by fear, that he might lose all, if matters went to extremities, he sent orders, prohibiting his Coorgs from encountering the troops of the Company, hence the easy advance of the latter.

A *subdivision of the Eastern Column* under Col. Stewart advanced on the 2nd April from Periapatna towards the Kávéri, opposite Rangasamudram, where the enemy was stationed in considerable force, but being plied with a few cannon shot, he left his entrenched position and retired across country, leaving six men dead. Col. Stewart crossed the Kávéri at Kondanghery and proceeded to Víréjpet, where he was to co-operate with the Western Column and open up communication with Mysore by way of Siddápur.

The *Northern Column* under the command of Col. G. Waugh, was composed of one Brigade 6 Pr. guns from Bellary, 300 Rank and File and Head-Quarters H. M. 55th Regt., 9th Regt. N. I., 31st Regt. Light Infantry, Rifle Company of 24th Regt. N. I., and 200 Sappers and Miners.

It marched on the 1st April from Hosacotta to Shanivár-sante. On passing the Coorg boundary river, Hémávati, the enemy's advanced posts had retreated and no molestation was offered until the force reached Codlipet, where an armed body of 200 men occupied an entrenched high ground, but on their flanks being turned, they speedily fell back and the advanced guard of the English encountered only one more slight opposition at Mudravalli, which was as speedily overcome. A far different resistance the troops met on the following day, when they were to join the Eastern Column at

Haringi. They had scarcely proceeded a few hundred yards beyond their encamping ground, when they found the road blockaded with felled trees, which rendered their progress exceedingly difficult and slow. As the column approached a village situated in a wood near the base of the pass in which the enemy's principal position was situated, a feeble fire was opened, but readily silenced. The stockade, known as the Buck-stockade, was exceedingly strong; outside protected by thick bamboos and trees and surrounded with a deep ditch and inside built of mud walls, faced with stones, and pierced with innumerable loopholes which commanded the approaches in every direction. The intrepid Coorgs who held it, were commanded by the present (1870) Head Sheristadar Madanta Appachu, a fine old Coorg, of tall stature and martial bearing, but ever since the British accession a most loyal and devoted servant of Government.

Determined to carry it by assault, as the stockade barred their advance, the troops under Major Bird of the 31st Light Infantry as Field-Officer of the day attempted every means of attack for four hours and a half, during which they were exposed to a most severe and raking fire; but in vain. A misdirected flank-movement of H. M. 55th Regt. under Col. Mill proved equally unsuccessful. Col. Mill was shot dead on the spot, likewise Ensigns Robertson of the 9th N. I. and Babington of the 31st N. I. Major Bird determined to withdraw the column and, with little additional loss, brought it under cover, and on account of the heavy list of wounded and for the sake of supplies and a more convenient camp he retreated several miles to the rear. In this most unfortunate affair about forty-eight were killed, including the three officers, and 118 wounded.

The *Western Column* marched from Cannanore on the 31st March and was under the command of Col. David Fowlis. It consisted of the following arms: Half a Company of Golundanze—four 6 Pr. guns—300 Rank and File and Head-Quarters H. M. 48th Regt.—20th and 32nd Regts. N. I. and 200 Sappers and Miners.

It was to reach Mercara after forcing the Heggala-Ghat and occupying Vírájpet. The Light Company of H. M. 48th Regt. and the Grenadier Company of the 20th Regt. N. I. proceeded on the 2nd April in advance beyond the Stony River into Coorg; their progress was checked by a party of Coorgs posted near the river, and Lieut. Erskine, a most promising young officer of the M. 48th, was killed. At six the following morning the main body broke ground and had to fight its way up the Pass every inch. The Coorgs had fortified it with three successive stockades, as well as with breast-works and felled trees at every hundred yards. The first stockade was taken with trifling loss; but from that time till four in the afternoon a series of hard conflicts was maintained in carrying the successive barriers which the enemy defended with bravery, maintaining at the same time a continued skirmishing from the wood. The last stockade was only captured by attacking it in reverse as well as in flank. In these achievements Capts. Butterworth and Macdonald greatly distinguished themselves. Also a volunteer, Thomas Bell, son of Col. Bell of H. M. 48th Regt. excited the admiration of the Commanding Officer for his "conspicuous bravery in every attack and skirmish with the enemy."

Next day, on the 4th April, as Col. Fowlis marched in advance and within a quarter of a mile of his camp, a flag of truce appeared, bearing a proposal from the Rája for a suspension of arms. He replied, that, if the Coorgs did not fire, his troops would also abstain from firing; but as his orders were to go up the Ghat, go he would. He accordingly effected this march without opposition and in the afternoon at two he passed through the East-Ukudu (guard-house) at Heggala, where he halted and was supplied with grain by the Coorgs.

His service was now completed with the loss of twelve killed and thirty-six wounded. On the 13th April a detachment of this column under Major Tweedie marched without opposition to Nalkanád and took possession of the Palace. It is rumoured, that part of the Rájah's hidden treasure there got wings after the arrival of the troops; but they did not find the Deván Kunta Basava, who was to be sent a prisoner to Mercara.

Thirty men of H. M. 48th Regt., two Companies of the 48th Regt. N. I., two Companies 20th Regt. N. I. and one 12 Pr. Howitzer with a detachment of Artillery men, were left at Virájpet under the command of Col. Brock of the 48th Regt. The main body of Col. Fowlis' Column marched on towards Mercara and remained encamped near the Muddaramudy river 7 miles south of Mercara. Col. Stewart's force which was to co-operate with and had joined the Western Column at Virájpet, was directed to proceed to open the Siddapur Pass into Mysore.

The *Western Auxiliary Column* under the command o Lieut. Colonel George Jackson and with the present Commander-in-Chief of Madras, then Capt. McCleverty H. M. 48th, as Brigade Major, consisted only of 150 Rank and File H. M. 48th Foot, the 40th Regt. N. I. (400 Rank and File) and 50 Sappers and Miners, who never joined but were retained at Cannanore and had not a single gun.

This column was intended to occupy the lower Taluqs of the Coorg dominions for the purpose of covering the Company's country and giving protection and confidence to such of the inhabitants as might be well disposed to the British Government. If possible it was to take up its position at the ruined fort of Sulya, at the foot of the Ghat, but was strictly enjoined, not to divide itself into small parties.

Col. Jackson advanced from Kumbla, a small town on the sea-coast south of Mangalore, on the morning of the 29th March at 3 o'clock 9 miles towards the east on an extremely difficult road, and his advanced guard fell in with the enemy's advanced piquet about half a mile distant from their stockade, where three prisoners were made, who said their piquet was under orders from the Rájah, not to fire unless first fired at. As, however, the Coorgs would not quit their post, unless force was employed and as they assembled at the gateway of the stockade, the Company's troops made an assault and carried it without difficulty or loss. On the 30th they marched to Uppanangalla, on the 31st to a Pagoda near Bellur, on the 1st April they reached the Ishvaramangala Pagoda, where Col. Jackson learnt, that a strong stockade obstructed the road on a hill in the midst of a thick jungle near Madhur and Bollary. A reconnoitering party, consisting of 4 officers, 40 European and 80 Native Infantry was sent to ascertain its locality. This duty was completed on the 3rd April, but the party was attacked on the spot, when it had received orders to retire and it reached the camp 5 miles distant at Ishvaramangala with the loss of 2 officers killed and wounded and more than half of the men, the greater proportion killed, Col. Jackson, after considering this loss and the reported strength of the position, thought it impossible to attempt carrying the stockade without further reinforcements and fell back towards Kumbla, but on learning that his retreat would be cut off by the Coorgs who outmarched him, he turned across country to Kásergóde, which place he reached on the 6th April with the remainder of his disorganized and disheartened force. His retreat was greatly harassed by crowds of skirmishers. The coolies and bearers decamped as well as they could; and at every favourable interval the enemy fell upon the followers, the sick and wounded, and massacred them with the most horrid barbarity. Part of the ammunition and public stores, the officers' tents and equipments fell into the hands of the Coorgs, while several of the officers' horses were shot. The casualties of this column amounted to thirty killed and thirty-six wounded. Col. Jackson was so overcome by the mortifying failure of his expedition, that he himself applied for an enquiry by a Court Martial into the cause of his failure.

In a General Order, dated Ootacamund 9th September 1834 the Commander-in-Chief concurred in the opinion expressed by the Committee of Enquiry respecting the conduct of Col. Jackson, viz. "The Court do not see reason to ascribe any blame to the Lieut. Colonel, and they would be doing him less than justice if they omitted to record their conviction, arising from the concurrent testimony of all the witnesses who have been examined, that he most zealously and most unremittingly exerted himself for the good of the service on which he was engaged, and that on every occasion, when his column came in contact with the enemy, he was to be found at the point, where danger pressed and where his presence was most required." It is very probable, that if the Court had been desired, to express an opinion on the wisdom of the authorities who sent a force so inadequate to the task imposed, its verdict would have been less favourable!

The issue of the war had already been decided by the success of the Eastern Column in occupying Mercara, the capital. Life and honorable treatment being offered him by Col. Fraser, if he would surrender, the Rájah availed himself of so favourable terms and returned within the stipulated time of three days from Nalkanád to Mercara after a vain attempt of gaining at least 15 days' time, to march in proper princely style with his women and baggage. He entered Mercara Fort at noon of the 10th April, accompanied by his unarmed attendants (Pahara Chowkee) and his women, and was received with due respect at the outer gate by the officer commanding the Fort. Col. Fraser thus reports to the Governor General his first interview with the Rájah on the evening of the 11th April:—

"The Rájah of Coorg having sent me a message yesterday morning, that he wished to see me, I called upon him at five in the evening and he detained me until past seven. When I first went in, I found the whole palace almost entirely dark, in consequence of the windows being closed and blinds let down all round it, for the purpose of preventing the inner of the palace being overlooked or its inmates seen by the officers and men of the Company of H. M. 39th Regiment doing duty in the Fort. The Rájah himself came out a moment afterwards from behind a veil which separated an inner appartment from the front verandah. He took me by the hand which he continued to hold, but seemed for some minutes so frightened and agitated, as not to know what to do or say. I addressed him in Hindustáni and enquired after his health, to which he replied in the usual terms. At length one of his attendants suggested to him to go to the upper part of the palace. To this he silently assented, and while he still held me by the hand, we proceeded through one or two passages and ascended a flight of steps, where all was so perfectly dark, that I was obliged to feel my way along the walls with my disengaged hand. Arrived in an appartment in the upper part of the building, where the windows were entirely closed, and where there was no light whatever but from a common lamp set upon the ground, he seated me by him on a sopha. It is impossible to repeat the desultory remarks which he continued to make to me for about two hours and he himself repeatedly observed, that he was weary and unwell, that his head was confused and he knew not what he was saying. The principal object he seemed to have in view was to justify his first proceedings in regard to his demand for the surrender of Channa Basava, founded, as he said it was, upon previously understood agreements, and the letter to him from the Resident in Mysore under date the 1st August 1828. He said, that he detained Kulputty Karnikára Manoon only because this person had promised to procure for him the surrender of the fugitives and that he thought, he would be a useful mediator between him and the British Government. To some remark I made upon this subject, the Rájah replied, that he was an ignorant man, and knew not, that he was doing wrong, or acting in a manner contrary to the usage of other countries. He spoke repeatedly and earnestly of the friendship which he and his ancestors had ever entertained for the English, and prayed for my intercession with the Governor General, that he might not be removed from his Fort, but allowed to remain and judged by the tenor of his future conduct. He often repeated, that he was young, that he was ignorant and unacquainted with the customs of the world, that he had never benefitted by the advantages of society and that in all his late proceedings he had been misled by evil councillors such as Abbas Ali and others, whom he plainly designated as villains. I am led to believe, that this account of himself is just, that he is a weak and ignorant person, spoiled by the possession of early power and that the feelings and superstition which nature gave him, instead of being perverted to evil purposes as they have been, might have taken a different and far better direction, had he been guided by judicious advisers and had a more frequent intercourse been maintained between him and the officers of the British Government.....

"In the course of my conversation I acquainted the Rájah, that the future determination of his fate depended not on the least on myself, but entirely on the pleasure of the Governor General; but in order to prevent his entertaining any hope of which the disappointment hereafter might in consequence be more painful, I acquainted him, that I had not the least hope, that under any circumstances whatever would he be permitted to remain in the Fort of his country."

Finding out that his deposition and removal were determined upon, he felt uneasy at the thought, that Kunta Basava, the accomplice of all his atrocities, was likely to be delivered or to give himself up to Col. Fraser, who had fixed a prize of one thousand Rupees upon his apprehension, for he looked upon him as "the worst and most dangerous character in the whole country." In all his enquiries about the Rájah's doings, Col. Fraser was constantly referred to Deván Basava for information, as if he was alone possessed of the secret of all the acts of murder that may have been committed, and as if the Rájah himself had been little else, than a young man devoted to his own idle or sensual pursuits, leaving to his Deván the exclusive charge and direction of any species of cruelty and convenient crime. Basava had betaken himself to the jungles and went to live with a Kuruba family in an inaccessible part of the western mountains, not far from Nalkanád; but he was apprehended and a Coorg man escorted him in the evening of the 14th April, to the Kagodlenád Kachery at the fort of the Mercara hill. A message was received there at nightfall from the Rájah. Basava was strangled by the men in the Kachery and hung up on a tree close by. Next morning the Coorg, who had delivered Basava, was sent about his business and a report made to Col. Fraser, that Basava had committed suicide, and had been found in the jungle at a distance of a mile and a half from Mercara. Dr. Grant of the 35th Regt. N. I. and the Provost Martial of the camp were sent down "to investigate as far as possible the circumstances of the Deván's death and especially to ascertain, whether it seemed likely, that he had died by his own hand or had been put to death by other persons." The Doctor duly reported, that he had no doubt but that the Deván committed suicide.—His determination must have been very firm, for the Doctor found him suspended by two ropes, and a third rope, a spare one, it must be supposed, was found at the foot of the tree!—The Rájah's scheme succeeded well enough. Col. Fraser fully believed in the suicide of Basava; all the Coorgs *seemed* to believe it—but those who knew, afterwards confessed the truth—and the Rájah was at liberty to shift all blame from himself upon the dead man! Kunta Basava was a Badaga of the lowest extraction, who had risen from a dog-boy to the Devánship under Lingarája and having ingratiated himself with Vírarája by pampering to his vicious propensities, he retained his post. He hated the Coorgs as much as he was hated by them and maltreated them, whenever he had an opportunity. Shortly before the outbreak of the war Kunta Basava assaulted the Deván Chepudira Ponappa in the presence of the Rájah, whom he dissuaded from fighting against the Company. With his clenched iron fist Basava gave him a blow on the temple, which sent him to the ground for dead. The accomplice of the Rájah's crimes perished with ignominy; Chepudira Ponappa became the principal man in the country under the British Government and was much respected both by his superiors and the people! His grandson Ch. Soobiah is now Assistant Superintendent of Coorg.

The object of the expedition having been attained, and no disturbance of the tranquillity of the country being anticipated, the Coorg Field-Force was broken up and only a body of troops kept in Mercara sufficient for any emergency. The prize-money distributed amongst the troops amounted to over ten lacs of rupees. Regarding the services of the Field-Force the following is the

"General Order, by His Excellency the Right Honorable the Governor General and Commander-in-Chief in India."

Head Quarters,

***Ootacamund** 17th May* **1834.**

The Governor General and Commander-in-Chief has much pleasure in expressing to Brigadier Lindsay C. B. his entire approbation of the manner in which the military operations under his general control against the Rájah of Coorg have been brought to a speedy and successful termination. His

Lordship had confidently anticipated this result from the Brigadier's long experience and established reputation.

To Lieut. Col. Stewart, who commanded a detachment from the main Column under Brigadier Lindsay the expression of His Lordship's satisfaction is also due for having successfully overcome all the obstacles opposed by the enemy to his progress and for having effected in obedience to his orders a junction with the Column under Col. Fowlis' command.

The Column under the command of Col. Waugh met with complete failure, the loss of many brave men is to be deplored and of none more than of the gallant Lieut. Col. Mill. The determined valour, displayed by the Officers and troops and more especially by His Majesty's 55th is the best consolation for this misfortune. (? !) His Lordship has carefully examined the detailed reports which he had required of the operations of this Column and is happy in generally concurring in the opinion of Brigadier Lindsay, that Col. Waugh is not justly chargeable with blame; that all his orders and arrangements appear to have been made with sound discretion and a due observance of correct military principles, and that the disaster may be ascribed to the extreme difficulty of the country and to those accidents, to which the best concerted schemes will occasionally be liable.

It may perhaps be regretted, that the attack was so long persevered in, but the good order in which the retreat was made to the ground occupied before the attack, proves that the arrangements were ably made, while the perseverance with which the main object of the operations of this Column was followed up, reflects the greatest credit upon Col. Waugh.

The good disposition made by Col. Fowlis in command of the *South-Western Column* for the attack of the Heggala Ghat and the gallantry with which it was carried, reflect the greatest credit upon that Officer and the Officers and men under his command.

Col. Fowlis' name will be brought to the particular notice of the Honorable Court.

To all the Officers and men, composing the several columns, above enumerated, His Lordship expresses his thanks for their zealous and gallant conduct, although the troops have had to engage an enemy much inferior to themselves, yet the excessive strength of the mountainous and densly jungle-country constituted a resistance which the greatest perseverance and courage could alone have surmounted. The army have the satisfaction of knowing that a sanguinary tyrant has been subdued and a valuable acquisition been made to the Company's territories.

To the excellent order and discipline of the troops may in part be ascribed the general desire expressed by the inhabitants, to become the subjects of the British Government.

The conduct of Lieut. Col. Jackson in command of the North-Western Column, being under investigation, His Lordship refrains for the present from making any remark upon the operations of that part of the Force. (Vide page 341.)

The Governor General cannot omit to mention in this place the eminent services of Lieut. Col. J. S. Fraser, to whom was entrusted the conduct of our negotiations with the enemy. By the judicious arrangement which that Officer adopted, the successes of the troops were ably seconded, while his subsequent measures in administering the affairs of the Coorg country have been so discreet and conciliatory as to gain for him the confidence of the inhabitants and to secure their entire and willing obedience.

By Command of His Excellency the Right Honorable the Governor General.

(Signed:) W. H. MACNAGHTEN,
Secretary to the Governor General.

As a mark of the King's approval Brigadier Lindsay's services, he nominated that Officer "to be Knight Commander of the Royal Hanoverian Guelphic Order."

IV. PART.

COORG

under the British Government

Since 1834.

A. HISTORICAL EVENTS.

1. THE RÁJAH'S DEPOSITION AND THE ANNEXATION OF COORG.

The representative of the Governor General now entered into negotiations with the remaining Deváns and other principal men, which must have puzzled them not a little, but which they turned to pretty good account, after having comprehended their novel position. They no doubt had expected, that the principality would, without ado, be converted into a Company's taluq, and indeed the Headmen of the lower Districts, of Amra-Sulya, at once petitioned for the annexation of their Districts to Canara. The Coorgs were surprised to find themselves treated almost as an independent body. The chief men being assembled in the unfinished palace—the site of which is now occupied by the Central School—Col. Fraser informed them of the deposition of the Rájah and called upon them "to express their wishes without apprehension or reserve, in regard to the form of administration, which they desired to be established for the future Government of the country" "The Devâns and Karnik, or principal accountant, a person of coequal rank with the Devâns then went round the assembled multitude, who sat in perfectly quiet and decent order, as is usual in native Durbars, and after taking the votes of all present, returned to the place, where I sat, and acquainted me, that an unanimous wish had been expressed to be transferred to the British Government and to be ruled in future by the same laws and regulations which prevailed in the Company's dominions." (Col. Fraser's Despatches to the Governor General.)

Not being quite sure, whether the Rájah would not, in the end, be allowed to remain in Coorg, and, wishing to be on the safe side, they added a proposal to permit the Rájah to stay amongst them at Mercara. When they were most positively informed, that he *must* leave the country, they were greatly relieved and readily acquiesced in the orders of the Sirkar. In other respects the Coorgs were treated, as if they were the masters of the country and were greatly pleased with the sudden change from abject servitude to a kind of consequential independence. The upshot was, that Col. Fraser issued a proclamation, which declared that Coorg was annexed, because it was the wish of the people to be ruled by the British Government!

It ran thus:

"Whereas it is the unanimous wish of the inhabitants of Coorg to be taken under the protection of the British Government, His Excellency the Right Honorable the Governor General has been pleased to resolve, that the territory, heretofore governed by Vírarâjendra Vodeya shall be transferred to the Honorable Company.

"The inhabitants are hereby assured, that they shall not again be subjected to native rule, that their civil and religious usages will be respected, and that the greatest desire will invariably be shown by the British Government, to augment their security, comfort and happiness."

(Signed:) J. S. FRASER,

Camp at Mercara, 7th May 1834. *Lt. Col. and Political Agent.*

Gradually light began to break in upon the darkness of Coorg affairs, as soon as it became known, that the Rájah was to leave the country. Col. Fraser wrote on the 7th June to the Governor General: "The Rájah is cunning, false, hypocritical and well capable of deceiving those around him, who happen not to be aware of the past events of his life. But, in my opinion, he has forfeited every claim to indulgence, and I think, that his atrocious character would render it discreditable to the British Government, to concede more to him, than was granted to him, life and honorable treatment."

The cruelty to his subjects and the massacre of his relatives were fully established and in reply to an official report on the subject the Governor General's Secretary wrote to Col. Fraser: "With regard to that portion of your letter, dated 29th May, which treats of the murders perpetrated in Coorg between the period of the flight of Channa Basava and his wife to Bangalore, up to that of the surrender of the Ex-Rájah, I am desired to observe, that these atrocities are of such a description as to render it exceedingly doubtful in the opinion of the Governor General, whether any indulgence beyond that of granting him his life should be extended to the author of them. At the time when the Ex-Rájah surrendered, no conception was formed, that his cruelties had been carried to so enormous an extent as would now appear to be the case, nor indeed would it seem possible for the imagination by any effort to ascribe to one individual the perpetration of so much wickedness as may now, with too great an appearance of reality, be imputed to the Ex-Rájah."

Col. Fraser, on being transferred to the Commissionership of Mysore, left Coorg in September 1834, on which occasion he received the following address, the contents of which and of his reply reflect great honor on the respective parties, and give us a just appreciation of their character:

Address of the Coorgs.

To

Lieutenant Colonel J. S. FRASER,

Commissioner for the affairs of Coorg.
&c. &c. &c.

Honorable Sir,

We, the undersigned natives and inhabitants of Coorg, would ever reproach ourselves for having omitted to perform a sacred duty, did we not adopt this mode of expressing, in the name of ourselves and our community, our sincere and deep regret at your approaching separation from us. We are aware that although your honour is going to Mysore to assume charge of the Residency to which His Excellency the Right Honorable the Governor General (may His Lordship be prosperous!) has been pleased to appoint you, yet you still retain the office of Commissioner for this country, and that its administration will be conducted under your orders and supervision. We should nevertheless, not permit you to separate from us without acknowledging the heavy debt of gratitude we owe to your honour.

You arrived in this country in the capacity of Political Agent to the Right Honorable the Governor General. After the deposition of the Rájah you were entrusted with the administration of this country. We are very much indebted to His Excellency for having selected a person of your excellent qualities to govern us. Although you never had a previous personal intercourse with us, yet all your acts and measures regarding this country were such as preserved inviolate our rights, civil usages and religion. Your abilities, and knowledge of the customs, manners and feelings of the people deserve our unqualified praise. Your name must ever be revered for the philanthropic and benevolent disposition and liberality, which you have evinced in all your proceedings. It is with pleasure we declare that you have always shown a scrupulous anxiety to maintain and protect us in religious usages, and a solicitude to improve our moral and intellectual faculties. We have seen your patience, benevolence, conciliating manners in your intercourse with us, your unwearied assiduity to ameliorate this country in every respect and make it flourish, and your desire to promote our interests and secure our happiness.

We recollect also with delight the humane disposition you have always shown in attending to the representations and grievances of the people; thus free access to you and the facility which you have afforded in obtaining justice. Your honour always consulted the inhabitants in the adoption of all measures connected with the administration of the country, and there is nothing which you have done ~~that~~ has not been consonant with the wishes of the community, a circumstance by which you have acquired the confidence, esteem and affection of the people of the country. It is impossible that we can adequately express our sense of obligation for all your benevolent acts, nor could a few words satisfy our minds, which feel more impressed than can be uttered by even the most laboured language. The numerous kindnesses and benefits which we have received from you are engraven on our hearts, and they will ever be most gratefully remembered not only by us, but by the whole population of Coorg, your name will be venerated, and handed down with honor and respect to the latest posterity.

In testimony of these our sincere sentiments, and as a lasting memorial of the high estimation in which we hold you, we respectfully request your acceptance of a *gold cup*, and *a Coorg dress*, which we have taken the liberty to present to your honour.

You will ever have our fervent wishes for your happiness and prosperity; and we will always offer our humble supplications to the Almighty that He may bless you and your family with health, long life and uninterrupted happiness.

Signed by the whole of the Native Officers and about 630 of the *Principal Ryots of Coorg*.

Lieutenant Colonel J. S. Fraser's

Reply to the Address of the Coorgs.

Deváns, Native Officers, and Inhabitants of Coorg.

I consider myself greatly honored by this address, and accept with pleasure the *gold cup* and *Coorg arms* which you have been pleased to present to me. I shall preserve them while I live as a highly flattering memorial of your friendship and kindness.

I think myself fortunate to have been brought by the commands of my Government into official connection and personal intercourse with a people like the brave Coorgs, for whom I entertain an unfeigned and cordial esteem.

I attach a peculiar value to these presents, because I regard them as indicating not merely a feeling of personal good will towards myself, but as conveying also a gratifying testimony that the Coorgs are entirely satisfied with the proceedings of the English Government, and an assurance that the sentiments of allegiance and fidelity which now unite this country to the British dominions will never be destroyed or impaired.

To advert to the points that are more particularly touched upon in this address, namely the mode of administration under which the affairs of the country are conducted, and the share which I have personally had in this administration, I have only to observe respecting the former, that in as far as it has proved satisfactory to the people of the country, they are indebted for it exclusively to the supreme British Government of India, under whose orders and guidance I have acted. The invariable object of those orders and that guidance has been the happiness of the people of Coorg. This principle of administration could scarcely fail of being attended with a prosperous issue under the direction of common prudence. But if it should be thought that success was still contingent on secondary agency, I can yet assume no merit for the performance of the subordinate part that has rested with me. Let the inhabitants of Coorg take that merit to themselves, for it is theirs.

They have been quiet, respectful, and obedient; open and frank in the declaration of their sentiments, and equally ready to receive the expression of mine. We have in fact acted in concurrence. We have proceeded hand in hand. And what has been the consequence? Why, this plain and obvious one; that since the first day on which I took charge of the country, I knew that all was right; that but one interest, one wish, one feeling prevailed; and that the Coorgs and myself, the governed and the instrument of Government, were associated in a common bond of union. Long may this be the established system here; for while it is so, the well-being of the country, and the happiness of its inhabitants are secured.

Farewell then for the present, my brave and estimable friends! I shall come and visit you sometimes, and shall always be happy to meet you again. But wherever I am, and in whatever circumstances I may be placed, be assured that the prosperity of Coorg will never cease to be an object of my sincerest wishes, and most anxious solicitude.

(Signed:) J. S. FRASER, Lieut. Col.

and Commissioner for the Affairs of Coorg.

2. THE RĀJAH'S EXILE AND DEATH. VICTORIA GAURAMMA

After a short stay in Mercara, the Rájah had to leave under an escort of the 35th and 48th N. I. commanded by Col. Stewart, who at Bangalore delivered him over to the charge of the Commissioner of Mysore on the 12th May 1834. The Ex-Rájah rode away through the town of Mercara, ordering the band to strike up "the British Grenadier," as if he had no sense of his fall. A number of his wives accompanied him. In their pálkies and his own he concealed vast sums of money in gold so that the bearers could hardly carry their loads. At the first halting place beyond the frontier of Coorg, at Sirlecote, he buried a great quantity of treasure, for he found the concealment no longer safe as he was allowed to carry away only ten thousand rupees. A certain Káryagára from Nálkanád who accompanied the Rájah afterwards helped himself to a large amount of this treasure and when the secret oozed out, he found it necessary to inform Capt. Le Hardy, that he knew of treasure secreted by the Rájah. An elephant was despatched to the eastward under the guidance of the honest Coorg, who faithfully delivered to the Company all he had left there and received a reward of Rs. 1000 for his loyal honesty! Gold coins were handed about rather freely at Nálkanád and are not yet scarce in certain houses.

From Bangalore the Ex-Rájah proceeded to Vellore and finally to Benares, where he drew a monthly pension of Rs. 6000 out of the Coorg Revenue. The British Government confiscated the money, deposited in Government securities by his uncle Dodda-Víraràja; still the Rájah was in possession of the valuable jewelry of his murdered cousin Dévammáji which together with the money carried away from Coorg, enabled him, to play, though under Government surveillance, the roll of a rich Indian Prince and to keep up through paid agents a secret correspondence with Coorg and to revive from time to time rumours of his return to the principality, which caused no little anxiety to the English Superintendents of Coorg.

When the Ex-Rájah was convinced of the hopelessness of ever regaining his principality, he demanded the payment of the capital of Rs. 680,000, the inheritance of his cousin Dévammáji, the interest of which he drew up to 1833 through Messrs. Binny & Co. in Madras. But in vain.

At last in 1852 he obtained leave from Lord Dalhousie, to visit England with his favourite daughter Gauramma who was then ten years old, in order to give her the advantages of an European education. Arrived there he expressed a wish to have her brought up in the Christian faith. Queen Victoria took an interest in the Indian Princess and at her baptism on the 30th June 1852 through the Archbishop of Canterbury, she stood sponsor and gave her the name "Victoria." By this achievement feeling himself strong in the royal favor, the Ex-Rájah commenced a Chancery suit against the East India Company for the recovery of the Rs. 680,000, but it dragged on a weary course, meanwhile in 1858 the Government of India was placed under the Crown and his suit fell to the ground.

The Coorg Princess *Victoria Gauramma* was by the Queen first placed in charge of the wife of Major Drummond and then entrusted to Sir John Login, formerly guardian of Dhulip Sing, in whose family she received a most careful and pious education. Unhappily married to an English Officer, she died on the 1st April 1864 and her husband and child have since mysteriously disappeared. Víraràja had died before and was buried in Kensal-Green, a London graveyard,—but as a heathen. True to his character in Coorg, he remained a stranger to the influence of Christian faith and morality in England.

Thus ended with Víraája Vodeya the *Royal House of Coorg, the line of the Rájahs of Haléri!*

3. VĪRARĀJENDER'S SONS AND RELATIVES.

CHANNA BASAVA.

Whilst in exile, six sons are said to have been born to Víraájender by his several wives, in addition to the baby boy, Chitrashékara, who was six months old, when his father left Mercara. At Vellore Lingarája and Sómashékara were born and at Benares: Vírabhadra, Nanjunda, Muddarája and Patmarája. Of these seven sons the first and the two last named are dead and the remaining four live at Benares on a small stipend from Government. A few years ago they sent emissaries to Coorg to obtain wives from amongst the leading Coorg families, though they themselves are Lingaites. They were evidently anxious to reawaken an interest amongst the subjects of their father; but their overtures were unsuccessful; the Coorgs one and all declined the proferred alliance.

Channa Basava and *Dévammáji* after their return from Bangalore had their confiscated farm at Appagalla with all its former belongings restored to them, and Government not only increased the land from 1596¼ to 2562¼ Butties, but gave them also a pension of Rs. 250 p. m. Yet they were not satisfied. Channa Basava, having received so much attention at Bangalore, flattered himself with the hope of eventually being seated on the Coorg throne as the only remaining male relative of the Ex-Rájah. On his return he assumed the title "Arasu" i. e. king, petitioned Government to grant him for a residence one of the three palaces at Mercara, Haléri and Nálkanád, as his house at Appagalla was like a "cow stable", "unhealthy" and "unpropitious." He also wanted the Punya or Rájah's farm at Nanjarájpatna and the charge of the Rájahs' tombs at Mercara, for the maintenance of which Government allowed Rs. 2000 per annum. But the Coorg Headmen exposed his designs so cleverly in an official report to Government, that it is quite refreshing to read their clear and telling arguments, which evince a most loyal disposition to the new Sircar. They plainly state it as their private opinion, "that Channa Basava is obnoxious to the Coorgs and that if he be aggrandized in any respect, a discontent will be created in the country." Thus he remained in his obscure position as a farmer at Appagalla. He died on the 3rd August 1868 at his farm. His widow, Dévammáji and his only son Sómashékarappa, are the only surviving legitimate relations remaining in the province. Two daughters are married to Polygars in Mysore.

Of the other members of the Rájahs' family, two relics of Tippu Sultan, *Dévammáji* and *Nílammáji*, cousins of Dodda-Vírajender, had the palace at Nálkanád assigned for their residence without, however, any claim or title to the property. Dévammáji died there before 1852 and was buried in the garden behind the Palace. Nílammáji followed her in 1865 and was buried by her side according to Mussulman rites.

There were three more distant female relations residing at the palace at Haléri, of whom Rájammáji, the widow of Vírappa, died on the 26th September 1868 and Lingavva, the widow of Nanjundappa, brother of Vírappa, and both sons of Appáji Arasu, younger brother of Dodda-Vírájender, on the 8th May 1869.

4. ABHRAMBĀRA, THE IMPOSTOR.

These two brothers, Vírappa and Nanjundappa, together with fourteen others of their relations were apprehended by order of the Ex-Rájah, immediately after his father's death in 1820, and confined in a building in the Fort of Mercara, called the Kótemane, where the whole of them died of starvation and misery within three months after their imprisonment. Rájammáji was at this period only 7 or 8 years of age and long entertained the idea, that her husband, Vírappa, had escaped and was still alive. This rumour circulated for the first time, when the British force entered Coorg, and it was said, that he accompanied the invading army to claim the Musnud. The report gained so much credit, that the Ex-Rájah despatched spies, to ascertain the fact. Rumour stated, that Vírappa had effected his escape from prison by the person who had been ordered to put him to death and who, as a proof of his having carried the order into execution, showed the Rájah a quantity of blood which he obtained from a wound, made in Vírappa's arm, that he proceeded to Mysore and remained for some time in the village of Avarti, till his wound was healed, when he wandered about as a Sanyási. In 1833, the news spread in Coorg and reached the Rájah, that a Sanyási, an extraordinary man, went about in the Manjerabad district, that he had a number of followers, performed miracles and composed extempore songs like Dasarapadas. Some of his verses were brought to Mercara and sung in the palace. The Rájah became curious to see the man. Abhrambára, this was the Sanyási's name, was desired to come to Mercara. On his arrival he was introduced to the Rájah. He was a tall and powerful man, sparingly dressed and wore a long beard looking more like a Mussulman Fakir, than a Hindu Sanyási. The Rájah asked him: "Who are you?" "A man," was the answer. R. "Where is your home?" S. "Here." R. "Who was your mother?" S. "The womb." R. "Who was your father?" The Sanyási continued to give the Rájah short, contemptuous and more and more indecent answers, so that he was greatly annoyed, but being afraid of maltreating him, he sent him abruptly away. Afterwards he regretted the measure and sent a messenger to bring him back, but Abhrambára had crossed the frontier and, though overtaken, refused to return. He was no more seen till after the establishment of the Company's Government, when in March 1835 he again appeared in the north of Coorg and was believed to be Vírappa. A person who knew the latter brought the information, that the Sanyási bore no resemblance whatever to Vírappa; others said the change in appearance had been caused by an attack of small-pox. No one could be found who had heard Abhrambára assert his identity with Vírappa. He appeared, indeed, to deny the truth of the story, but in a manner, calculated rather to confirm than to dissipate the report of his being Vírappa. His usual answers were, that he was only a poor Sanyási, that he was nobody, that he was the meanest servant of those by whom he was visited. The Coorg Deváns did not believe in the truth of the rumour and Capt. Le Hardy apprehended no danger, but made further enquiries and kept a watchful eye on the Jangama. About the end of May 1835 he was again wandering about the country, but without any followers except a few Brahmans and Jangamas. From Codlipet he proceeded to Sómwarpet and thence to Haringi, where he found accommodation in the house of the Dalavai (General) Venkatappa. His next visit was to Haléri Palace, in an outhouse of which he stayed a day and a night; after his return from Mercara he stopped there again and went back the same way he came to Kenchamane Hosakóte, accompanied by about 70 followers from Halérinád, Yedavanád and Yélusávirashíme, but only about 40 men went with him beyond the frontier and amongst these 11 only were Jamma-ryots and one a Kodaga. During his visit at Haléri Palace it could not be discovered, that any conversation or correspondence took place between him and Rájammáji, nor is there any proof of her having sent him a gold necklace during his stay at Subramanya. It is possible, that Abhrambára's only motive in going to the Haléri Palace was, to foster the belief of his being in correspondence with Rájammáji with the view of strengthening the report of his being her husband.

At Hosakóte his designs could no longer remain doubtful. His pretensions to the throne of Coorg were openly proclaimed by his followers. He assumed the headdress—a small cocked hat, and other insignia worn by the Rájahs of Coorg and circulated a proclamation. He is also said, to have predicted a disturbance that would shortly take place in Coorg and to have warned his followers, that by associating with him, they might possibly render themselves liable to punishment. Indeed two of his followers Kalyana Basava and Puttu Basava were seized at Baitur, in Malabar, and brought to Mercara. Laksmináráyana, one of the Deváns was also implicated in the Impostor's proceedings and eventually was sent prisoner to Bangalore. His brother at Sulya was at the head of the so-called Coorg insurrection of 1837. Abhrambára was at last caught and kept as a political prisoner in the Bangalore Jail. After 30 years' detention, he was set free and his first journey was to Coorg in July 1869. Being allowed but a passing visit under surveillance, he came again in June 1870 but was sent back to Mysore and died on his way at Seringapatam.

5. THE COORG REBELLION.

1837.

The so-called *Coorg Rebellion* was properly speaking a rise of the Gaudas, a tribe on the Western slope of the Ghats who resemble the Coorgs in many of their habits. These were disaffected to the Company's Government. After the annexation of Coorg, the districts of Amara Sulya, Puttur and Bantwála, the latter adjoining that of Mangalore, had been retransferred to the province of Canara, from which they had been taken. Under the Coorg Rájahs, the assessment had been paid in kind. The Collector of Mangalore now demanded cash payment. This was considered a grievance, as the farmers were laid under tribute by the money changers. One of the four Deváns, the above named Laksminárâyana, a Brahmin, who was displeased with the ascendancy of his Coorg brother-Deváns, made political capital out of the ill-feeling of the Gaudas. A brother of his at Sulya, in the low country, was in league with some rich and influential men of the malcontent Gaudas and he likewise entertained some intrigues with Abhrambára. The insurgents assembled at Sulya. They were a mere rabble, but they made a successful attack at Puttur on the Collector of Mangalore and two Companies of sepoys. A party of the rebels, whose courage and numbers increased after their unexpected success, advanced to Mangalore, opened the Jail and with the assistance of the prison fraternity, burnt and looted the Kacheri and some Civilians' houses, situated on the hills, overlooking the town. All the Europeans of the station were seized with a panic. The Civilians who fled on board a ship, bound for Cannanore, were spectators of the conflagration of their houses and thought the whole country was in arms. The Commanding Officer held a council of war and, deeming discretion the better part of valour, would have embarked the garrison, consisting of a Regiment, much weakened it is true, by the defeated detachment of several Companies, had boats been procurable, and ran away before a few hundred Gaudas, if so many, and the rabble of the Jail! Troops were immediately sent from Cannanore and Bombay; but when they arrived, they found nobody to fight with. The Mangalore garrison recovered their presence of mind and had no difficulty in maintaining their ground and restoring order.

Though this was altogether a Gauda-affair, a rise was also planned amongst the Coorgs at Nálkanád and Beppunád and amongst the Badagas in the Panje, Bellári and Subramanya districts and the northern parts of Coorg, inhabited by the late Rájah's trusted and favored Siváchâries. Also the late Deván, Kunta Basava's relatives, connections and ever ready tools were there. Formal proclamations were issued in the name of that mysterious personage, Abhrambára, who seemed to be everywhere and nowhere. The Coorgs and other inhabitants of the country were summoned to the service of the great prince of the Haléri house, who was about to take possession of his inheritance. A number of Coorgs about Talakávéri and Nálkanád believed the proclamations to which the Rájah's seal was attached and the assurances of the messengers who carried them. They took up arms and went down to the Head-quarters at Sulya. Abhrambára's letters patent were carried to Beppunád. The Coorgs there, officials and others, were taken by surprise, not knowing what to believe and unable to discern the safer side, they hesitated. After a day or two, a deputation from Vírájpet went to Mercara, to see the Deváns, to report to them and to ask for directions. Capt. Le Hardey, the Superintendent, was on the alert. After consultation with the Deváns, he left Ponappa at Mercara and marched with Bopu and a body of troops in the direction of Sulya as far as Sampáji, whither the insurgents were expected to move according to Bopu's information. When Capt. Le Hardey, after a long and tedious march, had reached Sampáji at the foot of the Ghats, no rebels were to be seen, and he learnt, that they had moved towards the Bisli-ghat and North Coorg. It was impossible to follow the insurgents through a tract of forest hills, difficult of passage even for travellers. He returned, therefore, to Mercara and marched to the supposed rendezvous of the rebels through the upper districts of Coorg. When he arrived there, still accompanied by Bopu, no insurgents were to be seen, and intelligence now reached his camp, that the enemy was at Sampáji. He forthwith marched to Sampáji by way of Kadamakall. Again no rebels. The Superintendent began to doubt the fidelity of his Deván. On his return to Mercara he was told by the other Deván Ponappa, who seems to have borne Bopu a grudge, that information had been received in the mean time of several of Bopu's relatives having joined the insurgents. Capt. Le Hardey's suspicions were thus confirmed. He called Bopu and charged him straight with treachery. "Go down to your friends, the rebels; be an open enemy; go, and I will come after you; and, if I catch you, you shall be hung." Bopu, who was as faithful a servant of the Company as his friend Ponappa, was terribly alarmed. Appearances were certainly against him; yet he was innocent. But how was he to gain the confidence of the Chief which he had evidently lost? The man broke out into tears and protested his fidelity with the eloquence of despair. "Do you stay, Capt. Le Hardey," he said, "and let me quell this miserable rebellion. If you give me liberty to act according to circumstances, and take all responsibility upon yourself, I will set out immediately and bring you the ringleaders alive or dead." Capt. Le Hardey felt, that the man was true and permitted him to do as he pleased. The Coorgs from Beppunád and other districts had in the mean time collected at Mercara. A party of some sixty men was despatched to the north under Subadar Appachanna the present (1870) Head Sheristadar. Bopu, with another troop marched straight down to Sampáji. Two "Lictors" of his own fashion preceded the "Coorg Consul," viz. two coolies, each of them carrying a load of fresh cut sticks. The Deván evidently intended to give the rebels a licking in the literal sense of the word. His best Nálkanád friends gathered around him; three of them marched a little in advance of the Deván to scour the way before him; for Chetty Kudiya, who had been the late Rájah's shooting master and great favourite, a man of the Male-Kudiya tribe, who could hit, it was said, the eye of a flying bird, had sworn to shoot Bopu dead the moment he saw him. The party had not proceeded further than the "Rájah's Seat" and were just descending the

Ghat, when they met two unlucky wights, a former Subadar, Muddaya and a late Párpadyagára, Appaya. They were well known to Bopu. They had failed to give him information of the insurrection; they must have known things and had they sent him a message in due time, it would have saved him the danger of utter disgrace and ruin, from which he had barely escaped. He, therefore, ordered some of his followers to seize the fellows and others to take out a fresh stick for each and give them a good blow up. The two unfortunates, at once seized by rude hands and stripped of their coats, demanded explanations; they were answered by blows. They protested their innocence, though no charge had been brought against them. Bopu did not stop to expostulate. Blows were the answer. They cried for mercy; fresh blows followed. After a while they were left half dead on the ground and Bopu marched on. Half way down the Sampáji pass, he met with a party of Nálkanád Coorgs, men of his own acquaintance; they were armed, but dared not fight the Deván; he at once ordered them all to be seized by his men, who were much more numerous and administered a severe castigation to all except one, who escaped by telling all he knew about the movements of the insurgents. Bopu went on gloriously. He did redeem the promise given to Capt. Le Hardey. The Subadar of Nálkanád had been drawn into this foolish affair. Bopu sent him word and then had a meeting with him, when he prevailed on him, without difficulty to withdraw from the rebels and to return to the allegiance he had sworn to the Company. The loss of so influential a man was a great blow and discouragement to the petty insurrection. It was put down with little shedding of blood beyond that which was drawn by the "Lictors" and from that time Coorg has been at peace. The Coorgs were most abundantly praised by Government for their loyalty and in recognition of their services of the recaptured treasure Rs. 20,000 were to be divided amongst those employed on the expedition; but they begged, that they might be honored with other distinctions in lieu; consequently they were rewarded with jaghir lands to a great extent and pensions for three generations, with horses, gold and silver medals, and broad cloth, according to their merits, or perhaps to the different degrees of relationship and friendship in which they stood to the Devâns. The "Coorg medal" in gold weighs 7 Tolas without, and 11½ Tolas with the chain and is two inches in diameter. On one side it represents a Coorg warrior in fighting attitude, and on the other it shows round a wreath which encircles the Coorg-knives—the Picha-Katti and the Odû-Katti—the following inscription in English: "For distinguished conduct and loyalty to the British Government Coorg. April 1837." The same inscription in Canarese is given on the reverse side. During the "Mutiny" in 1857 the Coorgs enjoyed the confidence of the local Government to such a degree, that after the suppression of the Rebellion, General Cubbon, the Chief Commissioner, issued to them the following Notification in English and Canarese, bearing at its head a medallion representing a Coorg in full warrior costume.

NOTIFICATION.

26th February 1861.

"In consideration of the exalted honour, loyalty and intrepidity, characteristic of this little nation of warriors and in recollection of its conspicuous services in aid of the British Government, it is my pleasing duty to notify hereby, for general information, in virtue of the power vested in me by the Government of India, that the provisions of the Act, commonly called the *Disarming Act* are not applicable to the gallant people of Coorg."

(Signed:) M. CUBBON,
Commissioner.

B. THE ADMINISTRATION OF COORG.

1. SUBDIVISION OF COORG FOR ADMINISTRATIVE PURPOSES, SKETCH OF THE SEVERAL TALUQS AND TOWNS.

On the assumption of Coorg by the British Government, the existing administrative organisation of the country, hallowed by age and routine, was as little as possible interfered with; but in progress of time such changes took place, as were deemed necessary for the better administration of the province. At present Coorg is divided into six taluqs and twenty-four náds, each of which is again subdivided into grámas or villages, which in "Coorg Proper" are made up of a number of vargas or farms rather, than of a number of houses joined into one community, for, as already observed, the Coorgs live on detached farms. In Yélusávirashíme— and part of Nanjarájpatna-taluq, the subdivisions are denominated "Hoblis" instead of náds, and in these two taluqs the greatest number of regular villages is found.

In the following table the divisions of Coorg are exhibited, together with the area in square miles, the number of villages and the seat of the Kacheri of each taluq and nád, from which statement it will be seen, that Coorg on an area of 1585 square miles contains 508 villages besides the towns: Mádapet (Mercara), Vírájpet, Fraserpet, Sómwárpet, Kodlipet and Ponnappet.

A Coorgman armed.

Lith by E Kaufmann, Labr

Name of Taluqs and Náds	Area.	No. of villages.	Seat of Kacheries.
I. Mercara-taluq	*209*	*57*	*Mercara.*
1. Mercara-Haléri-nád . .	49	15	Mercara.
2. Kagodlu-nád	40	6	Talatmáne.
3. Horur-núrokkal-nád . .	39	11	Boykeri.
4. Hudikéri-kanta-murnád . .	49	14	Murnád.
5. Ulugule-Mudikéri-nád . .	32	11	Sunticopa.
II. Padinálknád-taluq . .	*413*	*57*	*Napoklu.*
1. Padinálknád	142	12	Nálkanád Palace.
2. Katiednád	51	12	Bhávuli
3. Tavunád	139	9	Bhágamandala.
4. Benganád	42	11	Kolagadála.
5. Kuyinkéri	39	13	Pálur.
III. Yedenálknád-taluq . . .	*210*	*49*	*Virájenderpet.*
1. Yedenálknád	92	22	Virájenderpet.
2. Beppunád	41	8	Arméri.
3. Ammatnád	77	19	Cólepét.
IV. Kiggatnád-taluq	*400*	*63*	*Hudikéri.*
1. Anjikérinád	89	15	Hudikéri.
2. Thavalakérinád	110	15	Thavalakéri.
3. Hattugatnád	113	13	Ponnappet.
4. Betiednád	89	20	Kuntagráma.
V. Nanjarájpatna	*262*	*114*	*Fraserpet.*
1. Surlabi-Gadinád	113	21	Mádapur (Mahádévapur)
2. Yedavanád	94	37	Sómawárpet.
3. Nanjarájpatna-Hobli . . }	55	26	Fraserpet.
4. Rámaswámi-kanavé-Hobli }		30	Kampur.
VI. Yélusávirashíme-taluq.	*91*	*168*	*Saniwársante.*
1. Kodli-Hobli	27	55	Kodlipet.
2. Bilháda-Hobli	18	40	Saniwársante.
3. Nidhada-Hobli	46	73	Gaudhalli.
Grand Total . . .	*1585*	*508*	

Mercara-taluq with its 5 náds and 57 villages occupies the middle of Coorg and covers 209 square miles with a population of 15,556 souls, amongst whom there are only 2814 Coorgs. Within this small area all the essential features of the province are comprised:—ranges of high hills and solitary peaks, especially Nurokal-betta and Kóte-betta, fertile rice-valleys and parklike grassland, dense cardamom jungles and extensive coffee plantations, stately forest trees and clumps of graceful bamboos, innumerable clear mountain rills and ever flowing streams and rivers. With the exception of the most easterly portion of the taluq, the climate is everywhere healthy, and the soil fertile and well cultivated both for wet and dry crops. The principal ryots are Coorgs and Gaudas. The four highroads from Mysore, Cannanore, Mangalore and Manjarabád intersect the taluq at Mercara, hence also the great number of coffee plantations, especially in Mercara-Halérinád. Nearly the whole length of the Sampáji-ghat as far as the 16th mile the hillslopes are covered with the coffee shrub and there are some most successful plantations. On the north-eastern plateau of the ghat, in Horamalnád, the Coorg Coffee Company owns an estate of thousand acres. The oldest is the Mercara estate, further to the west, north and east from it are grouped the beautiful and valuable estates: "Glenmore" near the pretty Jessy-falls; "Beltamally" and "Hállery." Thousands of coolies are attracted to this taluq and on Sundays the Mercara bazaar is crowded with them. On the whole the ryots are of a poor class; the proximity of Head-quarters with its various demands seems to fall heavily upon them and to keep aloof richer farmers, besides the alluring temptations of the Mercara shops may induce the ryots to spend their money imprudently and help to impoverish them. The people of *Halérinád* have always been remarkable for their attachment to the Rájahs' family, since the dynasty originated there and in consequence assumed the title of "Haléri Samsthán".

The *Head Quarter Station* is *Mercara*, the capital of Coorg. Its geographical position is in Lat. 12° 26′ N. and Long. 75° 46′ E. It is distant from Madras via Mysore and Bangalore 352 miles, from Bangalore 147, from Mysore 75, from Cannanore 68, and from Mangalore 84 miles. Situated on a plateau and in a central position, the locality seems to have been chosen from its comparative difficulty of access in former days. Mudduraja selected the spot for a fort and in 1681—82 took up his residence there. Surrounded by an amphitheatre of undulating, grassy or slightly wooded hills—in former days covered with dense forests—the local position of the town, 3767 feet above the level of the sea and about 600 feet above the Kávéri-valley is extremely picturesque and beautiful. The Fort with its principal buildings: (vide p. 191 and 180) the Palace, the English church and the Superintendent's Kacheri, rises in the centre of the plateau. Outside the fort on the southern hill-slope stand: the *Regimental Hospital*, and in parallel rows, sheltered from the easterly and westerly winds, the newly constructed tiled *Lines* of the sepoys with the regimental bazaar and in the hollow beyond the Gaulika-village. Skirting the ridge to the southwest above the Lines, a parade-ground and promenade have been levelled and on the evenings, when the regimental band plays there, Mercara society is in the habit of frequenting the place. At its further end in a retired little garden is the "*Rájah's Seat*," the charming, homelike panorama from which attracts every lover of beautiful landscape. Close by is the *Burial-ground* of the Protestant community, where many an aspiring or weary European pilgrim has found his last resting place, among them Major Gustard, Superintendent of Coorg, and his two wives, Dr. Dunkan Macpherson, late Inspector General of Hospitals, and Major

Frank Vardon, the intrepid companion of Dr. Livingstone in South-Africa. He died on the 21st June 1860. At the junction of the three Ghat-roads rises the *Roman Catholic Church of St. Michael*, renovated a few years ago. Further on to the left of the Fraserpet road is a prettily designed, but badly executed long row of buildings, destined for native shops and Abkari-godowns; behind it, in modest retreat, stands the *Civil Dispensary*, and on the opposite side of the road on a beautiful spot the *Travellers' Bangalow*, where, though comforts may be wanting, a splendid view is ever present! Still further on near the first mile-stone is the site of the *Offices of the Public Works Department.* Dotted here and there, ensconced in wooded nooks or standing forth on knolls, boldly facing the monsoon storms, but commanding glorious views, the European houses are placed. In front of the Superintendent's Kacheri is the *Post-Office* and the *Jail-garden*, and below it the dome of the *Onkárésvara-temple* with its gilt orb peeps out from a hollow round which the dwellings of the Coorg officials and of Brahmins are clustered amid a dense mass of vegetation. Some of these houses are two storied and after European pattern. On the northside of the fort on a lower terrace stands the *Telegraph Office*, a building of the Rájahs' time which, after the successive metamorphosis into an elephant-stable, travellers' bangalow and school-house, attained its present destination in 1867. At a little distance and separated from it by a narrow rice valley crossed by a broad bund, stretches the native town, called *Mádapet* or *Mahádévpet* in honour of Mahádévamma, the favourite Ráni of Dodda-Vírájender. It consists of three streets, two of which are nearly parallel and the third branches off to the left at the beginning of the town, leading to the Sappers' lines. An addition to the Petta was attempted six years ago by allotting a new piece of ground for dwellings, but the scheme has not made much progress since. The new portion was to be called "Ránipetta" in honour of Queen Victoria. The town, which 15 years ago was almost entirely composed of wretched thatched mud-huts, bears now, in consequence of its profitable coffee traffic and exorbitant prices permitted by free trade, the stamp of prosperity. Out of its 850 houses 281 are tiled, most of them brick built and two storied and inhabited by merchants and tradesmen. The population of 3859 souls—without the Regiment—comprises 43 different castes, but no Coorgs live in the Petta. The Petta-*Subadar's Kacheri* occupies the highest point of the town and behind it are situated the Tombs of the Coorg Rájahs (vide p. 182). Under Capt. Cole's direction Lieut. Mackenzie, the Assistant Superintendent, has greatly interested himself in the amelioration of the sanitary condition of the Petta. The streets are broad and clean; two small tanks and a number of wells and running streams supply wholesome water. Every Friday there is a market, hence Mercara is also called *Shukravára-sante* (Friday-market). In the principal street—locally the High-street—the daily requisites for food and raiment are displayed. People from Nanjarájpatna and the Mysore country bring: dry grain—such as, rági, gram, rice of the superior sorts, dál, wheat, green gram, Bengal gram—, jaggory, tamarind, potatoes, chillies, onions, garlic, turmeric, mustard, coriander, oil seeds, castor oil, sesamum oil, tobacco, betel leaves, chunam, baskets, eggs, fowl, sheep, goats, etc. Máplas from Tellicherry and Cannanore import cocoanuts, arekanuts, cocoanut oil, and dry fish; Coorgs and other ryots bring clean rice, plantains, oranges, pineapples and straw; the merchants and petty dealers spread out in their shops or in the street their merchandise: cotton, silk and woolen fabrics; potters pile up their many-shaped vessels, tailors expose their gay, ready made clothes, money-changers squat before their stores of copper coins, liquor shops attract the crowd by their gaily ornamented brandy bottles and barbers ply their handicraft in retired corners of the road!

To the east of the town on a flat hill spur the *Government Central School* buildings and higher up some private dwellings are conspicuous. The "Westend" of Mercara was occupied by the *Sappers' Lines.* There are still some public offices left, to which some European cottages have been added to enliven that distant locality. Mercara can also boast of several *European Shops* which are well supplied to minister to the wants and luxuries of European habit and taste.

The hilly nature of the locality does not admit of a great *variety of drives,* but the Fraserpet and Manjarabad highroads are generally in a very good condition and the rides along the hills to the neighbouring coffee plantations are very enjoyable.

Padinálknád-taluq with its five Náds is twice the size of Mercara-taluq, but contains the same number of villages viz. 57 with a population of 20,303 souls, of whom 5611 are Coorgs and 13,256 other Hindus, 1029 Mussulmans and the rest belonging to other castes. This taluq, which extends westward of the Mercara-taluq, occupies the most hilly and wooded part of Coorg, and contains little arable, but plenty of hilly grass and forest land with the largest and most productive cardamom jungles. This part of Coorg is not opened up by Europeans, but many natives hold here coffee plantations, chiefly planted under shade. Rice cultivation, owing to the want of suitable land, is so deficient, that even the largest farms are not able to produce sufficient rice for their own consumption; the ryots in general have to buy rice for six months in the year and chiefly rely on the produce of their cardamom and coffee-gardens; but since both have not been very productive of late, the condition of the ryots in Padinálknád-taluq is far from flourishing. Containing the richly endowed Brahmanical Institutions at Bhágamandala and Tale-

Kávéri and a great number of other Dévasthánas and fine forests dedicated to sylvan gods, this division is the most unenlightened and uncivilised in Coorg. There are many jungle-people especially the Kádu-Maratties, who live on Kumari-cultivation (vide p. 108) and one tribe in the forests of Távunád, the Kádavas or Bodavas, whose women dress in Eve's fashion, but with the vanity of Eve's daughters change the leaves four times a day. The women never come out of the forest, only the men show themselves, covered with a coarse cloth. They are excellent marksmen with bow and arrow, and live on the chase, seldom working for hire." Their huts, which they frequently change, are of the rudest description, made of sticks and covered with Netti-Pai (leaves of the Netti palm). Nearly the whole population of Távunád consists of Tulu-gaudas; there and in Nálkanád Canarese is scarcely understood, the people speak Codagu, Tulu and Malayálam.

The ryots in Kuyinkéri-nád, chiefly influenced by the wealthy House of the Karanika, Kutteti Eyappa, are mostly Coorgs and much devoted to the Pálur deity (vide p. 174). But here as elsewhere in this taluq, the love of gain or, perhaps, necessity seems to overcome the superstitious scruples of the ryots; the venerated dévara-kádus (sacred jungles) which, having for ages remained intact, are generally the finest forests, are cautiously invaded by the natives' axe and planted with coffee; but to propitiate the fabled wrath of Pálurappa, Iggutappa, Maletámbirappa and Ayappa, the devoted planter pays from 8 As. up to 1 Rs. per Batti of coffee towards the worship of the despoiled sylvan deities; but with the disappearance of these sacred forests, the oblation will probably cease too!

Padinálknád-taluq, being skirted by the highest range of the Western Ghats with the broad based Tatiandamol, at the foot of which the Nálkanád-palace is built, is watered by the upper course of the Kávéri with its numerous tributaries.

Nápoklu is the seat of the Taluq-Kacheri, but otherwise an insignificant place. It is 15 miles from Mercara and on the Rájah's road to Nálkanád Palace. It possesses a flourishing Canarese School which will soon be enlarged into an Anglo-Vernacular School.

Yedenálkanád-taluq separates Kiggatnád from Mercara and Padinálknád-taluq. Its northern boundary is all along formed by the Kávéri. Within an area of 210 square miles, it contains 49 villages and one town. The population of its three Náds amounts to 14,153 souls and amongst them 4,802 Coorgs, 7,314 other Hindus, 1029 Mussulmans and the rest is made up of various classes. This taluq is considered as the focus of Coorg life. Most of the leading Coorg families reside here and as they resisted the temptations of the imposter Abhrambára in 1837, they came in for a large share of the Government rewards. It contains the most fertile paddy fields in Coorg and also extensive European and native coffee-plantations. The Carnatic Coffee Company held here large Estates. There are still fine forests on the Perambóti Ghat, and in Beppunád there is a dense Dévara-kádu, called Kariárbana (blackest jungle,) the residence of Beyturappa, which from superstitious fear is never entered by the natives. In the eastern portion of Ammatnád there are still many waste paddy fields. What in the same Nád is called the "Bamboo-district," is remarkable for its luxuriantly growing coffee-plantations, which, but for the devastations of the coffee-borer, would have been the most productive in Coorg. In this locality a new market has been opened for the convenience of the numerous coolies and the place has been called *Cólepet* in honor of our late Superintendent Capt. R. A. Cole. Another newly founded village in Ammatnád is Anandapur, the first Protestant settlement of a Christian Holeya congregation (1857).

The seat of the Taluq-Kacheri is at *Vírájenderpet*, a

flourishing town, 20 miles from Mercara, on the Cannanore high-road and four miles from its junction at Perambádi with the Mysore road. It is a place of some importance on account of its coffee, rice and cardamom traffic with the Western Coast. The population amounts to 3024 souls, of whom 1,255 are Mussulmans, 1296 Hindus, 156 Jains and 313 Roman Catholic Christians, who settled here as fugitives from Tippu Sultan's conquered dominions. The town was established in 1792 by Dodda-Vírájender in commemoration of a meeting that took place between himself and General Abercromby during the first campaign against Mysore in 1791.

The town proved very unhealthy, but since the rigorous introduction of sanitary measures by Lieut. Mackenzie, generously supported by a Native Municipal Board, the health of the people has greatly improved. Vírájpet is prettily situated at the foot of the Maletambira hill on the top of which there is a large square-built temple. The town may be divided into the Roman Catholic quarter, the main bazaar and the Mussulman streets. Every Wednesday there is market, which attracts a great concourse of Coorgs. The merchandise is similar to that at Mercara. Of public buildings the most attractive is the renovated *Roman Catholic Church*, which Father Guillon reconstructed in simple gothic style and with a copper roof. The inside is gaudily ornamented with paintings and statues in stucco, his handywork, greatly to the taste and admiration of the natives. The *New Offices* of the Assistant Superintendent, the Taluq and Nád Subadar's Kacheri behind the Traveller's Bangalow and above the town, promise to be an imposing and convenient structure, when completed. The *Traveller's Bangalow* surrounded by a high wall, is well situated on a knoll, which forms the highest point of the town. It was built of the material and on the site of the Rájah's palace, but without much regard to the convenience of European visitors who frequent the place. The

Government *English School* is a temporary building near the Bangalow and a more commodious and substantial School-house should be erected. Of the four *tanks* belonging to the town, Gauri-kere contains the purest water. It is at the head of the Petta and was excavated by the orders of Dodda-Vírájender, the founder of Vírájpet. At the expense of Pál-pare Rudaya it was repaired some years ago, but people being allowed to wash and bathe in the tank, the wholesomeness of the water must be greatly impaired, and Gauri-idol which is annually thrown into it at the Gauri-feast will not restore its purity! Good drinking water, but in a small quantity, is obtained from an enclosed spring at the foot of the Bangalow hill, close to the paddy fields. The site of Vírájpet being very rocky, the industry of the people in economising every foot of cultivable land is very remarkable, but the destruction of so many coffee and orange trees by the Borer has considerably marred the once luxuriant vegetation in and around Vírájpet. In the principal street there are a few straggling cocoanut trees, but the climate is not congenial to a fertile growth.

Communication with the eastern portion of the taluq and with Mysore is maintained by two bandy roads, one through Cólepet, Anandapur and Siddápur, the other towards Bittan-gala and Hattúr.

Kiggatnád-taluq extends with its four Náds over the whole of south-eastern Coorg and covers an area of 400 square miles with 63 villages and the rising town Ponappet. The taluq contains 17,650 inhabitants, of whom 5,480 are Coorgs, 5,709 other Hindus and 5,818 Jungle people, such as Kurubas and Yeravas; of the rest 417 are Mussulmans and 223 Amma-Codagas. Upon the whole the people of this taluq may be said to be in easy circumstances, as they are well provided with the necessaries of life. With the exception of the large and influential house of the late Deván Chepudira Ponnappa but little disparity in point of wealth exists amongst the ryots. The Kiggatnád rice-fields are extensive and fertile, the grass-lands parklike, the mountain streams numerous, and the forests and jungles rich in valuable timber and bamboos. The Marenád- and Brahmagiri-hills with their cascades of the Barapolle and Laksmanatírtha are picturesque and their shólas and dense forests give cover to a variety of game. Many of the undulating grass-hills (Báne), being almost bare of trees and free from stones, seem admirably suited for dry cultivation, besides there are large pieces of other waste land; but the population is rather scanty and hardly sufficient for the cultivation of their rice-fields, since the abolishment of slavery. There are both European and native coffee-plantations in the Marenád-hills; but the natives seem to derive the greater profit from them. This taluq is in great want of good roads. There is only the military highroad from Periapatna to Cannanore, which is joined at the Gonikopal bridge by a branch road leading to Ponnappet; a trace has been cut to the Taluq-Kacheri and on to Kúrchi to connect Coorg with Wynád, but the work has been stopped. From Marenád a steep ghat, called the Mépalé-ghat, leads into the Malabar country and is used by the Lumbánies and Koramárs, who once a year carry rice from and salt into Coorg. A footpath leads into Wynád over the Brahmagiris by way of Tiranelli.

The south-eastern corner of Kiggatnád is unhealthy and strangers can scarcely be induced to settle there, in spite of the nearness of Kuttadámma's famous sanctuary, which cannot render the place more salubrious; fever, spleen and dropsy are the local diseases.

The Taluq-Kacheri is in *Hudikéri.* The place is well selected, being central and in a healthy locality on the top of a beautiful grass hill, whence a fine view of the Brahmagiris and Marenád-hills is obtained. An English School has been lately established and is promising well.

The only town of the district is *Ponnappet*, so named in compliment to the late Deván Chepudira Ponnappa, the grandfather of the present Native Assistant Superintendent Ch. Soobiah. It was founded in 1835, but owing to the unhealthiness of the locality it had to be abandoned and a fresh site was selected on the ridge of a hill about 3 miles from the Gonikopal bridge and as far from the Taluq-Kacheri. The Nád-Kacheri has been established there and the Petta is springing up around it, most of the 33 houses have been built and are owned by the Deván's son Mádaya. Of the 124 inhabitants the greater number are Lingaites, but no Coorgs settle there.

Nanjarájpatna-taluq with its four Náds surrounds the northern half of Mercara-taluq and extends from the Bissly-ghat in the north to the Kávéri, the eastern boundary. It covers 262 square miles and contains 114 villages besides the towns of Fraserpet and Sómawárpet. In point of population, it is the largest taluq, numbering 20,997 souls, of whom 5,225 are Coorgs, 15,289 other Hindus and 427 Mussulmans. Here also the greatest number of cultivators is to be found, amounting to 15,384, whilst in Padinálknád-taluq on nearly twice the area, there are only 15,296 ryots. The taluq, as regards natural features and population, may be divided into the hilly tract of Surlabi—Gadinád and Yedavanád and into the champaign country of Nanjarájpatna—and Rámaswámi-kanavé-Hobli. The former resembles Mercara-taluq, but having its steepest declivities, from Pushpagiri to Katamakal, due west; the latter is like the adjoining portion of the Mysore country. The former tract is chiefly peopled by the Yedavanád Coorgs, who dress like the Coorgs proper, but are originally Canara and Manjerabad Vokkaligas. Though mostly Jamma-ryots, they are poor and have little influence in the country. Also in a moral and intellectual point of view, they hold a low position. They express little desire for education and when offered, do not exert themselves to retain the boon. However, their wants are not overlooked, a new school will shortly be re-established in Gadinád. These people, who with the exception of the inhabitants of Surlabi-Muttunád behaved badly towards the English Government in 1837, are much under the influence of the Jangams residing in these Náds. There are two Mathas of note here, Mádapur and Abbi-matha, where the Shivácháries possess rich endowments.

The Kanavé-Hoblis are inhabited by a set of people identical with that of the adjoining Mysore ryots. They are chiefly cultivators of dry land and produce horse-gram, rági, various kinds of beans, tobacco, bangh, flax, sesamum and also cotton. The sandalwood tree grows extensively in this taluq. In Yedavanád some rice-fields which have a good water-supply yield two crops; there the wild sago-palm is also carefully attended to for the sake of the toddy drawn from it and for the farinaceous substance, prepared for food by the poorer classes from the inner part of the tree. Honey of the best quality is largely collected in June and much appreciated by the people. Near the village Beradi-kanavé there was the Back-stokade from which the northern column of the Coorg field-force was repulsed in 1834. (Bakka, *Kg.* door-way to a narrow passage.)

Fraserpet is the seat of the taluq and Nád-Kacheri of Nanjarájpatna and the monsoon Head-quarters of the Superintendent. It lies 20 miles to the east from Mercara on an elevation of 3,100 feet above the sea. Situated on the left bank of the river Kávéri in a bent formed by a sudden turn of the river, opposite the Mysore frontier, with which it is connected by a fine stone bridge, and the country, though open, being dotted by rounded grass or wood-clad hillocks on which the European houses are built, Fraserpet offers a most varied and pleasing landscape, especially from the travellers' bangalow, which occupies a rocky eminence, the site of the former fort. It was a happy thought to select this spot for a travellers' bangalow, where after a weary journey over the monotonous Mysore-roads the traveller is placed in the midst of a charming scenery, a worthy introduction into Coorg!

From the position of Fraserpet its climate is hotter than that of Mercara, but during the monsoon it is extremely pleasant, as very little rain falls there and the heat of the sun is moderated by constant clouds and light fogs. The nights are cool and pleasant, nor is the sun ever very oppressive at any season, except for an hour or two at midday; after the monsoon, however, and especially after considerable inundations by the Kávéri, the place becomes feverish and is no inhabited by Europeans.

The town was named "Fraserpet" in honor of General Fraser, the first Commissioner of Coorg. It contains now 326 houses, mostly tiled, and a population of 1,213 souls, of whom 360 are Christians, 388 Mussulmans and 465 Hindus. The town can boast of a Roman Catholic Church, a newly built shrine, dedicated to Ganapati, with a very useful public well in front of it, an Anglo-Vernacular School, a native rest-house with a tank and a Government wood-yard, besides the European bangalows. The Roman Catholics are mostly native or East Indian pensioned soldiers and their families, a detachment of Sappers and Miners having been stationed there when employed in making the great road to Mercara and the bridge over the Kávéri.

Sómawárpet in Yedavanád is 26¾ miles to the north of Mercara and of the same elevation. It lies on the highroad to Manjerabad, but there is nothing remarkable connected with the Petta. Of its 197 houses 19 are tiled and 178 thatched. Of the 953 inhabitants 862 are Hindus and 91 Mussulmans. There are but few cultivators, most of them live on trade in various articles. Though fully alive to their material interests, the town-people have little desire for or perhaps little faith in education after European fashion. They seem to be quite content with the knowledge of their bazaar-routine. Every Monday there is market, hence the name of the place. (Sómawára=Monday.)

The place is greatly in want of a travellers' bangalow, for which a beautiful site could be obtained near the lodge of the road-overseer. The country about Sómawárpet is very picturesque, especially towards Shanthally, the Mukribetta with a flourishing coffee-plantation at its foot, and the rocks that enclose the Honammana tank. vide p. 15. On the summit of these rocks "Cairns" in excellent preservation have lately been found.

Yélusávirashíme-taluq occupies the northermost part of Coorg. It is a narrow strip of land, about 22 miles in length and 4 in width. Its total area comprises only 91 square miles; yet it contains in its three Hoblis, 168 villages and a population of 17,766 souls, of whom 17,623 are Hindus, 41 Mussulmans, and 98 Native Christians. There are no Coorgs in this taluq; the inhabitants are of the same class as the agricultural population in the adjoining taluq of Hassan. There is a striking contrast between the ryots of Yélusávirashíme and those of Central Coorg. Whilst the latter are well and warmly dressed, comfortably housed and abundantly fed, the former appear very poor and miserable, covered as they are only with a black coarse camlet. They are timid, credulous and submissive to the authority of the Patéls, who find them patient sheep for fleecing, but the Patéls with their connexions are noted as exceedingly litigious amongst themselves and rather troublesome to the Government in times past. The country was wrested from Mysore by the Coorg Rájah, Dodda-Vírappa, who died in 1736, and partakes of the natural features of the Manjarabad district. It is hilly, and some mountains, as the Málimbi and the Uru-uduvé (village-jungles) are densely wooded, other hills are bare and precipitous. The narrow valleys, in which rice-cultivation is carried on, are terraced to a considerable extent to enlarge their area. Only some well watered fields yield a scanty second crop. Transplanting is not much practised, the seed is sown broadcast in most instances. The cultivated lands of Yélusávirashíme possess none of the characteristic fertility of Yedenálknád- or Kiggatnád-taluq. The soil of the higher grounds consists of a thin stratum of gravelly earth, barren and arrid, producing only a few dwarfish shrubs especially the Dwarf-date-palm, (Phoenix farinifera), and a tall thin grass, the decay of which yields little humus, to enrich the paddy fields. The soil for the cultivation of dry grain consists generally of a light friable earth and the kind of produce especially tobacco is similar to that in the Kanavé districts of Nanjarájpatna-taluq, but not so good. Toddy is extensively drawn and forms the habitual beverage of the people.

The seat of the Taluq-Subadár and of the Subadár of Bilháda Hobli is *Saniwársante* (Saturday-market), a market-place of little importance, but prettily situated on the top of a broad hill, which towards the south presents a beautiful encamping ground. It lies on the highroad to Manjarabad, 12 miles from Sómawárpet and 38¾ from Mercara. Among its 483 inhabitants who live in 101 houses, of which 4 only are tiled, there are 46 families of weavers, who in the most primitive style ply their craft in the street, manufacturing coarse cotton fabrics.

Kodlipet, near the northern frontier of Coorg, is a small town on the Manjarabad highroad and 44¾ miles from Mercara. It lies in an elevated, open and healthy locality with a tank at its entrance. Its 141 houses, of which 87 are tiled, are arranged in broad streets and give the place a tidy, well-to-do appearance. It contains 730 inhabitants, mostly Lingaites who are busily engaged in trade. There are 31 cloth-merchants, 32 tobacco-sellers, 41 petty dealers, 8 jewel-makers and 4 money-changers and bankers, which shows, that the community must be a thriving one. A school containing about 50 children is also maintained by the inhabitants, but like those at Sómawárpet, they show little inclination to render assistance for the establishment of a Government English School, though they seem to be anxious to have one, if every thing is done for them.

2. ADMINISTRATION OF JUSTICE.

a. In the time of the Rájahs.

The Rájahs, having exercised sovereign power arbitrarily, never established any court of judicature, nor framed any code of judicial regulations. They published, however, a Hukum-náma (code) for the administration of revenue, to which they added a few paragraphs, simply defining the degrees of punishment which the district officials might in their judicial capacity inflict upon offenders without reference to the Huzur (Huzur, presence, highest authority). By usage (mámúl) the following judicial system became established:—

The Gauda, the headman of the village, enquired into the complaints preferred by the ryots residing in it, respecting civil cases or petty offences and settled them upon viva voce evidence either himself or through a Pancháyat (court of arbitration) according to circumstances. He was incompetent to adjudge cases of heinous crimes. The Gauda could try petty criminal offences, but had to commit the guilty person to the Kacheri of the Párapatiagár, who could award punishment not exceeding three days. Caste disputes were settled by the Kuláchára (guardian of the observances peculiar to caste), who had authority to punish to the amount of 12 fanams or Rs. 3 as. 8. The appeal from the Gauda or his

Pancháyat lay to the Párapatiagár or to the Deván's Kacheri. The Párapatiagár settled at his own responsibility or through a Pancháyat cases of small amount which, however, remained undefined.

When *theft* was committed in a village, the Gauda with the ryots exerted themselves to catch the thief and on apprehension carried him to the Párapatiagár's Kacheri, where an enquiry was made, the stolen property, if possible, recovered and restored to the owner with an award of half the value of the stolen property as a punishment of the thief. In default of payment, he was flogged or sentenced to work on the roads. *Corporal punishment* was not restricted to any class of crime or people; even Deváns, who had incurred the displeasure of the Rájahs, were subjected to the last, some times swung by the royal hand!

In *murder cases*, the Párapatiagárs and the Subadár of the district committed the criminal for trial to the Huzur, the officials of which, under orders from the Rájah, examined the prisoner and reported the result. According to circumstances the murderer would be pardoned, fined, whipped, mutilated or executed, agreeably to the Rájah's orders. In *cases of adultery* the guilty parties were severely and barbarously punished. *Manslaughter* committed in a state of intoxication or during hunting or whilst guarding the crops against wild beasts, was leniently dealt with, especially if the unfortunate man reported the accident voluntarily before the Huzur had been informed of it. *Eloping from the country* and *treasonable acts against the Sirkar* were considered as the most heinous crimes, and the culprit, if caught, seldom escaped capital punishment, dictated with a savage vindictiveness. Of the nature of these punishments it is difficult to credit the stories, that are told of their frequency and ferocity. The ordinary ones are said to have been: crushing to death by elephants, strangulation or decapitation by the large Coorg knife, a most efficient instrument for such an operation; others less expeditious but more cruel were: throwing the criminal over the precipice near the "Rájah's Seat" or nailing him to a tree and shooting him with arrows. In such a manner the Deván Kshouri Kariappanna was tormented to death by Lingarája. Punishments short of death were: dislocating the toes and fingers, suspending the offender by the ears, pounding out his teeth, amputating his nose and lips or otherwise mutilating his person. When of a capital nature, punishments were never public and every care was taken to conceal them from the people. The Rájahs' Siddi—or African—bodyguard acted as executioners. The sufferer was proclaimed as having deserted his home and a reward offered for his apprehension. If he was a man of consequence, instructions were given to make a diligent search after the fugitive, which of course proved ineffectual. when he was declared to have eluded pursuit and escaped to some of the neighbouring countries. Artifices of this nature could not long retain the power of imposing, but the danger of mentioning the transaction secured silence regarding it.

With so primitive and simple forms of judicial procedure, the enforcement of its precepts required no complicated system of police. Every villager was a voluntary policeman and every Jamma-ryot bound to render gratuitous service to the Sirkar. The limited extent of the country and the vigilant control over all its parts, enhanced by frequent communication by means of posted runners with all the Kacheris, kept the Rájahs well informed of any unusual occurrence and enabled them to send prompt orders to the district-officials.

b. Under the British Government.

From the Proclamation of Col. Fraser in April 1834 we have already seen, that he upheld the authority of the native officials, reserving to himself, as the representative of the

Governor General, the prerogative of the Rájah. On the 30th August 1834 he issued a set of "*Rules for the conduct of the District functionaries in Coorg*" from which we cite the following paragraphs as they contain the principles and routine of the English administration until lately modified by new Acts.

"Civil Justice."

Para 55. "Whereas it is necessary for the due administration of justice in the Coorg country, to introduce regularity in the system which has prevailed, and to define the judicial power of the district functionaries, the following rules have been enacted and are published for general information and guidance.

56. The custom of adjusting differences by mutual composition of the parties being highly commendable, the Sirkar will be glad, when parties settle their disputes in this manner; or by the arbitration of a referee selected from among their neighbours. If an adjustment cannot be effected by this means, they shall then have recourse to the Sirkar functionaries.

57. The Patéls are empowered to hear, try and determine on their own responsibility upon oral evidence such suits as may be preferred to them for sums of money or other personal property the amount or the value of which shall not exceed five rupees.

58. If the parties be dissatisfied with the decision of the Patéls, they may appeal to the Párapatiagárs. The jurisdiction of the Patéls is to extend to all civil suits to the amount above limited, which may arise between the parties residing within the villages.

59. The Párapatiagárs at the head of their Kacheri may hear the appeals against the decision of the Patéls. They shall try on their own responsibility causes not exceeding Rs. 50 upon recorded evidence, and all causes above that sum

and not exceeding 100 Rs. shall be investigated through a Pancháyat which they shall convene for that purpose. The Párapatiagárs shall take cognizance of all civil suits arising within their respective náds. Appeals against the decision of the Párapatiagárs lie to the Kacheri of the Subadár.

60. In hearing and determining civil suits the Párapatiagárs shall be assisted by the Shánabógas in writing the proceedings of the enquiry. The Shánabógas are to keep registers of the suits preferred to the Párapatiagárs, each complaint being entered in the order in which it may be received and will forward them after being signed by the Párapatiagárs to the Subadár's Kacheri.

61. The Subadár shall try and settle causes to the amount of Rs. 100 on his own responsibility; but in cases, where the sum in litigation may be above that sum and not exceeding Rs. 200, he shall assemble a Pancháyat and settle them. The Subadárs shall take cognizance of all suits arising within their respective taluqs.

62. In trying and determining suits, the Subadár shall be assisted by the Sheristadars and the Gumastas in writing the proceedings of the enquiry. The Sheristadars and the Gumastas are to keep registers of the suits preferred to the Taluq-Kacheri, entering each plaint in the order in which it may be received and forwarding them monthly to the Daryáft-Kacheri.

63. A Kacheri, denominated the Daryáft-Kacheri, and composed of one of the three Deváns and the Karanika or any two of these, accordingly as they may be engaged or otherwise in their respective and more specific duties, has been established at the Huzur. It shall hear all appeals against the decision of the Subadárs and determine them. This Kacheri shall decide on its own authority causes from Rs. 200 to Rs. 1000 upon recorded evidence.

64. All causes above Rs. 1000 and not exceeding Rs. 3,000 shall be inquired into and settled by a Pancháyat which

will be convened by the Daryáft-Kacheri. The Daryáft-Kacheri assisted by a Pancháyat shall make inquiry into causes beyond Rs. 3,000 and submit the proceedings to the Huzur and carry its orders into effect.

65. The Daryáft-Kacheri shall be assisted by two Mutsudies of the Deván-Kacheri in writing the proceedings of the inquiries they make. The Mutsudies are to keep registers of all suits decided by the Daryáft-Kacheri and preserve in regular order the records connected with that Kacheri, distinct from that of the Deváns. The Daryáft-Kacheri shall submit for the perusal of the Huzur these registers monthly.

66. The plaintiff and defendant in a cause shall be allowed to employ their relations or agents to plead before the Párapatiagárs, the Subadárs and the Daryáft-Kacheri, as also before the Pancháyats assembled by them, furnishing them with power for that purpose.

67. The plaints shall clearly state the name and residence of the complainant as well as of the person complained against, the grounds on which the complaint is founded, the amount of value of the property claimed and all such circumstances as may serve for the elucidation of the case.

68. The Párapatiagárs or Subadárs may send peons either with a verbal message or written summons (yádást) to the defendant, directing him to appear in order to answer the complaints preferred against him.

69. The complainant shall be directed to accompany the peons entrusted with the summons, or otherwise to send relations or agents for the purpose, indicating the residence of the defendant and identifying his person.

70. After the defendant makes his appearance the complaint shall be read over to him and he shall be directed to give an answer to it on a day which shall be fixed, he being furnished with a copy of the complaint.

71. On the delivery of the answer by the defendant who ought to state therein what he may have to say, a copy of it shall be sent to the plaintiff. The latter shall be required to give his reply within a prescribed time and after he delivers it, a copy of it shall be furnished to the defendant and he shall give a rejoinder. Afterwards the plaintiff and the defendant shall be directed to give in a list of the witnesses whom they wish to produce. The depositions of the witnesses shall be taken with all possible expedition and they shall be ordered to return to their homes or respective employments. The Párapatiagár or Subadár shall then decide the cause according to justice and the custom of the country.

72. In cases where the defendant may neglect to attend at the Kacheri on the day appointed, notwithstanding he is summoned, an enquiry shall be made whether the summons has been actually served or not. If it be proved that the summons has been served on the defendant and that he has wilfully neglected to give his attendance at the Kacheri, a notice shall be affixed at the door of his house intimating, that although he signed the summons, which had been served on him, yet he had neglected to give his appearance to answer the complaint which was preferred against him, that a time, however, of 10 days would still be allowed to him to appear before the district functionary or the Pancháyat to answer the complaint, and that, if he failed to do so, the functionary or the Pancháyat would proceed to decide the case ex parte. If he do not make his appearance to answer the complaint within the time fixed in the notice, the Pancháyat or the functionary shall examine the vouchers and decide the case ex parte.

73. Where Pancháyats are assembled for investigating any dispute, the parties shall be caused to give written agreements binding themselves to abide by the decision of the Pancháyat. After the award is passed, the parties shall be

caused to interchange Farigh khati and a Rázináma shall be taken from them.

74. Whenever a case is investigated by a Pancháyat, and an award is passed, if one of the parties refused to abide by it, he shall be asked to explain the reason and if he has reason to suppose, that undue means have been used to bias the Pancháyat or that the decision was partial, he shall be required to produce evidence to that effect and give a written obligation, binding himself to pay such penalty as the Sirkar may be pleased to direct, in the event of his assertions proving false. If this circumstance happens at the Kacheri of a Párapatiagár, he shall forward the proceedings together with the witnesses to prove the corruption of the Pancháyat to the Subadár, and if it should happen at the Kacheri of the latter, the Subadár shall send them to the Daryáft-Kacheri.

75. But in cases where the party, refusing to abide by the decision of the Pancháyat fails to bring forward witnesses to prove his allegation, the award shall be carried into effect.

76. In cases where a suit is preferred against an individual who is not subject to the jurisdiction of either the Párapatiagár or the Subadár of the nád or taluq, where the complainant is residing, the Párapatiagár or Subadár shall request by a letter the officer in authority at the place, where the defendant may be residing, to send him in order to answer the complaint, preferred against him. The same rule is applicable to cases where witnesses may be residing within another jurisdiction.

77. In cases where either the defendant or witnesses may be residing in another country, the district-servants are to report the circumstance to the Huzur, which will take measures by writing to the European Officer in authority at that place, either to cause the personal attendance of such defendant or witnesses or to obtain their defence or evidence respectively in writing as may seem to him advisable.

78. The Nád- and the Táluq-Pancháyats shall be composed of respectable inhabitants, or Chetties, or merchants. When the parties in suits are of different castes, the Párapatiagárs or Subadárs shall, if practicable, select an equal number of persons of the caste, to which each party may belong and also one or two of a caste different from that of either of the parties. The same rule shall be observed by the Daryáft-Kacheri.

79. Appeals against the decision of a Párapatiagár shall be made to the Subadár within 30 days from the date on which the award may be passed and given to the party; and those against the decision of the Subadárs shall be made to the Daryáft-Kacheri within 45 days. If after the expiration of this time the party appealing assign good and satisfactory reason for his delay, the appeal shall be admitted. Provided, however, that no appeal shall be admitted from any case decided by a Pancháyat, except on the ground of gross partiality or dishonesty on the part of the arbitrators.

80. The expense of summoning shall be paid in the first instance by the party by whom they are summoned; but the functionary or the Panchayat shall determine, when the award is passed, by whom the expense shall be finally borne according to the merits of the case.

Criminal Justice.

81. The Gauda is authorised to reprimand or admonish an offender for stealing vegetables, or a few seers of grain, or the commission of similar trifling offences within the jurisdiction of his village. He shall seize and make over all other offenders to the Párapatiagárs.

82. The Párapatiagár shall confine for 10 days, or fine in a sum not exceeding five rupees, according to the circumstances of the case, any offender charged with disobedience

of orders, or with assaulting another person, or using abusive language or with stealing property of the value of 10 rupees.

83. The Párapatiagár may release persons accused of the above offences on their finding bail.

84. All persons deserving higher punishment than what has been mentioned above, shall be sent to the Subadár by whom they shall be tried. The Subadár shall confine for 30 days, or fine in a sum not exceeding 16 rupees, according to the circumstances of the case, any person accused of having stolen property of the value of from 10 to 30 rupees, or charged with disobedience of orders or with assaulting another person or using abusive language.

85. The Subadár may release persons accused of these offences on their finding bail.

86. Offenders accused of thefts not attended with violence and of which the amount or value may be above thirty and not exceeding one hundred rupees, or of the other offences specified in para 84, but deserving a higher punishment than what is therein mentioned, shall be sent for trial to the Daryáft-Kacheri. In these cases the Daryáft-Kacheri is empowered to sentence an offender to imprisonment not exceeding two months, or to levy a fine not exceeding twenty rupees. This Kacheri may release persons on bail.

87. The Párapatiagárs and Subadárs are directed to send with the least practicable delay to the Daryáft-Kacheri all persons accused of thefts attended with violence or exceeding in amount or value thirty rupees, burglaries, highway or gang robberies, arson and murder, etc. after they are apprehended, together with their depositions.

88. The Daryáft-Kacheri assisted by the Pancháyat shall make enquiries into the aforementioned cases, and in the event of their finding the fact against the accused, they shall submit their proceedings to the Commissioner (respective Superintendent since October 1834) who shall pass judgment thereon.

89. The numbers of the Pancháyat shall in no case be less than five nor more than thirteen. The prisoner shall have the power of challenging any of the members as far as the number five, before the commencement of the enquiry, assigning reasons for the same, which shall be taken into consideration by the Daryáft-Kacheri. In the event of these reasons being deemed valid, the member who is challenged shall be removed and another substituted. The majority of the Pancháyat shall concur in the verdict, whether in civil or criminal cases, to render it valid.

90. Corporal punishment by the officers of Government is prohibited in every possible case throughout the whole of Coorg.

91. There are three modes of passing sentence of imprisonment. One is to sentence an offender to be confined and to be put to perform hard labour on the roads. The second is to sentence the criminal to be imprisoned and be made to work in the prison; and the third is to pass sentence of imprisonment only, without labour. These three modes may be adopted by the Daryáft-Kacheri in passing sentence against offenders according to the degree of guilt proved against them.

92. The Párapatiagár of each Nád shall send in monthly to the Subadár of his taluq a register of offenders punished by him.

93. The Subadár in like manner shall send a register to the Daryáft-Kacheri, which will submit to the Huzur an abstract of their registers, including the offenders punished by their own award.

94. All disputes relating to caste are to be settled by the heads of the respective castes according to the usage and custom of the country.

Police.

41. The police of the taluqs is to be considered under the charge of the Subadárs, and subordinately to them, of the Párapatiagárs and Patéls.

42. The district functionaries are to give at all times their utmost care and attention to prevent disturbances, assaults, and all other acts in breach of the peace; they are to apprehend and send to the Daryáft-Kacheri any person who may be accused of having committed robbery or violence.

43. The Patéls of the village and the villagers shall conjointly protect their villages from depredations of robbers. They shall always be on their guard and act with vigilance, so that no thefts or personal assaults may be committed.

45. If any person of a suspicious character makes his appearance in a village, the Patél shall make an enquiry about his name, place of residence and the purpose for which he has come to the village; and if the Patél be not satisfied with his answer, he shall send him to the Párapatiagár.

46. If any person in the village behaves improperly, the Patél shall persuade him to correct his conduct and give him the admonitions that may seem necessary.

47. If any theft or robbery be committed, the Patél and the villagers shall exert themselves to apprehend the robbers. If the robbers be found in the act of robbing and if they escape, they shall be pursued and seized. The Patéls of the neighbouring villages shall co-operate in ensuring the seizure of the robbers. But if the Patéls or others do not use their endeavours either to discover or apprehend the robbers, and if the Sirkar shall have reason to believe that the robbery was committed through the negligence of the Patéls, they will incur the displeasure of the Sirkar and be punished accordingly.

48. Whenever information is lodged of a person having

died a violent death, the functionaries shall proceed to the spot where the dead body may have been found. They shall examine the body and ascertain, whether there are any marks of violence upon it, or bruises, the number of them, and with what weapons the wounds or hurts may appear to have been given. The above inquiries shall be made in the presence of two or three creditable persons, and being committed to writing the proceedings shall be sent to the Daryáft-Kacheri, afterwards the functionaries shall endeavour to trace the persons who may have murdered the deceased and apprehend them.

49. The Subadárs of the taluqs on the frontier shall be particularly vigilant in apprehending robbers and vagabonds who may come to this district from the neighbouring countries to commit mischief.

50. The magisterial authority of the Subadárs does not extend to the pettas, where Kotwals are employed. The police of the pettas is entrusted to the charge of the Kotwals and they will preserve the peace there. In cases where Kotwals may require the assistance of the Subadárs or the Revenue officers who may be near the pettas, they shall be promptly furnished with the aid demanded.

51. In cases where any person of whatever caste may die a natural death without having relations or friends present, the Sirkar servants shall cause the corpse to be buried or burned according to circumstances at an expense of from one to three canterai fanams. But if the deceased leaves property and no relations to claim it, a sufficient portion of the property shall be appropriated for the performance of the funeral ceremonies, and the remainder lodged in the Public Treasury until claimed.

52. Any person who has laboured under the disease of leprosy shall not be buried in the earth. The corpse of such person shall be burned, or if the caste of the deceased do not

admit of the corpse being burnt, it shall be caused to be thrown into a river.

53. In case where a ryot, or a chetty or a merchant die, leaving young children, whether boys or girls, the Subadár or the Párapatiagárs shall make over the property of the deceased to his nearest relations, and after the children attain their majority, the property shall be caused to be made over to them. But in defect of relations, the Gauda or the headman of the village shall be directed to take charge of the property and bring up the children. An inventary of the property shall be taken, one copy of which shall be kept by the Patél and the other entered in the Dufters. The expense attending the education, maintenance or marriage of the children, shall be deducted from the property."

Coorg being a non-regulation province, these simple rules sufficed for many years for the judicial administration of the country, wielded by the able officers, by whom Coorg had the good fortune successively to be ruled. On Col. Fraser leaving Coorg in October 1834 to be "Resident of Mysore," Capt. Le Hardy was appointed "*Superintendent of Coorg*," the first of a line of 15 Superintendents up to date and all, with the exception of two, military officers of the Madras Army. Col. Fraser transferred to Capt. Le Hardy "the civil charge and administration of the District" and when the former became Resident of Travancore and Cochin in 1836, and Col.—afterwards General Sir—Mark Cubbon C. B. succeeded him as Commissioner of the Government of the territories of His Highness the Rájah of Mysore and "*Commissioner of the affairs of Coorg*," the Superintendent's relative position remained unchanged down to the present day

Sir Mark Cubbon, in whom India saw a noble type of the English gentleman, ruled Mysore and Coorg for a quarter of a century with great ability, vigour and judgment. Of his merits as a ruler, the Marquis of Dalhousie has borne a high and honorable testimony in a despatch, dated Fort William, 7th February 1856, which, however, is too long for us to quote. The administrative genius of Sir Mark Cubbon's successor, L. Bowring Esq., C. S. I., asserted itself in a different manner and shone in a peculiar light. With critical acumen and administrative skill of a high order he penetrated, analysed and reformed every branch of the existing administration and placed it on a level with the most advanced systems of modern Government in India. He left India for good in March 1870, highly esteemed and deeply regretted by the natives of Mysore and Coorg.

With the settlement of European Planters in Coorg during the last ten years the admission of pleaders into the Courts and the more elaborate and refined system of judicature consequent to the introduction into the province of the Indian Penal Code in 1861, the Criminal Procedure Code in 1862, the Indian Stamp Act in 1862, the Registration Act in 1865, the Indian Succession Act in 1865, the Criminal High Court Act in 1865, the Forest Act in 1866, and others, the establishment of a better constituted description of Courts became necessary.

Before the 1st December 1868 the Civil and Criminal Courts in Coorg were thus constituted:

The *Subadár's Court.* Each of the six taluqs was presided over by a Subadár exercising both civil and criminal jurisdiction. In addition to these were two Petta- or Town-Subadárs—formerly called Kotwals—stationed at the two principal towns of Mercara and Virájenderpet, who were vested with the same powers as the former. The civil jurisdiction of the Subadár extended to Rs. 200, and their criminal powers were those of a Sub-Magistrate of the Second Class. These officials were assisted in their revenue, magisterial and police duties by 24 Párapatiagárs, 13 of whom had been invested, from time to time, according as they had been considered qualified and competent to exercise the same, with criminal powers equivalent with those of the Subadárs, but they did not exercise any civil jurisdiction.

The *Daryáft-Kacheri* was in so far modified, that it was composed of a Moktasir (native judge) and four Pancháyatdárs who were selected by rotation from among the most intelligent of the various classes of the people and who received an allowance of a rupee a head per day for such days as the Court actually was sitting. It exercised original civil jurisdiction in suits, the value of which ranged from Rs. 200 to 3,000, and had appellate jurisdiction over the decisions passed by the Taluq-Subadárs. This institution which had a certain amount of time honored prestige amongst the Coorgs, was somewhat anomalous and exceptional in its character when compared with the system of judicature in force in the other parts of Her Majesty's territories.

In the *Assistant Superintendents' Courts*, presided over respectively by a Native and an Englishman, the former exercised the powers of a Sub-Magistrate, the latter had been vested with the full powers of a Magistrate.

In the *Superintendent's Court*, the Superintendent of Coorg exercised original jurisdiction in civil matters extending from Rs. 3000 to any amount and was the Magistrate of the District. Appeals from the decisions passed by the Daryáft-Kacheri were made to him

A *Sessions Court* was established by vesting the Superintendent of the Ashtagrám division of Mysore, with which Coorg had been incorporated for a short time (Nov. 1862—July 1863) with the powers of a Sessions Judge in disposing of cases, with which, as Assistant Sessions Judge under Act XV of 1862 the Superintendent was incompetent to deal. Though this was a somewhat inconvenient arrangement, yet it pleased the Coorgs better than the annexation of their country to

Mysore, against which measure they strongly protested, being greatly averse to any subordination to the Brahmin officials of Mysore on their immediate frontier.

The *Court of the Judicial Commissioner* was highest appellate Court, and exercised control over the judicial administration of the province in all its branches. Sentences of death passed by the Superintendent of Ashtagrám as Sessions Judge in Coorg, required the confirmation of the Judicial Commissioner. This office was first instituted in 1856 by the Supreme Government.

With the 1*st December* 1868 *the Coorg Courts' Act XXV of* 1868 *came into operation.* Its primary object was to settle and define the jurisdiction of the various civil and criminal functionaries in Coorg and the immediate occasion for it arose, when the two Assistants were appointed, whose powers it was necessary to determine. As a necessary consequence the Daryáft-Kacheri was abrogated, its last judge being the first Coorg pupil of the Central School in 1856, Colavanda Cariappah, now Subadár of Mercara taluq.

The civil jurisdiction conferred by the Act on Officers of various classes is limited as follows:

Subadárs of the 2nd class may determine suits to the value of	Rs.	100.
Subadárs of the the 1st class	„	300.
Assistant Superintendent of the 2nd class .	„	1000.
Assistant Superintendent of the 1st class . .	„	3000.

The Superintendent of Coorg without limit.

The Chief Commissioner may invest any Párapatiagár or Naib-Subadár with power to try certain kinds of suits for money or moveable property not exceeding in value Rs. 50. Appeals lie from the Subadárs to the Assistant Superintendents; from the Assistants to the Superintendent of Coorg; and from the Superintendent to the Judicial Commissioner. Special appeals lie from the decisions of the Superintendent and from those of the Assistants to the Judicial Commissioner; but in suits of the nature of Small Causes no special appeal is allowed for less than Rs. 300.

On the criminal side, the Act provides that for the purpose of criminal jurisdiction the Superintendent of Coorg shall be taken to be the chief Officer charged with the executive administration of a district in criminal matters. Appeals against the sentences of the Magistrates with full powers in Coorg shall lie to the Judicial Commissioner. The Sessions Judge, appointed by the Governor General, shall, as often as may be necessary for the trial of offenders, hold sessions in the province

However flattering the notion may be, that the judicial administration of Coorg is now on a level with the most advanced stage of judicial reform in India, one cannot, on seeing the backward state of civilization of the majority of the people for whom this refined apparatus of justice is intended, help regretting the disappearance of those simple and practical institutions, adopted by General Fraser, which best suited the wants and comprehension of the natives and, in the absence of stamp duties, secured to them cheap justice! However, as the Judicial Commissioner truly remarks, "the more complicated and difficult portions of the law affect, not the "simple mountaineer" so much, as the coffee planter and the trader; and when the business of life is at all complex, almost any ascertained rules must be preferable to no rule."

Of the *Jail* it need only be said, that its locality in an airy corner within the fort walls is healthy, and if the practicable alterations and improvements were carried out, good and sufficient accommodations for the small number of convicts, averaging 70 per annum, could be afforded without going to the expense of a palatial new building outside the fort as proposed. The Regimental Surgeon, in civil charge of the Jail, exercises the powers of a Magistrate over its inmates, who are superintended by a European Jailor.

The *Police*, with the exception of a small regular body of a miserable description in Mercara and Vîrájenderpet, still maintains its rural character, as best adapted to the country.

According to the returns of the annual "Judicial Reports," the inhabitants of Coorg are neither remarkable for their litigiousness, nor for an excess of criminality.

3. ADMINISTRATION OF REVENUE.

a. Land Revenue.

The Land Revenue constituted the chief source of the wealth of the Coorg Rájahs. It still forms the principal item in the annual income of Government. It will, therefore, be of interest to analyze the mode of assessment, peculiar to Coorg, for generations in use and still upheld by the British Government. The settlement was made in 1812 by Lingarájender, who caused the Shist accounts to be preserved in a kind of Domesday-Book in which all the vargas or farms are registered with great detail and accuracy, noting also the tenure under which each varga is held.

According to this *quasi settlement in perpetuity* we have to distinguish, besides the rentfree holdings, *four different kinds of tenures of land: Jamma, Sâgu, Umbali and Jódi-tenure*, an arrangement nearly allied to what is called "Shivappa Naik's Shist" i. e. an assessment fixed in the time of Shivappa Naik, a polygar of Naggara.

The *Jamma-tenure*, from the Sanscrit "janma," a word conveying the meaning of "hereditary by birth," is the holding of the privileged class, called *Jamma-ryots*, comprising: Coorgs, Amma-Coorgs, Hegadas, Eimbokalas, Airis, Koyavas, Moplas and Gaudas. The light assessment of Rs. 5 per 100 butties of wet land with its accompanying Báné and Bariké was made originally on condition of military and general service to the State. The Jamma-ryots are still liable to be called out to repel outward aggression or quell internal disturbances, and to furnish all Police- and Treasure-guards, escorts, etc. in time of peace. Excepting old men and boys, there are now 7070 active Jamma-ryots of whom 4910 are Coorgs and, next in number, 1244 Gaudas.

The *Butty account* is a peculiar one and dates from the time of Lingarájender, who in 1813 had all the ricelands measured and the result registered; 100 butties of wet land mean an area which produces 100 butties at 80 seers per butty of paddy or rice in the husk. Since this produce, however, is depending on the fertility of the soil, it is clear, that the area of 100 butties varies according to the nature of the ground. There are 7 different qualities of fields, ascertained or supposed to produce 8, 10, 12, 14, 16, 18, and 20 seers of paddy respectively on an area of land, containing 256 square feet or a square of one kólu (bambu) 16 feet long, the original measure used for determining this account. To produce then 100 butties or 8,000 seers of paddy from these seven different kinds of fields, 1000, 800, 660¾, 570, 500, 440¼, 400 times 256 square feet or about 5·87, 4·8, 3·92, 3·35, 2·93, 2·61, 2·35 acres respectively are required. As a fair average, therefore, 3 acres may be assigned as an equivalent of 100 butties of land.

Báné is the highland adjoining the ricefields and generally clothed with forest from which each farm obtains its firewood, manure, grass, etc.

Bariké is the low swampy portion of land adjacent to or below the paddy fields, it remains uncultivated and is used for grazing purposes.

No remission of the Jamma-rent is ever made, except under extraordinary circumstances, such as the death of several members of a family, the entire destruction of property by fire or the loss of a large number of cattle. In these cases and when the produce of their lands has been very meagre, the Jamma-ryots are allowed to pay Rs. 10 per 100 butties *for the quantity of land which has been cultivated*, instead of *five* rupees *for the whole farm*. It is also customary, under such circumstances, or when only women and young children are left in the house, to permit the whole of the Jamma-lands to be sublet on vára-tenure (division of the crop in equal halves between the tenant and landlord) for periods ranging from 1 to 5 years according to the particulars of each case. On being invested with the proprietary right to a farm, the Jamma-ryot has to pay a donation of Rs. 10 per 100 butties called "Nuzur Kánike," in 3 yearly instalments, and a fee of Rs. one termed the "Gatti-Jamma fee," on taking possession of the land. On the same terms a Jamma-ryot may claim as much available land, as he may like to cultivate, provided he takes an entire farm, failing which his Jamma-rent is doubled for the additional portion. He likewise may also resign his Jamma-land or Government may, for good reasons, resume it. When invested with the land, by the Superintendent of Coorg, a formula is spoken, intimating, that the holder has received the hereditary right to the land on the feudal conditions laid down, and at the same time a handful of the soil of the land he has applied for is given to him. Similarly when resigning land, the Jamma-ryot lays down before the Superintendent a handful of the soil as a sign of his relinquishment of all rights to the land. Except with the consent of the Government Jamma-land cannot be alienated and is never marketable, nor can it be mortgaged.

A Jamma-farm consists of from 10 to 1,500 butties of wet land, according to the extent of soil susceptible of cultivation and from ancient times it had an apportioned number of slaves as "glebae adscripti." These became liberated under the British Government, but for many years their freedom was merely nominal and the economy of the Coorg houses remained undisturbed. But the subsequent settlement of British planters rudely disturbed the dorment slave-question to the great inconvenience and loss of the Coorgs. Many slaves ran away from their masters who, unable to compete with the Planters' cash-payments, had no means of cultivating their farms. Government, though earnestly appealed to by the Coorgs, could not restore their slaves. The Coorgs then prayed, that they might be allowed, to sublet their Jamma-lands. The question with its various bearings was an important one both in the interest of Government and that of the Jamma-ryots. But the difficulty seems to have been judiciously and satisfactorily solved by Mr. Bowring, the late Chief Commissioner. It was decided, that one quarter of the entire holdings only should be allowed to be sublet on vára and that amongst the new tenants preferential claim should be given

1st to the holder of the farm,

2nd to the proprietor of the adjoining farm,

3rd to the cultivators of the same village,

so that, whilst the subletting Jamma-ryot is not relieved of his feudal obligation to Government, his more powerful or opulent neighbour has to contend against these preferential claimants.

That the measure affords relief to the ryots is proved by the fact, that on the 1st April 1870 73 Jamma-ryots had availed themselves of the boon to the extent of 12,642¼ butties of land. At the same time 112 ryots were allowed, on the plea of distress, to sublet Jumma-land amounting to 24,751¼ butties. It is assumed, that the expenses connected with the cultivation of 100 butties of wet land, when the ryot uses his own bullocks, amount to about 71 per cent of the whole out-turn, the land-tax on the holding is Rs. 5 per 100 butties, to which house-tax, Dhúli-paddy and other items. which bring up the total taxation to about 9 per cent, have to be added; so that the profits are about 20 per cent. The farms produce also oranges, vegetables and coffee, free of tax on plots of Báné-land less than ten acres, which add to the income of the proprietor; but on the other hand, as all the members of the family live under the same roof and subsist on the produce of the same farm, there is little real profit left. However light the assessment of the Jamma-ryots may appear to be, the changes effected in the general administration of the country and the imposition of various taxes have greatly modified the relative value of this tenure. The establishment of a number of departments, the officers of which with their subordinates are frequently on the move, imposes—almost of necessity—services on the Jamma-ryots for the performance of which formerly their slaves were used and which consequently now the masters with their crude notions of free trade very unwillingly perform. Of the Coorgs, whose pride as a martial race has always been fostered by Government, it can hardly be expected, that they should readily carry the camp-loads, etc. of the public functionaries, and the exigencies of the Sirkar, in this respect, might perhaps be fulfilled without too much wounding the self-respect of the Coorgs. Many Jamma-ryots, it is said, are on the point of resigning their Jamma—with the intention of holding their land on Ságu-tenure and thus escaping these vexatious services!

In 1869-70 the revenue from Jamma-lands amounted to Rs. 50,893—9—9.

The next holding is called *Ságu-tenure* (from the Canarese ságu, to be under cultivation) and should be considered as the *normal assessment*, all others being exceptional. The tenants pay Rs. 10 per 100 butties land-tax, are not bound by their tenure to render feudal service to the State and may claim remission of assessment for those fields of their farms, which they are unable to cultivate. It is estimated, that of their total produce the Government demand amounts to 14 per cent and their profits, after deducting all expenses, hardly exceed 7 per cent in good seasons.

Excepting old men and boys in both cases, the number of Ságu-ryots is nearly double that of Jamma-ryots, amounting to 13,500 of whom the greatest number are Gaudas viz. 3654, and next Holeyas, viz. 3605. There are only 40 Coorgs holding land on Ságu-tenure.

It may here be stated, that the late Rájah's twenty farms, called Panyas, which on the assumption of Coorg by the British in 1834 amounted to 46,872½ butties of land with 168 predial and 1055 disposable slaves were, at the recommendation of the Deváns, divided into the original vargas (farms) and disposed of like all other land held on Ságu-tenure, the predial slaves remaining attached to such estates as they belonged to and the others were entrusted to the care of respectable ryots, who were required to maintain them on the same terms as ordinary labourers, paying them the same rate of hire, demanding their attendance only during working hours, and especially allowing them the entire management and control of their family affairs and the settlement of their children's marriages. Some of the Panyas were allotted on Jódi tenure to religious establishments.

Waste land, now taken up for cultivation, is chiefly held on Ságu-tenure. Considering, however, the difficulty and expense of reclaiming waste land for wet cultivation, Government has sanctioned a certain progressive scale of taxation, according to the number of years, such farms have been lying waste. Thus land lain waste for 5-10 years, if brought under cultivation, pays one-fourth of the assessment the first year, half the second, three-quarter the third and the full amount of tax the fourth year. Besides this graduated assessment, for land left uncultivated from

10 to 15 years one year's assessment is remitted,
15 „ 25 „ two „ „ „

25 to 35 years	three year's assessment is remitted,	
35 „ 50 „	four „ „ „	
above 50 „	five „ „ „	

after which periods of remission the above scale of taxation comes into force.

If any ryot, who undertakes to cultivate lands on these conditions, declines before the expiration of his term to cultivate any longer, he will be liable on relinquishing his land, to pay one-fourth of the amount of tax, which he would otherwise have been exempted from in the first year, half of the amount for two years, three-quarter for three years and the full amount of tax to be paid for four and five years.

It often happens, that a Ságu-ryot transfers his land for a certain sum of money in favor of another tenant; but, whilst Government does not forbid the transaction,—for the money thus obtained may be a fair reward for the ryot's trouble and expense on the land—, it does not admit the ryot's claim to proprietaryship in the land. On the ryot relinquishing his land, the name of the first applicant for the same will be registered without reference to any private arrangement, but such transfers are generally satisfactorily settled.

It may be remarked, that in Yélusávirashíme the Ságu-tax is levied on a portion of wet land capable of producing 60 Kandagas of grain, or 120 butties by measure at the rate of 16 rupees

The total revenue from Ságu-holdings amounted in 1869-70 to Rs. 77,246—15—5.

Umbali-tenure (from the Can. umbali, a plot of ground free of rent) is held on account of services performed by certain ryots in the Rájahs' times and is lightly taxed at three rates viz: one, two and a half and three rupees per 100 butties, a sannad (titledeed) for the tenure having been given by the Chief Commissioner. The revenue from this tenure being in 1869-70 Rs. 6774—3—6 and assuming the average tax at the rate of Rs. 2—8 per 100 butties, the whole extent of Umbali-tenure would be about 448,900 butties.

An addition, at least in name, to these Umbali-holdings has been lately made at the recommendation of Capt. Cole, who proposed "that a fixed remuneration in the shape of a reduction in the assessment on the land, held by each Patél, be allowed to him as a "*Gaud-Umbali*" for the large additional work thrown on the Patéls by the effects of advancing civilization, by the opening out of the country and by the settlement of Europeans." This measure was hailed with satisfaction by the Patéls; most of them fixed the Umbali on the hereditary lands of their houses and in some cases the Umbali amounted to the entire assessment on their lands, which by this remission became virtually Jhágir or free, so that the "Gaud-Umbali" should be classed with the Inám-lands or freeholds.

The *Jódi-tenure* (from the Can. jódi, a favourable quit-rent) is the holding of land which has been alienated to the office of the Patéls in the Yélusávirashíme- and Nanjarájpatna-taluq and for the maintenance of religious establishments, in all parts of Coorg. Half of its original assessment having been relinquished in favour of the holders, the Sirkar receives only Rs. 5 per 100 butties as from Jamma-land. Like this the former cannot be sublet and, if left uncultivated, it is at the disposal of the district officers and may be given by them to any ryot on Ságu-tenure, when 5 Rs. of the land-tax are paid to Government and the other 5 Rs. to the religious establishment to which it belongs. The revenue of the Jódi-tenure in 1869-70 was Rs. 5,930—5—7.

All these different holdings were liable to three additional taxes payable to Government viz: ghee-house- and Dhúli-paddy-tax.

The *ghee-tax* amounted to half a seer of ghee for every 100 butties of land and was paid in consideration of the Sirkar's expense on feasting the Coorgs, who assembled at the Huttari- and Gauri-feast at the Rájah's palaces for exhibiting their national dance, accompanied by singing and instrumental music. At the general request of the people it was abolished, as the English Government neither fed nor gave the dancers presents on these occasions.

The *house-tax* is paid by every farmer at the rate of 9 As. 7 P. per family, Pariahs paying only half that sum. Merchants and other classes pay according to their caste or trade from 3 As. 2½ P. to 3 Rs. 10 As. 10 P. per house.

The *Dhúli-paddy-tax* was originally of an eleemosynary character, being voluntarily given to the Haléri-Jangam who first pretended to be satisfied with an offering of the refuse paddy (Dhúli *Can.* dust) but, who on having usurped the Coorg Samsthán, imposed the tax by right on all ryots, vide p. 230. Since 1834 the rule was, that ryots, cultivating from 25 to 50 butties of wet land, had to pay ¾ of a butty of paddy—but no refuse!—and for 50 and upwards 1¼ butty of paddy to Government. In Gadinád and Yedavanád the ryots paid three Hannies or six seers in addition to every rupee paid for the land rent instead of the Dhúli-paddy-tax.

The paddy thus collected amounted in 1835 to 3,323 butties and in 1868-69, when this impost was commuted into a money payment of Rs. 3—3—7 per 1¼ butty or 120 seers,—this being the average market price of paddy for the 5 previous years—, it yielded Rs. 18,304—6—3 which at the above rate represents 8,516 butties, an increase of nearly 2¼ times and a considerable item in the land revenue!

The *Inám-holdings*, or rentfree lands, are either granted to religious institutions or for service rendered to the State and represent a nominal land-tax of Rs. 17,298—8—4. For *Dry-cultivation* the land is divided into fields and pieces of ground, denominated in the Registers respectively "Sargas" and "Tundus," each of the latter measuring from one to two cawnies and the former comprising from one to eight tundus.

Though the name, situation, size and extent of each tundu is minutely specified in the Registers, no mention is made of their estimated produce. Practice has, however, established the rule, that Government should receive one sixth of the gross produce, which in 1869-1870 effected a revenue of Rs. 9,362—3—5. When several families unite in cultivating pieces of dry land, each ryot contributing his share of labour and agricultural stock according to his means and receiving a corresponding proportion of the produce, such a farm is called "Hola-kula" or family field. The house-tax is, however, collected from each ryot.

With the year 1866-67 a new source of land revenue arose from the *assessment on land* taken up *for coffee cultivation.* After much deliberation and correspondence on the part of the "*Coorg Planters' Association*" and *Government*, the latter finally resolved in October 1863, to abolish the "Halut" or excise duty of 4 as. per maund of 28 lbs., or one rupee per hundredweight of clean coffee and to substitute on acreage rental on the following terms:

From the first to the fourth year the land is rentfree from the date of acceptance by the District Officer of the tender for the grant.

From the fifth to the ninth year one rupee per acre on the whole area, except a certain proportion of waste grass land.

From the tenth and subsequent years two rupees on the same area.

The Planters' Association (in September 1864) expressed itself entirely satisfied with these Rules which on the whole were considered both "just and liberal." A six years' experience, however, under adverse circumstances of bad seasons, Bug and Borer convinced the Planters, that the assessment, having been fixed upon too sanguine expectations of coffee-produce and therefore wrong premises, had turned out to be unjust and illiberal, and in some instances had become actually oppressive. Government has therefore been addressed by the Association to relieve the distress of the Planters by reducing the assessment to eight annas per acre on the whole area, instead of two rupees.

The total revenue from coffee assessment amounted for 1869-70 to Rs. 89,942—1—5 against Rs. 91,251—12—5 for the year previous.

With regard to the *disposal* of *waste lands* the following Rules have been framed by Government:

I Waste lands in which no rights of private proprietorship, or exclusive occupancy exist, and which may not be reserved as hereinafter (Rule XVIII) provided, may, until further notice, be sold under the following rules.

II. Applications for land under these rules, shall be addressed to the Superintendent of Coorg, and shall comprise the following particulars:—

a) The estimated area of the lot applied for.

b) The situation of the lot and its boundaries as accurately as can be stated.

III. No lot shall exceed 500 acres. Within the limits of towns, the maximum extent of a lot shall be 10 acres. But any person may apply for several contiguous lots, each not exceeding the above limits.

IV. Every lot shall be compact and shall include no more than one tract of land, capable of being surrounded by a ring fence, and when the lot touches a public road, the length of the road frontage shall not exceed one half of the depth of the lot.

V. No lot shall be sold until the area has been estimated by the Taluq authorities. Before a title-deed is granted the lot shall be surveyed by the Government Surveyors.

VI. If on receipt of an application under Rule II, the Superintendent has reason to believe, that the lot applied for is saleable under these Rules, he shall call upon the applicant to deposit with him the estimated cost of surveying the lot and of marking it out with boundary marks, unless the land has been already surveyed and demarkated. The Superintendent will refund to the depositor any portion of his deposit which may not be actually expended in the survey and demarkation, and the depositor shall pay any deficiency.

VII. If the applicant fails to deposit the sum required under Rule VI within six weeks from the date of demand, his application shall be null and void.

VIII. On receipt of the deposit required under Rule VI, the Superintendent shall, as soon as possible, cause the area of the land applied for to be estimated by the Taluq authorities. He shall then advertise the lot for sale on a given day, to be fixed as to admit of the notice, required in Rule IX, being given.

IX. The advertisement shall be in English and in Canarese, and shall specify the locality, extent and boundaries of the lot, the annual assessment, and the place, time and conditions of sale. It shall be posted for three months at least on the land itself, as well as in the neighbouring villages, in the Offices of the Superintendent and the Subadár of the Taluq and the nearest Post Office. The Superintendent shall at his discretion fix the time and place of sale and may alter both, if necessary, provided that not less than 14 days' notice be publicly given of every such alteration, and that no land be sold, until it has been advertised, as aforesaid, for three full months at least.

X. The Superintendent shall send written notice of the place and time of sale, as also of any alteration under the provisions of Rule IX to the applicant; but no sale shall be disturbed in consequence of the nonreceipt of such notice or delayed in consequence of the nonappearance of the applicant.

XI. An applicant withdrawing his application prior to the sale of the lot, will be entitled to the refund of so much only of his deposit under Rule VI, as may not have been expended. If it should prove that the lot is not saleable under these Rules, the applicant must still pay the expense attendant on ascertaining the estimated area under Rule VIII.

XII. On the withdrawal of an application, it shall be discretional with the Superintendent to proceed with the sale of the lot or not, as he considers best for the public interests.

XIII. The upset price shall in all cases be two rupees an acre, to include all survey expenses. If the original applicant be the purchaser, he shall receive credit for his deposit in payment; otherwise the amount of deposit shall be paid to him at once from the sale proceed.

XIV. If, before the time of sale, no claim of private proprietorship, or of exclusive occupancy or of any other right incompatible with the sale of the lot under these Rules be preferred, the lot shall as advertised be put up to auction and sold to the highest bidder above the upset price, subject to an annual assessment after four years from 1st May in the year of sale of one rupee an acre, and after nine years of two rupees an acre on the whole area.

XV. The successful bidder shall, immediately on the sale being declared, pay down 10 per cent of the price and the residue of the purchase money shall be paid in full within 30 days. The sale shall be conducted under and subject to the following conditions of sale:—

XVI. 1. The highest bidder above the upset price shall be the purchaser of the lot, and if any dispute arise between two or more bidders at the same price, the lot shall immediately be put up again at the last preceding undisputed bidding and resold.

2. If the purchaser shall pay to the said Superintendent the residue of his purchase money, he shall thereupon be placed in possession of the lot pending survey.

3. All persons desirous of becoming purchasers are to satisfy themselves as to the identity and correct description and the estimated area and bounderies of the lot, previous to the sale, as by having the lot knocked down to him, the purchaser thereof shall be held to have waived all objections to any mistakes that may afterwards appear to have been made in the description of the lot, as well as to any other error whatever in the particulars of the property.

4. If the purchase shall not be completed by the thirtieth day from the day of sale, the purchaser shall pay to the Superintendent interest at the rate of 12 Rs. per cent per annum; on the remainder of his purchase money from the day of sale until the purchase shall be completed without prejudice nevertheless, to the right of resale reserved by the fifth condition, if not paid within one year.

5. If the purchaser shall neglect or refuse to comply with the above conditions, or any of them, his deposit money shall be forfeited and retained by Government, and the Government shall be at liberty to resell the lot either by public auction or private contract, without the necessity of previously tendering a conveyance to the purchaser at the present sale, who shall so neglect or refuse as and for liquidated damages.

XVII. If before the time of sale a claim of private proprietorship, or of exclusive occupancy or of any other right incompatible with the sale of the land under these Rules, shall be preferred to the lot or any part of it, the Superintendent shall postpone the sale of the lot until such claim shall be disposed of in due course of law.

XVIII. Reserves of grazing and forest land, of land for the growth of firewood, for building sites, and for land required for other special purposes, are not to be sold under these Rules without the express sanction of the Government.

XIX. As soon as the actual area of the lot purchased has been ascertained by survey, a grant shall be made to the purchaser (provided he shall have paid his purchase money in full) in the form hereto annexed and marked

A. Should the actual area as ascertained by survey be more than $\frac{1}{10}$ less than the area as estimated before the sale, the purchaser shall be refunded a proportionate part of his purchase money in respect of such deficiency beyond $\frac{1}{10}$. Should the actual area be more than $\frac{1}{10}$ in excess of the area as estimated, such excess beyond $\frac{1}{10}$ shall revert to Government, and the purchaser shall forthwith yield up possession thereof.

XX. The annual assessment on lands sold under these Rules, may at any time be redeemed by the owner, by payment of a sum equal to 25 times the annual assessment of two rupees an acre on the whole area, and the lands so redeemed shall thereafter be for ever free from all demand on the part of the State on account of land revenue. On payment of the redemption money, the owner of the land shall be furnished with a deed in the form annexed to these Rules and marked B.

XXI Arrears of annual assessment shall be recoverable in the same manner as arrears of Ryotwári-land-revenue are, or may be recoverable by the law for the time being in force in Coorg.

XXII Lands sold or redeemed under these Rules, shall continue subject to all general taxes and local rates payable by law or custom.

XXIII. The existing and customary rights of Government, of other proprietors, and of the public in existing roads and paths and in streams running through or bounding lands sold under these Rules, are reserved and in no way affected by the sale of such lands under these Rules.

XXIV. Nothing contained in these Rules shall be held to debar the Government from granting waste land on Puttah, Cowle, or otherwise at their discretion as heretofore.

FORM A. (1).

By this deed made the ____day of ___ between the Secretary of State for India in Council of the one part, and A. B. of ____of the other part, in consideration of the purchase money or sum of Rs. ____duly paid by the said A. B.

The said Secretary of State hereby grants to the said A. B., his heirs, representatives and assigns, the parcel of Government land situated in the village of in____ of the ____ taluq in the District of Coorg and included within the following boundaries: ________

Excepting and always reserving out of the said grant, to the said Secretary of State in Council, his successors and assigns, all such timber growing or to grow on the said land as by any rule or decision of the Government Forest Department for the time being, and from time to time, shall be determined or declared to belong to Government.

And it is hereby declared, and the said A. B. for himself, his heirs, representatives and assigns, hereby agrees that the Government revenue assessed on and hereafter payable in respect of the said land is as follows: From the 1st May 18 — to 30th April 18— no assessment. From the 1st May 18 — to 30th April 18— annually one rupee per acre on the whole area. From 1st May 18— two rupees annually per acre on the whole area.

And that this grant shall not in any way affect the rights of the Government of any adjoining proprietor in respect to any road or stream running through or bounding any part of the said land, and that the said A. B., his heirs, representatives and assigns shall not cultivate any of the land within 5 yards of a public road, nor destroy any brushwood or grass forming a natural fringe or revetement to any road, nor dam up or contract any waterway made by the Public Works Department, and also shall and will at all times hereafter maintain in good repair at his and their own cost, the boundary marks of the said land erected by the Government Surveyor.

Signed, sealed, and delivered by the Commissioner for the Affairs of Coorg for and on behalf of the said Secretary of State and by the said A. B. The day and year first above written.

FORM A. (2.)

The same throughout as Form A. (1); instead of the third paragraph, however, beginning with: "And it is hereby declared etc." the following is substituted:

' Which said parcel of land shall henceforth be held by the said A. B. his heirs, representatives and assigns, freed and discharged from all claim in respect of Government revenue".

FORM B.

By this deed made the   day of ___ between the Secretary of State for India in Council of the one part, and A. B. of the other part, in consideration of Rupees_____duly paid by the said A. B., the said Secretary of State hereby absolutely and freely releases to the said A. B., his heirs, representatives and assigns, all Government land revenue hereafter accruing for or in respect of the parcel of land situate in the village of_____ in the taluq _____ and comprised within the following boundaries, (give the survey boundaries) and such parcel of land shall henceforth for ever be held by the said A. B., his heirs, representatives and assigns, free of any Government rent.

Signed, sealed, etc. as in Form A.

The Registration of these Assurances according to Act XVI of 1864 appears not to be much appreciated by the natives, who shrewdly remark, that, if the Chief Commissioner's signature to their title-deeds cannot assure their validity unless registered by a local Official, what is the good at all of these documents; in fact they do not seem to care for them and are likewise prejudiced against the obligatory registration of their Jamma-sannads.

Amended Rules for carrying out the substitution of an acreage on Coffee lands for the Halut or excise duty.

I. Surveyed estates, held free since 1st May 1860 are liable to be assessed at one rupee an acre on the whole area from the 1st May 1864.

II. Unsurveyed estates held free since 1st May 1860 to be assessed according to the proprietors' estimated area subject to adjustment of rent, if more or less than $\frac{1}{10}$ difference on the survey reaching them.

III. All Government unassessed lands granted for Coffee cultivation, whether cultivated or waste, to count for assessment from date of grant, or the land to be given up and the grant resigned.

IV. Every Coffee holding on Government Cardamom land of which the Cardamom rent has ceased to be paid, will count for assessment at one rupee an acre on the whole area from the 1st May in that year when the rent ceased.

V. Cardamom plots taken up for Coffee cultivation but still waste, and paying rent to Government annually until expiration of lease in 1865-66, will be assessed at one rupee an acre on the whole area from the first May 1866 or lapse to Government on that date.

VI. Cardamom plots wholly cultivated will be assessed (as if on the fifth year) from the year on which Cardamom rent ceased to be paid.

VII. All lands now liable to assessment will be charged upon the estimated area in acres, as returned last year, unless corrected by the tenants at time of assessment, which in each case will be subject to adjustment on survey.

VIII. In all cases of adjustment of rent, whether to credit of Government or the tenant, to take place from the first instalment of rent due after the land has been surveyed.

IX. In all cases when the survey papers and title-deed are ready for delivery, the cost of the survey must be paid at the Superintendent's Treasury, before the papers are handed over.

X. Every title-deed should have entered on its back the years and rates of assessment payable to the Government on the land which it represents.

XI. The assessment when directed to be commenced should be conducted at Mercara by the Superintendent, by Taluqs and Náds, one Register for each Nád being completed before proceeding to another on the basis of the Registry of areas of coffee lands taken last year.

XII. The Báne-lands of the Coorgs being included in their Sannads as part of a tenure with a permanently fixed rent, and assigned hereditarily to them for ever, not to be subject to the assessment of coffee lands; unless when cultivation is over 10 acres, such land be separated from the varga or farm.

XIII. Coffee gardens, backyards, and fields in and around the suburbs of towns, if one acre or upwards in extent, to be assessed under the new Rules.

XIV. Valuable timber in forests already in possession and about to be felled, to be purchased by the tenant paying a royalty upon each tree.

XV. The Settlement-Office to commence a Register by Taluqs and Náds, taking the Survey Register at Mercara for a basis, but completing all the holdings in each Nád without reference to the survey having reached them or not.

W. H. KERR,
Superintendent.

Superintendent's Office,
Mercara, 4th August 1864.

Until lately, when, to swell the meagre returns of the Forest Department, the *rents from cardamom jungles* were transferred to its accounts, this assessment formed a legitimate item of the land revenue and amounted in 1869-70 to Rs. 32,796—2—2. Lieut. Connor states, that in Lingarájender's time the revenue from this source amounted to Surat Rupees 100,800. Dr. Moegling mentions Rs. 80,000 as the average return in the time of the Rájahs. (vide p. 91.) To explain the great difference between these returns, the natives say, that the item in the Rájahs' accounts does not represent a rent but the profit made by the sale of the cardamoms which were Sirkar monopoly. If this statement is correct, it is rather surprising, that the English Government was less successful in its profits from the same monopoly!

General Fraser in his "Rules" or Hukumnáma of August 1834 promulgated in Para 31:

"As some of the ryots are in the possession of cardamom grounds, they shall as hitherto deliver their whole produce to the Sirkar. They shall be paid at the rate of 20 Rs. per maund of the first sort, 17 Rs. for the second sort, 15 Rs. for the third and 12 Rs. per maund, if the cardamom seeds have been removed from the capsules. They are prohibited from selling their cardamoms to any other person but only to the Sirkar. If they violate this rule, they shall be fined in a sum equal to double the value of the cardamoms which they have offered for sale to other persons".

Yet in turning to the Revenue Statistics of 1834-35 the entry under "Cardamoms" shows only Rs. 7,348—4—11, and in 1842-43 it sank as low as Rs. 3,744—4—0; but in 1856-57, when the cardamom jungles were leased by Government, the revenue suddenly rose to Rs. 26,512—12—8. May the falling off of this revenue be perhaps accounted for by Capt. LeHardy's arrangement as proposed in para 159 of his Jammabandi Report of 1834-35?

"There are at present five separate establishments employed in superintending the cardamom grounds; but, it appears that the duties of three of these may with advantage be transferred to the Párapatiagárs of Náds bordering on the Western Ghats on giving the latter a small increase of establishment."

This arrangement must have weakened the control over the most exposed and productive jungles. Cardamoms being worth in the market from Rs. 50 to 65, the Government rate of payment viz. Rs. 12 to 20 per maund offered a strong inducement to smuggle the spice beyond the Ghats and to sell it in Malabar!

Drawing the administration of land revenue to a close, we may remark, that the routine of collecting the revenue and the class of functionaries engaged in the work are much the same as organised by General Fraser in 1834. According to his Hukumnáma

Para 12. "The Subadárs Párapatiagárs and Sheristadárs are to pay particular attention to the cultivation of their respective Taluqs. The increase of the land revenue being entirely dependent on the exertions and activity of the Subadárs and Párapatiagárs, they shall use their best endeavours to extend cultivation by giving every encouragement to the ryots."

P. 13. "In the months of January and February the Subadár and Sheristadárs in conjunction with the Párapatiagárs shall visit every village in the Náds and make an enquiry through the Patéls into the state of the village and the circumstances of the ryots. They shall ascertain whether the whole of the ryots of the villages are capable of bringing under culture the uncultivated land. In cases where the ryots may not be able to cultivate the whole of the land which they possess, they shall be encouraged, and advances shall be made to them for buying bullocks, seed, ploughs and other implements of husbandry, the same being reported to the Huzur. The amount of these advances shall be recovered from the ryots after the crops are reaped."

P. 19. "The Subadárs and the Párapatiagárs shall administer the revenues of their districts in such a manner as may be advantageous both to the Sirkar and to the ryots and which may increase the happiness of the people and the prosperity of their respective Taluqs and Náds. They should not hesitate to suggest to the Sirkar such measures as may, in their opinion, be calculated to improve either the revenue or in any other respect the well-being of the country."

P. 20. "In the months of June, July and August the Párapatiagárs shall again go to the villages and institute an investigation assisted by the Patéls into the state of the cultivation and send reports to the Subadárs, who shall submit an abstract thereof to the Huzur."

P. 21. "In October and November the Subadárs, Sheristadárs, Párapatiagárs and Shánabhóga shall visit the villages and Náds and inspect the crops and send an arzi (report) to the Huzur, reporting the degree of improvement which may have been made in cultivation, the state of the crops and also the damages, if any, which the crops may have suffered from any accident, either from the overflow of nullahs (streams) or depredations of elephants, etc."

P. 24. "In December the Subadárs and Sheristadárs are to repair to the Huzur Kacheri and assist in the preparation of the Jammabandi accounts in the usual manner. They shall according to custom give an agreement (kei-kágada) stating that they will collect the kists (instalments of revenue) from the ryots and remit the amount to the Huzur."

For the supposed convenience of the ryots Government allows them now to pay:

2	Annas	of each Rupee	of assessment	in	January
3	„	„	„	„	February
4	„	„	„	„	March
4	„	„	„	„	April
3	„	„	„	„	May.

On the Superintendent's annual tour of inspection—*Jammabandi*—throughout the province, a halt is made for two or three days in each Nád to review and settle its accounts etc. The business consists generally of little more, than the mere form of reading over to the ryots the detailed statements of the quantity of land cultivated and amount of assessment payable by each.

As Head-quarters move on, the Superintendent is accompanied by the Jamma-ryots of the Nád and preceeded by a native band of musicians. On approaching the boundary of another division, long files of stalwart peasantry are marshalled on the border to receive and conduct him through their Nád. On a bamboo frame-work prasáda (offering of food) is spread in his honor, consisting of oranges, plantains, coccoanuts and flowers, the Párapatiagár and Patéls offer limes and flower-wreaths, kind words are interchanged, local wants discussed and the Queen's honored representative marches on to his encamping ground, which is always the most picturesque spot of the Nád.

Since 1834 the steady progress of the land revenue, exclusive of cardamom and coffee, is exhibited in the subjoined quinquennial statement.

1834-35	Rs.	89,915.	1854-55	Rs.	128,917.
1839-40	„	102,270.	1858-59	„	145,949.
1844-45	„	108,498.	1864-65	„	167,803.
1849-50	„	127,118.	1869-70	„	150,661.

b. *Forest Conservancy.*

A glance at the Coorg Forests and their general Flora, as stated in page 16 ff., will show, that the formation of a Forest Conservancy Department in 1864 was an absolute necessity, and it is only to be regretted, that it was not five years earlier in operation, before some of the finest forests fell under the Planters' axe. There is, however, still scope enough for the energy and talents of a well trained Forest Officer in Coorg, and the more a scientific system of working the reserved forests is introduced such as was originated by Dr. Brandis and carried out in Burmah and other parts if India, especially in the Madras Presidency under the able direction of Dr. Cleghorn and Major Beddome, the better will be the prospects of an ever increasing revenue from this department, which seems not yet to be in a very flourishing condition. Being left without rules fixed by law, the Forest Officer cannot act with that authority which is due to his position and necessary to the interests of Government.

Of the trees reserved by Government, Sandal and Teak are its monopoly, the Kuve or Poonspar is sold at the rate of Rs. 20 per tree, Blackwood and Anjili are sold at Rs. 10 and Ebony, Hone and Irupu at Rs. 6 per tree. All other timbers, bamboos and firewood are allowed free to the ryot paying land revenue to Government and also to all Government servants in Coorg whose pay does not exceed 10 Rs. per mensem, without written permission or any prohibition whatever, except that only mature trees must be cut and that the timber must be used solely for bona fide agricultural and building purposes and not for sale. For the same kind of trees which are free of charge to the ryots, traders have to pay from Rs. 3 to Rs. 4—8 per tree and Rs. 6 per 1000 bamboos, whilst non-ryot residents, if for their own use, pay only half price.

The Assistant Conservator in charge of the department is under the general control of the Superintendent of Coorg and in fact his Revenue Forest Officer, but departmentally he is a third Assistant to the Conservator of Forests in Mysore. His functions hitherto have been the inspection of and report on those forests which were applied for by coffee planters, the inspection and working of reserved forests, the cultivation of tree-nurseries and the superintendence of the collection and sale of sandalwood and forest produce, the latter comprising resin, pepper, tamarind, soapnut, gallnut, bees' wax and areca nut. The forest receipts in 1869-70 amounted to Rs. 92,668—1—6 and are thus accounted for:

1. Timber . .	Rs.	13,645—15—11.
2. Sandalwood . .	„	45,027—14— 3.
3. Forest produce	„	1,198— 1— 2.
4. Cardamoms . .	„	32,796— 2— 2.
		92,668— 1— 6.

c. *Revenue Survey.*

In the time of Lingarája, from October 1815 to October 1817, a topographical survey of Coorg, which then also comprised the two taluqs Puttúr and Sulya, was completed by Lieut. Connor at the request of the Rájah. To judge from the "Memoir of the Codugu Survey," written by him, and his beautifully executed map on a scale of one mile to an inch, Lieut. Connor's task, accomplished in so short a time, is a giant's work and a lasting memorial of his energy and high professional skill. On an area of 2,165 square miles, then far more densely wooded than at the present time, he made no less than 118 triangulations, ascertained and measured 732 boundary stations and took the bearing and distance of 454 villages from fixed trigonometrical points; and on his map, every plot of cultivated land was carefully laid down.

The extensive cultivation of coffee and the consequent acreage-assessment rendered a Revenue-survey necessary and the Field-establishment organised in 1863 under the superintendence in succession of Mr. Plumb, Lieut. W. Freeth and Lieut. R. M. Clerk has ever since been at work. A detailed revenue survey of thousands of petty holdings is, however, a far more laborious and tedious task than a topographical survey, and consequently requires much more time. As a beginning of a new topographical survey of Coorg, Horurnúrokkalnád in Mercara-taluq has been completed by Lieut. Freeth, and the work is continued by Lieut. Clerk along with the revenue survey. The reasons given for the delay in completing the operations of the survey are the reduction of the establishment, interruptions from heavy monsoons, subordinates being prostrated with fever etc. added to the incorrectness of the data upon which calculations were based.

The mapping of the field-work is executed in the Madras Central Office.

Memo. shewing the number of estates surveyed, mapped etc. from the commencement of Survey in 1863 up to 31st March 1870.

Estates Surveyed.	European.		Native.		No. of estates mapped.	No. of estates lithographed.	Remarks.
	No.	Area in acres.	No.	Area in acres.			
2365	168	64809	2197	29496	1592	1164	Horur-núrokkalnád topographically surveyed and mapped—Area 20856 acres, at a cost of Rs. 2075 or 1 As. 7 P. per acre.

There are still about 21 European and 1,753 native estates to be surveyed. The cost to the Planter of surveying his estate has been fixed by Government at the rate of three annas per acre.

d. Abkári.

Abkári, or the revenue derived from the manufacture or sale of intoxicating liquors and drugs, has, in spite of the best intentioned repressive measures of Government, proved a very expansive financial source, showing an increase of revenue since 1834, which indicates a most lamentable rate of consumption of spirituous liquors in so small a country:

Abkári revenue.

In 1834-35	Rs. 4,445.	In 1854-55	Rs. 20,022.
„ 1839-40	„ 17,409.	„ 1858-59	„ 32,266.
„ 1844-45	„ 15,646.	„ 1864-65	„ 140,491.
„ 1849-50	„ 25,983.	„ 1869-70	„ 75,146.

A Government Distillery having been erected at Fraserpet and rented to licensed contractors who within its walls manufacture arrack of a certain strength and pay for the monopoly a still-head-duty; it is assumed, that no other native liquor is produced in the country; but there can be no doubt, that many ryots distil a superior article from rice for feasts and home-consumption in general; this practice is, of course, interdicted and punishable, but who dares to denounce trespassers!

In the Rájahs' times a few people only knew the secret of distilling rice-brandy, and drinking was kept down by rules enforced in Coorg fashion, besides, it was dangerous in those days to get drunk; for if, according to the ancient adage "In vino veritas," there is truth in a bottle of wine, there must be a great deal of it in a bottle of brandy! Words spoken in an unguarded moment, if conveyed to head-quarters by one of the numerous channels of espionage, might cost the man his tongue, nose or head. There is no such fear now before the eyes of the Coorg inhabitants. They are prosperous, their climate favours the evil habit and drunkenness, in its very nature, is a growing vice. Moreover since the influx of so many European settlers in Coorg, the natives have become familiar with the strongest European drinks and the liquor dealers are not slow in improving their opportunities to the ruin of the people. Beer- wine- and brandy-shops are scattered over the country.

It is hard to say how Government ought to deal with this vital Abkári-question and what measures might be adopted, to stem the torrent of vice and ruin. The old barriers, raised against the moral and physical plague of drunkenness by the laws of Hindu religion and of caste, have been broken through and cannot be repaired. The system of Government monopoly appears at first sight most objectionable; yet the abolition of it would have consequences still more deplorable. There is one panacea and one only, against this, as against every other moral evil in individuals or nations—a renovation of moral life and strength through the Gospel. All else is quackery!

4. THE DEPARTMENT OF PUBLIC WORKS.

It was not until the year 1862, that the wants of Coorg were sufficiently recognised, to induce Government to organize a regular establishment for the execution of Public Works in Coorg. A detachment of Sappers and Miners having been stationed in the Province since 1834, all the needful Public Works were carried out by them and after they had been withdrawn, an European Overseer took charge of the roads etc. The present effective establishment with an Executive Engineer (R. E.) at its head wants only funds to carry out large and important works, especially an iron bridge over the Kávéri with new highroads through Southeast Coorg into Mysore and Wynád.

Coorg is crossed by two trunk-roads from east to west and from north to south, intersecting each other at Mercara, and by a branch-road near Vírájpet the western and eastern highroads are connected.

Previous to the occupation of the country by the British in 1834, the roads were in a primitive state, wholly impracticable for wheeled carriges and scarcely less so for bullocks, it having been part of the policy of the Rájahs, to render their country as little accessible as possible, from an idea common to the mountaineers in all parts of the world, that the chance of invasion and conquest was thereby diminished. For the same reason some of the more direct and practicable lines, leading to Mercara were shut up and travelling by them prohibited.

The *Eastern trunk-road* from Mysore enters Coorg at Fraserpet, where it crosses the Káveri, which is spanned by a fine masonry bridge of 7 arches and 516 feet in length. The part of the line between Fraserpet and Mercara is 19½ miles in length and was commenced in January 1835 and completed in 1837 by a detachment of Sappers under Capt. Underwood, Lieuts. Rundall, Doria and Fast. The Káveri-bridge, however, was built in 1846-48 by Capt. Ch. J. Green with the material of the dismantled Fort at Fraserpet. It bears the inscription: "The Most Noble George Marquis of Tweeddale, Governor of Madras, Major-General Mark Cubbon Commissioner of Mysore. Fraserpet Bridge. The first stone of this bridge was laid on the 1st day of January 1846 by Capt. W. G. Onslow, Superintendent of Coorg and it was opened to public traffic on the 12th day of May 1848. Charles James Green, Capt. in the Madras Engineers, Architect."

To break the distance of 19½ miles, there is a Traveller's Bangalow at Suntikoppa, 9 miles from Mercara. The elevated situation is pretty. but the present condition of the Bangalow wretched.

The upper portion of this road near Mercara has in several places too steep a gradient and should, as the Chief Engineer proposes, be reconstructed. The *Sampáji-Ghat* or the line from Mercara towards Mangalore, which, however, ought to be called "*Fast's Ghat*" in honor to the professional skill of the young Engineer Officer who planned and executed this great work and who fell a victim to jungle-fever, was commenced after the monsoon in 1837 and offered considerable engineering difficulties, as it followed for many a mile through dense jungle. It is for the most part very direct; the soil is generally good and, except in two places, so gentle is the slope down the Ghat of 19½ miles in length, that for bandy traffic it offers no difficulty. Between the 9th and 10th miles only the gradient for a very short distance is as much as 1 in 12 and 1 in 6 or 7. The total fall in the first 15 miles of this Ghat is about 2900 feet, which gives 1 in 37 for the whole line. From the foot of the Ghat to Sampáji, 4½ miles, the fall is only 55 feet. The cost of cutting out the roadway of these 19½ miles, including the removal of rocks, trees, etc. but without bridges amounted to about 3500 Rs. per mile, exclusive of the pay of the Sappers and cost of tools. Whithin a short time the cost of the road was more than covered by the increase of the Salt Revenue on the coast, whilst the easy access to a market gave stimulus to the agriculture of Coorg and with the advent of coffee-planters, whose extensive estates line both sides of the road, its importance became invaluable.

The stages on this road from Mercara are: 6 miles to Madyanád, 14 to Sampáji, 13½ to Sulya, 11 to Káu, 10½ to Puttúr, 15 to Pánemangalore, 7 to Feringapet and 9 to Mangalore with a Traveller's Bangalow at each stage and all in healthy localities except that at Sampáji.

The road from Cannanore into Coorg through the Periambády Ghat and the Anachaukur road were finished some twelve years later, chiefly for military purposes. The line from Víréjpet to Mercara was made shortly afterwards. A continuation of this line to the north of Coorg from Mercara to Kodlipet was commenced in 1862 and opened for traffic in 1868.

Considering the *Cannanore-road*, its first 2½ miles leading out of Mercara are excessively severe, in several places the gradients being 1 in 9. The total fall in this descent of 2½ miles is about 550 feet, giving 1 in 24 over all. Beyond the 7th mile a high arched bridge leads over the Muttaremutha and between the 9th and 10th miles the well situated, clean and comfortable Bangalow at Murnád invites the traveller. Beyond the 12th mile the river Kávéri is crossed by a ferry and thence to Víréjpet, the road is pretty level and throughout in excellent condition. Four miles from Víréjpet the Periambády Ghat commences which was laid out by Capt. Francis and is down to Urti about 10 miles in length with a fall of 2682 feet. From the head of the Ghat, which is 3141 above the sea level, the descent varies from 1 in 18 and 20 to 1 in 30, but two miles from the head to the Wottekolli public bangalow, a distance of three quarters of a mile, there is a distressing gradient of 1 in 10 and 12. The road after this is easy and level in places to beyond the fourth mile from which it drops down to Urti—6 miles from Wottekolli—with generally far too steep a gradient. On the Coorg frontier the Kalla-hole, a mountain torrent coming down from the western slope of the Ghats, is to be crossed by a good bridge. Urti is 38 miles from Cannanore and 459 feet above the sea. There is no public bangalow, but a pretty one at Gunot, 7 miles further on near the united Kalla-hole (stony-river) and Bara-pole which river flows at a little distance behind the bangalow and offers attractive sport to the lover of the "gentle art." As to a journey down the Ghat, it is replete with ever varying charms, reminding the tourist of the finest mountain scenery of Scotland, Wales or the Black Forest in Baden. And such glorious forest trees of Poon, Sampige, Red Cedar Anjili, Hone, etc.! To see them and travel under their shade is worth a long journey. From Gunot to Cannanore or Tellicherry the road runs level and affords easy travelling. Near Ulil or Chávachári, 22 miles from Cannanore, a large wooden bridge resting on high stone pillars crosses the Gunot-river, but a public bangalow is only found at Shalot, 12½ miles from Cannanore.

At the head of the Periambády Ghat a highroad branches off into Mysore by way of Bittangala 5 miles, Hattúr 3 miles, Tittimatti 9 miles, Anechaukur 4 miles, Panchally 6 miles, Honasur 11½ miles, 4 miles from which place it meets the Mysore-Fraserpet road. Except between Anechaukur and Tittimatti the road is easy and generally in good condition, and since the Gonikoppa-bridge near Hattúr has been finished, at the sacrifice of the life of Mr. R. Hunter, a most promising Engineer Officer, there is no difficulty for wheeled carriages from Mysore to Cannanore, a distance of 113 miles. The public bangalows on this line are excellent in the Mysore country, but very indifferent in Coorg and Malabar.

To cut off two sides of a triangle a branch road, 3 miles long, has been constructed from Vírájpet to Bittangala for the Mysore cart-traffic. It is hoped, that the Mysore railway may yet extend to the eastern frontier of Coorg!

The *Northern highroad*, lately constructed by Mr. Stottard, connects Mercara with Manjerabad by way of Sómawárpet and Kodlipet, 44½ miles to the latter town. The line having been laid out under stringent regulations in regard to gradient, and the trace receiving great attention by Capt. W. Campbell, the result is a road with uniformly the easiest gradients in the Province. Most of the roadway is 18 feet wide. The smaller streams are all bridged over; for the Choran-hole a three-arched masonry bridge of 65 feet is proposed; for the Mattapúr a single-arched, and for the Hatte-hole a three-arched bridge. For the present these rivers are crossed in the dry season by rough stone causeways, but during the monsoon no carts can pass. There is no public bangalow on this line. During the last few years avenue trees at regular distances have been planted by the ryots along these high-roads and future generations will enjoy the benefit of this benevolent measure.

A line of equal importance, but unfinished though practicable for carts, is Col. Stuart's (vide p. 339) road from Vírájpet into Mysore by way of Anandapur and Siddápur, whence a branch, traced by Messrs. Stoddard and Gramatzki and opened out by Mr. J. Hunt, leads on the right bank of the Kávéri to Fraserpet. To avoid the steep Mercara ghat-roads for the through-traffic from Mysore to Mangalore, a new trace has been cut by Lieut. Clarke and Mr. Gramatzki to connect the Periapatna-Siddápur road with the Sampáji-ghat-road, placing in its line the iron girder bridge which is to span the Kávéri; but under the present financial difficulties the scheme has been postponed; likewise the opening up of a cart-road through Kiggatnád into Wynád, the trace of which only has been cut by the same engineers. Roads proposed are those from Bhágamandala to Sulya, from Bhágamandala to Nálkanád and Virájpet and Bhágamandala to Mercara. The Rájah's road from Mercara to Nálkanád is still in use, but it is impracticable for carts. Here and there it is still lined with stately avenue trees.

In addition to the roads, designed and carried out from Imperial funds, others have been constructed by planters from private sources without any Government assistance, so that, for pack-bullocks at least, the country is opened up in every direction, but for the increasing traffic better means of communication are required and the proposed roads would supply every want.

5. POST OFFICE AND TELEGRAPHS.

Besides the regular postal service with Offices at Mercara and Vírájpet, there is a local post called Anché, originally established by the Rájahs and still principally used for official communication between the district functionaries and the heads of departments, who are exempt from postage, but it is open also to the public both for letters and packages on the same terms as the Queen's Post. By its means 160,999 letters, etc. have been despatched in 1869-70, whilst the Queen's Post at the two offices transmitted 147,309 letters, etc. over the three lines, Mercara—Mysore,—Cannanore,—Mangalore. For the Anché-tappál there are five lines:

1.	from Mercara to	Fraserpet	20	miles.
2.	" "	Kiggatnád	35	"
3.	" "	Kodlipet	46	"
4.	" "	Nálkanád	20	"
5.	" "	Madyanád	5	"

In localities away from these lines postal communication is very imperfect and public business much impeded and often seriously inconvenienced.

Mercara has lately become the Head-quarters of the Malabar Coast Division of the *Government Telegraph Department* and consequently the Bangalore, Cannanore, and Mangalore lines are here united and Mercara is brought into telegraphic communication with all parts of the civilized world. During 1869-70 1595 messages have been received and despatched, and yielded an income of Rs. 1,798—8.

6. MILITARY DEPARTMENT.

Considering the military services rendered by the Jammaryots in the times of the Coorg Rájahs and their martial spirit and loyalty, so often applauded by the English Government, it may cause surprise, that no advantage has hitherto been taken of such excellent material ~~for local~~ military service, by organising all able-bodied men into a Coorg militia under English Officers and keeping a small body of men for short periods on duty at Mercara, instead of a Sepoy-Regiment, especially since it was the loyal Coorgs and not the Sepoys, who suppressed the insurrection anno 1837. Lately some proposal was indeed put forward to abolish Mercara as a military station, but the strategical position of the country, adjoining the foreign territory of Mysore on the one side and the Mopla inhabited districts of Madras on the other, was deemed of sufficient importance, to continue its occupation by a Regiment of Madras Native Infantry.

Mercara having been declared a *Military Cantonment*, (vide page 1009 Fort St. Georg Gazette 1856) the following are the specifications of bearings and distances of its boundaries.

Station.	Compass bearing.	Distance in feet.	REMARKS.
1	210°	312	Station 1. Opposite entrance to Fort. Boundary follows outer side of main road to station 5. Station 5. Opposite the gate of the Roman Catholic Priest's house; boundary leaves the main road and ascends the hill in rear of the Roman Catholic Priest's house, skirting the compound which it leaves outside the limits, it continues to follow the crest of the range of hills overhanging the Mangalore ghat till it reaches Station 18. Station 18. A slightly elevated peak intersected by a Coorg ditch and rampart, boundary follows this ditch down the slope of the hill to the burying ground which it encloses, traversing its west and south side to station 20 and thence descending the valley in which the Lines are situated to station 21. At 330 feet it strikes the bank of a Nullah along which it continues to station 23. From 23 to 24 it runs through enclosed gardens
2	201	225	
3	174	315	
4	121	288	
5	261	150	
6	181	173	
7	126	77	
8	148	73	
9	200	374	
10	285	130	
11	275	191	
12	178	318	
13	261	184	
14	218	165	
15	259	90	
16	212	162	
17	185	181	
18	285	485	
19	23	175	
20	41	215	

Station.	Compass bearing.	Distance in feet.	REMARKS.
21	9	720	and thence follows a pathway till it reaches the Artillery drivers-lines which it encloses. It here skirts the edge of a hill (from station 29) and joins a bandy-rord on the borders of a semicircular excavation at station 35. From station 35 boundary follows the bandy-road above alluded to till it joins the main road by a zigzag path at the commencement of the causeway leading to the town at station 39. From station 39 boundary follows the outer side of the main road to the north corner of the Artillery bullock shed compound; it then turns to the south enclosing the main road at station 42, continues along its outer edges as before till it terminates at station 1.
22	347	280	
23	307	315	
24	0	200	
25	324	175	
26	337	95	
27	352	250	
28	358	238	
29	39	238	
30	65°30′	188	
31	103	105	
32	145	150	
33	80	128	
34	51	27	
35	41	172	
36	81	78	
37	99	20	
38	70	240	
39	105	220	
40	77	310	
41	166	265	
42	201	340	

(Signed:) A. CUPPAGE, Lt. Col.
Comdg. Mercara.

Mercara,
26th Sept. 1856.

G. M. MARTIN,
Offg. Supt. of Coorg.

True Copy.

(Signed:) H. O'CONNELL Capt.
Ag. Dy. A. Qr. Mr. Genl. of the Army.

7. MEDICAL DEPARTMENT.

The requirements of the Military and Civil service in Coorg render the presence of a Medical Officer indispensable; it has been even proposed, to constitute Mercara into a separate charge of a Civil Surgeon, but Government thought the Military Doctor sufficient for all the wants of the station, considering probably, that the European settlers in the province should make their own arrangements, a supposition which has proved impracticable, as there is not enough remunerative work for a private practitioner. Besides the Military Hospital there is a Civil Dispensary; but it does not receive that ready support from the wealthier natives, which would render so needful and benevolent an institution a more comfortable asylum for the sick poor.

There seems to be a more charitable spirit in Víráјpet, where Ráyanna Shetti, a merchant, has undertaken to erect and maintain a similar institution and Government granted a native medical subordinate for its charge. At the Mercara Dispensary 4,787 patients were aided during 1869-70 at a cost of Rs. 4,484, towards which Government contributed Rs. 2,916, whilst the private subscriptions and donations amounted only to Rs. 897.

Vaccination is attended to by two native vaccinators each at Rs. 15 pay per mensem, under the medical officer's control, but, though the Coorgs at least are very anxious to have their children vaccinated, the operations seem not to be very successful and small-pox remains still a much dreaded epidemic.

To accord to the natives of Coorg a readier access to medical aid, it has been proposed to educate a few Coorg lads for the medical profession, to practise hereafter, either as subordinates in the Civil department, or independently as "Native Doctors," and there is every prospect that the scheme will be carried out.

About the climate of Coorg and its influence upon human health vide p. 85 ff.

8. EDUCATION.

It speaks well for the Coorgs, that no sooner were they brought under the English rule, than they expressed an anxiety for the education of their children. It was, however, in those days a difficult task for Government, efficiently to satisfy their wants. In 1834 an English and a Canarese School were established in Mercara and Vírájpet and a Canarese School only in Kiggatnád at a monthly cost of Rs. 90 for the whole educational establishment. The result was in due proportion. The Vírájpet School collapsed in 1842 and the teacher's pay was appropriated for the maintenance of five Canarese Schools. For a number of years this state of affairs continued and the annual educational Report ran thus in stereotyped fashion:—"There are (25) boys learning English and (429) learning native languages, making a total of (454) showing an increase (or decrease) of (8) boys in the English and (17) in the native schools." This was the beginning, middle and end of the educational Reports, excellent in their way, short and businesslike, entailing no waste of time in writing or reading them! They said every thing that could be said, testifying to the number of names appearing on the different school-rolls. As for learning English, there were some difficulties. The Schoolmaster, could not, of course, be expected to know more, than reading and writing English as well as the copyist in the Kacheri who was better paid. After 20 years of English tuition, there was not one Coorg who could write an English letter or make a tolerable translation from Canarese into English, no one who had acquired any kind of knowledge human or divine through the medium of the English language.

The teaching of the native languages, Hindustani at Mercara, and Canarese in the districts, consisted in reading and writing of the alphabets, getting by heart of multiplication tables and, when the scholars had further advanced, the reading and writing of petitions (Arjis). Education there was none, nor was it wanted. The great men in the Kacheris felt quite happy in their complete ignorance, being cunning enough to look after their own interests. What more could be required? Their only care was to keep every thing in statu quo and to oppose every thing like innovation. This, happily, is an account of the past.

In 1855, encouraged by Sir Mark Cubbon, Dr. Moegling, the first Protestant Missionary in Coorg, established an English School at Mercara, the charge of which was placed into the hands of the Rev. G. Richter in May 1856 and in February 1857 the Supreme Government sanctioned a liberal grant for its support. Maintaining its missionary character, the Coorg Headmen, one of whom felt in particular its christianizing influence upon his sons, at first opposed the school with all their might, but the Head-sheristadar, Nanchappa, having been reconciled to the new order of things, the School began to flourish and gain the favour of the people. Unfortunately for Coorg and the School, the Deván Nanchappa, who was a high spirited and influential leader of his people and would have done much for the advance of education, suddenly died by a fall from his horse.

On the departure of Dr. Moegling to Germany in December 1860, Mr. Richter was nominated by Government Principal of the School and with the year 1861 a new period commences in the educational affairs of Coorg.

The educational scheme, proposed by the Principal and heartily approved of by the Director of Public Instruction, the Chief Commissioner and the Supreme Government, has ever since been gradually carried out and comprises, when fully established, the following features:—an unlimited number of Vernacular district-schools, five Anglo-vernacular schools and the Mercara Central School with boarding establishments for Coorg boys and girls.

The number of *Vernacular district-schools* was raised to 25 and the teachers, nearly all of them Coorgs, were trained by the Principal four at a time for 3 or 4 months at the Central School, which served as a Normal School. After a successful examination the teachers' former pittance of Rs. 2¼ per mensem was increased to a monthly salary of Rs. 7 with the prospect of Rs. 12 p. m. after five years' satisfactory service. The remodelled Schools were placed under the control of the Principal, who under the immediate orders of the Director of Public Instruction is also Inspector of the Coorg Schools. Once in 3 or 4 months all the teachers assemble in Mercara for a conference with the Principal to give an oral report in each other's presence on the state of their work and to receive further instruction in educational topics.

The school-houses are ordinary native buildings, erected by the ryots who also keep them in good repairs and therefore no school-fees are collected from the scholars.

The lessons, taught in the Canarese language, comprise: reading of manuscript papers and of the prescribed printed prose and poetical books, the latter being a collection of extracts from the best native authors; elementary arithmetic with the current weights and measures; copy-writing and dictation, composition; a short geography and history of Coorg and of India and the map of the world.

It is a most pleasing feature, that nearly one-tenth of the number of pupils is made up of Coorg-girls who in their lessons advance equally with the boys and who are not unfrequently quicker in their answers.

The total number of scholars in these 25 schools amounted on the 31st March 1870 to 1158 of whom 890 were Coorgs, including 92 girls.

The *Anglo-vernacular Schools,* three of which have been

established at Vírájpet, Kiggatnád and Fraserpet with a total of 245 pupils are to serve a double purpose. Being affiliated to the Central School, they form for the younger children in the distant Náds convenient seminaries to learn near home the elements of English and in time supply the Central School with a better prepared class of scholars, who will at once join the third form. With the opening of two more Schools at Padynálkanád and Kodlipet, each taluq will have an English School. The teachers, with one exception are pupils of the Central School.

The *Central School at Mercara* gradually advanced to its present position, the first decisive step having been taken in 1862, when the Coorg Headmen petitioned Government for assistance. A copy of their Petition will show both the earnestness of the Coorgs and the extent of the scheme:—

From the Headmen of Coorg

To

Capt. JOHN CAMPBELL,

Superintendent of Coorg.

Sir,

We, the undersigned Headmen of Coorg, being the representatives of our countrymen, beg most respectfully to lay before you what is now uppermost in our minds and what appears to us of the greatest importance for the welfare of our people. If our humble petition should meet with your favourable consideration and approval, we would further beg you, to convey our wishes to the Chief Commissioner of Mysore and Coorg, J. Bowring Esq., with such recommendations and improvements as you may deem proper.

Though the noble generosity of the late lamented Chief Commissioner, General Sir Mark Cubbon, K. C. B., the blessing of education has been extended to us six years ago, though we did not appreciate it then, as we do now. Our minds were darkened and full of prejudice as to its possible effect; but the influence of the established English School at Mercara. its steady progress and the temperate, judicious and devoted manner in which it has been carried on for the last six years, have disarmed all our fears and we earnestly desire, that all our children should be benefitted by the instruction there given. The great influx of European settlers into our country makes the education of our children appear to our minds doubly necessary, since our own ignorance renders our intercourse with the Planters difficult and disadvantageous to us.

The peculiar circumstance, however, that Mercara, though the capital of the province, contains but a few Coorg-houses, enables only a limited number of Coorg boys to attend the school. To remedy this disadvantage, we have resolved to collect a sum of money amongst ourselves sufficient to build and endow a boarding house for about 100 boys.

The Coorg officials and the Pensioners (vide p. 365) are ready to contribute half a month's pay, which together with the subscriptions of the Coorg farmers will amount to about Rs. 6,000. This is all we can do at present; but we earnestly desire, that also our daughters should receive some education and for them we would have to build a similar house.

The question now arises, where to build the houses. Certainly near the School. The present English School, however, is on a slope of the hill on which the Fort is built and within military limits, it is enclosed by two roads, the compound belonging to it very small and in the vicinity no suitable spot available. The school-house itself, which was originally the Rájahs' elephant's stable and had afterwards been turned into a travellers' bangalow, has no suitable arrangements for schoolrooms and does not admit of an increased number of scholars. It was the generous gift of Sir Mark Cubbon for the school and has answered its purpose very well for the beginning, but now it is too small and larger premises are required.

We therfore most humbly beg, that Government may give us a helping hand to carry out our plans. We propose to have all the School buildings required within the same compound and under the eye of the resident Principal, and for this purpose no other spot in Mercara seems to us in every respect more suitable than the site of the old palace. It is central, spacious and healthy. The few remaining walls would yield some building material and the foundations might serve for the new school-house with the Principal's dwelling; the compound would afford an extensive playground and gymnasium and enough room for a garden, to be cultivated by our children. We beg that this piece of ground be granted to us for this purpose.

We estimate the cost of the school-house, the Principal's dwelling, the boarding house and out-houses, the gymnastic apparatus and the laying out of the garden at about Rs. 20,000; towards which we bind ourselves to collect Rs. 6,000; the sale of the present school-house may yield Rs. 3,000 and if Government would grant the rest, we should feel deeply grateful.

Mr. Richter, the Principal of the English School, who has conducted it for the last six years and won our entire confidence, has not only given the first impulse to this movement, but also declared himself with his esteemed partner most willing, to carry out the proposed plans and since both have hitherto acted as father and mother towards our children, we have not the least hesitation in confiding them also for the future to their parental care; the inner arrangements of the boarding houses, however, will be managed by our own people.

On the proposed site our Rájahs built a palace for the sole accommodation of their English friends during their visits at Mercara, whom they hospitably entertained and amused with all the wild sports of our native country (vide p. 297 ff.); how much nobler would be the task of our present benevolent Rulers, if on the ruins of the same palace they assisted us in erecting the desired buildings for the accommodation of our sons and daughters and entertained them in the halls of wisdom and knowledge with sublimer sport than the wild jungles of Coorg could furnish; and while even these palace ruins are in some degree honorable to our late Rájahs, we are fully convinced, that the new buildings will be a more lasting and brighter memorial to the honor of the paternal Government of India!

From the kind interest, which we rejoice to hear, the present Chief Commissioner entertains towards us and especially in educational matters, we have great hopes of a favourable result of this Petition.

Assuring Government of our heartfelt gratitude for received favors and of our devoted loyalty, we subscribe ourselves

Sir,

&c. &c. &c.

Mercara, 26th August 1862. 65 Signatures.

In transmitting the Petition to the Secretary to the Chief Commissioner, Capt. J. A. Campbell remarked:—

"I have the greatest satisfaction in being the medium of bringing this most interesting movement on the part of the people of Coorg to the notice of Government, and I beg to bear my testimony to the genuineness of the feeling expressed in this petition, both as regards the earnestness of the people to progress in knowledge, their readiness to make sacrifices in the cause, and the esteem in which they hold the present Headmaster and his wife, to whom they have already given so much of their confidence."

The Petition was forwarded by the Chief Commissioner to the Secretary to the Government of India, accompanied by the following letter:—

Sir,

I have particular pleasure in submitting to His Excellency the Viceroy and Governor General in Council, the accompanying copy of a letter from the Officiating Superintendent of Coorg together with a request, which may be deemed a national one, on the part of the Coorg people to be admitted to those benefits of education which others in more favoured positions have already received.

There is a genuineness of expression about this address, which I beg to send in original, that, I feel assured, will secure the hearty approval of the Government of India. It has probably rarely happened in India that a whole race has come forward in this manner, putting aside traditional prejudices, to meet half way the earnest wish of their Rulers, that they should educate themselves, and it is especially remarkable among mountaineers in this country, as the hill races are generally far below those of the plains in their acquisition of knowledge.

I have informed the Officiating Superintendent of Coorg, that I would lose no time in laying the address before His Excellency in Council, and that I feel convinced, that the Government will receive with peculiar pleasure the spontaneous expression of the good will borne by the Coorg race towards their Rulers.

In respect to the site solicited, there is no difficulty, and I have signified my assent to its being made over for the School in conformity with the existing practice in regard to building grants at Mercara.

With reference to the sum required to enable the people to carry out their wishes, I have no hesitation in soliciting that the sanction of Government may be accorded to the project being undertaken, so that the Coorgs may receive early intimation, that their earnest wish for their own enlightenment has been made known to and has been approved of by the Viceroy in Council, as the knowledge of the interest, taken in their welfare by the Head of Her Majesty's Government cannot but be an additional link to bind them to British rule. The detailed accounts required for the Budget can be estimated for in due course.

The Government of India may perhaps also be pleased to make known their approval of Mr. Richter's exertions.

I have etc. etc.

Bangalore 27th October, 1862. (Signed) L. BOWRING, *Commissioner.*

In the extract from the Proceedings of the Right Honorable the Governor General of India in Council in the Home Department, under date 15th January 1863 after a summary of the preceding correspondence: "The Governor General in Council is pleased to sanction the grant of a sum of money not exceeding Rs. 11,000 for the purpose indicated." "His Excellency in Council also notices with approbation the exertions of Mr. Richter, the Head Master of the School in question, who is stated to have won the 'entire confidence' of the people, and to have been the means of giving the first impulse to the present movement."

Rejoiced at the good news, the Coorgs enabled Mr. Richter to set at once to work. A building committee was formed consisting of the late Superintendent, Major Martin, and the three Head-Coorg-Officials, and having received the needful instructions at Head-quarters in Bangalore, the Principal planned and executed within the next five years under the most trying difficulties the proposed buildings at an outlay of Rs. 32,548—11—7, towards which the Coorgs subscribed Rs. 9,721—15—5, the Europeans in Coorg Rs. 471, the sale of the old school-house produced Rs. 6,500 and the balance was liberally paid by the Government.

The boys' boarding-house is now being fitted up for occupation in the beginning of 1871 and the girls' boarding-house will shortly be ready too. It is being built by Colovanda Cariappah, the first Coorg pupil of the English School of 1856, and now Subadár of Mercara-taluq and always with his friend, Chepudira Soobiah, the staunchest and most liberal supporter of the cause of education amongst his people.

The Basel Missionary Society, in whose connection Mr. Richter hitherto stood, observed with uneasiness the extraordinary educational movement in Coorg and were apprehensive of being thereby involved in responsibilities which they considered foreign to their missionary operations; they came, therefore, to the resolution of dissolving in the most friendly manner, his connection with them, and Mr. Richter, since October 1863, fully entered the Government service in the Coorg Commission and the Society withdrew from any further interference and obligation in educational matters in Coorg.

The new Central School was opened in May 1869 and contains now 176 pupils of whom 12 are girls. Besides 93 Coorgs, there are 14 Christians, 28 Mussulmans, 3 Parsees and the rest other Hindus.

The course of instruction, here adopted, aims at a practical education, yet keeping in view the standard of the Matriculation test for the highest class. Divided into six classes, of which the Hindustani and Canarese classes are at the bottom, elementary instruction is first imparted by means of the Vernaculars, which in the higher classes gradually give way to English instruction and Canarese is studied only as a language. The girls, of whom seven are Coorgs, form only for needlework under Mrs. Richter's instruction a separate class, their other lessons they learn with the boys. In the lower and middle classes history is taught in Canarese and consequently the boys are well grounded in an intelligent knowledge of the subject. In geography a thorough knowledge of Coorg in Canarese prepares the pupils for a better understanding of India, Asia, and the Map of the World. Geometrical linear drawing with definitions lays the foundation for Euclid of which the First Book is taught in Canarese in the middle class, whilst the first class absolves the Third Book with deductions and mensuration of plain figures and of solids. Arithmetic leads up to decimals, the compound rule of three and evolutions; Algebra includes simple equations. The study of English comprises: Grammar, composition and analysis of prose and poetical selections; in the same way Canarese is studied in the two upper classes.

At the request of Government, "Botany" has been added to the list of lessons of the first class. Singing is a general lesson for the musical boys and upwards of 60 Canarese and English songs are practised. The Gymnasium engages twice a week the whole School and the exercises are very popular. A library and some philosophical apparatus are aids for evening lectures for the further instruction of studious youths who left the School.

On the whole the Coorg boys, though eager for learning and diligent and persevering in their studies, have not that quickness of perception and brilliancy of intellect which generally distinguishes Brahmin youths. They are slow and lack imagination, but are solid in their acquirements and gifted with sound common sense. In a competitive examination, the quick-witted Brahmin, though not half so well informed, will outstrip the Coorg lad; but give the latter time and he will maintain his place due to his real worth. Coorg lads and others, trained in the Central School, are now found in every office of the various departments of Government in Coorg and some fill important posts; but it is to be regretted, that many of them did not complete the course of education offered to them. Some time ago the openings in the offices were so many, that the young men could not resist the temptation of well paid employments under Government and relinquished their studies. For the same reason none of the first class pupils has yet attempted to pass the Matriculation examination, though, in the opinion of the Director of Public Instruction, "if these boys were to remain another year under instruction, they might all be prepared to pass the Matriculation test of the Madras University." (vide his Report of 1869-70.)

Foreseeing the difficulty of permanently supporting the boarding-houses without the aid of public charity or Government assistance, the general speculation in coffee in Coorg suggested a source of revenue, which was thought both legitimate and profitable. Some of the most public spirited and liberal minded Coorgs took up the idea and the following is the agreement concerning the proposed Endowment-Plantation:

"We the undersigned, Headmen of Coorg, taking a lively interest in the intellectual enlightenment of the sons and daughters of our countrymen, have by the advice of the Rev. G. Richter agreed upon and resolved to carry out the following plan:—

1. Having obtained as a free gift from the Chief Commissioner of Mysore and Coorg, L. Bowring Esq., the two jungles Paramádu and Punchi in Yedenálknád,—a claim to which having been relinquished by the late Subadar, Colovanda Soobiah, in favour of the present undertaking—we bind ourselves by this document to raise at five per cent interest per annum from amongst ourselves and other Coorgs who are willing to join us, a sum of money sufficient for the purpose of opening a Coffee-plantation as an endowment for the Mercara Central School and its boarding-houses.

2. The subscribers choose amongst themselves six Coorgs as a committee, who together with the Principal of the Mercara Central School undertake the management of the whole business and who have power to fill up vacancies.

3. No part of the money thus lent can, before the execution of the plan, be withdrawn by any subscriber unless his subscription is refunded by a substitute. When the estate comes into bearing, from the proceeds of the year's crop a sum of money, sufficient for the working expenditure of the current year, is to be first deducted; of the remainder the interest of the subscribed money is to be paid to each subscriber and of the balance the capital is to be repaid in proportion to the amount of each share. The Plantation, however, remains mortgaged to the subscribers until their advances have been repaid.

4. After the loan has been repaid, the Plantation will be for ever the property of the Mercara Central School and held in trust for the same by the appointed committee, but *the annual net profits can only be applied to educational purposes.*

5. The *disposal* of the money accruing from the Plantation rests solely with the managing committee, but the propositions of expenditure are made by the Principal of the Central School as the representative of Government and his vote is decisive, whenever the division of committee-members is equally balanced. The Principal will also carry out the resolutions of the committee.

6. If after due notice, four of the committee-members, the Principal included, are present at a meeting, they may pass final resolutions.

7. What money is required for every three months' operations, may be called up from the subscribers through the Secretary after one month's notice. The Principal of the Central School may convene a meeting of the committee once every three months or whenever circumstances render it necessary.

Clause. As the present Principal of the Central School has taken so great an interest in the welfare of the Coorgs and we may expect him to do the same also in future, we cheerfully accord him his position in our committee, but in case of the present Principal retiring from his post, his successor will have no claim to the same privileges and can be admitted only with the consent of the committee.

Mercara, 17th October 1863.

Chepudira Soobiah, **2nd Assist. Supt.**
Colorunda Cariappah, **Subadár.**
Madandu Appachoo, **Head-Sheristadar.**
Konganda Appeya, **Judicial Sheristadar.**
Kotanda Appachoo, **Muktasir.**

Bitianda Cariappah, Head-Munshi.
Kuttetira Eyappa, Treasurer.
Korovanda Ponnappa.
Shamana.
Chaurira Appeya.
Timappeya Appeya.
Bittandra Mutteya.
Appaneravana Acheya."

The Plantation not succeeding so well as was anticipated, though it is now in a hopeful condition, the Principal suggested another plan and in September last (1870) the Coorg Headmen passed and submitted to Government for sanction the following resolutions:—

1. "With the sanction of Government an *Educational Cess* should be levied on the ryots of Coorg in the shape of a plough-tax, the mode and extent of levying which is to be left with the Superintendent's approval and authorization, to the Headmen as on former occasions.

2. From the children of the ryots thus taxed, no schooling fees should be levied; the fees from other children in the *Anglo-vernacular Schools only* should be added to the local-cess-fund

3. The money thus raised, which may amount to Rs. 3 or 4000, is not to supersede, but to supplement the ordinary educational Budget-grant and should be spent upon the *maintenance of the Mercara boarding-houses, the upkeep of the Vernacular and Anglo-vernacular school-houses and the extension of Vernacular education throughout Coorg.*

4. The management of the Cess-fund should be vested in the Principal of the Central School conjointly with the three principal Coorg Officials and the eight Subadárs."

Thus the Government system of education in Coorg may be said to be of a comprehensive and an expansive character, resting on the sure and proper basis of Government assistance and conjoint local exertions and claiming the interest of all classes of the Coorg population. The work is still in its infancy, but promises well for the future.

Of *private institutions*, aided by Government, there are the German Mission School at Anandapur and the Roman Catholic Boys' and Girls' schools at Vírájpet. Regarding *private unaided schools*, it is difficult to obtain reliable information as to their number and attendance. They are generally of a temporary and very insignificant character.

Of the 1,545 pupils at School in March 1870, 1,422 were in Government Schools and 1,082 children Coorgs. Assuming that the present population of Coorg is 120,000, of whom about 25,000 are Coorgs, the number of children under education in the Government and aided schools, gives a proportion of one child at school for every 78 people of the whole population or nearly 13 per thousand; and as 1,082 Coorg boys and girls attend these schools, of one Coorg child for every 23 people of that race or 43 per thousand, the proportion in the case of the latter being unusually large and satisfactory.

C. CHRISTIAN INFLUENCE UPON THE COORGS.

1. THE ROMAN CATHOLIC SETTLEMENTS

Whatever the moral and political vices of the Coorg Rájahs may have been, in religious matters they showed a tolerant and liberal spirit, which at the time put to shame the intolerance of many Christian Governments. Dodda-Vírájender extended his protection to the poor fugitive Roman Catholics who fled from the claws of Tippu Sultan, when in 1792 Lord Cornwallis besieged Seringapatam. They were Konkanis from the western coast, had incurred Tippu's particular displeasure for their assistance in provisioning General Mathew's army and had come into his power after the fall of Bednore and the siege of Mangalore in 1783, when he settled them in and about his capital. The Konkanis are noted for their industry and skill of adapting themselves to circumstances. Dodda-Vírájender eagerly welcomed them into his depopulated country, granted them land at Vírájpet, procured for them a Priest in the person of Father John de Costa, a native of Goa, assisted in building a chapel and allotted to its maintenance a stipend of 84 butties of paddy and a certain amount of oil and candles, which allowance his successors continued and which the English Government since 1835 commuted into a monthly grant of Rs. 20, "its continuance being dependant not only on the Priest's conduct, but that of his flock, in as far as he may justly be considered responsible for it." This stipend is now looked upon as the Priest's salary from Government and attempts have been made, to get it increased, but Sir Mark Cubbon declared: "that the amount, the Priest enjoyed, had no doubt been deemed proportioned to the ordinary duties of his office, but if called to the discharge of any extra duties by the requisition of the members of his congregation, the Commissioner conceived that the latter should contribute the means of enabling the Priest to meet such extra-official calls."

Pastoral jurisdiction having been claimed by the Archbishop of Goa, the Rev. F. Bernardino De Sta. Ágnes, Bishop-Coadjutor, Vicar Apostolic at Mangalore addressed in 1846 the Superintendent of Coorg in the following letter:—

The Mission of Coorg, by a Firman passed by the Rájah in 1805, was founded to remain always under the jurisdiction of the Bishop, Vicar Apostolic of Bombay, who has ultimately transferred it to me. No jurisdiction over it was ever or is now possessed by the Archbishop of Goa. The jurisdiction of His Grace does not extend beyond that Portuguese territory as shewn by various Bulls which have emanated from Rome regarding the same, but the Archbishop, actuated by certain national presumption, pretends to possess something like an omnipotence in the spiritual throughout the whole of India and therefore sends his emissaries to excite dissensions and disturbances among the Roman Catholics, subject to the Vicars Apostolic, and he has accordingly sent one to Coorg named Francesco Pacheco, who endeavours to take forcible possession of the Church there."

Now the Roman Catholic establishments in Coorg are under the spiritual charge of the Bishop at Bangalore, the See at Mangalore having declined about ten years ago to send Priests to so unhealthy a locality as Vírájpet.

In 1835 a grant of Rs. 1500 was sanctioned by Government for the restoration of the delapidated church at Vírájpet and in 1866 a new grant of Rs. 2,500 for rebuilding the same edifice, which after completion is said to have cost Rs. 15,000 (vide p. 375). The Priest's dwelling and the school-houses for boys and girls are on the same premises. The streets of the Christian quarter look clean and tidy and the houses like those of the better class of other natives in the place are substantial and comfortable. The number of Roman Catholic Christians in Vírájpet amounts to 313, and there may be as many more in the neighbourhood. The mortality amongst those, the town has of late years been very considerable.

As stated by Mr. Kerr, the late Superintendent of Coorg and himself a Roman Catholic, "the Christian colony at Vírájpet is not a mission-establishment in the ordinary acceptation of the term," and no Coorg and hardly any other caste people of Coorg have ever joined it. The Christians, away from their pastor's eye, seem to be more influenced by the surrounding heathenish superstition, than to exercise any renovating influence by their Christian life and testimony upon the heathen; but socially as well as morally they appear now to be in a better condition than they were, when Lieut. Connor saw them in 1817 and drew a picture of the colony in the following sketch:—

"The Christians here are under the Church of Bombay, a small chapel has been built and its services are performed by an ecclesiastic from that place; the condition of his flock, however, is far from flourishing, the greater portion of them are employed in the manufacture of arrack from rice, an avocation that bespeaks the estimation in which they are held. Christianity has impressed no very awful sense of religion on its rude followers, who are subject to all the degradation, attaching to a profession of it in eastern countries; but a small share of the morality it inculcates is observable, and its votaries seem still to retain most of their ancient superstitions; indeed, if either the condition or character of these followers of it be taken as a criterion, the most sanguine could scarcely hope much good to result from a more general conversion to its divine doctrines."

A church and native congregation, chiefly of Tamil-Christians, the servants of Europeans, and pensioned sepoys, especially Sappers and Miners, have been established at Mercara and Fraserpet at which places periodically a European or Native Priest resides.

2. THE ENGLISH CHAPLANCY IN MERCARA.

Mercara containing a greater number of Europeans than Mangalore and offering a more salubrious residence, the chaplain of the latter station removed to the former in 1854 and Mercara was ever since under the spiritual care of a clergyman of the Church of England. His congregation, comprising civilians, military officers and planters, numbers over hundred souls. Through subordinate agency native Christians, especially Tamulians, have likewise been benefitted by the successive Chaplains and the heathens around have at least an opportunity of witnessing in a chaste church (vide p. 192.) the pure and simple worship of a Protestant congregation; and should all who profess and call themselves Christians be led in the way of truth and hold the faith in unity of spirit, in the bond of peace and in righteousness of life, what amount of good might thus be effected even by those who cannot speak to the natives in their tongue! There would certainly be less cause for taunting the Christian missionary with want of success!

The first resident Chaplain at Mercara, the Rev. Mr. Prosnett.

was appointed here in 1852. The Rev. Mr. Fennell B. A. succeeded him early in 1853, and the Rev. M. O. Deane B. A. took charge in December 1866, and was followed by Rev. J. Wynch M. A. in December 1868, who left in December 1869, when the chaplaincy was vacated till December 1870 and then filled by the Rev. C. H. Deane M. A.

3. THE PROTESTANT MISSION OF THE BASEL SOCIETY.

When the account of the reduction of Coorg arrived in England, considerable interest was awakened in behalf of the inhabitants of the new Province, whom British arms had delivered from cruel bondage, and whose brave and frank character seemed to establish a peculiar claim upon the sympathies of the friends of Indian missions.

General Fraser on the 10th June 1834 in a letter to Mr. McNaughton, the Secretary to the Government of India remarks:—

"There is not probably a spot of ground in all India of this limited extent capable of so much improvement as Coorg. The people appear to have little or no attachment to the debasing superstition of the country and their minds seem to me to be more open than those of any other Indians, I have seen, to be prepared for receiving the light of the Christian religion, while their intellect may be expected rapidly to expand under the influence of that education, they are themselves soliciting." The noble-hearted General offered his share of the prize-money as an endowment of a Protestant Mission and the Wesleyan and the London Missionary Societies were inclined to extend their operations to Coorg, but both Societies subsequently found, that they could not spare men for a new Mission at a distance from their older stations, and thus a good opportunity was lost. General Fraser subsequently established a school at Fraserpet which he endowed with a sum of Rs. 300, the interest of which goes towards the teacher's pay. The school is now under Government management and incorporated with the Anglo-Vernacular School.

In the year 1834 the Basel Missionary Society commenced operations on the western coast, in the neighbourhood of Coorg, and extended their stations to the north and south. Mercara and Víráǰpet were now and then visited; but no proposal was made to the Committee to occupy Coorg. Thus the country remained nearly twenty years under British rule without the establishment of a Mission. until Dr. Moegling in 1852 was in an unforeseen and singular manner led to commence the long delayed work.

Being on the point of returning to Germany to recruit his shattered health, he was visited by a Coorg man, disguised as a Sanyási, who applied for instruction in the Christian doctrine. He was an intelligent and astute Coorg and the story of his life highly interesting. Having been baptized on the 6th January 1853, Stephanas Someyah of Almanda in Beppunád. returned unexpected and unnoticed to his house. His wife received him with great joy and declared that she would live and die with him. On the following day Stephanas took formal possession of his house, and Dr. Moegling, who had accompanied him, resolved on standing by the family and becoming security to the creditors, who speedily assembled for the liquidation of the debts of the convert. Two days afterwards his neighbours and relatives drove him and his family out of their house at night and forced them to take refuge with the missionary at Víráǰpet. The Superintendent enquired into the case and the Chief Commissioner, Sir Mark Cubbon, to whom the matter was referred gave the following decision:—

To

THE SUPERINTENDENT

of Coorg.

Sir,

The Commissioner, having had under consideration your various communications regarding the reception on his return to Coorg of one, Somiah who has left his caste, I have the honor, by his advice to convey to you his instructions as to the manner in which this and similar cases should be dealt with.

In the first place it seems to be admitted on all hands, that but for the fact of his having left his caste, Somiah, as the rightful head by inheritance of his branch of his family, had nothing to do but to return to Coorg and take quiet possession of his house and lands. There would have been no aggrieved party in this case, and it requires to be shown, that there is an aggrieved party in the case as it really happened.

If it be true, as stated in the papers under notice, and the Commissioner sees no reason to doubt that it is so, that several instances exist of individuals having become outcasts from their own religion and even converts to Mahomedanism and yet been allowed to remain in quiet possession of their estates; it is clear that degradation from caste for misconduct or on voluntary change of faith is not of itself regarded in Coorg as involving the deprivation of hereditary or self-acquired property. It is therefore evident in the present instance, that neither on national nor on caste grounds could there have been an aggrieved party, unless perhaps in the event of his wife and childern and the other inmates of the house which he came to occupy, having felt themselves polluted by his neighbourhood. So far, however, is this from being the case, that it appears, that one and all of them preferred being turned out in his company in the middle of the night, to remaining under shelter of the roof without him; and it is moreover subsequently reported, that the wife and children lost no time in following his example and making a public renunciation of the faith in which they had been brought up.

Under these circumstances the Commissioner must regard the act of those people who violently ejected him from the house, of which he had been in quiet possession for nearly three days, as a gross and flagrant insult to the Government, only to be excused by their ignorance and their having been led away to a certain extent by the evil example of their Subadár Appachoo. Of the conduct of Appachoo himself, there can be but one opinion, but the Commissioner is not unwilling to overlook for once the error of an old and able servant of the Government and trusts, that Appachoo will justify his good opinion of him by the cheerful alacrity with which he will replace Somiah in possession of the house and lands of which he was so illegally and violently deprived.

You will be good enough, carefully to explain the whole of the foregoing to all the parties concerned and at the same time inform them, that the civil courts are open to them, should they still consider that there are any legal grounds for depriving this convert of his inheritance."

&c. &c. &c.

The Coorg-family returned to their home in June; Dr. Moegling remained in their neighbourhood during the monsoon. With the beginning of the cold season he made preparations for building a little church and a dwelling-house on a piece of ground given by Stephanas to the Mission and the work of preaching at the principal market-places was commenced. Having taken all these steps without the Society's sanction, the founder of the Mission had to bear all the burden of its support and arrangement as well as the evangelistic labour for six long years. Strong in faith, however, he cheerfully and regardless of his prostrate health, devoted himself to his Master's work who did not forsake him in his daily wants. The publication of the "Coorg Memoirs" and the periodical reports of his work in the "Madras Christian Herald" greatly helped to interest the South-Indian public in his Mission.

A new Mission seldom thrives well under regulations unadapted to its peculiar circumstances and requirements and Dr. Moegling had the courage to trust, that he might be able unembarrassed to labour on, and his experience was, that he could gratefully and rejoicingly say, that no man should be discouraged by mere want of money from doing his duty! Whilst standing alone with his Mission, he still continued in connexion with the Basel Committee in everything except financial support and obedience to the rules of their conference as applied to the older stations.

Meanwhile two more Coorg families joined him and Dr. Moegling, notwithstanding repeated attacks of jungle fever, remained at his post and continued to labour assiduously, preaching on market-days at Víràjpet and Mercara, visiting the scenes of the Coorg annual festivals and engaging in literary labours for the Government and the Bible Society. He was treated with great kindness and encouragement by the English Officials and by the other residents in Mercara. In 1856 he married the widow of a brother-missionary, who was herself practised in all the branches of mission work including translation into Canarese, and she proved to him in all his various labours a true and worthy helpmate.

In the same year a number of families, comprising 130 souls, of the Holeyas or agricultural slave-caste (vide p. 112), who had assisted in building the Almanda church, applied for instruction. They were received and located in Ammatnád on a waste farm, which was taken from Government for the purpose, where they might maintain themselves by its cultivation under the direction of Stephanas. The farm was held by Dr. Moegling's spiritual son, the Rev. A. Kaundinya, one of the first Brahmin converts of Mangalore, who cheerfully undertook the risk and responsibility. The new settlement was named Anandapur (city of joy) and a simple residence and chapel were erected. In 1858, the departure one by one of the tried friends who had known the work from its beginning, and the altered circumstances of India after the Mutiny, induced Dr. Moegling to seek substantial connexion with the Church Missionary Society and he went to England and offered himself and the Mission to their acceptance. He was very kindly received by the Committee, but, after full deliberation, they considered it better, that he should make another effort to continue attached to Basel and, meantime, they gave a liberal grant of 500 £ to his work. Encouraged with this help, he returned to Coorg in January 1859 after having effected a new connexion of the station with the Basel Society and so it still continues. Dr. Moegling in 1860 had to part with his excellent wife, who was ordered to Europe in broken health, and at the end of the same year he had himself to follow in thoroughly shattered health and reached Württemberg just in time to nurse her in her last illness. His own state of health did not allow him to return to India.

The work has been carried on by his successors: Revs. Kittel, Stokes, Kaufmann, Kaundinya and Schnepf with varying success and under great trials and disappointments. The Christians built for themselves new houses, the proprietor of the farm erected by his manager, Mr. Hahn, a substantial dwelling and a new church towards which the Government contributed Rs. 1,000; he also opened out a small coffee plantation to give additional and permanent employment to the colony, but though very hopeful at first, the devastation by the Borer was here so complete, that the whole plantation was destroyed.

Unfortunately the locality of Anandapur being in a bamboo district and only partially and newly cleared, has not proved a healthy one; the native as well as the European residents were frequently prostrated by fever, the Missionaries Kittel, Stokes and Schnepf and Mr. and Mrs. Hahn had to leave the station on account of ill-health from severe attacks of fever and both the late pastor Mr. Kaufmann and his wife fell victims in 1869 to the Coorg fever, contracted at Anandapur.

According to the last census of the Coorg mission in 1869-70 there are 50 communicants and 7 non-communicants, 42 children, 12 catechumeni, and the parochial school is attended by 23 children.

Considering the abject and degraded position of most of these Christians before their conversion, the social, intellectual and religious standing of this colony cannot be expected to be very high; but, in spite of much weakness and grievous shortcomings, evidences are not wanting of visible and genuine christian and spiritual life.

Of the nine Christians from amongst the Coorgs, and of Stephanas in particular, not much good can be said, in fact several of them disgraced by their conduct the christian name among their own people and proved to them a stumbling block. Stephanas, being insincere and of a divided heart, as it seems, from the very beginning, was at last found out in his secret course of wickedness and had to be excommunicated. He is suspected, to have afterwards in a fit of revenge set fire to the Almanda chapel and dwelling-house in 1867 both of which were utterly demolished, and then disappeared from the country without any trace of his whereabouts. Perhaps he has again become a Sanyási! His son, now in the Mangalore Theological Seminary, will perhaps strive, to redeem his father's discreditable Christian career. Stephanas' two married daughters at Mangalore lead a becoming christian life. Their mother died, her last years being beclouded by insanity.

Thus far General Fraser's hopeful view of the Coorgs' preparedness for embracing the Christian religion, when the opportunity was offered to them, has not been realised. To what causes this failure may be ascribed, it is difficult to say. The unpalatable defeat of some of the Coorg headmen in Stephana's affair, the loss of the 130 Holeyas of Beppunád who joined the Missionary, the Coorgs' jealousy of the moral and social improvement of their former slaves, their fancied apprehension of their own degradation to an equal footing with them on becoming Christians, the inconsistent life of some of the Coorg converts, the natural propensity of the Coorgs to, and success in material prosperity of late years and the concomitant selfindulgence, their more frequent intercourse with Europeans, the increasing influence of Brahmins upon the superstitious Coorgs—these and other circumstances may have led to such a result. Perhaps General Fraser formed his opinion, before he had sufficiently made himself acquainted with the Coorg character, though he was a very shrewd observer, or perhaps the providential time has not yet come for such a decisive step by the whole Coorg-clan and his opinion may still be an unfulfilled prophesy; but however this may be, we believe, that Dr. Moegling's labors in Coorg have not been in vain. The good seed, sown by his evangelistic and educational efforts, has struck ground and others will with joyful hearts reap the fruit of his prayers and tears and at the harvest time will cherish, with grateful recognition of his merits, the memory of Dr. Moegling, the accomplished, devoted and faithful founder of the Coorg Mission!

In connexion with the "Mercantile Association" of the Basel Mission, there is at Mercara a mercantile establishment under a European married agent, which, while serving the secular interests of the Mission, gives useful employment to a number of native converts and teaches them also in this path of life to honor their calling as Christians.

Appendix I.

Statement shewing the dates of assumption of charge of the Chief Commissioners and the Superintendents of Coorg.

Date of assumption of charge.	Names of the Chief Commissioners.
3rd March 1834	Lieut. Col. J. S. Fraser.
18th January 1836	Lieut. Col. Mark Cubbon.
1st March 1861	C. B. Saunders Esq., C. B.
21st April 1862	L. B. Bowring Esq., C. S. I.
10th September 1866	C. B. Saunders Esq., C. B.
11th November 1867	L. B. Bowring Esq., C. S. B.
21st February 1870	Col. R. J. Meade, C. S. I.
	Names of the Superintendents.
2nd September 1834	Captain C. F. Le Hardy.
11th March 1843	do. G. Haines.
2nd March 1844	do. W. C. Onslow.
7th June 1846	do. H. F. Gustard.
16th January 1855	do. G. M. Martin.
27th October 1856	Major H. F. Gustard.
31st December 1856	do. G. M. Martin.
21st June 1859	Captain H. M. Elliott.
31st December 1861	do. F. M. Mc. Hutchin.
8th March 1862	do. Tredway G. Clarke.
28th April 1862	do. J. A. Campbell.
6th May 1862	Lancelot Ricketts Esq.
5th July 1862	Captain J. A. Campbell.
17th November 1862	do. Ralph N. Taylor.
20th July 1864	William Hobart Kerr Esq., M. C. S.
3rd March 1865	Captain Robert Andrews Cole.
13th October 1865	William Hobart Kerr Esq., M. C. S.
23rd February 1866	Captain R. A. Cole.
2nd July 1869	Lieut. Edmund S. Ludlow.
6th October 1869	Captain R. A. Cole.
2nd December 1869	Major Hugh Gordon Thomson.

Appendix II.

COMPARATIVE STATISTICS OF THE COORG REVENUE.

Sources of Income.	1834—35.			1839—40.			1849—50.			1859—60.			1864—65.			1869—70.		
	Rs.	As.	P.	Rs.	As.	P.	Rs.	As.	P.	Rs.	As.	P.	Rs.	As.	P.	Rs.	As.	P.
Land Revenue	89,915	6	3	102,270	9	4	127,118	14	10	162,664	12	7	182,859	15	8	286,560	4	9
Forest	7,348	4	11	65,032	12	10	13,950	1	5	38,522	12	10	102,218	10	4	106,658	8	6
Excise on Spirits and Drugs	4,445	0	0	17,609	8	0	25,983	13	4	32,266	0	0	142,510	10	10	66,374	11	7
Assessed Taxes, etc	5,797	13	4	8,076	6	7	9,733	15	9	10,955	3	11	13,333	7	5	3,027	13	0
Stamps	0	0	0	0	0	0	0	0	0	0	0	0	17,262	8	3	33,741	14	1
Post and Service Lables	0	0	0	0	0	0	0	0	0	0	0	0	0	0	0	6,129	8	2
Post Office	0	0	0	0	0	0	0	0	0	0	0	0	0	0	0	880	1	2
Electric Telegraph	0	0	0	0	0	0	0	0	0	0	0	0	0	0	0	1,863	12	0
Law and Justice	0	0	0	0	0	0	0	0	0	0	0	0	0	0	0	5,075	2	1
Registration Fees	0	0	0	0	0	0	0	0	0	0	0	0	0	0	0	1,847	4	0
Public Works	0	0	0	0	0	0	0	0	0	0	0	0	0	0	0	70,480	3	2*
Miscellaneous	3,591	0	4	4,054	2	3	3,939	9	6	6,339	7	9	10,638	12	4	7,302	3	10
Local Funds	0	0	0	0	0	0	0	0	0	0	0	0	0	0	0	4,518	15	2
Sáyers or Inland Customs	5,923	14	2	8,267	8	6	0	0	0	0	0	0	0	0	0	0	0	0
Grand Total	117,021	7	0	205,310	15	6	180,726	6	10	250,748	5	1	468,824	0	10	594,460	5	6

Note:—Forest includes Cardamoms and Sandalwood.

Assessed taxes inclıde Mohaturfa or tax on houses and shops, Income-tax and License-tax.

* Nearly the whole amount is a mere treasury-transaction for the accommodation of the Mysore Government.

Appendix III.

COMPARATIVE STATISTICS OF CHARGES AGAINST THE COORG REVENUE.

Heads of Expenditure.	1834—35.			1839—40.			1849—50.			1859—60.			1864—65.			1869—70.		
	Rs.	As.	P.	Rs.	As.	P.	Rs.	As.	P.	Rs.	As.	P.	Rs.	As.	P.	Rs.	As.	P.
Civil Establishments	63,949	4	10	64,510	10	7	62,515	2	7	60,021	1	6	127,513	8	11	154,763	4	4
Judicial	1,841	0	11	5,191	8	1	7,570	15	8	7,696	15	2	12,827	9	0	19,308	4	5
Stamps	0	0	0	0	0	0	0	0	0	0	0	0	831	0	5	2,532	9	5
Police	0	0	0	0	0	0	0	0	0	0	0	0	0	0	0	1,152	0	0
Public Works	0	0	0	75,350	11	11	51,519	15	10	21,446	1	1	92,595	0	4	124,651	7	10*
Education	626	6	4	1,080	0	0	1,080	0	0	3,870	0	0	18,160	8	0	14,088	7	5
Post Office and Anche	0	0	0	0	0	0	0	0	0	0	0	0	4,188	0	0	5,385	13	7
Superannuation and retiring allowances	0	0	0	0	0	0	0	0	0	0	0	0	0	0	0	1,972	12	0
Ecclesiastical	224	10	8	240	0	0	240	0	0	240	0	0	2,876	8	0	4,836	7	6
Allowances and assignments under treaties & engagements	127,946	6	7	141,801	7	11	93,216	3	10	25,670	3	10	26,661	9	9	21,469	11	5
Miscellaneous	0	0	0	0	0	0	0	0	0	0	0	0	15,788	3	1	7,873	1	4
Local Funds	0	0	0	0	0	0	0	0	0	0	0	0	0	0	0	2,322	2	5
Grand Total	194,587	13	4	288,174	6	6	216,142	5	11	118,944	5	7	301,441	15	6	360,356	1	8

*These charges are debited to the Imperial Revenue.

Appendix IV.

MERCURIAL BAROMETER-OBSERVATIONS AT MERCARA

REGISTERED BY REV. G. RICHTER WITH BLAND AND LONG'S INSTRUMENT.

Months.	1866.			1867.			1868.			1869.			1870.			Average.		
	6 A.M.	3 P.M.	Mean.	6 A.M.	3 P.M.	Mean.	6 A.M.	3 P.M.	Mean.	6 A.M.	3 P.M.	Mean.	6 A.M.	3 P.M.	Mean.	6 A.M.	3 P.M.	Mean.
January . .	26·44	26·56	26·50	26·43	26·55	26·48	26·40	26·59	26·50	26·49	26·55	26 51	26·34	26·50	26·43	26·42	26·55	26·48
February . .	— 42	— 58	— 50	— 43	— 55	— 48	— 40	— 60	— 49	— 45	— 60	— 50	— 40	— 52	— 45	— 53	— 57	— 48
March . . .	— 44	— 57	— 50	— 45	— 60	— 50	— 40	— 55	— 50	— 45	— 60	— 50	— 41	— 53	— 49	— 43	— 57	— 49
April . . .	— 42	— 54	— 48	— 40	— 50	— 45	— 40	— 60	— 46	— 44	— 55	— 49	— 37	— 50	— 43	— 40	— 54	— 46
May . . .	— 32	— 52	— 42	— 26	— 48	— 38	— 34	— 55	— 47	— 35	— 55	— 44	— 32	— 45	— 39	— 32	— 51	— 42
June . . .	— 22	— 45	— 34	— 25	— 40	— 37	— 15	— 47	— 35	— 30	— 47	— 35	— 29	— 40	— 35	— 24	— 42	— 35
July . . .	— 30	— 42	— 36	— 30	— 45	— 36	— 29	— 40	— 35	— 30	— 45	— 36	— 28	— 38	— 31	— 29	— 42	— 35
August . .	— 27	— 44	— 36	— 29	— 45	— 34	— 25	— 45	— 36	— 29	— 40	— 34	— 30	— 40	— 34	— 25	— 43	— 35
September .	— 30	— 42	— 36	— 28	— 50	— 39	— 33	— 45	— 39	— 25	— 45	— 37	— 31	— 40	— 35	— 29	— 44	— 33
October . .	— 15	— 50	— 39	— 35	— 47	— 41	— 35	— 48	— 44	— 35	— 42	— 39	— 20	— 40	— 34	— 25	— 45	— 39
November .	— 41	— 54	— 47	— 40	— 59	— 49	— 35	— 50	— 47	— 40	— 50	— 45	— 30	— 52	— 42	— 37	— 53	— 46
December .	— 40	— 58	— 49	— 50	— 58	— 51	— 47	— 52	— 50	— 40	— 50	— 45	— 42	— 59	— 50	— 44	— 55	— 49

Appendix V.

THERMOMETER-OBSERVATIONS AT MERCARA

TAKEN BY REV. G. RICHTER, WITH PASTORELLI & CO.'S AND NEWMAN & SON'S INSTRUMENTS.

Months.	1866.			1867.			1868.			1869.			1870.			Average.		
	Min.	Max.	Mean.	Min.	Max.	Mean.	Min.	Max.	Mean.	Min.	Max.	Mean.	Min.	Max.	Mean.	Min.	Max.	Mean.
January	52°	75°	63°	51°	79°	64°	51°	80°	67°	56°	76°	67°	50°	76°	63°	52°	77°	65°
February	54	84	70	58	85	70	52	85	67	52	81	69	54	79	66	54	83	67
March	54	85	70	55	85	71	54	85	70	54	84	70	56	82	69	54	84	70
April	59	82	70	61	79	70	60	84	73	54	86	72	56	85	71	58	83	71
May	67	76	72	64	78	71	62	83	72	61	81	72	59	81	71	62	80	72
June	61	80	68	63	77	67	61	81	66	60	75	66	59	79	68	61	78	67
July	61	70	64	61	75	66	60	77	65	61	75	65	58	67	63	60	73	65
August	62	70	66	62	71	68	60	73	65	59	78	67	58	75	67	60	73	66
September	61	76	66	58	75	65	60	78	66	60	70	65	58	74	67	59	74	66
October	59	76	64	62	77	68	57	73	68	58	74	66	55	75	66	58	76	66
November	51	77	66	51	81	66	50	75	64	50	74	64	53	74	66	51	76	65
December	52	77	65	53	80	65	53	76	65	53	75	63	51	75	63	52	76	64

Appendix VI.

RAINFALL AT MERCARA IN INCHES AND CENTS,

REGISTERED BY REV. G. RICHTER WITH MURRAY AND HEATH'S PLUVIOMETER.

Year.	Jan.	Febr.	March.	April.	May.	June.	July.	August.	Sept.	Oct.	Nov.	Dec.	Total.
1863	0	0	0·45	1·25	2·30	4·78	41·74	39 46	22·95	10·08	10·98	1·40	134·99
1864	0	0	0	1·52	4.72	24·79	74·40	19·00	11·22	3·55	0·98	1·40	141·38
1865	0	0	1·23	2·50	9·33	21·17	64·82	36·91	9·08	2 84	2·28	0	150·16
1866	0	0	0	1·63	2 41	38·59	23·52	17·66	9·14	14·68	0·13	2·28	110·01
1867	0	0	3·70	1·46	8·56	19 89	37 47	19·80	14·02	6·07	0·03	0	111·00
1868	1·33	0	1·39	1·92	3·49	30 98	19 80	25·92	4·55	4·35	1·52	0	95·25
1869	0	0	1·22	2·12	2·05	26·24	44·18	14·14	11·75	9·86	1·90	0·20	113·66
1870	0 38	0	3 54	0·10	2 24	30·21	32·29	19·66	11·68	6·64	1·82	0	108 56
Average	0·21	0	1·44	1·56	4·39	24·58	42·27	24·07	11·79	7·23	2·45	0·66	120·65

Note: The difference in the average total, stated here and on p. 84, is explained by the additional year 1870 being taken into account.

Appendix VII.

GENERAL METEREOLOGICAL ABSTRACT FOR THE THREE SEASONS

DEDUCED FROM THE PRECEDING TABLES.

SEASONS.	Mercurial Barometer.			Thermometer.			Rainfall.		WIND.
	6 A.M.	3 P.M.	Mean.	Min.	Max.	Mean.	Inches.	Cents.	
Cold Season, October—January . . .	26 29	26·51	26·45	54°	76°	65°	10	55	N. E. and E.
Hot Season, February—May . . .	26·33	26·44	26·37	57°	82°	70°	7	39	E. and S. W.
Wet Season, June—September . . .	26·21	26·34	26·27	60°	74°	66°	102	71	W.
Average for the year.	26 28	26·43	26·36	57°	77°	67°	120	65	

Appendix VIII.

STATEMENT OF THE EUROPEAN COFFEE-ESTATES IN COORG,

THEIR REPUTED PROPRIETORS AND MANAGERS IN 1870.

I. In the Mercara-taluq.

No.	Names of Estates.	Acreage.		Proprietors.	Managers.	Remarks on Estates.
		Total.	Cultivated.			
1	Aberdour	337·21	120	J. Russell	J. Russel	
2	Abyal	344	not known	Major G. M. Martin	K. Chittyanna	
3	Angare-kolli	183·8	do.	W. U. Arbuthnot	F. H. Baker	
4	Baliátre	130 97	90	Herbert Taylor	H. Taylor	
5	Beauvoir	44·63	44·63	Rev. A. Fennell	Rev. A. Fennell	
6	Belta-male	476·70	450	do.	do.	
7	Belta-male	380·8	300	W. S. Boyd	W. Bidie	
8	Bhaktana-kotte	612·42	0	S. Jup	do.	resigned.
9	Bhíma-kandi	859 58	0	Donald Stewart	J. Woodman	
10	Boykéri	80	80	H. Taylor	H. Taylor	
11	Cheppe-kád	125·86	125	J. P. Hunt	J. P. Hunt	
12	Closeburn	231·46		Major Martin and Dr. Kirkpatrick	P. Pearson	
13	Coorg-Coffee-Company	2095·46	800	Coorg-Coffee-Company	F. Rylett	
14	Culdees	1023 64	165	H. Bain	Scobie	
15	Edrington	46 71	not known	Capt. Marshall	Jaganath	
16	Fanny-vale	205·76	175	D. Stewart	J. A. Young	

No.	Names of Estates.	Acreage.		Proprietors.	Managers.	Remarks on Estates.
		Total.	Cultivated.			
17	Fisher	489·91	400	W. U. Arbuthnot	F. H. Baker	
18	Glen-Coorg	3012·52	400	Donald Stewart	J. Woodman	
19	Glen-more	173	132	J. P. Hunt	J. P. Hunt	
20	Háleri-kótekád	161·18	150	H. A. Mangles	F. Mangles	
21	Helen-hally	467·79	100	S. G. Tipping	S. G. Tipping	
22	Horumale-nád	455·53	300	H. Mann	C. M. Grant	
23	Horúr-kótekád	369·12	150	A. C. Campbell		
24	Kadien-kád	118·27	118	Rev. A. Fennell	Rev. A. Fennell	
25	Kagodlu-nád	174·66	174	H. Mann	J. Brewer	
26	Kánan-kád	107·80	25	J. P. Hunt		
27	Kapale-kád	184 84	~~180~~	A. C. Campbell, A. Fowler and Mr. N. A. M. Denoon	James Fowler	
28	Káre-kolli	461·22	0	late Dr. Macpherson		abandoned.
29	Kimade-male	214·13	175	H. Mann	J. Brewer	
30	Knoli	93.21		Major Martin	Major Martin	
31	Do.	40·49		do.	do.	
32	Kunni-motte	136·40	136	Henry Mann		
33	Kundalam-kolli	203·32	175	F. W. Hill		
34	Lilford	113·93	95	W. Drummond	H. Drummond	abandoned.
35	Lower Kimale	198·52		Nicol Duckworth and Co.	J. H. Young	
36	Lower Belta-male	245·8	190	W. S. Boyd	A. G. Allay	
37	Made-nád	341·13	290	H. Mann	J. W. Finlayson	
38	May-male	369·71	300	W. S. Boyd	A. Stephen	
39	Mercara-Estate	243·65	190	Mrs. A. M. Denoon, A. Campbell & J. Fowler	J. Fowler	
40	Pachanda-male	566·69	250	W. S. Boyd	A. G. Allen	

41	Padachi-kád	155·30	155	J. P. Hunt and J. W. Hill		
42	Pándi-male	435·66	300	H. Mann	A. G. Aspinall	
43	Salop	299·91	220	Nicol William and Co.	F. H. Hayes	
44	Sampige-kolli	197·47	140	W. T. Drake and A. R. Alston	W. T. Drake and A. R. Alston	
45	Sunti-koppa	372·50		late Dr. Macpherson		resigned.
46	Upper-kimale	488·24	280	Nicol Duckworth and Co.	J. H. Young	
47	Wóte-ko.li	480·74	250	Donald Stewart	J. Russel	

II. *In the Padinálknád-taluq.*

1	Anepáre-kád	455·88	167	Ch. Grant and Aspinall	A. Wheeler	
2	Athumarada-Dére	204·42		J. W. Finlayson		
3	Banada-kolli	200		Nicol Duckworth and Co.		
4	Banter	364·59	170	W. U. Arbuthnot and 3 others		
5	Chetti-male	235·76	200	J. W. Finlayson	Turner	
6	Eyenkallia-male	200	80	W. Burnett and A. Stephen	A. Stephen	
7	Eyenkanungandi-kád	100		J. W. Finlayson		
8	Itiakutumbe-male	417·54		do.		
9	Kartha-kád	85·70	70	C. Grant and Aspinall	A. Wheeler	
10	Kutanganda-Dére	94·51		J. W. Finlayson		
11	Mechanda-Dére	94·52		do.		
12	Mukati-kád	100		do.		
13	Padiche-male	327·45	10	C. Grant and Aspinall	A. Wheeler	
14	Patti male	811·29	150	Capt. R. Taylor	Whish	
15	Thórikád	197 62	42	C. Grant and Aspinall	H. A. Wheeler	
16	Umale	283 2	150	Edg. Ludlow		
17	Waveney Valley	282·50	100	H. L. Johnstone and Brewer	J. Morgan	

III. *In the Yedenálknád-taluq.*

No.	Names of Estates.	Acreage.		Proprietors.	Managers.	Remarks on Estates.
		Total.	Cultivated.			
1	Alitópu I.	268·49	180	G. R. Evans	F. Marsden	
2	Do. II.	329·16		F. Marsden	do.	
3	Allathan-kád	580·16		D. Stewart		
4	Anandapur	96 82	25	Rev. H. A. Kaundinya	David	
5	Bari-kád	816·23	165	Marquis Viviano	W. Rose.	
6	Beechlands	732·8		J. Tanner	Pudicombe	
7	Clutha	426 95	400	Nicol Duckworth and Co.	A. Mc. Innes	
8	Eyan-bataratu-kád	300		G. MacGregor		waste.
9	Fairlands and Oaklands	386 3	380	J. Wright of Edinburgh	J. Chisholm	
10	Fowler	808 6		Mrs. A. M. Denoon		uncultivated.
11	Do.	300		do.		do.
12	Do.	120 95		do.		do.
13	Glen Moriston	282 81	130	James Fowler and Co.	James Fowler	
14	Glen Urguhart	211·80		James Fowler		abandoned.
15	Hanchi-betta	168·17	0	Rev. H. A. Kaundinya		resigned.
16	Handi-gutta-betta	260·60		N. Stewart		
17	Kabarádu-male	300		Major Beddock and Mrs. Hearn		
18	Kákunda	862·28	500	Donald Stewart		
19	Kayem-kád	491·78	40	late Dr. Maxwell	C. Lawrence	
20	Kávéri-Estate	289·4	150	Kávéri-Coffee-Company	Pereira	
21	Kembu-kolli	376·61	250	W. R. Arbuthnot and J. Young		
22	Kunchuri		75	Rev. G. Richter and J. Haller	J. Haller	

23	Mathada-kád	195·88		N. Stewart		
24	Muskalbora	141·66	50	late P. James and P. Kennedy		
25	Nallu-kóte	296·66	250	N. Stewart	W. T. Simpson	
26	Periambádi	266·54	140	late Dr. Maxwell	W. Rose	
27	Píli-betta	315·93	240	R. St. John Shaw	R. Shaw	
28	Polle-kád	43 90		Donald Stewart		
29	Polle-betta	1066 38	700	H. P. Minchin and W. R. Arbuthnot	H. P. Minchin	
30	Rockliffe	960·44		J. Stewart		resigned.
31	Rockville	151·52		F. Brown		
32	School-Plantation	301	50	Central-School-Endowment	Rev. G. Richter	
33	Siddhapur	165·70		J. P. Hunt		waste.
34	Strathmore	1011·74	320	Nicol Duckworth and Co.	C. Macdonald	
35	Tanada-betta	387·33		H. Forman	H. R. Craig	
36	Thanir-halla	506 87		N. Stewart		waste.
37	Woodside	508 95		D. Stewart	J. Miller	
38	Wodder-halli	303 34	150	J. P. Hunt	Hobbert	
39	Yemmegundi	785 33	450	W. R. Arbuthnot and J. Young	W. Turnbull	

IV. In the Kiggatnád-taluq.

1	Athol I.	176 96	140	J W. Savage and	
2	Do. II.	152 64	90	H. J. Marsden	J. W. Savage
3	Bambu-kád	158 17	45	J. W. Hayes	
4	Benlomond	252	170	A. C. Burnett and G. Ross	A. Burnett
5	Burnside	277·76		G. Anderson	
6	Clifton	233·70	150	Alex. Denoon	James Fowler
7	Cluny	368·70		Cols. A. Cadell & Barrow	H. P. Drummond
8	Cudial	114·03	100	Maj. Renton, Capt. Magrath & H. A. Ross	H. A Ross

No.	Names of Estates.	Acreage.		Proprietors.	Managers.	Remarks on Estates.
		Total.	Cultivated.			
9	Eygunda	418·48	300	Capt. R. Taylor	F. Jaques	
10	Karia-male	1032·99	435	H. G. Roberts, D. Rose, and D. Peebles	J. Rose	
11	Kayim-kolli	667 62	147	R. St. John Shaw	R. Shaw	
12	Kikád	106·45	80	Maj. Renton, Capt. Magrath & H. A. Ross	H. A. Ross	
13	Koku-male	894·55	160	McGregor and J. Martin	J. L. Martin	
14	Kokéri	103·62		H. P. Gordon	H. P. Horton	
15	Mathigód	488·94		D. Stewart		waste.
16	Peggadi-male			H. J. Roberts, D. Rose and D. Peebles		
17	Paletód	1565·12	400	C. W. Dawson		
18	Ponnambáre			W. V. Drummond		waste.
19	Rosemath		45	W. Rose	J. Rose	
20	Shulankéri	193 75		Nicol Duckworth and Co.		resigned.
21	Singe-mane			do.		do.
22	Sávirabatti-kád			G. Wilson		

V. *In the Nanjarájpatna-taluq.*

1	Alle-katte	151·18		H. A. Mangles	G. F. Deeds	
2	Battada-rási	238·84	100	Col. Cunningham and Barrett	S. Barrett	
3	Carton	278·81	200	R. P. Carr		abandoned.
4	Hamyal	1461·29	120	Campbell and Fowler		
5	Lowden valley	460·18	100	Mrs. E. Wright and W. Wright	W. Wright	
6	Kumbu-kád		145	H. R. East	H. R. East	
7	Kuvina-kolli	212·21	20	H. A. Mangles	G. F. Deeds	

CORRIGENDA.

Page	Instead of	Read
wherever	"w" in native words	"v"
VI	seperate	separate
5	doures	downs
8	Bisly-pass	Bisilu-pass
14	Chóvanhole	Choran-hole
20	Thimbergia	Thunbergia
25	draft	draught
31	Tamaind	Tamarind
38	beautiful spots	beauty-spots
42	clows	claws
99	stable-manure.	stable-manure,
116	exculants	exiles
118	waist	wrist
118	Kokaládi	Kokadádi
120	rein	rim
121ff	Doddi Auwa	Dodda-Auva
166	cobra capella	cobra di capella
168	favour	the favour
172	and pressure	(drop these words)
175	Omkarésvara	Onkarésvara
180	the Coorg shall	the Coorgs shall
181	Cutcherry	Kachéri
184	hands?	hands.
185	on Báne	on a Báne
241	Harige Shíme	Itterige Shíme
259	end his life	end of his life
259	Lingrája	Lingarája
268	frobearing	forbearing
291	purpose	propose
336	Shanivár-sante	Sanivár-sante

Page	Instead of	Read
347	approval Brigadier	approval of Brigadier
356	Punya	Panya
367	Kuyinkéri	Kuyinkéri-nád
367	Nanjarájpatna	Nanjarájpatna-táluq
367	Kampur	Rampur
374	Perambóti	Periambádi
376	and G i-idol	and the Gauri-idol
397	ten years the	ten years, the
400	cheap justice	cheap and speedy justice
401	neither remarkable	remarkable neither
401	in 1812	in 1813
421	if India	of India
422	one mile to an inch	one inch to a mile
438	Though the noble	Through the noble
451	in 1854	in 1852
451	what amount	what an amount